How to do Linguistics with R

How to do Linguistics with R

Data exploration and statistical analysis

Natalia Levshina

Université catholique de Louvain

John Benjamins Publishing Company

Amsterdam / Philadelphia

DOI 10.1075/z.195

Cataloging-in-Publication Data available from Library of Congress:
LCCN 2015016708 (PRINT) / 2015019027 (E-BOOK)

ISBN 978 90 272 1224 5 (HB) / ISBN 978 90 272 1225 2 (PB)
ISBN 978 90 272 6845 7 (E-BOOK)

John Benjamins Publishing Co. · https://benjamins.com

*To my mother, Alevtina Pavlovna Levshina (née Krasikova),
and all women with a passion for numbers*

Table of contents

The companion website can be found at:
http://dx.doi.org/10.1075/z.195.website

Acknowledgements

This book is a result of my experience in teaching R and statistics to students and colleagues in different parts of Europe: the Friedrich Schiller University of Jena (Germany), the Philipp University of Marburg (Germany), the Palacký University of Olomouc (the Czech Republic) and the Catholic University of Louvain (Belgium). I thank them for their open-mindedness, enthusiasm and numerous difficult questions, which have helped me to improve this book, both thematically and didactically.

My life as a statistician began at the University of Leuven. I'm grateful to my ex-supervisors, Dirk Geeraerts and Dirk Speelman, for encouraging us, their Ph.D. students, to jump into the ocean of statistics and R and helping us not to get drowned. My thanks also go to all ex-colleagues at the research unit of Quantitative Lexicology and Variational Linguistics with whom I had an opportunity to discuss statistical secrets and solve R riddles. As a young quantitative linguist, I was particularly inspired by work of such pioneers as R. Harald Baayen, Stefan Th. Gries and Dirk Speelman. In this book, I discuss some of their innovative approaches, as well as other popular methods from psycholinguistics, collocation analysis, dialectometry, register variation studies and other domains.

This book would have never been written without the vast and vibrant R community – all those people who have created and supported R software, documentation, textbooks, online tutorials and discussion forums. I'm particularly grateful to the anonymous reviewer for highly valuable and extensive comments on the previous version of the manuscript, as well as to Dagmar Divjak, Martin Hilpert, Yves Peirsman and Björn Wiemer for their encouragement and constructive feedback on selected chapters. Of course, all remaining imperfections are solely mine.

Introduction

1. Who is this book written for?

Statistics lies at the heart of scientific investigation. It helps the researcher to formulate and test theoretical hypotheses, making generalizations about a population of interest based on a limited sample. It is indispensable at all stages of the empirical cycle of research, from formulation of a hypothesis and data collection to data analysis and hypothesis falsification. Although statistics has played an important role in many hybrid linguistic disciplines, such as psycholinguistics, sociolinguistics, applied, computational and corpus linguistics, it is only recently that the awareness of its importance has reached the more traditional theoretical areas of linguistics. Slowly but surely, statistical methods are becoming a more common sight in linguistic teaching programmes, at conferences, in research articles and books.

This book is for you if you want…

- to learn how to operationalize and test your linguistic hypotheses
- to know which statistical method to choose in which situation
- to understand statistical terminology and participate in methodological discussion
- to get your message across with the help of clear and informative graphs
- to participate actively in making linguistics a more rigorous scientific discipline
- to get acquainted with a new programming language, R, and become a member of the dynamic international R community.

The book is intended mostly for researchers and students of usage-based or functional linguistics, although the methods are generic and can be applied in any field, regardless of one's theoretical persuasion. Without complicated jargon, but with detailed explanations, the book presents the most important statistical procedures and tests. The book also pays special attention to small-scale and non-normal data, which are so frequent in linguistic research. It shows how one can use non-parametric approaches and special techniques, such as bootstrap and permutation, to deal with small and irregular samples.

Most methods described in the book are well established in usage-based linguistics, such as logistic regression or distinctive collexeme analysis. However, some approaches are not yet mainstream. An example is Semantic Vector Spaces (Chapter 16), which originate in Computational Linguistics and can be used as a convenient tool to measure semantic relatedness of words, word forms or constructions.

Although some methods are more 'prototypical' than others in solving specific tasks, the suggested methods should not be regarded as the ultimate truth. Firstly, the development of tools that adequately solve theoretical problems in linguistics is still work in progress, although some approaches have already become a *de facto* standard in particular fields (see examples in Newman 2011). Secondly, the methods are often complementary and allow one to see a phenomenon from different perspectives. The ultimate goal of the book is to encourage creativity by offering a set of classical and cutting-edge techniques that can be used to explore linguistic data.

Although R is a popular tool for extraction of information from corpora, this aspect is not covered in the textbook. For an introduction to corpus linguistics with R, see Gries (2009). We will not discuss the programming aspects of R, either. Those interested can consult textbooks, such as Chambers (2008) and Matloff (2011), as well as numerous online tutorials.

2.   The quantitative turn in linguistics

In recent years, linguistics has been undergoing a quantitative turn, with statistical procedures gaining in popularity in many subfields, from usage-based morphology to Cognitive Semantics, and from phonology to discourse analysis. This has not always been the case, however. In fact, linguistics in the twentieth century has been dominated by idealist mentalist theories, which were alien to a rigorous empirical methodology. The most influential ones were (and still are, in some fields) Linguistic Structuralism and Generativism, which can be regarded as a modification of the former. Both assumed that the true object of linguistic investigation is some invariable structure, be it a system of oppositions, or innate linguistic competence. There was no need to resort to frequencies or probabilities since linguistic categories (at least, in one language), were assumed to be invariable, discrete and clear-cut. Every linguist could consider his or her linguistic knowledge a source of all necessary information about the entire language, which lead to the predominance of introspection and self-invented examples as the main type of evidence. As a consequence, statistics was thought to be unnecessary:

> Large groups of people make up all their utterances out of the same stock of lexical forms and grammatical constructions. A linguistic observer therefore can describe the speech-habits of a community without resorting to statistics.
>
> (Bloomfield 1935:37)

> I think we are forced to conclude that grammar is autonomous and independent of meaning, and that probabilistic models give no particular insight into some of the basic problems of syntactic structure.   (Chomsky 1957:17)

Today the situation is rapidly changing. On the one hand, these changes are in line with the recent theoretical shifts. One of them is connected with the spread of the usage-based approach, which originates in Langacker's work (1987). The main idea behind this framework is that linguistic knowledge is shaped by language usage. Importantly, when speakers learn the language, they subconsciously analyse and store a vast amount of information about co-occurrence frequencies of words and constructions. When doing so, they act as 'intuitive statisticians' (Ellis 2006: 1). Frequency effects, which will be discussed in Chapters 5–7, play a crucial role in language use, acquisition and change. They are rooted in fundamental cognitive and social mechanisms. On the cognitive side, there is massive evidence that human categories have probabilistic structure and fuzzy boundaries, as shown by postclassical theories of categorization, such as Prototype and Exemplar Theories (cf. Chapter 19). From the social perspective, common linguistic categories (as well as shared conceptual structures) emerge as a result of linguistic alignment of speakers and hearers, which results in incremental strengthening of some representations and weakening of others over time. This process is the driving force of language evolution (Steels 2012). Obviously, the resulting inter- and intraspeaker variation can only be modelled statistically.

To implement the holistic approach to language use, variation and change, one needs multifactorial models. This approach reflects a general trend in linguistics labelled as 'recontextualization', which follows a long period of decontextualization in linguistic theory and practice (Geeraerts 2010). For example, one can test whether the speaker's choice between two or more linguistic alternatives in a particular context may be influenced by conceptual, social, stylistic, discursive, cultural and historical factors. Such models can be only created with the help of advanced multivariate methods, which are discussed in this book (see Chapters 12 to 14). Of course, when we deal with actual linguistic behaviour, there is always some degree of unpredictable variation, which is common in all types of social behaviour (Itkonen 1980: 350). This has to do with the complexity of the object of investigation, but should not discourage one from doing quantitative research.

On the other hand, even linguists who support theories that traditionally use introspection as the primary source of evidence begin to explore different types of data. As Kepser & Reis put it,

> [e]vidence involving different domains of data will shed different, but altogether more, light on the issues under investigation, be it that the various findings support each other, help with the correct interpretation, or by contradicting each other, lead to factors of influence so far overlooked.
> (Kepser & Reis 2005: 3)

Clearly, comparing different kinds of evidence from corpora, experiments, questionnaires, etc. requires an up-to-date methodological toolkit, which should necessarily include a broad range of statistical techniques.

Finally, the computer era has brought a huge number of freely available corpora, databases and other sources of linguistic evidence. Nearly every linguist nowadays has some experience with corpus data, even if this experience amounts to finding an unfamiliar expression in Google. Quantitative data analysis is indispensable when one needs to discover patterns in large data sets and corpora.

3.   How to use this textbook

The textbook consists of four large parts. The first two chapters are preparatory. Chapter 1 introduces basic statistical concepts, whereas the main purpose of Chapter 2 is to help the reader get started with R. If you are new to R and statistics, this part of the book is indispensable.

The next two chapters are dedicated to the first descriptive analyses of quantitative (Chapter 3) and qualitative (Chapter 4) variables. They also discuss such basic notions as the mean, median, mode, standard deviation, proportions, and many more, and introduce a variety of standard plotting functions in R. This part of the book is also highly recommended for those who take their first steps in quantitative research.

The third and the largest part of the book explains main statistical tests and analytical statistics, from the t-test in Chapter 5 to the correlational analysis in Chapter 6 and linear regression in Chapter 7, followed by a discussion of different types of ANOVA in Chapter 8. Chapters 9–11 focus on association measures between two categorical variables and discuss collocational and collostructional methods, such as distinctive collexeme analysis (Chapter 11). Chapters 12 and 13 introduce logistic regression with binary and multinomial outcomes, respectively. These models are widely used in multifactorial probabilistic grammar and lexicology. Chapter 14 deals with additional classification tools, namely, conditional inference trees and random forests, which can be of help when regression analysis is not appropriate or the model is too complex to interpret. To get acquainted with some of the most popular hypothesis-testing techniques and measures of effect size, one may be well-advised to study Chapters 5, 6 and 9.

The last part of the book is dedicated to exploratory multivariate methods, which can be used to discover underlying structure in the data. Chapter 15 and 16 discuss some ideas behind distributional approaches to semantics: Behavioural Profiles and Semantic Vector Spaces, respectively. They also deal with various distance metrics and clustering techniques. Chapter 17 focuses on Multidimensional Scaling and shows how the method can be applied in variational linguistics. Chapter 18 is dedicated to Principal Components Analysis and Factor Analysis, which are used in multidimensional analysis of register variation. In Chapter 19, Simple and Multiple Correspondence Analysis are introduced and illustrated with case studies of lexical category structure and variation. Finally, Chapter 20 shows how one can visualize constructional change with the help of motion charts. Although the methods introduced in Chapters 15 to 19 are to some extent interrelated, each of these chapters can be studied on its own.

Every chapter contains R code and R output, including graphs. Executable R code is usually placed after the symbol '>' on a separate line, for example:

```
> a <-3
```

The '>' symbol should not be typed. Sometimes a short commentary is provided after the sign '#', for example:

```
> a <-3 # this is an example of a commentary
```

Appendix 1 summarizes the basic operations with a few most popular data types in R, whereas Appendix 2 offers an overview of numerous graphical parameters and plotting functions. It also introduces the package ggplot2, which enables one to produce high-quality graphs.

The book comes with a companion R package Rling, which is freely downloadable from the online platform for the textbook at http://dx.doi.org/10.1075/z.195.website (file *Rling_1.0.tar.gz*), see instructions in the file *read.me*. In addition, the online platform offers exercises and multiple choice questions that will help you master the basic statistical notions, specific methods and R code introduced in each chapter. The keys to the exercises and questions can be found online, as well as the R code for each chapter.

In every chapter you will see several boxes with additional information. The icons at the top of a box have the following meaning:

Additional information and reading suggestions.

A warning: it is easy to make a mistake.

Tips on writing up the results of a statistical test for publishing.

Practical recommendation or tip for fixing a problem.

Advice on how to create an enhanced version of a graph with the help of ggplot2.

The code provided in this textbook is based on R version 3.2.0. R is very dynamic and keeps changing and improving. This is why some coding details may change while this book is being published, as well as later on. Normally, when deprecated code is used, R gives a warning message and suggests an alternative. The readers would be well-advised to read such messages carefully and adjust the code accordingly.

CHAPTER 1

What is statistics?

Main statistical notions and principles

What you will learn from this chapter:

> What is statistics? What can and cannot statistics do for you? How to formulate
> and test research hypotheses? What kind of statistical tests are there? These and
> many other questions are discussed in this chapter. In addition, you will also learn
> about different types of variables, parametric and non-parametric tests, *p*-values
> and many other things which you will need in order to understand explanations
> provided in the following chapters.

1.1   Statistics and statistics

Not many people know that the English word **statistics** is in fact ambiguous. This can
cause some confusion. On the one hand, it is a mass noun in the singular, which designates
a discipline, like mathematics, physics or economics. Broadly speaking, statistics is a set
of techniques and tools for describing and analysing data. On the other hand, the word is
often used in the plural to refer to values derived from a sample, as opposed to the entire
population. A **population** is a group that represents all objects of interest. For example,
if we want to compare the speech rate of speakers of Dutch spoken in Belgium and in
the Netherlands, the corresponding population will include all Dutch speakers in the two
countries. The values obtained from a population are called **parameters**. An example of a
parameter is the mean speech rate of all Belgian Dutch speakers. Of course, it would be too
time-consuming, expensive and tedious to measure the speech rate of every Belgian Dutch
and Netherlandic Dutch speaker. This is why linguists normally deal with **samples** which,
as they hope, are representative of the population. So, **statistics** in the plural are measures
obtained from samples. An example of a statistic is the average speech rate obtained for a
sample of one hundred Belgian Dutch speakers.

Statistics (both in the singular and in the plural) can be subdivided into descriptive and inferential. **Descriptive statistics** can be used to describe the characteristics of
a sample. An example is the above-mentioned average speech rate in the sample of one
hundred Belgian Dutch speakers. **Inferential statistics** allows the researcher to use the
characteristics of a sample in order to make conclusions about the population in general.
If we compare the average speech rates of Belgian Dutch and Netherlandic Dutch speakers,

inferential statistics can tell us if the difference is statistically significant or it can be merely attributed to chance. Inferential statistics allows us to make an amazing leap from the sample to the entire population and infer to all Dutch speakers in the two countries, given the results based on a small sample. If not for inferential statistics, one would have to measure the speech rate of all Dutch speakers. And now imagine how much time and money you could save if you had to carry out a similar study on speakers of English or Chinese.

Certainly, in order to make this leap from a sample to the population, one has to be sure that the sample is representative of the population. The difference between a sample statistic and the corresponding population parameter is called the **sampling error**. The smaller the sampling error, the closer the sample represents the characteristics of the population. The higher the sampling error, the more difficult it will be to extend the results of your study to the population. This is why it is very important that your sample should represent the population as closely as possible. The best sampling method is random sampling. This means that every member of the population has equal chances to be selected. In the speech rate example, we would have to make a random selection from the list of all Belgian and Netherlandic Dutch speakers. Of course, this approach is not always feasible, although it is considered the most reliable. Alternatively, one can use so-called representative and convenience sampling. Representative sampling means that the researcher draws a sample in such a way that it matches the population on certain characteristics. For example, one may create a sample of Belgian Dutch speakers by reproducing the same ratios of men and women, older and younger speakers, different ethnic groups and dialects, etc. This method is slightly inferior to random sampling because there is risk of omitting some important variables. Finally, there is convenience sampling, the least reliable, but probably the most widely used method. One can simply make recordings of different speakers of Dutch only in a few easily accessible cities. Of course, the less random the sampling procedure, the higher the risk of a bias.

1.2   How to formulate and test your hypotheses

1.2.1   Null and alternative hypotheses

Before beginning any statistical analysis, it is necessary to formulate a research hypothesis. It is an 'educated guess', which usually posits some difference between groups or relationship between variables. Consider the example with the speech rate. You might have heard several Netherlandic and Belgian Dutch speakers, and you might feel that the former speak a bit faster than the latter. The hypothesis would be then that Dutch speakers in the Netherlands speak on average faster than Belgian Dutch speakers (in fact, this is exactly what was found by Verhoeven et al. [2004], who also controlled for other demographic factors). The research hypothesis, which is also called, probably counterintuitively, the **alternative hypothesis**, always goes together with the **null hypothesis**, which says that there is no difference between different groups, or no association between different variables, etc. In our example, the null hypothesis is that there is no difference in the average speech rates between the Dutch speakers in these two countries. Below are a few other examples:

A. H_0 (the null hypothesis): There is no difference in the number of lexemes that denote snow in Eskimo and Yucatec Maya.

   H_1 (the alternative hypothesis): There are more lexemes that denote snow in Eskimo than in Yucatec Maya.

B. H_0 (the null hypothesis): there is no relationship between the frequency of a word and how fast it is recognized in a lexical decision task.

   H_1 (the alternative hypothesis): the more frequent a word, the faster it is recognized in a lexical decision task.

C. H_0 (the null hypothesis): there is no difference in the relative frequencies of meta-phoric expressions used by men and women when they speak about sex.

   H_1 (the alternative hypothesis): there is a difference in the relative frequencies of meta-phoric expressions used by men and women when they speak about sex.

The alternative hypotheses in A and B are called **directional**. They posit a direction to the inequality assumed by the researcher because they contain expressions like 'X is more than Y' and 'the greater X, the greater Y'. In contrast, the alternative hypothesis in C is **non-directional**. The researcher has no expectations about the frequencies of metaphoric expressions used by men and women. She simply expects to find a difference between the sexes. It can be expressed as 'X does not equal Y'.

Why do we need the null and alternative hypotheses? This is because contemporary science is based on the logic of falsification. It is impossible to prove that something is right, but it is possible to reject the opposite. Consider an example. According to Universal Grammar, all human languages have recursion, i.e. one can embed clauses within sentences endlessly, e.g. *This is the cat that killed the rat that ate the malt that lay in the house that Jack built...* It is impossible to prove that all human languages have recursion. After all, even if one checks all living languages, there is no way to analyse the extinct ones and future ones. However, it is possible to falsify the hypothesis if you find at least one language that does not have recursion. In fact, it seems that such a language has been found. It is Pirahã, a Brazilian Amazon language. It is claimed that cultural factors have made linguistic recursion in that language unnecessary (Everett 2005). Therefore, you should not try to prove that your research (alternative) hypothesis is right. Instead, you should try to reject its opposite, that is, the null hypothesis.

1.2.2 Those mysterious *p*-values...

You know now that one should try to reject the null hypothesis, but how can one do it in practice? In statistics, rejection or non-rejection of the null hypothesis depends on the value of the corresponding test statistic, such as t, χ^2, W, F., etc. The test statistic is computed on the basis of a sample. If the test statistic is beyond some critical value, one can suspect that this may not be due to mere chance. Therefore, the null hypothesis should be wrong.

How can we decide whether the test statistic is extreme enough to suggest that something is going on? This is possible because statisticians know how test statistics are distributed. A **distribution** is a collection of scores, or values, on a variable. It is common to represent distributions as scores arranged from the smallest to the largest ones with varying likelihood of occurrence. Let us imagine that we have collected the heights of all adult hobbits[1] in a hobbit village. The heights can be represented then as points on the horizontal axis ranged from the smallest to the largest ones, as shown in Figure 1.1. The vertical axis represents the so-called probability density. To put it simply, the plot shows that heights around 110 cm are much more likely to occur than heights around 60 or 160 cm.

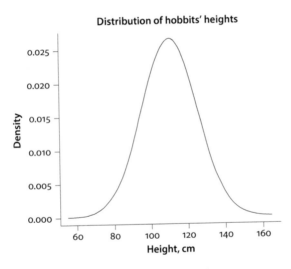

Figure 1.1. Imaginary probability distribution of hobbits' heights

It is worth mentioning that this kind of nicely symmetric bell-shaped distribution is called normal, or Gaussian (after the name of Carl Friedrich Gauss, a great German mathematician). It is a very important concept in statistics because many tests, which are called parametric, assume that the data are distributed normally (see Section 1.4). Of course,

---

1.   Hobbits are small human-like creatures with hairy feet from Tolkien's novels.

there exist a variety of other important distributions with a different shape, such as the F-distribution or χ^2-distribution.

A very useful thing about knowing the shape of a distribution is that one can compute the exact probabilities for a range of x. The entire area under the curve corresponds to the probability of 1 (or 100%). That is, if you measure the height of any random hobbit, there is 100% probability that his or her height will be somewhere under the curve. One can also say that the probability that a random hobbit's height is under 110 cm (the left shaded area on the plot in Figure 1.2) is 0.5, or 50%, because this is a half of the entire area under the curve. Of course, this will hold only if the distribution is symmetric. It is also possible to estimate the probability of meeting a hobbit who is 150 cm tall or taller (the small shaded area on the right in Figure 1.2), around 0.038, or 3.8%.

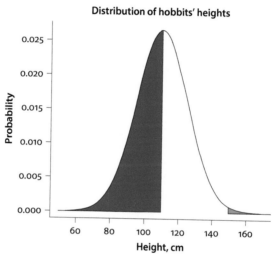

Distribution of hobbits' heights

Figure 1.2. Probability distribution of hobbits' heights and different probabilities of observing particular values. Large shaded area under the curve on the left: probability of finding a hobbit shorter than 110 cm (50%); small shaded area under the curve on the right: probability of finding a hobbit taller than 150 cm (3.8%)

Therefore, if one knows what distribution the data come from, it is possible to obtain the probability of observing the actual statistic (and more extreme values) by chance. This is crucial for hypothesis testing. You can compute a test statistic and see the probability of obtaining it and more extreme results by chance alone, that is, under the assumption that the null hypothesis is true. This is what the p-value means.

The p-value shows the probability of obtaining a given test statistic value or more extreme values if the null hypothesis is true.

If a *p*-value is smaller than some conventional level (usually 0.05 or 0.01), then the null hypothesis is rejected, and one has grounds to believe that the result is not due to chance. Therefore, one can conclude that there is a true difference between the groups, association between the variables, etc., depending on the research hypothesis and statistical test. If the *p*-value is larger than this conventional value, then the null hypothesis cannot be rejected, and you can conclude that there is no sufficient evidence that the groups are different (or the variables are correlated, associated, etc). The values 0.05 or 0.01 are called the **significance level**. This is the degree of risk you are willing to take that you will reject a null hypothesis that is actually true. It is crucial that the significance level is decided on *before* the statistical analysis, not after it.

Degrees of freedom

In addition to the test statistic value, one also has to know the number of degrees of freedom (often designated as *df*) in order to compute the *p*-value. In a nutshell, this is the number of values that are free to vary. For many basic statistical tests, it is the sample size minus one. For example, you have three observations with the scores of 3, 4 and 8, and you are interested in their average score, which is 5. You can freely change only two scores without changing the average. The third value is not free. In this example, if you replace the first score with 1, and the second score with 10, your third score can only be 4. Any other third score will change the average. For five scores, you have four degrees of freedom; for ten scores, you will have nine, and so on. For a 2-by-2 table with fixed marginal totals (i.e. the totals of each row and each column), the number of degrees of freedom is $(2 - 1) \times (2 - 1) = 1$. This means that only one cell is free. You can calculate all other cells from the marginal totals.

Degrees of freedom are crucial because they tell us what the distribution of a test statistic ought to look like. For different numbers of degrees of freedom, the **critical values** of the test statistic (that is, the values that correspond to a given significance level, e.g. 0.05 or 0.01) will be different. The number of degrees of freedom is usually reported along with the test statistic and the *p*-value, e.g. $\chi^2 (1) = 7.47, p = 0.006$. The number in brackets displays the number of degrees of freedom (1).

1.2.3 Type I and Type II errors

The significance level says how much risk you agree to take that you discard a null hypothesis that is in fact true. This is called the Type I error, 'false alarm' or 'false positive'. An example is when a doctor diagnoses a disease, but the patient is healthy. Or you think you have found difference between two experimental conditions, but the result is due to sampling error and there is no real difference. If the level of significance is 0.05, it means that there is a 5% chance of rejecting the null hypothesis when it is in fact true.

A Type II error, also called 'false negative', is committed when the researcher accepts a null hypothesis which is in fact false and there is true difference between groups (or association between variables, etc.). An example is when the patient is sick, but the doctor fails to identify the disease. A Type II error is related to the notion of statistical **power**. The more powerful (in the statistical sense) the test, the higher the likelihood that it will reject the null hypothesis when it is false. If you commit a Type II error, this means that your statistical analysis lacked power, which may have to do, for example, with an insufficient sample size.

Note that decreasing the significance level (e.g. from 0.05 to 0.01) will decrease the chances of a Type I error and increase the chances of a Type II error, other things being constant. In contrast, if you raise the significance level (e.g. from 0.05 to 0.1), you will increase the chances of a Type I error and decrease the chances of a Type II error. In general, most linguists and other researchers use the 0.05 level as a trade-off, and one should have very good reasons for changing it.

1.2.4 One-tailed and two-tailed statistical tests

It has been mentioned above that an alternative hypothesis can be directional (e.g. 'X is greater than Y') or non-directional (e.g. 'X is different from Y'). This distinction is very important when one chooses an appropriate statistical test. Most tests (not all!)[2] come in two flavours: one-tailed and two-tailed. If the alternative hypothesis is directional, it is correct to use a one-tailed test. If it is non-directional, one should normally use a two-tailed test. Why is that important? As discussed above, hypothesis testing involves computing a test statistic (e.g. t, T, W or F) and deciding whether it is extreme enough to be expected by pure chance. The reason for distinguishing between one-tailed and two-tailed tests is that you will need different minimum or maximum test statistics in order to obtain a significant result. Recall that the probability of observing a test statistic value under the null hypothesis should be 0.05 or less if the result is significant. In case of a directional one-tailed test, we should look only at one tail of the test statistic

---

2. For example, the F-test in ANOVA is always one-tailed.

distribution, as shown in the left panel of Figure 1.3. If your alternative hypothesis is 'X is greater than Y', the test statistic should be somewhere in the shaded area (the region of rejection). If your hypothesis is 'X is smaller than Y', the test statistics should be located on the left, in a region of the same size.

In contrast, if your hypothesis is non-directional, that is, 'X is different from Y', you can observe an extreme result either in the left or right tail. This is why the 0.05 value will be split into 0.025 (for the left tail) and 0.025 (for the right tail), as shown in the right panel of Figure 1.3. The shaded areas correspond to the critical regions of the values of the test statistic.

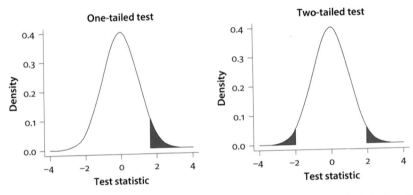

Figure 1.3. One-tailed and two-tailed tests. Left: one-tailed; right: two-tailed. Shaded: the critical region(s) of the test statistic values, which lead(s) us to reject the null hypothesis

Decide on your tails first!

The difference in the size of critical regions for one-tailed and two-tailed tests has important consequences. If you have a directional alternative hypothesis, you need a less extreme value of your test statistic to discard the null hypothesis than if you have a non-directional one. One may be tempted to change the original non-directional alternative hypothesis to a directional one when the one-tailed test yields a significant result, and the two-tailed test does not. Doing such things is scientifically unethical! It is crucial that you formulate your alternative hypothesis and make your choice between the one- and two-tailed tests **before** you compute any test statistic.

1.3   What statistics cannot do for you

Although statistics can help you test your hypotheses, describe your data and do many other things, you cannot let your statistical software do all research for you. Let us imagine that you test a hypothesis, and it is supported by the data. Well done! However, that is not always the case. If we find, as in our example, no significant difference between the speech rates in two national varieties of Dutch, should we give up, or change anything about our research design, data, methods, and so on? Such a decision is not always an easy one. A famous case is Michelson-Morley's series of experiments in the end of the 19th century, which were meant to prove the existence of aether, or the so-called fifth element, which was believed to fill the regions of the universe and conduct light (see an interesting discussion in Geeraerts 1999). The first experiment in 1881 did not bring the expected results. Michelson and Morley decided that the lack of results was due to flaws in the experimental settings and repeated the experiment some years later with a very sophisticated design, all in vain. The second opportunity, however, would be to reject the initial hypothesis, as was done later by Einstein. As this example shows, the ultimate decision is always the researcher's responsibility.

Another thing that one cannot expect from statistics is that it will answer the question 'why'. Causality is always imposed by the researcher on the basis of her theoretical considerations, empirical data and common sense. There is a well-known saying, 'correlation does not imply causation'. Sometimes even a strong and statistically significant correlation may be entirely spurious. For example, according to the website *Spurious Correlations*,[3] the number of people who drowned by falling into a swimming pool in the USA from 1999 to 2009 correlates with the number of films Nicholas Cage appeared in during the same period. Another example is a correlation between the number of world-wide non-commercial space launches and the number of sociology doctorates awarded in the USA from 1997 to 2009.

In some cases there may be a third factor that influences both phenomena in question. For example, if one finds a correlation between the number of infants and storks in a neighbourhood, this does not mean that one causes the other. Both variables can be related to a third factor, which can be described as the degree of urbanization. Birth rates and the populations of storks are usually higher in the country than in urban areas. Consider another example. Ember and Ember (2007) found a positive correlation between sonority of sounds in a language and the frequency of extramarital sex in the corresponding linguistic community. Does it mean that louder speech sounds encourage intimate contacts? Or the other way round, can sexual freedom influence the free flow of voice during

---

3.   See http://www.tylervigen.com/ (last access 11.06.2015).

articulation? Maybe these variables are manifestations of some other underlying cultural and ecological factors? These are questions that statistics alone cannot answer.

1.4   Types of variables

To use statistical methods correctly, one has to know which type of data they are dealing with. At this point it is necessary to introduce the notion of **variable**, i.e. some property of the objects that can vary and that can be measured or described. For instance, if you have a set of words, you can compare them according to the following characteristics: length, grammatical word class, semantic class, frequency of use, register, origin, morphological complexity, and so on. All those characteristics can become your variables. The simplest way is to think of your dataset as a spreadsheet like in Microsoft Excel or OpenOffice Calc with individual subjects or observations as rows and variables as columns. Depending on the number of variables per each item, your data can be univariate (one variable), bivariate (two variables) and multivariate (three and more variables).

Variables in a study may have different status, which depends on how you model the relationships between them. The outcome variable, or the one which changes as a function of some other parameters of interest, is called the **response**, or **dependent variable**. The variables that influence the outcome are called **explanatory**, or **independent variables**.[4] If we carry out an experiment to find out whether the frequency of a word influences how quickly it is recognized in a lexical decision task, the explanatory variable will be the frequency, and the response variable will be the reaction time. Remember that the relationship of causality is something that is imposed by the researcher based on theoretical considerations. Such a relationship is possible, but not necessary. For example, in multivariate exploratory methods (see Chapters 15–19) the notions of dependent or independent variables are irrelevant.

Moreover, all variables vary along different scales of measurement: nominal, ordinal, interval and ratio. This classification is crucial for a correct choice of statistical tests.

– **Nominal** variables are two or more categories that are mutually exclusive. If the number of categories is only two, one speaks of a **binary** variable. For example, a speaker of a language can be male or female, native or non-native; possession may be expressed by the Saxon genitive (*the people's voice*) or the Norman genitive (*the voice of people*). Examples of a greater number of categories are numerous, as well. For instance, a simple clause in many languages may be intransitive, transitive or ditransitive;

---

4.   Some statisticians avoid using the term 'independent variable' because the variables that we consider independent in an experiment or corpus analysis may in fact depend on other variables. Moreover, most corpus-based analyses are correlational and do not assume any (direct) causal relationship between variables.

a nominal phrase in German may be in the nominative, genitive, dative or accusative case; languages can be accusative, ergative, neutral or mixed, displaying split ergativity. Nominal variables represent the least precise and informative level of measurement, in comparison with the ones that follow.

– The categories may be ordered. In that case, we deal with **ordinal** variables. An example is answers in a questionnaire on a five-point Likert scale, e.g. 'strongly disagree' – 'disagree' – 'neither agree nor disagree' – 'agree' – 'strongly agree'. The categories thus differ in order, but we do not know yet by how much. We cannot say, for example, that the difference between 'disagree' and 'neither agree nor disagree' is the same as the difference between 'strongly disagree' and 'disagree'. Different subjects can be using different internal scales. Although sometimes you can see numbers that represent the responses (from 1 to 5), equal intervals on the scale do not represent equal differences between the responses.

– If equal intervals on the scale represent equal differences between the points on the scale, we deal with an **interval** variable. A common example is temperature on the Celsius or Fahrenheit scale. The difference between 20 and 25 degrees is the same as the difference between 25 and 30 degrees. However, it is important that interval variables do not include a zero point, or, if they do, it is arbitrary.[5] That is, the temperature of 0 degrees Celsius does not mean that there is no temperature. This is why it does not make sense to say that twenty degrees Celsius is twice as warm as ten degrees.

– **Ratio** variables are very similar to interval ones, but they include zero on the scale, and the zero point is meaningful, not arbitrary. For example, consider the frequency of the word *aardvark* in a text. One can also very well imagine that a text contains no occurrences of *aardvark*. In that case, zero is perfectly meaningful. As a result, ratio variables allow for multiplication. For example, if the word *aardvark* occurs a hundred times in text A and only ten times in text B, it means that the word is ten times more frequent in text A than in text B.

These scales of measurements are displayed in Figure 1.4 as a set of steps, with the most informative ratio-scaled variables at the top, and the least informative nominal variables at the bottom. It is always possible to go down the ladder from a higher to a lower level of measurement. For example, word frequencies in a corpus can be subdivided into high, medium and low. In that case, we would go down from the ratio scale represented by the frequencies to the nominal level. However, one should go down the ladder only when this is absolutely necessary because every step down means a loss of information. In addition, ratio- and interval-scaled variables can be subdivided into **continuous**,

---

5. Celsius chose the point at which water freezes as the zero, whereas Fahrenheit used the temperature of a mixture of ice, salt and water, or, according to another version, the coldest temperature he could observe in his home town Gdańsk (Danzig).

when the scale of measurement is meaningful at all points between the numbers given (e.g. height in centimeters/feet or reaction times in milliseconds) and **discrete,** when the units of measurement cannot be split up (e.g. corpus frequencies or the number of phonemes in a language). Ratio- and interval-scaled variables are also often called **quantitative**, or **numerical**, whereas nominal and ordinal variables are called **qualitative**, or **categorical**.

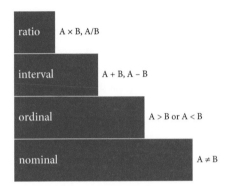

Figure 1.4. Scales of measurement. Every level above adds new information about values A and B, and includes all information at the levels below

If you have ratio or interval data, and they meet some assumptions, such as normality, homogeneity of variance, etc., you will normally be able to use a **parametric test**. Parametric tests are based on some assumptions about the underlying distribution. However, if these assumptions are violated, the resulting test statistic may be meaningless. In such cases, a **non-parametric** test is a more appropriate option. Non-parametric tests do not assume any specific distribution of the data. Since linguistic data are frequently non-normal and small-scale, this book pays special attention to non-parametric tests and situations when one should use them. In this book you will also learn some methods of statistical inference based on resampling (e.g. bootstrap and permutation), which allow one to validate their conclusions without collecting new data.

1.5   Summary

This chapter discussed the most important statistical notions and terms. It began from the distinction between a sample and a population and continued to show how data from a sample can be used to make inferences about the properties of the entire population. The distinction between descriptive and inferential statistics was introduced. Next, you learnt about the logic of hypothesis testing, and got acquainted with the notions of distribution, *p*-value, significance level and Type I and Type II errors. Finally, different types of variables and measurement scales were discussed, and the distinction between parametric and non-parametric statistics was mentioned. These notions will be crucial in the next chapters. There are also two important lessons to learn: first, do not let statistics do the thinking for you; second, formulate your hypothesis and decide on the type of test (one- or two-tailed) before you begin your statistical analysis.

More on basic statistical notions

You can find more information about the notions introduced in this chapter in a variety of introductory statistical textbooks, for example, N. J. Salkind's *Statistics for People Who (Think They) Hate Statistics* (2011) or T.C. Urdan's *Statistics in Plain English* (2010). See also Chapter 1 in Gries' *Statistics for Linguistics with R* (2013).

CHAPTER 2

Introduction to R

What you will learn from this chapter:

In this chapter you will learn to install the basic distribution of R, as well as add-on packages. The chapter also introduces the basics of R syntax and demonstrates how to perform simple operations with different R objects. Special attention is paid to importing and exporting your own data to and from R and saving your graphical output. You will also be able to interpret error messages and warnings that R may give you and search for additional information on R functions.

2.1 Why use R?

In the old days, statistical tests were performed with pencil and paper. Today we are lucky to have computers, which can do complex calculations with amazing speed. This book will show how to use R for statistical analyses and creation of graphs. Although R is also a programming language (that is, one can write their own functions and execute them in R), this aspect is not covered in this book. Its goal is to demonstrate how to use the most popular functions written by other programmers and statisticians and interpret the output.

Why use R? The reasons are manifold. First, R seems to have become the *de facto* standard tool in many areas of linguistics, especially corpus-based and computational studies. Many leading quantitative linguists use R. Second, R offers a wealth of various functions and packages for specific tasks written by professional statisticians and specialists in different fields (at the moment of writing, the number of downloadable packages in the CRAN repository was 6050). Although it takes some time to master the basics of R syntax, you will be rewarded by its amazing flexibility and wealth of useful information. In case of questions or problems, one can rely on the support of the vast and dynamic R community. And last but not least, R is freely available for download. Created and supported by thousands of enthusiasts all over the world, it is distributed under the GNU General Public License, which gives end users the right to use, study, share and modify the software.

2.2   Installation of the basic distribution and add-on packages

If you are a Windows or Mac OS X user, you can install R from http://cran.r-project.org/. CRAN is the Comprehensive R Archive Network. It is a collection of sites (mirrors) all over the world that carry identical material (packages, documentation, etc.). The purpose of mirrors is to reduce network load. Click on *Mirrors* in the main menu on the left and select the mirror site that is the closest to your location. Choose the binaries for base distribution that match your OS and download the Installer package. When the download is completed, double-click on the Installer and follow the directions of the setup wizard. If you use a 64-bit version of Windows, it is recommended to choose the 64-bit version of R when the installer asks you to make the choice between the 64-bit and 32-bit versions. This will make large computations run faster. In addition to the base packages, it is strongly recommended to install the documentation.

If you use Linux, you should check with your package management system, since R is part of many Linux distributions. However, such prebuilt copies of R may be outdated. To obtain the latest version, you may want to get the distribution directly from CRAN. Two scenarios are possible in that case. For some Unix and Unix-like platforms, you can find precompiled binary distributions. To install them, follow the directions available on the website or in the corresponding README files. The second option is to build the distribution package yourself from the source file (you will need a C compiler and a FORTRAN compiler or *f2c* to do that). For detailed instructions, see the manual on R Installation and Administration at http://cran.r-project.org/ and the corresponding FAQ section. In most cases, especially if you are a beginner, it makes more sense to install a precompiled distribution than to build R from scratch.

The basic distribution of R contains many useful functions developed by the R Core Team. There also exist add-on packages developed by statisticians all over the world for specific tasks. It is possible to install an add-on package by typing in the following command in the R console (see next section):

```
> install.packages("cluster")
```

The name of the package is enclosed in the quotation marks. Note that you need to have Internet access. First, R will prompt you to select the nearest CRAN mirror. Next, you will be able to select and install the package. However, you will not be able to access the data and functions from the package yet. First, you need to load it. For example, for the package cluster, the command will be as follows:

```
> library(cluster)
```

You will have to load all add-on packages that you need for your work every time you open your R workspace. If you work with the R GUI (Graphical User Interface), it is also possible to install, update and load packages via *Packages* in the main menu of the R console. Managing packages is also very easy with RStudio (see Section 2.5).

This textbook comes with a companion package `Rling`. It contains the datasets that are discussed in the textbook and a few functions. The package can be downloaded from the online platform at http://dx.doi.org/10.1075/z.195.website (file *Rling_1.0.tar.gz*) and installed on your computer by following the instructions provided in the file *read.me*. Next, it should be loaded:

```
> library(Rling)
```

The list of all packages that should be installed and loaded will be given at the beginning of every case study. To be able to access a dataset from an add-on package, use `data()` with the name of the dataset in parentheses, for example:

```
> data(ldt)
```

How to cite R and add-on R packages

It is important that you acknowledge the enormous work of R creators and maintainers by making proper references to the software. To obtain the citation information on your base distribution, type in the following:

```
> citation()

To cite R in publications use:

R Core Team (2015). R: A language and environment for statistical
computing. R Foundation for Statistical Computing, Vienna,
Austria. URL
http://www.R-project.org/.
[output omitted]
```

If you use someone's add-on package for your research, follow the example below:

```
> citation("cluster")

To cite the R package 'cluster' in publications use:

Maechler, M., Rousseeuw, P., Struyf, A., Hubert, M., Hornik,
K.(2015). cluster: Cluster Analysis Basics and Extensions. R
package version 2.0.1.
[output omitted]
```

2.3   First steps with R

2.3.1   Starting R

In Windows, R can be started by clicking on the *R* icon on your desktop (if you have agreed to create it during the setup) or from the *Start* menu. Users of OS X can click on the *R* icon in the *Applications* directory. This will open the R GUI, or R console, shown in Figure 2.1. If you work with Linux/Unix, type *R* to start an R session.

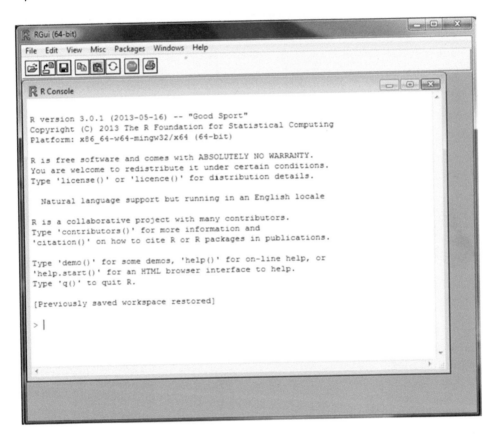

Figure 2.1. A screenshot of the R console

2.3.2   R syntax

After you have started R, you will see some text that gives you information about the R version and some useful commands. The > sign indicates the prompt line where you can type your code. Unlike some other statistical packages, R requires that the user types in his or her commands in the prompt line. Pressing *Enter* will get them executed. For example, one can type in an arithmetic expression and press *Enter* to get the result:

```
> 2 + 2
[1]  4
```

The result appears on the line below the command. The number in square brackets [1] shows the index number of the element in the output. This information can be useful when one has a long string of elements that does not fit in one line. For example, if you type in month.name, you can get the following output (the actual output on your computer depends on the size of the active screen):

```
> month.name
[1]  "January" "February" "March"    "April"         "May"
[6]  "June"    "July" "August"        "September" "October"
[11] "November" "December"
```

It is also possible to type several commands on one line. The commands should be separated by a semicolon:

```
> 2+2;4+4
[1]  4
[1]  8
```

Common arithmetic operations in R

Addition	`2 + 2`
Subtraction	`10 - 5`
Multiplication	`5*5`
Division	`10/2`
Raising to the power	`3^4`
Quadratic root	`16^(1/2)` or `sqrt(16)`
Cubic root	`27^(1/3)`
Natural logarithm $ln(x)$ to the base $e \approx 2.178$	`log(10)`
Logarithm to the base 10 $log_{10}(x)$	`log(100, 10)` or `log10(100)`

An example of combining several operations:

```
> -10 + (56 + 76)/12 + 3^4 - 16^(1/2) + 200*0.01
[1]  80
```

(Continued)

Do not forget to use parentheses to specify the order of operations where necessary:

```
> 16^(1/4)*(12+68)/(211 + 9)
[1] 0.7272727
```

Importantly, R can store objects created by you. This is convenient when you have complex analyses involving many steps. As a very simple illustration, we will create an object a that equals 3:

```
> a <- 3
```

This time R does not give any output. It simply 'remembers' the new object. To call a stored object, simply type its name:

```
> a
[1] 3
```

The new object can be used in other operations:

```
> a + 5
[1] 8
```

It is also possible to assign a value to a variable with the help of =.

```
> a = 3
> a
[1] 3
```

However, in some cases, this may create problems, so it is recommended to use <- for assignment, as shown above.

Double equal sign

In the following chapters you will also see the double equal sign ==. Unlike the single equal sign, which can be used for assignment, the double sign is used for testing if all elements of an object meet a certain logical condition. Consider the following example:

```
> a = 3 # creates an object a with the value 3, an alternative
to a <- 3
> a == 3 # tests if a equals 3
[1] TRUE
```

```
> a == 10 # tests if a equals 10
[1] FALSE
```

You can also perform different operations with the stored objects and combine them with other objects. Be careful with capital and small letters. R interprets them as different symbols.

```
> b <- 7
> a + b
[1] 10
> a + B
Error: object 'B' not found
```

The list of all objects that have been created can be accessed as follows:

```
> ls()
[1] "a"        "b"
```

To remove an object, you can use the rm() function:

```
> rm(b)
> ls()
[1] "a"
```

The code below removes ALL objects, so you should be very careful when using it:

```
> rm(list = ls())
```

Such expressions as sqrt(), rm(), ls() are called **functions**. To use them, one can provide arguments in parentheses, e.g. sqrt(16), or use the default ones. Every function has its unique arguments, such as numbers, characters, previously created R objects, other functions, etc. To check which arguments are needed, one can use Help files (see Section 2.3.4).

How to save time typing your R commands

You can always go back to your previous commands by using the *Up* and *Down* arrows on your keyboard. This will make the previous code appear on the command line. Instead of typing in your code again, you can simply use your previous commands. You can also edit them if necessary. It is recommended to copy and paste elaborate code in a separate file, so that it can be easily accessed again.

2.3.3   Exiting from R or terminating a process

In Windows and OS X, you can exit the R GUI by selecting *File → Exit* from the main menu, or by clicking on the red cross in the top right corner of the window frame. If you use Linux/Unix, press *Ctrl-D*. In all systems, you can always exit from R by typing in the following command:

```
> q()
```

R will ask you if you want to save your workspace. If you choose this option, R will save your workspace with all user-defined objects to an .RData file. This is the recommended option if you plan to continue working with the created objects in the future. By default, the file will be stored in your current working directory. Note that the previous .RData file will be overwritten. To identify your current working directory, type in

```
> getwd()
[1]  "C:/Users/YourName/YourDirectory"
```

When you want to open the saved workspace, you can do so by opening R or by double-clicking on the .RData file in your working directory. If you have several workspaces stored at different locations, you can open the one that you need either by double-clicking on the .RData file in the corresponding directory, or by typing in the path to the file in your R console:

```
> load("C:/Users/YourName/YourDirectory/yourFile.RData")
```

RStudio offers a convenient environment for managing several projects (see Section 2.5). Another useful file that you will find in the working directory after saving your workspace is .Rhistory, which contains the commands that you have entered.

Sometimes one needs to stop a computation process, which has been running for a long time. In this case, you can press *Esc* or click on the red *STOP* sign (Windows or OS X), or press *Ctrl-C* (Linux/Unix). By doing so, you will stop the process without exiting from R.

2.3.4   Getting help

Very often it is necessary to check which arguments are required by a function, or to search for a relevant function. R documentation provides a lot of useful information. For instance, if you want to find out how to use the function cor(), which returns a correlation coefficient, you can type in the following command:

```
> help(cor)
```

Alternatively, you can use

```
> ?cor
```

Very often, however, one does not remember or know the name of specific function. Suppose you want to learn how to measure correlation between two variables. In that case, one can use the following code:

```
> help.search("correlation")
```

or, more simply

```
> ??correlation
```

This will return a list of all functions available in your documentation, which contain the expression.

Important guidance is also provided in warnings and error messages. An error message indicates that the command was not successful. For example, the following code did not work because of a typo in the function name:

```
> corr.test(x, y) #do not run; only provided as an example
Error: could not find function "corr.test"
```

In this situation, one can correct the code by typing `cor.test(x, y)`. Unlike errors, warning messages do not mean that the operation was unsuccessful. Instead, they indicate some problematic issues that need to be double-checked. Consider an example with a data object d:

```
> chisq.test(d) # do not run
    Pearson's Chi-squared test with Yates' continuity correction
data: d
X-squared = 3.865, df = 1, p-value = 0.0493

Warning message:
In chisq.test(d): Chi-squared approximation may be incorrect
```

The chi-squared (χ^2) test is not robust when at least one expected value in the table is smaller than 5 (see Chapter 9). It is recommended to use another test (e.g. the Fisher exact test) in such cases.

If the documentation is not sufficient or clear, one can look for help in the global R community. The easiest way is googling for specific keywords. The chances are that someone has already been struggling with a similar issue. One can also post a question on mailing lists, e.g. the R-help list. See https://stat.ethz.ch/mailman/listinfo/r-help for further instructions.

2.4   Main types of R objects

Uni-, bi- and multivariate data can be represented in R by different objects. Single variables are most commonly represented by vectors and factors. **Vectors** can be of two main types:

numeric (sequences of numbers) and character (sequences of character strings). Below is a numeric vector called vnum, a sequence of integers from 1 to 5, which was generated with the help of the colon operator.

```
> vnum <- 1:5
> vnum
[1] 1 2 3 4 5
```

Another way of creating a vector is by using the function c(), which combines individual elements:

```
> fibonacci10 <- c(1, 1, 2, 3, 5, 8, 13, 21, 34, 55)
> fibonacci10
[1] 1 1 2 3 5 8 13 21 34 55
```

The resulting vector is a sequence of ten Fibonacci numbers, where each subsequent number is the sum of the previous two.

Now consider an example of a character vector, a sequence of words in Gertrude Stein's famous sentence:

```
> stein <- c("a", "rose", "is", "a", "rose", "is", "a", "rose")
> stein
[1] "a"     "rose" "is"   "a"    "rose" "is"   "a"    "rose"
```

Character strings should be enclosed in quotation marks. It does not matter whether you use double or single quotation marks in R, as long as you use the same type in the beginning and at the end of your character string.

Character vectors will be rarely used in this book, however. Nominal variables are best represented by **factors**. One can create a factor from a character vector as follows:

```
> stein.fac <- factor(stein)
> stein.fac
[1] a rose is a    rose is    a    rose
Levels: a is rose
```

The factor levels represent the categories a, is and rose. Note that the levels are arranged alphabetically by default.

The frequencies of factor levels can be represented in a **table**:

```
> table(stein.fac)
stein.fac
  a  is  rose
  3   2    3
```

The result of this operation is a one-dimensional table with frequencies of each level. In the corpus linguistics terminology, these are the **token frequencies** of the words in this small text, whereas the factor levels (words) represent **types**.

Several numeric vectors can be combined in a **matrix** (mathematically speaking, a two-dimensional array). Consider an example:

```
> m <- cbind(1:5, 10:6)
> m
     [,1] [,2]
[1,]  1    10
[2,]  2     9
[3,]  3     8
[4,]  4     7
[5,]  5     6
```

The function cbind() combines two or more vectors or factors as columns. Its counterpart is rbind(), which combines different rows.

In real research, data are often represented as **data frames**. A data frame is a list of vectors and/or factors of various types, or other objects. It is usually displayed as a table with rows, which normally correspond to individual cases, and columns, which represent variables. Below is an imaginary example of experimental data. The cases (rows) are four participants in an experiment, and the variables (sex and reaction time in milliseconds), are columns. The data frame is constructed from two vectors, one of which is a character vector with information about the participants' sex, and the other is a numeric vector with reaction times:

```
> sex <- c("f", "m", "m", "f")
> sex
[1] "f" "m" "m" "f"

> rt <- c(455, 773, 512, 667)
> rt
[1] 455 773 512 667

> df <- data.frame(sex, rt)
> df
  sex   rt
1  f    455
2  m    773
3  m    512
4  f    667
```

When building a data frame, R automatically turns a character vector (sex) into a factor, as can be seen from the output of str(), which can display the internal structure of any R object.

```
> str(df)
'data.frame':        4 obs. Of 2 variables:
$ sex: Factor w/ 2 levels "f","m": 1 2 2 1
$ rt: num 455 773 512 667
```

R offers many convenient tools to explore, edit and subset data frames. For example, one can easily select a column in a data frame as follows:

```
> df$sex
[1] f m m f
Levels: f m
```

For more information on how to manipulate these and other R objects, see Appendix 1. Finally, if you do not know which type an object belongs to, use the function is(), for example:

```
> is(m)
[1] "matrix"  "array"      "structure" "vector"
```

2.5   RStudio

RStudio is an integrated environment for R. It can run both locally and on a web server. It is very convenient for managing one's numerous research projects. RStudio enables one to easily access the R console, R code, data, plots, packages, etc., which are represented in separate panels and tabs (see Figure 2.2). You can view and edit your data, execute your code directly from the code editor, search in your R history, and do many other useful things. RStudio is freely downloadable from http://www.rstudio.com/ and available for different platforms.

2.6   Importing and exporting your data and saving your graphs

2.6.1   Importing your data to R

When doing your own research, it is crucial to be able to import and export your data to and from R. Many linguists store their datasets in Excel or similar spreadsheets. Consider an example, a fictitious dataset in Figure 2.3. The dataset contains a list of imaginary subjects, their sex, dialect (American or British English) and their reaction times in an experiment (in milliseconds). The first row contains the names of variables.

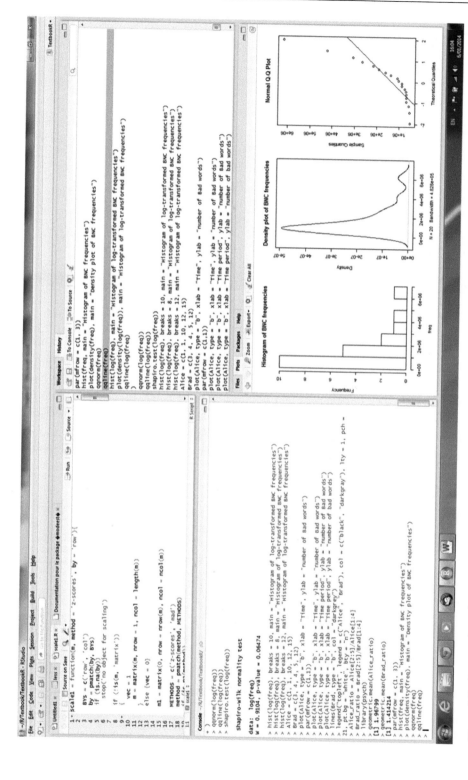

Figure 2.2. A screenshot of RStudio

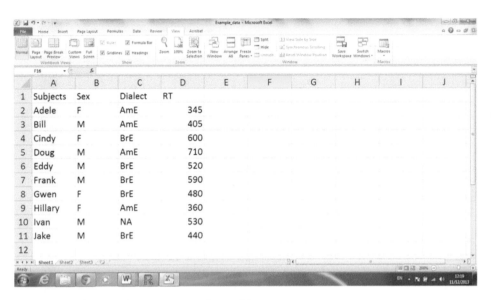

Figure 2.3. A fictitious dataset in an Excel spreadsheet

It is important that your table should not contain any empty cells. Note that Ivan has a missing value for *Dialect*. Missing values should be coded as "NA".

You can save your spreadsheet in several formats by using *File → Save As*. The most popular ones are the tab delimited text file (.txt) and the comma-separated values file (.csv). Let us assume you have used both options and created two files, *Example_data_tab.txt* and *Example_data_csv.csv*. See the screenshots in Figure 2.4. Note that the.csv file may also contain semicolons rather than commas, depending on the spreadsheet software you are using.

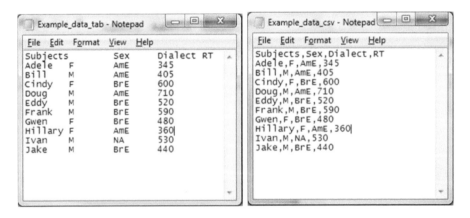

Figure 2.4. Screenshots of the files with tab-separated (left) and comma-separated values data (right)

Now you can import the data to R with the help of `read.table()` or `read.csv()`. You will have to specify the path (if you save the file in your working directory, then you can only provide the file name). For the tab-delimited file, the code will be as follows:

```
> data_tab <- read.table("C:/Your/Directory/Example_data_tab.txt",
header = TRUE)
```

The expression `header = TRUE` tells R to treat the first line as the names of variables.

For Windows users: Beware the backslash!

If you are a Windows user and you have to specify a file location in some directory, you should avoid using backslashes. For instance, if your path is

`C:\My\Directory\mydata.txt,`

you should use either double backslashes, as below:

`"C:\\My\\Directory\\mydata.txt",`

or single forward slashes:

`"C:/My/Directory/mydata.txt"`

The function `head()` enables you to see the first six elements (here, rows in the table). R also provides names for rows: here, the row names are numbers from 1 to 10 (only the first six are shown).

```
> head(data_tab)
  Subjects  Sex  Dialect  RT
1 Adele      F    AmE      345
2 Bill       M    AmE      405
3 Cindy      F    BrE      600
4 Doug       M    AmE      710
5 Eddy       M    BrE      520
6 Frank      M    BrE      590
```

Let us use `str()` to examine the structure of the data frame:

```
> str(data_tab)
'data.frame': 10 obs. Of 4 variables:
$ Subjects:    Factor w/ 10 levels "Adele","Bill",..: 1 2 3 4 5 6 7
                8 9 10
$ Sex:         Factor w/ 2 levels "F", "M": 1 2 1 2 2 2 1 1 2 2
$ Dialect:     Factor w/ 2 levels "AmE","BrE": 1 1 2 1 2 2 2 1 NA 2
$ RT:          int 345 405 600 710 520 590 480 360 530 440
```

Again, you can see that R has interpreted the subjects' names, sex and dialect variables as factors.

Non-ASCII characters in data frames

Using non-ASCII characters in R may be problematic. Consider an example. You collect experimental data about the linguistic development of several Russian children. Their names are written in Russian (the first column in your dataset). You save the data as a tab-delimited text file in Unicode, or UTF–8. When you import the data in R, you should specify the encoding:

```
> rus <- read.table("rus.txt", encoding = "UTF-8") # do not run
```

However, the data may be displayed unintelligibly when you try to look at the entire dataset:

```
> rus # do not run
V1 V2
1                       〈U+FEFF〉〈U+0410〉〈U+043D〉〈U+044F〉 28
2                       〈U+0412〉〈U+0430〉〈U+043D〉〈U+044F〉 16
3                       〈U+041C〉〈U+0438〉〈U+0448〉〈U+0430〉 22
4       <U+041D〉〈U+0430〉〈U+0442〉〈U+0430〉〈U+0448〉〈U+0430〉 31
5                       〈U+041F〉〈U+0435〉〈U+0442〉〈U+044F〉 30
6                       〈U+042F〉〈U+043D〉〈U+0430〉 25
```

Yet, if you look only at one variable, you can see the values (the children's names):

```
> rus[, 1] # do not run
[1] Аня      Ваня   Миша   Наташа Петя   Яна
Levels: Аня Ваня Миша Наташа Петя Яна
```

You can also see the original data if you transform the data into a matrix:

```
> as.matrix(rus) # do not run
       V1          V2
[1,]  "Аня"       "28"
[2,]  "Ваня"      "16"
[3,]  "Миша"      "22"
[4,]  "Наташа"    "31"
[5,]  "Петя"      "30"
[6,]  "Яна"       "25"
```

The output may also depend on the local settings of your OS. Unfortunately, data frames are easy to use if you have ASCII characters only.

To open the comma-separated file, use `read.csv()` instead of `read.table()`. In that case, you do not have to specify `header = TRUE` because it is the default option. If the file is saved with the semicolon as the delimiter, you can use `read.csv2()`.

Dealing with spaces in your data

In case you have a tab-delimited file and you have spaces in some of the values, you should tell R to use the tab as a delimiter; otherwise it will treat spaces as delimiters, as well. Let us add a new line to the data with the following values (shown with formatting signs):

Subjects   → Sex → Dialect → RT¶
Kate ·Emma → F   → BrE   → 570¶

"Kate Emma" is a double name written with a space, and it represents one subject in the experiment. If you now save the dataset as a tab-separated file *Example_data_space.txt* and try to read it in R, you will get an error message:

```
>  data_space  <-  read.table("C:/Your/Directory/Example_data_
space.txt", header = TRUE)
Error in scan(file, what, nmax, sep, dec, quote, skip, nlines,
na.strings,:
line 11 did not have 4 elements
```

(Continued)

This happens because line 11 has five elements instead of the expected four. To fix this, add sep = "\t" (the default separator is any 'white space', that is, one or more spaces, tabs, newlines or carriage returns):

```
> data_space <- read.table("C:/Your/Directory/Example_data_
space.txt", header = TRUE, sep = "\t")
```

2.6.2   Exporting your data from R

After you have created or edited your dataset in R, you might want to export it. To export a data frame, you can use the function write.table():

```
> write.table(data_tab, file = "C:/Your/Directory/Exported.txt",
quote = FALSE, sep = "\t", row.names = FALSE)
```

The first argument is the name of the data frame. It is followed by the path where you want to save the file. The next argument is quote = FALSE, which tells R not to put the character strings or factor values in quotation marks (it does so by default). The code also says that the field separator is the tab character (the default separator is white space). Finally, row.names = FALSE tells R not to save the row names (numbers from 1 to 10). In this example, they are not very informative. Of course, if the row names are important, you should keep them. In that case, you should simply remove row.names = FALSE from the code. The default is to save the row names, as well as the column names. The new file can be easily opened in Excel or a similar application. See more options on the help page of write.table(). If you want to save your data in the comma-separated values format, you can use write.csv().

Choosing files interactively

If you find it inconvenient to type long paths, you can choose files interactively with the help of file = file.choose(), e.g. read.table(file = file.choose()). You will see a file selection window, where you can choose the location and specify the name of the file.

2.6.3   Saving your graphs

R offers many functions that can be used for making graphs. After you have entered the code with those functions, an R graphical device window will be opened. If you use the R GUI, the easiest way to save your graphical output is to select *File → Save As* from the main menu and then choose the desired format. Another way of doing it, which is also available on Unix-like systems, would be as follows:

```
> png("C:/My/Directory/myplot.png")  # opens a plot device. You
should specify the path and the name of the file. Alternatively, use
file = file.choose(), as shown in the previous section.
> plot(1:5, 11:15) # makes a scatter plot
> dev.off()# closes the graphics device
null device
         1
```

You can also use `jpeg()`, `tiff()`, `bmp()`, as well as `pdf()` to save your output in a specific format. See `help(jpeg)` for more information about how to control different graphical parameters, e.g. the size of the plot (arguments `width` and `height`) and background colour (`bg`). RStudio offers a convenient interface for copying and saving plots in different formats and sizes.

Dealing with other data formats

- If you have tabular or CSV data from the Web, HTML tables and MySQL databases, see Teetor (2011) for guidelines.
- To learn how one can read and write individual vectors, factors, lists and matrices, see the help pages of `scan()` and `cat()` or `write()`. See also Gries (2013:69–71, 80–81).
- If you deal with more complex data structures, see Recipe 4.12 in Teetor (2011).
- If you want to store an R object for later use, or to transfer it from one computer to another, see Recipe 4.14 in Teetor (2011), as well as the help pages of `load()` and `save()`.

2.7 Summary

In this chapter you have learnt how to install the basic R distribution and add-on packages. We have discussed some operations with the main data types in R. You have also learnt how to import and export your own datasets to and from R. For further analyses discussed in this book, the author recommends that you use RStudio, although this is not necessary. You should be able now to install and load the add-on packages required for the subsequent case studies, including the companion package Rling. Now that you are equipped with the basic principles and tools, we can begin doing linguistics with R.

More on R basics

You can find more information on R basics and operations with various R objects in Crawley (2007: Ch. 1–7). Teetor's (2011) *R Cookbook* is a convenient task-based reference book. See also Appendix 1 for more operations with basic R objects.

CHAPTER 3

Descriptive statistics for quantitative variables

What you will learn from this chapter:

> This chapter shows how to compute basic descriptive statistics for a quantitative variable. You will learn the most popular measures of central tendency (the mean, the median and the mode) and dispersion (variance, standard deviation, range, IQR, median absolute deviation). The chapter will also demonstrate how to produce different graphs (box-and-whisker plots, histograms, density plots, Q–Q plots, line charts), which visualize univariate distributions and help one determine whether a variable is normally distributed. From the case studies you will learn how to analyse the distribution of word lengths in a sample, to detect suspicious values in subjects' reaction times in a lexical decision task, and to correct some problems with the shape of a distribution.

3.1 Analysing the distribution of word lengths: Basic descriptive statistics

3.1.1 The data

To be able to reproduce the code in this section, you will need two add-on packages: Rling and modeest. See Chapter 2 (Section 2.2) to find out how to install the former. To install the latter, you should do the following:

```
> install.packages("modeest")
```

When you have both packages installed, you should load them:

```
> library(Rling); library(modeest)
```

The first case study analyses the distribution of word lengths (in letters) in a sample of words. The dataset that we will use in this case study is ldt from Rling. If you want to work with a dataset from an add-on package, it is necessary to load it into the workspace:

```
> data(ldt)
```

The dataset contains 100 randomly selected words from the English Lexicon Project data (Balota et al. 2007). The English Lexicon Project provides behavioural and descriptive data from hundreds of native speakers for over forty thousand words in American English, as well as for non-words. The dataset contains three quantitative variables:

- *Length*: word length in letters;
- *Freq*: word frequency according to the Hyperspace Analogue to Language frequency norms (Lund & Burgess 1996), based on the HAL corpus, which consists of about 131 million words gathered from Usenet newsgroups, also known as Google groups;
- *Mean_RT*: average reaction times in a lexical decision task, in milliseconds. A lexical decision task is an experiment where subjects are asked to classify stimuli as words or non-words.

In R data frames, individual observations or items are usually represented as rows, and variables as columns. You can access the first six words and their values by using the function head():

```
> head(ldt)
             Length  Freq  Mean_RT
marveled        8     131   819.19
persuaders     10      82   977.63
midmost         7       0   908.22
crutch          6     592   766.30
resuspension   12       2  1125.42
efflorescent   12       9   948.33
```

To learn more about the dataset and its structure, one can use the function str():

```
> str(ldt)
'data.frame': 100 obs. of 3 variables:
$ Length: int 8 10 7 6 12 12 3 11 11 5 …
$ Freq: int 131 82 0 592 2 9 14013 15 48 290 …
$ Mean_RT: num 819 978 908 766 1125 …
```

The function returns the type of R object (data frame), the number of observations (100) and variables (3), as well as the class of each variable and its first values. The abbreviation int stands for a numeric vector with integers only (numbers like 1, 2, 3, 4, 100…). Word length in letters and word frequency, as discrete variables, contain only integers. The abbreviation num designates a numeric vector with non-integers (numbers like 1.2, 5.84, 9.946 etc.). R may also store integers as num objects, but this should not be a matter of concern.

In this case study we will analyse the distribution of word lengths. When analysing a quantitative variable, it is necessary to estimate the central tendency and dispersion. The measures of central tendency tell us which values tend to be the most typical. The measures of dispersion show how variable the data are.

3.1.2 Measures of central tendency

Which values are the most typical of a distribution? This question can be answered in different ways. Perhaps the most popular measure of central tendency is the **mean**, or **average**. For example, one can speak about average income in a country, average number of children in a family, or average life expectancy. In R, the mean is computed straightforwardly with the help of mean(). The average word length in the sample is obtained as follows:

```
> mean(ldt$Length)  # equivalent to mean(…, na.rm = FALSE), i.e.
by default, NAs are not removed. If there is a missing value, the
function returns NA. See box 'Handling Missing Data' below.
[1] 8.23
```

So, on average a word in the sample contains 8.23 letters.

How to attach and detach a dataset

If you do not want to type the name of your dataset every time you refer to the variables that it contains, you can simply attach it, so that R will be able to access the objects in the dataset directly:

```
> attach(ldt)
> mean(Length)
[1] 8.23
```

If you do not want R to access the objects directly (for example, if you have another dataset with similar variable names), you should detach the dataset:

```
> detach(ldt)
> mean(Length)
Error in mean(Length): object 'Length' not found
```

Another useful measure of central tendency is the **median**. This notion requires some explanation. Let us first sort all values in the vector of word lengths in increasing order:

```
> sort(ldt$Length) #equivalent to sort(…, decreasing = FALSE)
 [1] 3 3 4 4 4 4 4 5 5 5 5 5 5 5 6 6 6 6 6 6 6 6
[23] 6 6 6 6 6 7 7 7 7 7 7 7 7 7 7 7 8 8 8 8 8 8
[45] 8 8 8 8 8 8 8 8 8 8 9 9 9 9 9 9 9 9 9 9 9 9
[67] 10 10 10 10 10 10 10 10 10 10 10 10 10 10 10 10 11 11 11 11 11 11
[89] 11 11 11 11 11 12 12 12 13 14 14 15
```

The median is the value that is found in the middle of the ordered values. So, if we have 100 data points, the first half will include the first fifty values, whereas the values ranked 51 to 100 will constitute the second half. The middle point is thus found between the values with the ranks 50 and 51. Both of them equal eight. The median is then the sum of eight and eight divided by two, that is, eight. If we had 99 observations, the median would be the 50th value. If we had 101 observations, the median would be the 51st value. In R, the median can be obtained as follows:

```
> median(ldt$Length) #equivalent to median(…, na.rm = FALSE)
[1] 8
```

In some situations the median gives a better idea of the most typical value than the mean. The problem with the latter is that it is easily influenced by outliers, i.e. scores with unusually high or low values. For example, if twenty employees in a company have net salaries of €2000 a month, and the CEO's salary is €50000, the mean salary will be €4286, and the median will be €2000. The median gives a more realistic idea of the salaries in the company than the mean because the CEO's salary is exceptional.

The median can also be defined in terms of **percentiles** and **quartiles**. They represent values below which a given percentage or fraction of observations in a distribution falls. The median is a value below which we can find 50%. In other words, the median is the 50th percentile. We can also obtain the 33rd percentile, 67th percentile, 99th percentile, and so on. If we cut the data into four quarters, we will obtain quartiles. The point that separates the first quarter, or 25% of observations, from the rest, is called the first quartile, or the 25th percentile. Its counterpart is the third quartile, which separates the first three quarters, or 75% of observations, from the remaining 25%. It can also be called the 75th percentile. The median is then the second quartile, because it separates the two first quarters from the remaining two.

The generic term for percentiles and quartiles is **quantiles**. They are usually expressed as fractions from 0 to 1. For example, the 0.5 quantile corresponds to the median, or 50th percentile, or second quartile. The correspondences between different terms are summarized in Table 3.1. Computation of quantiles in R is straightforward. For example, one can obtain the 0.25 quantile, or the first quartile, or the 25th percentile, as follows:

```
> quantile(ldt$Length, 0.25)
25%
6
```

Another way to obtain the median, or the second quartile, or the 50th percentile, or the 0.5 quantile, is as follows:

```
> quantile(ldt$Length, 0.5)
50%
8
```

Finally, one can compute the third quartile, or the 75th percentile, or the 0.75 quantile:

```
> quantile(ldt$Length, 0.75)
75%
10
```

Quantiles, especially quartiles, will become crucial when one has to interpret graphical representations of distributions, such as box plots (see Section 3.1.4).

Table 3.1 Correspondences between different types of quantiles

Quartiles	Percentiles	Quantiles	Median	Meaning
First quartile	25th percentile	0.25	–	¼ of all ranked scores are below this value
Second quartile	50th percentile	0.5	median	½ of all ranked scores are found below this value
Third quartile	75th percentile	0.75	–	¾ of all ranked scores are found below this value

A third measure of central tendency is the **mode**. It is the most 'popular' value in the data. To find the mode, one can tabulate all possible values with the help of `table()`:

```
> table(ldt$Length)

 3  4  5  6  7  8  9 10 11 12 13 14 15
 2  5  7 13 12 16 11 16 11  3  1  2  1
```

The function displays all word lengths (the upper row) and how many times each length occurs in the data (the bottom row). One can see that the maximum frequency is 16, which occurs twice: when the length is equal to eight and ten letters. The distribution therefore has two modes, eight and ten. Such distributions are called bimodal.

This method of obtaining the mode, however, is not always very practical. When the number of values is large or when the data are continuous, one can use the function `mlv()` in the package `modeest`. If the data are continuous, the function will find the value that corresponds to the peak of the probability distribution (see Chapter 1). In this example it returns the same values, eight and ten:

```
> mlv(ldt$Length)
Mode (most frequent value): 8 10
Bickel's modal skewness: -0.17
Call: mlv.integer(x = ldt$Length)
```

More measures of central tendency

The list of central tendency measures is by no means restricted by the mean, the median and the mode. One can also compute the harmonic mean, the trimmed mean, the crude mode, and many more. See Huck (2009: 4–6).

A useful command to get most of the above-mentioned statistics at once is `summary()`, which also includes the minimum and the maximum:

```
> summary(ldt$Length)
  Min.  1st Qu.  Median  Mean  3rd Qu.  Max.
  3.00  6.00     8.00    8.23  10.00    15.00
```

The function for obtaining the maximum value only is `max()`. If you need the minimum value, you can use `min()`:

```
> max(ldt$Length)
[1] 15
> min(ldt$Length)
[1] 3
```

Handling missing data

In real life, we often have to deal with missing data. Consider an integer vector *x*, where the last value is missing ('NA'):

```
> x # do not run the code in this box
[1] 1 2 3 4 5 6 7 8 9 10 NA
```

To test if your data contain missing values, you can do the following:

```
> is.na(x)
[1] FALSE FALSE FALSE FALSE FALSE FALSE FALSE FALSE FALSE FALSE
TRUE
```

If there are missing values, this can produce NA's in the output of many standard functions, for example:

```
> mean(x)
[1] NA
```

For some functions, you can fix this by adding na.rm = TRUE to make R ignore all missing values:

```
> mean(x, na.rm = TRUE)
[1] 5.5
```

To create a new vector without missing values, you can do the following:

```
> x1 <- x[!is.na(x)]
> x1
[1] 1 2 3 4 5 6 7 8 9 10
```

For data frames, it is also possible to remove all observations with at least one missing value with the help of data[complete.cases(data),].

Sometimes removal of observations with missing data points is undesirable. An alternative is to assign a specific value instead of a missing one:

```
> x2 <- x #creates a new vector identical to x
> x2[is.na(x2)] <- 0
> x2
[1] 1 2 3 4 5 6 7 8 9 10 0
```

This approach will work for a matrix, as well.

Note that some functions remove observations with missing values automatically, so it is recommended to check the help page of the relevant function to be sure that the default option is what you really need.

3.1.3 Measures of dispersion

Although the measures of central tendency provide useful information, they do not show the entire picture. There is an old statistical joke that illustrates this idea, 'If your head is in the freezer, and your feet are in the oven, on average you're quite comfortable'. The mean, the median and the mode cannot say anything about how much variation we have in our data. For this purpose, we need measures of dispersion.

The simplest measure of dispersion is the **range**. It represents the difference between the maximum and minimum values. In our case, the range of word lengths equals 15 – 3 = 12. To obtain the minimum and maximum lengths simultaneously, one can use the following command:

```
> range(ldt$Length)
[1]  3 15
```

Probably the most popular measures of dispersion are variance and standard deviation. Mathematically speaking, **variance** is the sum of squared deviations of the observations from the mean divided by the number of observations minus 1.

$$s^2 = \frac{1}{n-1}\sum_{i=1}^{n}(x_i - \overline{x})^2$$

where n is the number of observations, $x_1, x_2, \ldots x_n$ are individual scores and $\bar{x}$ is the mean. From this follows that the further the individual cases are on average from the mean, the larger the variance. Note that the deviations (i.e. differences between the individual scores and the mean) are squared. There is a simple explanation to that. If an individual score is greater than the mean, the deviation will be positive. If it is smaller than the mean, the deviation will be negative. As a result, all deviations will sum up to zero, which is not particularly informative. The solution is to get rid of the sign by squaring all deviations. This operation also gives more weight to large deviations. To compute variance, one can use the function var():

```
> var(ldt$Length) # equivalent to var(…, na.rm = FALSE)
[1]  6.259697
```

However, it is more conventional to report the **standard deviation**, which is the square root of variance. By taking the square root, we come back to the original units:

```
> sqrt(var(ldt$Length))
[1]  2.501939
```

The standard deviation can also be computed directly with the help of sd():

```
> sd(ldt$Length)
[1]  2.501939
```

Another measure of dispersion is the **interquartile range (IQR)**, which represents the difference between the third (75%) and the first (25%) quartiles. In our sample, the IQR is 10 – 6 = 4. Alternatively, it can be computed as follows:

```
> IQR(ldt$Length)
[1]  4
```

The IQR can be regarded as a more robust measure of dispersion than variance and standard deviation. When individual deviations are squared, the impact of outliers, i.e. observations that strongly deviate from the mean, becomes even stronger.

Yet another measure is the **median absolute deviation** (MAD). To compute it, one needs to put all absolute deviations from the median in ascending order and then select the median value of these deviations. Since this measure is the median of deviations from the median, it is extremely robust. It can be computed in R as follows:

```
> mad(ldt$Length, constant = 1)
[1]  2
```

Standard deviation should be used for normally distributed data; otherwise, report IQR or MAD.

Obtaining statistics for rows or columns in a matrix

We have discussed how one can compute basic descriptive statistics for one numeric vector. But how to obtain mean reaction times, standard deviations, etc., for many columns or rows in a dataset at once? For this purpose, one can use apply(). For example, if you want to compute the mean for every row in your data (a matrix or a data frame with only quantitative variables), you can use the following command:

```
> apply(data, 1, mean) # do not run
```

The number 1 tells R to apply the function (mean) to every *row*. If you want to compute the standard deviation for each column, you can type in the following:

```
> apply(data, 2, sd) # do not run
```

The number 2 says that you want to apply the function sd to every *column* of data. The argument na.rm = TRUE should be added if you have missing values in the matrix and want R to ignore them.

Unfortunately, some studies report statistics of the central tendency (e.g. the mean or the median), but fail to report dispersion statistics. This can lead to misinterpretation. Consider two countries with a similar average income per capita. In one country the variance and standard deviation are relatively small because the finances are distributed fairly, whereas in the other they are very large because of several billionaires and many extremely poor people. Although the means are identical, the life in these two countries will differ dramatically.

More measures of dispersion

There exist many other measures of dispersion. For example, Gries (2013: 120–125) discusses such measures as relative entropy, average deviation and variation coefficient.

3.2   Bad times, good times: Visualization of a distribution and detection of outliers

The focus of this case study is reaction times in a lexical decision task. They are available as the variable Mean_RT from the data frame ldt, which was introduced in the previous case study. The dataset is available in the Rling package:

```
> install.packages("ggplot2") # if you have not done so previously
> library(Rling); library(ggplot2)
> data(ldt)
```

Note that we deal with *mean* reaction times averaged across many subjects who performed the task.

It is important to know how a variable is distributed and what the distribution looks like because it will influence the choice of appropriate statistical tests. There are several types of graphs that allow one to visualize a distribution. A popular way of visualizing a univariate continuous distribution is a **histogram**. To create a histogram, the entire range of values is first divided into several intervals. Next, rectangles are drawn for every interval. The height of every rectangle is proportional to the observed frequency of the values in the interval. You can create a histogram of the mean reaction times as follows:

```
> hist(ldt$Mean_RT, main = "Histogram of mean reaction times", xlab
= "reaction times, ms")
```

The result is displayed in Figure 3.1 (left). The first argument is a numeric vector of interest. It is followed by two graphical parameters that specify the title of the plot (`main`) and the label of the horizontal axis (`xlab`). Note that all text labels in R should be enclosed in quotation marks. The quotation marks may be single or double. Make sure you use the same type of quotation marks in the beginning and at the end of your expression. More graphical parameters for standard plots are available on the help page of `par()`.

How many bins do you need?

The representation of a distribution by a histogram depends on the number of bins (rectangles). One can experiment with different number of bins in order to select an optimal representation by using the argument `breaks`, e.g. `hist(v, breaks = seq(min(v), max(v), length = 10))`, where `v` is a numeric vector. This argument specifies the position of the breakpoints between the rectangles, including the outward boundaries (one can also try using `breaks = 10`, but this does not always return the exact number of bins). In this example, you will have ten breakpoints and nine rectangles.

There exist different methods of determining the optimal number of bins. One of them is implemented by default when you run `hist()`. Alternatively, you can use the following formula: number of bins = $1 + 3.32 \times \log_{10} n$, where n is the number of data points (Gries 2013: 113). In our example with mean reaction times, the number of bins can be computed as follows:

```
> nbins <- 1 + 3.32*log10(length(ldt$Mean_RT))
> nbins
[1] 7.64
```

A **density plot** shows the ordered numerical values of a variable x on the horizontal axis, and the probability density of x on the vertical axis (see Chapter 1). The result is smoothed, so that one can see the general shape of the distribution. The plots can be created with the help of the simple `plot()` function and embedded `density()` function. The `xlab` argument allows one to specify the text labels for the x-axis. The result is shown in Figure 3.1 (centre).

```
> plot(density(ldt$Mean_RT), main = "Density plot of mean reaction
times", xlab = "reaction times, ms")
```

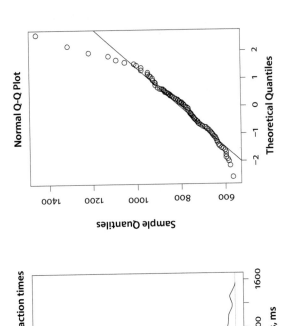

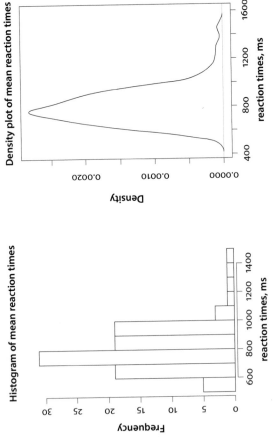

Figure 3.1. Histogram, density plot and Q–Q plot of mean reaction times

A very useful graph for diagnostics of normality is the **Q–Q (quantile-quantile) plot**. It represents the ordered sample values (the *y*-axis) against the quantiles of the standard normal distribution, which will be introduced below (the *x*-axis). First, one creates a plot, and then adds a straight line to it. The closer the points to the line, the more similar the observed data are to the normal distribution.

```
> qqnorm(ldt$Mean_RT)
> qqline(ldt$Mean_RT)
```

What can one infer from the plots? The histogram and the density plot reveal a long 'tail' on the right. This means that there may be one or several untypically large scores on the higher end of the distribution. Some words took the subjects very long to recognize. These words will be identified below. Such distributions with 'heavy' tails on the right are called **positively skewed**. The observations with untypically large values usually inflate the mean, so that it will become greater than the median.[1] This is what one can observe in the data, where the mean is 808.3, and the median is 784.9:

```
> summary(ldt$Mean_RT)
   Min.   1st Qu.   Median    Mean   3rd Qu.   Max.
  564.2   713.1     784.9    808.3   905.2    1459.0
```

Conversely, a distribution with a heavy left tail is called **negatively skewed**. The mean of such a distribution tends to be smaller than the median.

How to create a density plot, a histogram and a Q–Q plot with the help of ggplot2

From this chapter on, the book will provide code for advanced versions of the most important plots. These versions are created with the help of the package ggplot2. The code is very different from the standard plotting functions in R, and consists of several blocks: ggplot(), where you should specify the data frame, geom_...(), which specifies the kind of plot, aes(), which allows one to control 'aesthetics', such as colours, shapes, sizes, etc., and some others. To create a density plot, a histogram and a Q–Q plot of the reaction times with the help of ggplot2, you can use the following code:

(Continued)

---

1. But see Huck (2009: 25–28), who discusses exceptions from this rule.

```
> binsize <- diff(range(ldt$Mean_RT))/nbins # computes binwidth
for n bins. Here, we'll use nbins that was computed above.
> ggplot(ldt, aes(x = Mean_RT)) + geom_histogram(binwidth =
binsize, fill = "white", colour = "black") # creates a histogram
> ggplot(ldt, aes(x = Mean_RT)) + geom_line(stat = "density")
#creates a density plot
> ggplot(ldt, aes(sample = Mean_RT)) + stat_qq() # creates a Q-Q
plot
```

Unfortunately, there seems to be no easy way of adding a Q–Q line to the Q–Q plot.
Figure 3.1a shows the three plots.

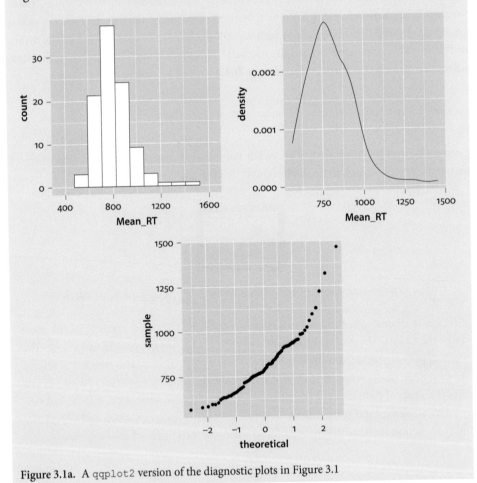

Figure 3.1a. A qqplot2 version of the diagnostic plots in Figure 3.1

In order to choose an appropriate test, it is often important to know whether the data
come from a normal distribution or not. Consider Figure 3.2. It shows a histogram, a density plot and a Q–Q plot of variable *x*. The vector contains 100 values that were randomly

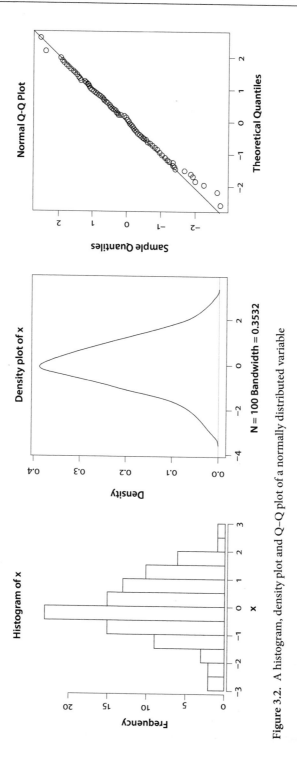

Figure 3.2. A histogram, density plot and Q–Q plot of a normally distributed variable

sampled from the standard normal distribution with the mean of 0 and standard deviation of 1. Normally distributed data are represented by a peculiar bell shape, which is observable on the histogram (left) and the density plot (centre). The closer the value of x to the mean (zero), the higher the probability density (see Chapter 1). Thus, the mean coincides with the mode. A normal distribution is also symmetric. From this follows that the mean also coincides with the median, which divides the distribution into two halves. The Q–Q plot shows that the points are very close to the line. The minor deviations at the ends can be disregarded.

The graphs in Figure 3.1 demonstrate that the mean reaction times are not normally distributed. In some situations, it may be difficult to decide whether the deviations are serious enough. There is a more formal way of testing whether a sample comes from a normal distribution, namely, the Shapiro-Wilk test for normality:

```
> shapiro.test(ldt$Mean_RT)
  Shapiro-Wilk normality test

data: ldt$Mean_RT
W = 0.9201, p-value = 1.418e-05
```

W is the Shapiro-Wilk test statistic. It is used to derive the p-value. Recall that if the p-value is greater than 0.05, the null hypothesis cannot be discarded. The null hypothesis of the Shapiro-Wilk test is that the sample comes from a normally distributed population. The alternative hypothesis is that the data deviate from normality. The p-value is displayed in the scientific notation, which is used to represent very small or very large numbers. The number 1.418e–5 is equal to 1.418 multiplied by 10 at the power of –5. To obtain a 'normal' notation, one can 'move' the decimal delimiter to the left by five decimal places: 0.00001418. Since the p-value is below 0.05, we can discard the null hypothesis of normality. In other words, we have enough reasons to believe that the distribution is non-normal, as one can see from the graphs. Note, however, that a visual inspection, especially examining a Q–Q plot, should be preferred to the Shapiro-Wilk test, since the latter is influenced by the sample size. If the number of observations is high, it is 'easier' for the algorithm to find deviations from normality than when the sample is small.

How to disable scientific notation

Scientific notation, e.g. 2.083e–10, can be disabled in R with the help of the following command:

```
> options(scipen = 999)
```

This command tells R to prefer fixed (normal) notation, unless it is 999 digits longer than the expression in scientific notation.

Thus, the mean reaction times are not distributed normally. There seems to be extremely long reaction times for some words. Observations with unusually high or low scores are called **outliers**. The presence of outliers may signal problems with data collection or design. There are different ways of identifying outliers. This section will discuss three criteria: relationship to the IQR (available in a box plot), z-scores and MAD-scores.

Let us first create a **box plot** (or, more precisely, a box-and-whisker plot) with the help of boxplot(). The first argument of the function is a vector, whereas the second argument is the graphical parameter which specifies the title of the plot.

```
> boxplot(ldt$Mean_RT, main = "Mean reaction times", ylab = "reaction
time in ms")
```

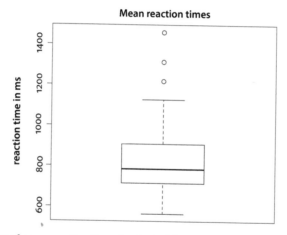

Figure 3.3. Box plot of mean reaction times in a lexical decision task

How to create a box plot with **ggplot2**

One can create a ggplot2 version of the box plot in Figure 3.3 as follows (see the result in Figure 3.3a):

(Continued)

```
> ggplot(ldt, aes(x = 1, y = Mean_RT)) + geom_boxplot() + theme(axis.
title.x = element_blank()) + scale_x_continuous(breaks = NULL)
```

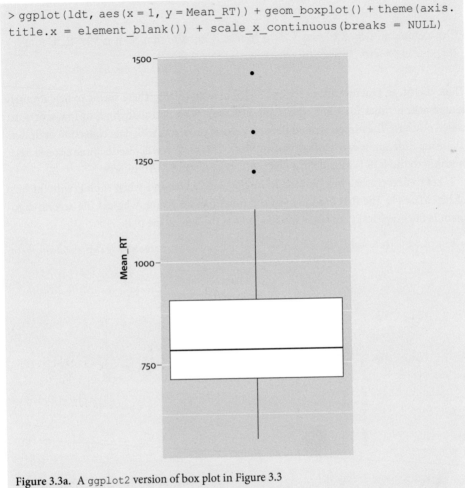

Figure 3.3a. A ggplot2 version of box plot in Figure 3.3

Note that the x-axis has neither a label nor breaks, since these are irrelevant.

A box plot shows the statistics that should be already familiar to the reader from the previous sections. The thick line inside the box corresponds to the median. The lower and upper boundaries of the boxes are called hinges. They show the first and third quartiles, respectively. The size of the box corresponds to the IQR, which represents the difference between the third (upper) and the first (lower) quartiles. The 'whiskers' (the dashed lines) are never longer than 1.5 times the IQR. All observations beyond that value are represented as dots and can be considered outliers. To find out which words these values represent, one can use the following command:

```
> ldt[ldt$Mean_RT > 1200, ]
                Length  Freq  Mean_RT
dessertspoon      12     11   1314.33
acquisitiveness   15      4   1216.81
diacritical       11    162   1458.75
```

You can also obtain the extreme values by typing in the following:

```
> boxplot.stats(ldt$Mean_RT)$out
[1] 1314.33 1216.81 1458.75
```

These words were on average identified slower. One can consider the unconventional spelling of the first word, length and morphological complexity of the second word, and terminological character of the third word as possible explanations of the longer reaction times.

Another way of detecting outliers, which is probably the most popular one, is by using z-scores, also known as standard scores. To compute a z-score from an individual score, or, in other words, to standardize the latter, one can subtract the mean from the score, and divide the result by the standard deviation:

$$z = \frac{x_i - \bar{x}}{s}$$

where x_i is an individual score, $\bar{x}$ is the mean, and s is the standard deviation.

To transform the reaction times into z-scores, you can use the scale() function in the base distribution. However, here we will use the function normalize() from Rling because it also allows one to compute MAD-scores, i.e. scores based on median absolute deviations. This measure of dispersion was introduced in Section 3.1.3. A further discussion will be provided below. First, however, we will compute the z-scores of the mean reaction times. The use of the function is straightforward:

```
> normalize(ldt$Mean_RT)
  [1] 0.07138544 1.10554648 0.65249726 -0.27383532 2.07019341
[output omitted]
```

The scores are now centred around zero. There are different rules of thumb as to which z-scores should be treated as suspicious. The most popular absolute values are 2 (not very conservative), 2.5 (moderately conservative) and 3 (very conservative). The higher the cut-off point, the fewer observations have the chance of being detected as outliers. Let us find the points whose absolute z-scores are equal to or greater than 2.5. Absolute values are non-negative values regardless of the sign. For example, 3 is the absolute value of both 3 and –3. Absolute values can be obtained with the help of abs().

```
> ldt[abs(normalize(ldt$Mean_RT)) >= 2.5,]
                Length  Freq  Mean_RT
dessertspoon      12     11   1314.33
```

```
acquisitiveness    15         4    1216.81
diacritical        11       162    1458.75
```

This expression returns the observations whose absolute z-scores are greater than or equal to 2.5. The outliers detected with the help of the z-scores method are identical to the ones we found with the help of the box plot.

Although z-scores are arguably the most popular method, using them to detect outliers sounds somewhat paradoxical, since z-scores are based on the mean and the standard deviation, which are sensitive to the presence of outliers. A more robust approach is based on MAD-scores (Leys et al. 2013). One can obtain the MAD-score outliers as follows:

```
> ldt[abs(normalize(ldt$Mean_RT, method = "mad")) >= 2.5,]
                 Length  Freq  Mean_RT
dessertspoon       12     11   1314.33
acquisitiveness    15      4   1216.81
diacritical        11    162   1458.75
```

Note that this method is acceptable only for the data that look normally distributed if you ignore the outliers. If the overall shape of the distribution represented on a diagnostic plot is different from the bell curve, one is advised to examine the outliers outside of the 1.5 × IQR region on the box plot.

After the 'suspects' have been detected, one should decide on what to do with them. First, it is necessary to check whether there are any coding errors and correct them, if possible. If all your data are correct, Field et al. (2012: 190–191) suggest three options: removal of the case(s), data transformation and assigning of new scores. Let us examine them one by one.

1. Remove the case(s). This should be done only in very special cases, for example, if there is a sampling mistake and the observation actually comes from a different population than your target population. For instance, you have got a non-native speaker in an experiment where you want to test only native speakers' performance. To create a new dataset without the outliers, you can take the following steps. First, you need to identify the row IDs of the outliers. For example, if you want to remove all outliers with absolute MAD-scores equal to or greater than 2.5, you can first obtain the row numbers of the suspicious observations with the help of which() containing the expression that has been used for identification of the outliers:

```
> outliers <- which(abs(normalize(ldt$Mean_RT, method = "mad")) >=
2.5)
> outliers
[1] 29 70 100
```

Thus, the outliers' row IDs are 29, 70 and 100. If you want to remove the outliers, the next step is as follows:

```
> ldt_remove <- ldt[-outliers,] # or ldt[-c(29, 70, 100),]
> dim(ldt_remove)
[1] 97 3
```

The function `dim()` returns the dimensions of the data: the number of rows and the number of columns. Its output shows that the data frame has now only 97 rows, instead of the original 100.

2. Use a transformation. This method should be applied when your data are very skewed (asymmetric). It is described in the next section.
3. Assign a different score, e.g. the mean plus or minus two standard deviations: `mean(data) + 2*sd(data)` for right-tailed, positively skewed data, or `mean(data) - 2*sd(data)` for left-tailed, negatively skewed data. For example, if you want to assign the mean plus two standard deviations from the mean, you can first compute the score:

```
> mean(ldt$Mean_RT) + 2*sd(ldt$Mean_RT)
[1] 1114.666
```

Next, you can create an identical data frame under a different name and replace the values in the outlier rows and the third column (reaction times):

```
> ldt_new <- ldt
> ldt_new[outliers, 3] <- 1114.666
```

Let us check the result:

```
> ldt_new[outliers,]
                Length  Freq  Mean_RT
dessertspoon       12    11   1114.666
acquisitiveness    15     4   1114.666
diacritical        11   162   1114.666
```

How to compute z-scores and MAD-scores for rows or columns in a matrix?

The function `normalize()` from `Rling` can also compute z-scores and MAD-scores for all rows or columns in a matrix. For example, if you want to compute the MAD-scores for each column, you can use the following command:

(Continued)

```
> normalize(data, method = "mad", by = "col")
```

To compute the *z*-scores for each row, you can use the following:

```
> normalize(data, method = "z-scores", by = "row")
```

or simply

```
> normalize(data)
```

The *z*-score method and standardization by row are the default options.

3.3   Zipf's law and word frequency: Transformation of quantitative variables

To reproduce the code in this case study, you will need two packages: Rling and ggplot2. If you have not installed the latter yet, you can do it as follows:

```
> install.packages("ggplot2")
```

Next, you will need to load the packages:

```
> library(Rling); library(ggplot2)
```

The dataset for this case study is again ldt from Rling. You should load it into you current workspace if you have not done so already.

```
> data(ldt)
```

The third variable in the dataset is Freq, which we have not examined yet, shows the word frequency in a large corpus. Let us first obtain the basic statistics:

```
> summary(ldt$Freq)
   Min. 1st Qu. Median  Mean    3rd Qu.  Max.
   0.0   53.5    310.5  3350.0  2103.0   75080.0
```

As one can see, the frequencies have a very broad range, from zero to 750,80. Let us explore the distribution visually by plotting the values in descending order, from high-frequency words to low-frequency ones (the function sort() with the option decreasing = TRUE):

```
> plot(sort(ldt$Freq, decreasing = TRUE), type = "b", main = "Zipf's
law", ylab = "Word frequency")
```

The result is shown in Figure 3.4. The position of data points is determined by their values on the *x*- and *y*-axes, which represent two numeric vectors. If there is only one vector, as in our case, then the scores are represented by the vertical axis, and the horizontal axis shows the scores' indices (in our case, ranks). This graph is called a line chart because it displays data points connected by lines. By default, the function `plot()` usually creates a scatter plot with points only. If one adds `type = "b"`, the points will be connected by lines. Adding `type = "l"` will display only lines.

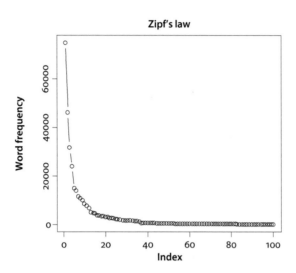

Figure 3.4. Line chart with word frequencies, displayed in descending order

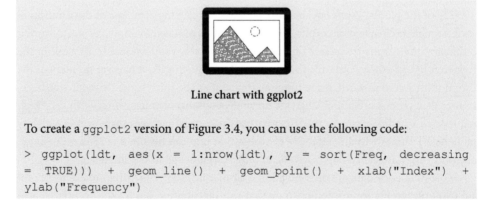

Line chart with ggplot2

To create a `ggplot2` version of Figure 3.4, you can use the following code:

```
> ggplot(ldt, aes(x = 1:nrow(ldt), y = sort(Freq, decreasing
= TRUE))) + geom_line() + geom_point() + xlab("Index") +
ylab("Frequency")
```

(Continued)

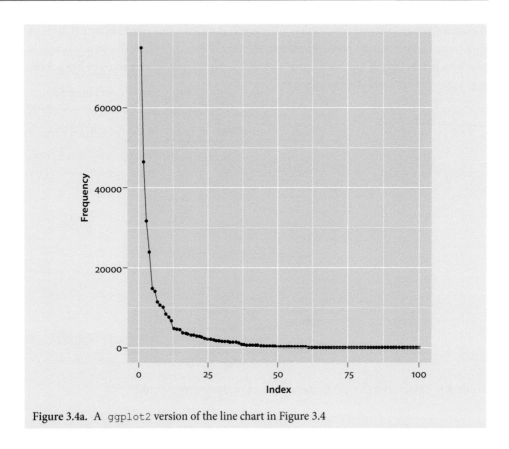

Figure 3.4a. A `ggplot2` version of the line chart in Figure 3.4

The title of the plot is 'Zipf's law' because it illustrates an empirical law of distribution of word frequencies in a text or corpus, which was first formulated by Zipf (1935). According to this law, the corpus frequency of any word is inversely proportional to its rank in the frequency list. In other words, the first word on the frequency list is twice as frequent as the second most frequent word, three times as frequent as the third most frequent word, etc. As a result, a corpus of natural language normally contains very few words with very high frequencies, which account for the larger part of the corpus, and very many words with low frequencies. This is why the majority of words that one can find in a corpus occur there only once. They are called *hapax legomena* (*hapax legomenon* in the singular).

Most frequency data are distributed in a similar fashion. The histogram, density plot and Q–Q plot in Figure 3.5 demonstrate that this distribution has a very peculiar shape. The plots were created with the help of the following code:

```
> par(mfrow = c(1, 3)) # allows to create several plots in one
device: the first number (1) stands for the number of rows, and the
second (3) for the number of columns
> hist(ldt$Freq, main = "Histogram of word frequencies", xlab = "Word
frequency in a corpus", ylab = "Relative frequency in the sample")
```

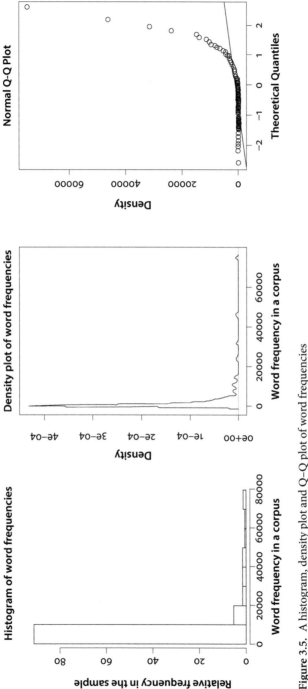

Figure 3.5. A histogram, density plot and Q–Q plot of word frequencies

```
> plot(density(ldt$Freq), main = "Density plot of word frequencies",
xlab = "Word frequency in a corpus")
> qqnorm(ldt$Freq)
> qqline(ldt$Freq)
```

Frequency data are usually logarithmically transformed. However, some frequencies are equal to zero. Since the natural logarithm of zero `log(0)` is minus infinity, this causes a problem:

```
> log(0)
[1] -Inf
```

To solve this problem, one can add 1 to each frequency score and compute the logarithms of the new scores. In R, this transformation can be done by using the function `log1p()`. Let us visualize the transformed data:

```
> hist(log1p(ldt$Freq), main = "Histogram of log-frequencies", xlab
= "Log-transformed word frequency", ylab = "Relative frequency in
the sample")
> plot(density(log1p(ldt$Freq)), main = "Density plot of log-
frequencies", xlab = "Log-transformed word frequency in a corpus")
> qqnorm(log1p(ldt$Freq))
> qqline(log1p(ldt$Freq))
```

As shown in Figure 3.6, the distribution of the log-transformed frequencies is now very similar to normal. The same conclusion can be made after using the Shapiro-Wilk test of normality:

```
> shapiro.test(log1p(ldt$Freq))

  Shapiro-Wilk normality test

data: log1p(ldt$Freq)
W = 0.9814, p-value = 0.1699
```

Other popular power transformations include the square root transformation `sqrt(yourVector)`, which can be helpful for moderate positive skews, the square transformation `(yourVector)^2` for negatively skewed data, and the reciprocal transformation, e.g. `1/(yourVector + 1)`, which can help in cases of distributions that look like the letter J or its mirror image. More details can be found in Field et al. (2012:191–201) and Sheskin (2011:483–488). The best way is to try different transformations and visualize them with the help of the plots that we have just discussed.

Applying power transformations has its costs and benefits. On the one hand, you can use many traditional well-understood parametric methods with normally distributed data. These tests will be introduced in the following chapters. On the other hand, overly sophisticated transformations make the results of statistical tests less interpretable. Moreover, there has been increasing interest in non-parametric methods, especially the ones

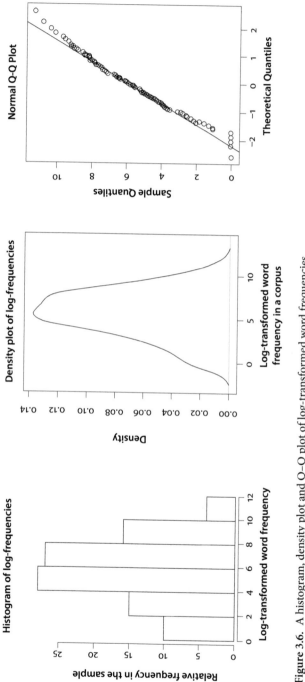

Figure 3.6. A histogram, density plot and Q–Q plot of log-transformed word frequencies

based on resampling, such as bootstrap and permutation. These approaches, which will be introduced in the following chapters, allow one to test statistical hypotheses on non-normal data.

3.4 Summary

This chapter has shown many basic operations that can help you explore univariate quantitative data. Data exploration is the first step in any statistical analysis. Its importance cannot be overestimated. This chapter has introduced the basic descriptive statistics (measures of central tendency and dispersion) and various graphical tools that enable one to investigate how the data are distributed. Several popular approaches to detecting outliers have been discussed, as well as some transformations that can be used in order to make the data more normal. The next chapter will demonstrate how basic diagnostics can be performed for qualitative, or categorical variables.

CHAPTER 4

How to explore qualitative variables

proportions and their visualizations

What you will learn from this chapter:

> This chapter demonstrates how to explore a categorical variable with the help of tables of counts and proportions. As in the previous chapter, graphs (pie charts, bar plots and dot charts) will play a very important role. You will also learn how to change values of a categorical variable. In addition, we will discuss how one can use Deviation of Proportions to measure dispersion of words in a corpus. This approach will be illustrated by a case study of the Basic Colour Terms in English.

4.1 Frequency tables, proportions and percentages

To reproduce the code in this and the following case studies, you will need two packages: Rling and ggplot2.

```
> install.packages("ggplot2") #unless you have already installed
the package
```

To be able to access the data and functions, you should load the packages:

```
> library(Rling); library(ggplot2)
```

This section investigates imaginary data with twenty simple clauses. Each of them is coded as intransitive, transitive or ditransitive. The data are available in the dataset sent in the package Rling. The structure of the dataset is the following:

```
> data(sent)
> str(sent)
'data.frame': 20 obs. of 2 variables:
$ clause: Factor w/ 3 levels "Ditr","Intrans",..: 3 3 1 3 2 2 3 …
$ subj: Factor w/ 4 levels "Abstr","Animal",..: 3 1 1 3 1 3 4 …
```

As one can see, the data frame contains twenty observations coded for two variables, *clause* and *subj*. The first variable, *clause*, is a factor with three levels: 'Ditr' (ditransitive), 'Intrans' (intransitive) and 'Trans' (transitive). The variable subj is a factor with four levels, which correspond to four semantic classes of the subject. Note that the function summary(), when applied to a factor, returns a vector with the frequencies of each level:

```
> summary(sent$clause)

  Ditr   Intrans   Trans
   2       10        8
```

Alternatively, one can use the function `table()` to see the frequencies:

```
> table(sent$clause)

  Ditr   Intrans   Trans
   2       10        8
```

For convenience, let us create a table with frequencies, which can be later used for various computations:

```
> sent.t <- table(sent$clause)
> sent.t

  Ditr   Intrans   Trans
   2       10        8
```

When analysing frequency data, it is often useful to compute proportions or percentages. Proportions are usually expressed as decimals that range from 0 to 1. To compute a proportion, one divides each value by the total frequency, which can be accessed with the help of `sum()`:

```
> sent.t/sum(sent.t)

  Ditr   Intrans   Trans
  0.1     0.5       0.4
```

Alternatively, one can use the function `prop.table()`, which turns raw frequencies into proportions:

```
> prop.table(sent.t)

  Ditr   Intrans   Trans
  0.1     0.5       0.4
```

Proportions of one category

If you only need the proportion of one category, for example, that of intransitive clauses, you can use the code below:

```
> mean(sent$clause == "Intrans")
[1] 0.5
```

How can this be possible? Let us look closer at the code. The expression in parentheses returns a vector of Boolean values (TRUE or FALSE):

```
> sent$clause == "Intrans"
 [1] FALSE FALSE FALSE FALSE TRUE TRUE FALSE FALSE FALSE TRUE
[11] TRUE FALSE TRUE TRUE FALSE FALSE TRUE TRUE TRUE TRUE
```

In the numerical form, the values TRUE are represented by 1's, and FALSE is represented by 0's:

```
> as.numeric(sent$clause == "Intrans")
 [1] 0 0 0 0 1 1 0 0 0 1 1 0 1 1 0 0 1 1 1 1
```

Since the function mean() coerces the Boolean values into 1's and 0's, the mean of this vector will be equal to the proportion of intransitive clauses: $(0 + 0 + 0 + 0 + 1 + 1 + 0 + 0 + 0 + 1 + 1 + 0 + 1 + 1 + 0 + 0 + 1 + 1 + 1 + 1)/20 = 0.5$.

One can also express proportions as percentages. To do so, one should multiply each proportion by 100, for example:

```
> prop.table(sent.t)*100

  Ditr   Intrans   Trans
  10     50        40
```

This means that intransitive clauses constitute 50% of the observations, transitive ones account for 40%, and ditransitive clauses represent 10% of the data.

Caution: Proportions and ratios (odds)

It is easy to confuse proportions with ratios. If we have two categories, a and b, the proportion of a in the data will be equal to $a/(a+b)$. The minimum proportion is 0, and the

(Continued)

maximum is 1. If *a* and *b* have equal values, their proportions will be 0.5. In contrast, a ratio (in probabilistic terms, **odds**) of *a* to *b* can be expressed as *a/b*. For example, the ratio of intransitive to transitive clauses in our data is as follows:

```
> 10/8
[1] 1.25
```

And the other way round, the ratio of transitive to intransitive is as follows:

```
> 8/10
[1] 0.8
```

If *a* and *b* are equal, the ratio is 1. If *a* > *b*, the ratio is greater than 1. If *a* < *b*, the ratio will be in the range from 0 to 1.

An important related concept is **odds ratio**. It will be discussed in Chapter 9.

4.2   Visualization of categorical data

It is often useful to visualize frequencies and proportions. R offers many different tools for that purpose. This section will introduce three popular types of graphs: pie charts, bar plots and dot charts. We will continue to work with the same data frame `sent` and the table `sent.t` that were introduced in the previous section.

A **pie chart** displays proportions as sections of a circle (to be entirely correct, a disc). The greater a proportion, the greater the size of the section. A simple pie chart can be produced as follows:

```
> pie(sent.t)
```

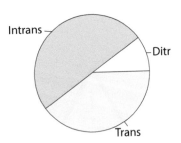

Figure 4.1. Pie chart of clause type proportions, simple version

The result is shown in Figure 4.1. However, it may be worth knowing how to create a customized version with a title, percentages as labels, a legend, and customized colours, as shown in Figure 4.2. To provide the labels, one has to compute the percentages first:

```
> sent_labels <- prop.table(sent.t)*100
> sent_labels

    Ditr Intrans    Trans
    10      50      40
```

Next, one should paste the numbers and the '%' symbol, which should immediately follow the numbers. The last argument, `sep = ""`, 'tells' R to insert nothing between the numbers and the '%' symbol (by default, R will add a space).

```
> sent_labels <- paste(sent_labels, "%", sep = "")
> sent_labels
[1] "10%" "50%" "40%"
```

The labels are ready. The next step is to make a customized list of colour names, which will be used to fill in the segments. We will use black for the first frequency value (ditransitives), 'grey40' (darker grey) for the second frequency value (intransitives), and 'grey80' (lighter grey) for the third frequency (transitives). The complete list of colours available in R can be accessed by typing in `colours()` or `colors()`.

```
> sent_colours <- c("black", "grey40", "grey80")
```

Now it is time to put all elements together and to produce an enhanced pie chart with the title, labels and customized colours:

```
> pie(sent.t, main = "Pie chart of clause types", labels = sent_
labels, col = sent_colours)
```

The final task is to add a legend at the right-hand side. The position of the legend is specified here by coordinates 1 (horizontal) and 0 (vertical). The coordinates usually have their origin (0, 0) at the bottom left corner and then increase in the right direction (horizontal) and to the top (vertical). In this pie chart, the horizontal 0 corresponds to the location of the pie centre. The text for the legend will correspond to the factor levels, and the customized colours will be used for the fillings:

```
> legend(1, 0, legend = levels(sent$clause), fill = sent_colours)
```

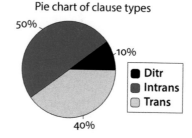

Figure 4.2. Pie chart of clause type proportions, enhanced version

How to make a pie chart with the help of `ggplot2`

To make a pie chart with `ggplot2`, you can use the following code:

```
> ggplot(sent, aes(x = factor(""), fill = clause)) + geom_bar()
+ coord_polar(theta = "y") + scale_x_discrete("") + scale_fill_
manual(values = c("black", "grey40", "grey80")))
```

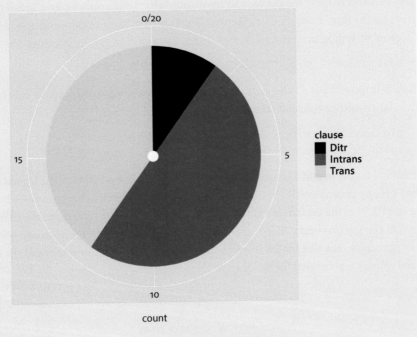

Figure 4.2a. A modified `ggplot2` version of the pie chart in Figure 4.2

The next graph is the **bar plot**, which represents quantities as vertical or horizontal bars. The code below can be used to reproduce the graph in Figure 4.3:

```
> barplot(sent.t, main = "Bar plot of clause types", col = "grey50",
cex.names = 1.2, xlab = "Clause type", ylab = "Frequency")
```

The argument `col` specifies a new shade of grey, whereas `cex.names = 1.2` is added to increase the size of the text labels in comparison with the default (1). Finally, `xlab` and `ylab` specify the labels of the axes.

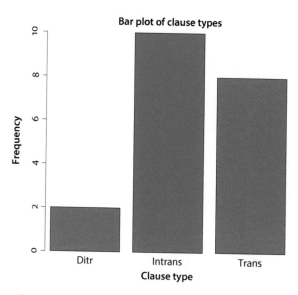

Figure 4.3. Bar plot of clause type frequencies

How to make a bar plot with the help of `ggplot2`

To create a `ggplot2` version of a bar plot of counts, you can use the code below. To make the bars more visible on the grey background, one can make them white and add a black outline, as shown in Figure 4.3a.

```
> ggplot(sent, aes(x = clause)) + geom_bar(fill = "white", colour
= "black") + xlab("Clause type") + ylab("Frequency")
```

(Continued)

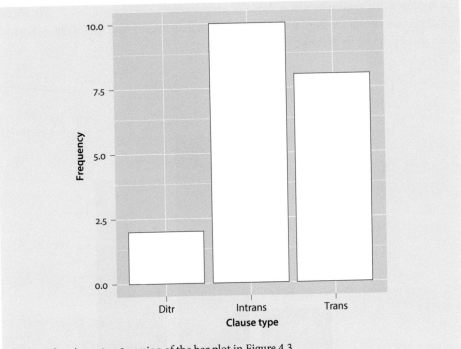

Figure 4.3a. A `ggplot2` version of the bar plot in Figure 4.3

How to edit factors

Editing factors in R is, unfortunately, not always easy. Let us first create a new factor, a copy of `sent$clause`, and use it to try different transformations:

```
> clause1 <- sent$clause
> head(clause1)
[1] Trans    Trans Ditr   Trans  Intrans Intrans
Levels: Ditr Intrans Trans
```

Imagine now that the first observation contains an error. Instead of 'Intrans', the value should be 'Trans'. To correct this mistake, one can specify the index of the observation (`[1]`) and assign the correct value:

```
> clause1[1] <- "Intrans"
```

```
> head(clause1)
[1] Intrans Trans   Ditr   Trans  Intrans Intrans
Levels: Ditr Intrans Trans
```

However, the task becomes more complex when one wants to add a new category, which does not correspond to any existing factor level. Let us try to change the value of the second observation from 'Trans' to 'Copula':

```
> clause1[2] <- "Copula"
Warning message:
In '[<-.factor'('*tmp*', 2, value = "Copula"):
invalid factor level, NA generated
> head(clause1)
[1] Intrans ⟨NA⟩     Ditr   Trans  Intrans Intrans
Levels: Ditr Intrans Trans
```

Our actions produce a warning message and a missing value. In this situation, one first has to add the new level to the list of factor levels:

```
> clause1 <- factor(clause1, levels = c(levels(clause1), "Copula"))
> summary(clause1)
  Ditr  Intrans  Trans  Copula  NA's
   2      11      6       0      1
```

Now it is possible to assign the new value:

```
> clause1[2] <- "Copula"
> head(clause1)
[1] Intrans Copula Ditr Trans Intrans Intrans
Levels: Ditr Intrans Trans Copula
```

Sometimes it is necessary to conflate two or more levels in one new level. Imagine you want to replace two old categories, 'Copula' and 'Intrans' with one some new value, e.g. 'NonTrans'. In that case, one has to add the new level first, and only after that can one replace all values 'Copula' and 'Intrans' with the new value:

```
> clause1 <- factor(clause1, levels = c(levels(clause1),
"NonTrans"))
> clause1[clause1=="Intrans"|clause1=="Copula"] <- "NonTrans"
> summary(clause1)
  Ditr  Intrans  Trans  Copula  NonTrans
   2      0       6       0       12
```

(Continued)

The sign '|' tells R to replace any value that is equal either to 'Intrans' or 'Copula'. Now these two levels have zero frequencies. To remove them, one can simply use `factor()`. This will drop the levels that do not occur:

```
> clause1 <- factor(clause1)
> summary(clause1)
  Ditr  Trans  NonTrans
   2     6      12
```

One often needs to reorder the levels of a factor. By default, the levels of a factor are ordered alphabetically. New levels (here, 'NonTrans') are appended at the end of the list:

```
> levels(clause1)
[1] "Ditr"   "Trans" "NonTrans"
```

Imagine that you want to change the order of the levels for some subsequent analyses. In that case, you can again use `factor()` and specify the preferred order of levels:

```
> clause1 <- factor(clause1, levels = c("Trans", "NonTrans",
"Ditr"))
> levels(clause1)
[1] "Trans"  "NonTrans" "Ditr"
```

Another useful command is `relevel()`, which reorders a factor so that the level specified by `ref` comes first and the other ones are moved down. For example, one can make 'NonTrans' the first level, which is also called the **reference level**:

```
> clause1 <- relevel(clause1, ref = "NonTrans")
> levels(clause1)
[1] "NonTrans" "Trans"    "Ditr"
```

This function is particularly useful when one wants to investigate categorical variables in regression analysis (see Chapters 7 and 12).

The final type of graph discussed in this section is **Cleveland's dot chart** (Figure 4.4). Although dot charts may be more useful in the situations when there are many different scores, let us create one here as an illustration:

```
> dotchart(sent.t, main = "Dot chart of clause types", xlab =
"Frequency", ylab = "Clause type", lcolor = "black", pch = 16, xlim
= c(0, 12))
[warning message omitted]
```

The argument `lcolor` specifies the colour of the horizontal lines, whereas `pch` specifies the type of points. The argument `xlim` provides the limits, i.e. the minimum and the maximum values, for the horizontal axis. See Appendix 2 for more options. There is also a warning message because we use a table instead of a numeric vector or a matrix, but this is not dangerous.

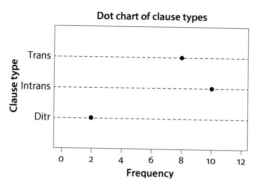

Figure 4.4. A dot chart of clause type frequencies

How to make a dot chart with the help of ggplot2

To make a ggplot2 version of the dot chart in Figure 4.4, you can use the following code:

```
> ggplot(sent, aes(x = clause)) + geom_point(stat = "bin", size
= 5) + xlab("Clause type") + ylab("Frequency") + coord_flip() +
ylim(0, 12) + theme_bw() + theme(panel.grid.major.x = element_
blank(), panel.grid.major.y = element_line(colour = "grey60",
linetype = "dashed"))
```
(handwritten annotation: *count* above "bin")

The result is shown in Fugure 4.4a.

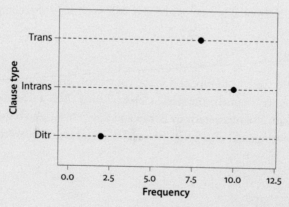

Figure 4.4a. A ggplot2 version of the dot chart in Figure 4.4

(Continued)

Some do's and dont's for producing graphs

-   avoid using 3D-effects, fancy graphical patterns, flashy colours and other distrac-
    tors; follow the rule 'less is more' and let your data speak for themselves
-   provide clear and informative labels
-   do not use tricks, such as manipulating the scale to make differences more or less
    visible
-   do not use red and green symbols on the same graph, as up to 5% of your audience
    may be colour-blind people

There is an opinion that pie charts are not optimal for representation of quantitative
differences because humans are not good at estimating and comparing angles (Gries
2013: 109), so do not use pie charts when the differences between numerical values
are too subtle.

4.3   Basic Colour Terms: Deviations of Proportions in subcorpora

4.3.1   The data and hypothesis

To reproduce the code in this case study, you will need only the companion package,
`Rling`.

```
> library(Rling)
```

The aim of this case study is to pinpoint usage constraints on a universal conceptual and
linguistic phenomenon, namely, the Basic Colour Terms (BCT). The research of colour
categories began with a seminal study by Berlin and Kay (1969), who suggested a universal
hierarchy in the development of colour terms across languages of the world. This hierarchy
looks as follows:

white   green   < blue < brown <   purple
                                                    pink
      < red <
black   yellow   grey
                                                    orange

The hierarchy constrains the inventory of colour terms in languages. If a language has a colour category, it will also have all terms that are found on the left from this term. For instance, if a language contains a term for blue, it will also have words for white, black, red, green and yellow. It has been assumed for a long time that the basic colour categories are universal and are grounded in the neurophychological mechanisms of perception that are shared by most humans (e.g. Rosch Heider & Olivier 1972). This evidence was important in the theoretical battle over the Whorfian hypothesis, which says that different languages cut the conceptual space in arbitrary ways, and the universalist paradigm promoted by Generative Linguistics. Today most researchers would agree that neurophysiological, psychological and cultural factors simultaneously play a role in the way we learn, process and use colour categories (see an overview in Anishchanka 2013).

The dataset that will be used in this case study is called colreg. It contains the frequencies of eleven BCT in four registers from the Corpus of Contemporary American English, or COCA (Davies 2008 –).[1] Only the adjectival uses of the colour terms were counted.

```
> data(colreg)
> colreg
           spoken   fiction   academic   press
black      20335    41118     26892      73080
blue       4693     22093     3605       21210
brown      1185     10914     1201       11539
gray       1168     12140     1289       6559
green      3860     14398     4477       26837
orange     931      3496      474        5766
pink       962      7312      584        6356
purple     613      3366      429        3403
red        7230     25111     5621       34596
white      14474    40745     26336      54883
yellow     1349     10553     1855       10382
```

We will focus on the difference between primary and secondary BCT. The primary BCT are black, white, red, green, yellow and blue. The secondary ones are brown, purple, pink, orange and grey. It is believed that the primary colours are directly determined by neural responses, whereas the secondary ones are generated by additional cognitive operations on these neural responses (Kay & McDaniel 1978). This means that they can also be more prone to cultural constraints in their use. Thus, we can expect that the register biases will be greater for the secondary BCT than for the primary BCT, whereas the primary BCT will

---

1. The frequencies are available at http://www.wordandphrase.info/frequencyList.asp (last access 11.06.2015).

be more evenly distributed. These biases will be measured with the help of Gries' (2008) Deviations of Proportions.

4.3.2   Deviation of Proportions as a measure of dispersion

In the previous chapter you learnt a few popular measures of dispersion: range, variance, standard variation, IQR and median absolute deviation. In corpus linguistics, one also speaks about dispersion of words in a corpus, which serves as a measure of familiarity, or entrenchment of a word, in addition to corpus frequency. For example, one can use the number of texts in a corpus where a word occurs. If a word occurs in very many texts, it is highly entrenched. If it occurs in only one or two texts, it is less spread, even though it may have a high frequency due to a large number of occurrences in those few texts. Thus, information about dispersion provides a useful addition to corpus frequency.

Counting the number of texts where a word occurs works well if the number of texts is very large (hundreds or thousands) and the texts are of comparable size. However, in our case all colours are found in all registers, and the total numbers of tokens in each register are different. This is a normal situation: more often than not the sizes of texts that constitute a corpus vary substantially. Presumably, a word will have more chances to occur in a larger text than in a smaller one. How can one take this into account? A convenient and intuitive measure of variation is the so-called Deviation of Proportions, or DP (Gries 2008; Lijffijt & Gries 2012). This measure compares the actual proportion of occurrences of a word in a given text or group of texts (as compared to the other texts or groups) with the expected occurrences of the word given the size of the text. To compute it, we need the total sizes of the texts (registers). This information can be found in the COCA documentation. On the basis of this information, we can create a vector with the total number of words in each of the four registers:

```
> freqreg <- c(95385672, 90344134, 91044778, 187245672)
> freqreg
[1] 95385672 90344134 91044778 187245672
```

To obtain the proportions of each register in the corpus, one can use the function `prop.table()`. These proportions are called **expected proportions** because they represent the probability of a word to occur in a particular register by mere chance. The vector of expected proportions for all colour terms (or any other words that occur in the corpus) looks as follows:

```
> exp_prop <- prop.table(freqreg)
> exp_prop
[1] 0.2055636 0.1946987 0.1962086 0.4035291
```

The press has the greatest proportion (about 0.40) because it is the largest subcorpus, whereas the three other registers have nearly equal proportions. To compute a DP, we will also need the observed proportions for each colour term. Let us begin with *black*. The frequencies of this adjective in the four registers are as follows:

```
> colreg[1,]
          spoken   fiction   academic   press
  black    20335    41118     26892     73080
```

These frequencies should be transformed into the so-called **observed proportions** with the help of prop.table():

```
> black_obs <- prop.table(colreg[1,])
> black_obs
  spoken   fiction     academic     press
  black    0.1259718  0.2547189  0.1665913   0.452718
```

Now we are ready to compute the DP of *black*. DP is the sum of absolute differences between the observed and expected proportions of a word or a group of words, as in this case, divided by two. The function abs() returns the absolute value, regardless of the sign (plus or minus).

```
> DP_black <- sum(abs(black_obs - exp_prop))/2
> DP_black
[1] 0.1092091
```

It can be useful to normalize the DPs by dividing a DP by one minus the smallest proportion in the expected values, as suggested by Lijffijt & Gries (2012). In that case, the distribution of DP values will range from 0 to 1.

```
> DP_black_norm <- DP_black/(1 - min(exp_prop))
> DP_black_norm
[1] 0.1356127
```

The normalized DP can be interpreted as follows. If the value is close to 0, then the word is distributed across n subcorpora as one should expect given the sizes of the subcorpora. A DP close to 1 indicates that the word has a strong preference for some subcorpora, and strongly 'disfavours' others. The value 0.136 indicates that *black* is quite evenly distributed.

Let us now repeat the same procedure and compute the normalized DP score for *gray* (with the American English spelling):

```
> gray_obs <- prop.table(colreg[4,])
> gray_obs
         spoken       fiction      academic       press
  gray    0.05520892   0.5738325   0.06092834   0.3100303
> DP_gray <- sum(abs(gray_obs - exp_prop))/2
> DP_gray
```

```
[1] 0.3791338
> DP_gray_norm <- DP_gray/(1 - min(exp_prop))
> DP_gray_norm
[1] 0.4707974
```

The register bias of *gray* is thus much greater than that of *black*.

This study focuses on the aggregate differences between the primary and secondary BCT. To obtain and compare the aggregate DP scores, one should first compute the sum frequencies of the primary and secondary colour terms. For convenience, let us create two subsets of the initial data, one with primary terms, and the other with the secondary terms. The subsetting is done by listing the row numbers of the corresponding terms (see more on subsetting in Appendix 1).

```
> primcol <- colreg[c(1, 2, 5, 9:11),]
> primcol
          spoken  fiction  academic  press
black     20335   41118    26892     73080
blue      4693    22093    3605      21210
green     3860    14398    4477      26837
red       7230    25111    5621      34596
white     14474   40745    26336     54883
yellow    1349    10553    1855      10382
> seccol <- colreg[-c(1, 2, 5, 9:11),]
> seccol
          spoken  fiction  academic  press
brown     1185    10914    1201      11539
gray      1168    12140    1289      6559
orange    931     3496     474       5766
pink      962     7312     584       6356
purple    613     3366     429       3403
```

The next step is to compute the column sums with the help of a special function colSums().

```
> primcol_sums <- colSums(primcol)
> primcol_sums
spoken   fiction  academic  press
51941    154018   68786     220988
> seccol_sums <- colSums(seccol)
> seccol_sums
spoken   fiction  academic  press
4859     37228    3977      33623
```

Now one can obtain the observed proportions with the help of prop.table():

```
> primcol_obs <- prop.table(primcol_sums)
> primcol_obs
```

```
spoken          fiction        academic       press
0.1047762       0.3106874      0.1387561      0.4457803
> seccol_obs <- prop.table(seccol_sums)
> seccol_obs
spoken          fiction        academic       press
0.06097607      0.46717783     0.04990776     0.42193833
```

The final step is to compute the DP values and their normalized versions for the primary and secondary terms.

```
> DP_primcol <- sum(abs(primcol_obs - exp_prop))/2 #simple DPs for
primary BCT
> DP_primcol
[1] 0.1582399
> DP_seccol <- sum(abs(seccol_obs - exp_prop))/2 #simple DPs for
secondary BCT
> DP_seccol
[1] 0.2908884
> DP_primcol_norm <- DP_primcol/(1 - min(exp_prop)) #normalized DPs
for primary BCT
> DP_primcol_norm
[1] 0.1964978
> DP_seccol_norm <- DP_seccol/(1 - min(exp_prop)) #normalized DPs
for secondary BCT
> DP_seccol_norm
[1] 0.3612168
```

The DPs show that the secondary terms are less evenly distributed in the corpus than the primary ones. This means that cultural factors have a stronger influence on the use of the secondary BCT than on the use of the primary BCT, in accordance with the theory-based expectations.

4.4 Summary

This chapter has presented different statistical and graphical tools for exploratory analysis of univariate categorical data. The key notions were counts (frequencies) and proportions. A case study of the Basic Colour Terms has also demonstrated how proportions can be used to measure dispersion of a word in a corpus. In addition, you have learnt how to edit factors, e.g. introduce new levels and remove unnecessary ones. The simple exploratory techniques described in this and previous chapters play a very important part in statistical analysis, as you will see in the next part of the book, which is dedicated to inferential statistics and hypothesis testing.

CHAPTER 5

Comparing two groups

t-test and Wilcoxon and Mann-Whitney tests for independent and dependent samples

What you will learn from this chapter:

> Do language learners who are taught by an innovative method show better results than those who are taught traditionally? Do speakers of one language variety speak faster than speakers of another variety? Do people of one gender use more hedging constructions than people of another? In this chapter, you will learn how to make such comparisons using the parametric *t*-test and the non-parametric Wilcoxon and Mann-Whitney tests for dependent and independent samples. You will learn how to compute the standard error and confidence intervals for the mean. The case studies will involve differences between high- and low-frequency nouns with regard to the number of associations that they trigger and their abstractness/concreteness scores.

5.1 Comparing group means or medians: An overview of the tests

This chapter introduces the *t*-test and its non-parametric version, the Wilcoxon test, which is equivalent to the Matt-Whitney test, also known as the *U*-test. These tests compare the measures of central tendency in two groups. More specifically, the *t*-test can tell us whether the group means are different, and the non-parametric tests are usually regarded as tests of the differences between the group medians.

All these tests exist in two versions: dependent (paired) and independent (unpaired). A **dependent**, or **paired** test is performed when the observations in two groups are paired. That is, an observation from one group has a related observation in the second group. Such observations may come from the same subject or be related to the same experimental stimulus. For example, one can measure learners' proficiency in a language before and after they are taught by a new teaching method, and investigate if the method has had any effect on their performance. In this case, every learner will have two scores, before and after the experiment. If there is no such connection between the scores in two groups, the test is called **independent**, or **unpaired**. An example is a test of the differences in vocabulary size of two groups of learners, where every learner is tested only once and has only one score.

To choose between the *t*-test and the non-parametric options, one should check a number of assumptions, i.e. the criteria that the data should meet so that the test returns meaningful results. The assumptions of the dependent and independent tests are slightly different. The parametric *t*-test for **independent** samples has the following assumptions:

– *The samples have been randomly selected from the populations they represent.*
– *The observations are independent, both between the groups and within the groups.*
– *The variable should be at least interval-scaled.*
– *The data in both samples are normally distributed, and/or the sample sizes are greater than 30.*[1]
– *The variances of the samples should be homogeneous.* That is, the variances in both groups should be equal. However, the standard implementation of the *t*-test in R includes Welch's adjustment, which provides a correction for unequal variances (see Field et al. 2012: 373 for more detail). This is why we will not be concerned about this assumption in this chapter. In Chapter 8, we will discuss the Levene test and the Fligner-Killeen test, which can be used for comparing group variances.

The test assumptions of the *t*-test for **dependent** samples are as follows:

– *The subjects have been sampled randomly.*
– *The data are at least interval-scaled.*
– *The differences between the pairs of scores (not the scores themselves!) are normally distributed, and/or the sample size is greater than 30.*
– *The variances in the underlying populations that represent two groups or conditions are equal.* As in the previous case, we will rely on the built-in correction for heterogeneous variance, which is implemented in the default version of the *t*-test in R.

If these assumptions are not met, one should use the non-parametric Wilcoxon or Matt-Whitney tests. They have less strict assumptions:

– *Each sample has been drawn randomly from the population.*
– *The observations are independent, within each sample only* (the dependent test) *or both within each sample and between the samples* (the independent test).
– *The measurement scale is at least ordinal.*
– *The underlying distributions need not be normal, but they should be of a similar shape.*

---

1.   Behind these two conditions is, in fact, one assumption, which requires that the sampling distribution should be normal. However, since we do not have access to this distribution we have to rely on the data at hand. See a definition of the sampling distribution in Section 5.2.4 and a detailed discussion in Urdan (2010: Ch. 6).

Finally, all above-mentioned tests exist in two versions: **one-tailed** and **two-tailed**. These notions were discussed in Chapter 1. Recall that a one-tailed test should be used when the alternative hypothesis is directional. For example, it contains expressions 'X is more than Y' or 'the greater X, the greater Y'. In contrast, if the hypothesis is non-directional, e.g. 'X does not equal Y', it is correct to use a two-tailed test. It is crucial that the choice between a one-tailed and two-tailed test should be made before the test statistic and the p-value are computed.

The remaining part of the chapter is organized as follows. Section 5.2 discusses the independent one-tailed t-test. Section 5.3 explains the non-parametric independent two-tailed Wilcoxon test. Section 5.4 demonstrates how one can perform the paired two-tailed t-test for dependent samples. Finally, Section 5.5 provides a short summary and suggestions on writing up the results of these tests.

5.2 Comparing the number of associations triggered by high- and low-frequency nouns with the help of the independent t-test

5.2.1 Data and hypothesis

To access the data and functions used in this case study you will need to have the following add-on packages installed:

```
> install.packages(c("ggplot2", "gplots"))
> library(Rling); library(ggplot2); library(gplots)
```

You will need two data frames, which are available in the `Rling` package under the names `pym_low` and `pym_high`. The data come from a well-known experimental study of 925 English nouns by Paivio et al. (1968). The subjects were asked to rate the nouns on concreteness, imagery and so-called meaningfulness. Concreteness is the most transparent parameter: concrete words are those that denote tangible objects, materials or persons that can be easily perceived with the senses. Imagery scores reflect how quickly and easily the word arouses a mental image defined as sensory experience, such as a mental picture or sound. The subjects were asked to rate concreteness and imagery on a scale from 1 (minimum) to 7 (maximum). Finally, meaningfulness represents the number of associations provided by the speakers in 30 seconds after they were shown the words. Paivio, Yuille and Madigan also used information about word length in syllables and letters.

```
> data(pym_high)
> data(pym_low)
```

The sample in `pym_low` contains 51 nouns sampled from the words with the frequency from 1 to 20, whereas `pym_high` contains 50 nouns with the frequency greater than 50.

These two samples were randomly produced by an online word list generator (Friendly 1996). The frequencies were taken from the Brown corpus (Kučera & Francis 1967), which was contemporary to the experiment, although it looks very small by the modern standards. The word list generator also returns the values for all variables of interest.

The data frames have similar structure. The observations are individual words, which are represented by the row names. Each dataset contains five variables. The first variable *syl* specifies the number of syllables for each word. The second one *let* is the number of letters. *Imag* is the average imagery score, which ranges from 1 (the lowest score) to 7 (the highest score). Likewise, *conc*, which is the average concreteness score, ranges from 1 to 7. The final variable *assoc* represents the average number of associations provided by the speakers for every word.

The first six rows of `pym_high` look as follows:

```
> head(pym_high)
          syl   let   imag   conc   assoc
time       1     4    4.13   2.47   7.00
life       1     4    4.07   2.96   6.78
home       1     4    6.50   6.25   6.88
church     1     6    6.63   6.59   7.52
mind       1     4    3.03   2.60   5.88
door       1     4    6.60   7.00   7.96
```

You can see the structure of the data frame with the help of `str()`:

```
> str(pym_high)
'data.frame': 50 obs. of 5 variables:
$ syl: int 1 1 1 1 1 1 2 1 5 2 ...
$ let: int 4 4 4 6 4 4 7 4 10 8 ...
$ imag: num 4.13 4.07 6.5 6.63 3.03 6.6 6.2 6.87 6.53 4.1 ...
$ conc: num 2.47 2.96 6.25 6.59 2.6 7 6.38 6.83 5.87 3.63 ...
$ assoc: num 7 6.78 6.88 7.52 5.88 7.96 7.28 5.12 7.2 5.8 ...
```

One can see that the first two variables, *syl* and *let*, are integer vectors, since they contain only discrete values, and the other variables are non-integer numeric vectors, which contain mean scores averaged over many different subjects.

The main question of this and the following case study is whether there is a difference between the high- and low-frequency nouns with regard to the experimental scores. There is substantial evidence of frequency effects in language use, acquisition and change (see Diessel 2007 for an overview). The evidence suggests that language learners are sensitive to frequencies of words and expressions that they encounter.

An important contribution to study of frequency effects was made by Zipf (1935), who discovered several frequency-related regularities. One of them, known as Zipf's law, was discussed in Chapter 3. In addition, Zipf found that the length of a word is in inverse relationship to its relative frequency (he called it the Law of Abbreviation).[2] Frequency also affects semantic functions of a word or construction. Frequent expressions have chances of being used in very diverse contexts, and therefore can acquire new grammatical and pragmatic functions. As a result, the higher the frequency of a word, the more semantically versatile it is. This correlation was pinpointed by Zipf (1949) in his Principle of Economic Versatility. From this follows that one can expect the high-frequency words to trigger on average more associations than the low-frequency ones, since the former are used in a greater number of diverse contexts. This will be the alternative hypothesis of the present study. The null hypothesis is that there is no difference between the frequency groups with regard to the number of associations. To see whether our expectations are supported by the data, we will first perform some exploratory analyses and visualizations, and next, will turn to the discussion of possible inferential statistics.

5.2.2   Descriptive statistics and visualizations

It is always recommended to begin statistical analyses by looking at the data distribution with the help of the methods introduced in Chapters 3 and 4. First, let us get the most important descriptive statistics by using the summary() function:

```
> summary(pym_high$assoc)
  Min.  1st Qu. Median  Mean  3rd Qu.  Max.
  4.88   5.69    6.24   6.38   7.16    9.12
> summary(pym_low$assoc)
  Min.   1st Qu. Median  Mean   3rd Qu.  Max.
  3.000  5.345   5.920   5.857  6.460    8.000
```

All statistics shown in the summary are higher in the high-frequency sample than in the low-frequency sample.

A useful visual tool for comparison of two and more groups is the box-and-whisker plot. Chapter 3 showed how to create a box plot for one sample. One can also put several boxes for two or more samples side by side in one graph and compare them (see Figure 5.1):

---

2.   There exist two main explanations of the reduction effect, and they are not mutually exclusive. On the one hand, frequent use of a word results in automation of production processes, which has influence on articulation (Bybee 2001). On the other hand, according to Diessel (2007), the more frequent a word, the more distributional information about the word is available, and therefore the more predictable it is from the context. As a result, even when a word is strongly reduced, the hearer can still restore it from the context. So the speaker can afford to be 'lazy' without the risk of being misunderstood.

```
> boxplot(pym_high$assoc, pym_low$assoc, names = c("high", "low"),
main = "Box plots of average numbers of associations", xlab =
"Frequency group", ylab = "Average number of associations")
```

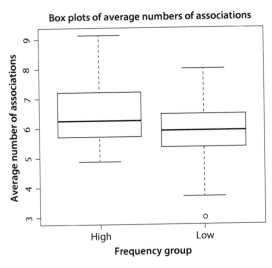

Figure 5.1. Box plots of average numbers of associations for the high- and low-frequency nouns

How to create a box plot of two or more groups with the help of ggplot2

To make a box plot of two vectors, one first has to combine the vectors with association scores for the high- and low-frequency nouns in one data frame, also creating a column that specifies the frequency group ('high' or 'low'). The function rep() repeats the same character strings.

```
> pym_assoc  <-  data.frame(assoc  =  c(pym_high$assoc, pym_
low$assoc), freq = c(rep("high", 50), rep("low", 51)))
> head(pym_assoc)
    assoc   freq
1   7.00    high
2   6.78    high
3   6.88    high
4   7.52    high
5   5.88    high
```

```
6  7.96    high
```

Now you can create the box plot (see Figure 5.1a):

```
> ggplot(pym_assoc, aes(x = freq, y = assoc)) + geom_boxplot() +
xlab("Frequency group") + ylab("Average number of associations")
```

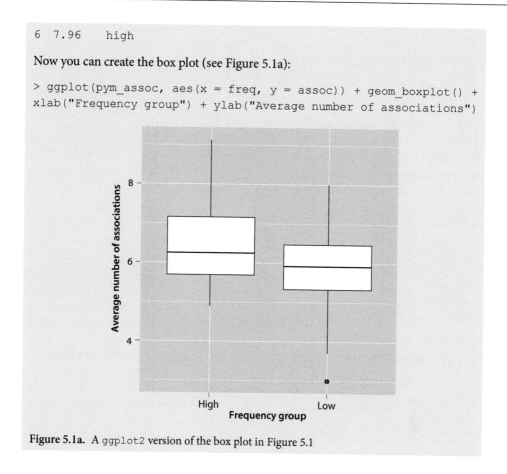

Figure 5.1a. A ggplot2 version of the box plot in Figure 5.1

One can see from the plot that the scores of the low-frequency sample are distributed slightly more symmetrically around the median than those of the high-frequency sample. However, the low-frequency sample has an outlier with a very low score. It is represented by a dot. One can identify this observation by first retrieving its score, and then selecting the row with this score from the data frame:

```
> boxplot.stats(pym_low$assoc)$out
[1] 3
> pym_low[pym_low$assoc == 3, ]
            syl  let  imag  conc  assoc
criterion   4    9    1.83  1.93  3
```

The outlier is the Greek loan word *criterion*. This noun also has the lowest imagery score (1.83) and the third lowest concreteness score (1.93) (see the box *How to sort data frames* to find information about detecting the highest- and lowest-ranking scores in a data frame).

How to sort data frames

In order to sort data frames, you can use the function `order()` within the subsetting square brackets. For example, one can sort the observations (rows) by the imagery scores in ascending order as follows:

```
> pym_low[order(pym_low$imag),]
             syl  let  imag  conc  assoc
criterion    4    9    1.83  1.93  3.00
impropriety  5    11   1.87  2.08  3.75
allegory     4    8    2.13  2.56  4.48
hypothesis   4    10   2.40  2.25  5.36
gender       2    6    2.90  3.63  5.41
[output omitted]
```

To sort in descending order, one adds the minus sign before the name of the column:

```
> pym_low[order(-pym_low$imag),]
           syl  let  imag  conc  assoc
lip        1    3    6.57  6.93  5.32
priest     1    6    6.53  6.59  6.88
tower      2    5    6.53  6.96  6.42
potato     3    6    6.50  7.00  7.13
nail       1    4    6.50  6.96  6.08
meadow     2    6    6.43  6.69  8.00
[output omitted]
```

To sort by more than one column, for example, by the number of syllables and then by the number of letters, simply list all these columns in the order that you prefer:

```
> pym_low[order(pym_low$syl, pym_low$let),]
       syl  let  imag  conc  assoc
lip    1    3    6.57  6.93  5.32
rod    1    3    5.97  6.62  6.04
fur    1    3    6.23  6.69  7.36
deed   1    4    3.63  4.19  5.32
lump   1    4    5.63  6.20  5.44
[output omitted]
```

5.2.3   Choosing an appropriate test to compare the measures of central tendency in two groups

The descriptive statistics and the paired box plot support our hypothesis that high-frequency nouns trigger more associations than low-frequency nouns. However, it may well be possible that this difference is due to chance only. If this is so, the results cannot be extrapolated to the entire population. In other words, if other researchers replicated the analyses on new samples of low- and high-frequency nouns, the results could be different. This is why one needs inferential statistics. To decide on the type of test, one has to answer three questions, which were already mentioned in Section 5.1:

1) should one use the test for dependent (paired) or independent (unpaired) data?
2) is the t-test or its non-parametric version more appropriate?
3) should the test be one- or two-tailed?

Since there is no connection between the scores in the high- and low-frequency samples, there are no reasons to assume that the observations are dependent. Thus, an independent (unpaired) test should be used. The next question is whether the independent t-test or its non-parametric version is more appropriate. Let us check if the assumptions of the t-test are met. For convenience, the assumptions are repeated below.

–   *The samples have been randomly selected from the populations they represent.* This assumption is met.
–   *The observations are independent, both between the groups and within the groups.* Since we do not have good reasons to believe that the number of associations triggered by some words depends on the number of associations triggered by others, we can consider this assumption to be met.
–   *The quantitative variable should be at least interval-scaled.* Since the data are on the ratio scale, this assumption is met, as well.
–   *The data in both samples are normally distributed, and/or the sample sizes are greater than 30.* To find out whether the samples are normally distributed or not, one can use visualization tools (histograms, density plots and Q–Q plots) and the Shapiro-Wilk test of normality. All these diagnostic tools were introduced in Chapter 3. However, the number of observations in the samples is 50 and 51, so we do not need to worry about normality.

Finally, would it be correct to use a one- or two-tailed test? Recall that the alternative hypothesis is directional. The high-frequency nouns are expected to trigger more associations than the low-frequency ones, so we should prefer the one-tailed version.

To summarize, the data and alternative hypothesis suggest that we should use the independent one-tailed t-test. The test, as well as its dependent and two-tailed versions, is implemented in the `t.test()` function. By default, the test is independent (`paired = FALSE`), but one can change that by typing in `paired = TRUE` if the samples are paired. The default test is also two-tailed (`alternative = "two.sided"`). If the alternative hypothesis is directional, one has two options. One can use `alternative = "greater"` if one expects that the first sample has a greater mean than the second sample, or `alternative = "less"` if one expects the first sample to have a smaller mean than the second sample. In our case, the code is as follows:

```
> t.test(pym_high$assoc, pym_low$assoc, alternative = "greater")

        Welch Two Sample t-test

data: pym_high$assoc and pym_low$assoc
t = 2.6717, df = 98.281, p-value = 0.004417
alternative hypothesis: true difference in means is greater than 0
95 percent confidence interval:
0.1977777     Inf
sample estimates:
mean of x mean of y
6.380000 5.857451
```

The most important line is the one that contains the *t*-statistic (2.6717), the degrees of freedom (98.281) and the *p*-value (0.004). Since the *p*-value is smaller than the significance level, we can reject the null hypothesis of no difference between the means. High-frequency words indeed trigger more associations than low-frequency words, and this difference is statistically significant. The algorithm also returns the 95% confidence interval of the difference in means. If a confidence interval includes 0, then it is possible that the difference between the means may be zero and therefore our result may be due to chance. In our example, the confidence interval ranges from approximately 0.198 to infinity. This is another indication that the difference in the number of associations triggered by high- and low-frequency words is significant. More information about the notion of confidence intervals will follow in the next subsection.

A column with groupings and formula interface

It is possible that your original data have a different format. Instead of two vectors, you may have two columns: one with numerical values and the other with information about the group membership. An example is `pym_assoc`, the data frame, which was created in the `ggplot2` box in the previous subsection:

```
> head(pym_assoc)
     assoc   freq
1    7.00    high
2    6.78    high
3    6.88    high
4    7.52    high
5    5.88    high
6    7.96    high

> tail(pym_assoc)
      assoc   freq
96    5.40    low
97    6.72    low
98    6.00    low
99    4.92    low
100   3.75    low
101   6.00    low
```

The column *assoc* shows the average number of associations, and the column *freq* displays which of the two frequency groups every nouns belongs to. In this case, you can use the *t*-test (and many other tests) with the formula interface:

```
>    t.test(pym_assoc$assoc    ~    pym_assoc$freq,    alternative    =
"greater")
[output omitted]
```

Note that the first (reference) level of the factor `freq` ('high') is compared with the second level of the factor ('low'):

```
> levels(pym_assoc$freq)
[1] "high" "low"
```

By default, the reference level is the one that comes first alphabetically. This is why one should use `alternative = "greater"` if one expects the high-frequency nouns to trigger more associations that the low-frequency nouns. If the reference level were 'low', one should use `alternative = "less"`.

Note that it is perfectly possible to swap the first two arguments and use `alternative = "less"`. The results will be identical, except for the reverse order of the means and the negative sign of the *t*-statistic and the confidence interval boundaries:

```
> t.test(pym_low$assoc, pym_high$assoc, alternative = "less")

        Welch Two Sample t-test
```

```
data: pym_low$assoc and pym_high$assoc
t = -2.6717, df = 98.281, p-value = 0.004417
alternative hypothesis: true difference in means is less than 0
95 percent confidence interval:
        -Inf -0.1977777
sample estimates:
mean of x mean of y
5.857451 6.380000
```

To conclude, our analyses reveal that the average number of associations per word is greater for high-frequency nouns than for low-frequency ones. The results of the test give us grounds to believe that the difference is not due to chance.

How to report *p*-values correctly

A common mistake made by beginners is to report *p*-values with excessive precision, e.g. *p* = 0.000123456. It is not recommended to go beyond three decimal places, e.g. *p* = 0.047. If your *p*-value is smaller than 0.001, you should write *p* < 0.001. Check the style sheet of your publisher for more precise guidelines. Also, you should specify whether the test is two-tailed or one-tailed. This is absolutely necessary in case of a one-tailed test.

5.2.4   Confidence intervals and standard errors

As was shown above, the *t*-test returns **the 95% confidence interval** of the difference between the means, and one should check whether the confidence interval includes the zero. But what are confidence intervals? A 95% confidence interval means that if we repeated the estimation process again and again on different samples from the population, there would be 95% probability that the given confidence interval is one containing the true parameter value (here, the difference of means), of all constructed confidence intervals. One can also encounter 99% and 90% confidence intervals, which correspond to the probability of 99% and 90%, respectively.

Confidence intervals are also commonly applied for estimation of the mean. To compute a confidence interval around the mean, one needs two things: the mean and the

standard error (SE), which should not be confused with the standard deviation. The latter is a dispersion measure that describes the average deviation from the mean (see Chapter 3). In contrast, the standard error is the standard deviation of the sampling distribution of the statistic, e.g. the mean. A **sampling distribution** is the distribution of a statistic calculated for many samples drawn from the same population. The standard error of the mean can be calculated by dividing the standard deviation of the sample by the square root of the number of observations in the sample:

$$SE_{\bar{x}} = \frac{s}{\sqrt{n}}$$

where $\bar{x}$ is the sample mean, s is the standard deviation, and n is the number of observations in the sample.

The computation of confidence intervals around the mean depends on the sample size. If the sample size is large (according to a rule of thumb, greater than 30), the lower boundary of a 95% confidence interval is computed as the sample mean minus 1.96 times the SE. The upper boundary is the sample mean plus 1.96 times the SE. The constant 1.96 is the value which corresponds to the significance level of 0.05 in the standard normal distribution with the mean of 0 and the standard deviation of 1. It is also known as the z-distribution (recall z-scores, which were discussed in Chapter 3). In the z-distribution, 95% of z-scores will be located between -1.96 and 1.96. If you need a 99% confidence interval, the constant is 2.58. For a 90% confidence interval, the constant is 1.64. The general formula for the lower and upper boundaries of a confidence interval looks as follows:

$$CI = \bar{x} \pm z_{\frac{1-p}{2}} \times SE$$

where $\bar{x}$ is the sample mean, SE is the standard error, p is the probability that you want for your confidence interval (e.g. 0.95 for a 95% CI, 0.99 for a 99% CI, etc.), and z is the z-score, which can be computed for a 95% confidence interval as follows:

```
> qnorm((1 - 0.95)/2, lower.tail = FALSE)
[1] 1.959964
```

If the sample size is small (less than or equal to 30), the t-distribution is used instead. The problem with small samples is that the scores are more spread out. The general formula for computing the confidence intervals for small samples is as follows:

$$CI = \bar{x} \pm t_{\frac{}{}, \, df = n-1} \times SE$$

where $\bar{x}$ is the sample mean, SE is the standard error, p is the probability that you want for your confidence interval, and t is the t-score for the probability and the number of degrees of freedom, which is equal to the sample size minus one. The *t*-score can be obtained as follows (the example is given for the number of associations triggered by the high-frequency nouns):

```
> qt((1 - 0.95)/2, df = length(pym_high$assoc) - 1, lower.tail =
FALSE)
[1] 2.009575
```

Let us now compute the standard error and the 95% confidence interval (CI) for the number of associations triggered by the high-frequency nouns. Since the sample is greater than 30, we will use the approach based on the *z*-distribution.

```
> se.high <- sd(pym_high$assoc)/sqrt(length(pym_high$assoc))  #SE
for the high-frequency nouns
> se.high
[1] 0.1315214
> ci.lower.high <- mean(pym_high$assoc) - 1.96*se.high # the lower
boundary of the 95% CI around the mean for the high-frequency
nouns
> ci.lower.high
[1] 6.122218
> ci.upper.high <- mean(pym_high$assoc) + 1.96*se.high # the upper
boundary of the 95% CI around the mean for the high-frequency nouns
> ci.upper.high
[1] 6.637782
```

Next, let us do the same for the low-frequency nouns:

```
> se.low <- sd(pym_low$assoc)/sqrt(length(pym_low$assoc))  #SE for
the low-frequency nouns
> se.low
[1] 0.1447616
> ci.lower.low <- mean(pym_low$assoc) - 1.96*se.low # the lower
boundary of the 95% CI around the mean for the low-frequency nouns
> ci.lower.low
[1] 5.573718
> ci.upper.low <- mean(pym_low$assoc) + 1.96*se.low # the upper
boundary of the 95% CI around the mean for the low-frequency nouns
> ci.upper.low
[1] 6.141184
```

Now we have the lower and upper boundaries of the confidence intervals. It is common to visualize them on bar plots, such as the one shown in Figure 5.2. To create the graph, we will create a vector with two means:

```
> means <- c(mean(pym_high$assoc), mean(pym_low$assoc))
> means
[1] 6.380000 5.857451
```

Next, create a vector with the 95% CI lower boundaries and a vector with the 95% CI upper boundaries. Be careful and keep the same order: first, the statistics of the high-frequency nouns, and then those of the low-frequency nouns:

```
> ci.lower <- c(ci.lower.high, ci.lower.low)
> ci.lower
[1] 6.122218 5.573718
> ci.upper <- c(ci.upper.high, ci.upper.low)
> ci.upper
[1] 6.637782 6.141184
```

Finally, we will use the function `barplot2()` from the package `gplots` to create a bar plot of means and their confidence intervals. The argument `plot.ci` should have the TRUE value, `ci.l` specifies the vector with the lower boundaries, and `ci.u` the vector with the upper boundaries.

```
> barplot2(means, plot.ci = TRUE, ci.l = ci.lower, ci.u = ci.upper,
main = "Bar plot with 95% confidence intervals", xlab = "Frequency
groups", ylab = "Average number of associations", names = c("High",
"Low"))
```

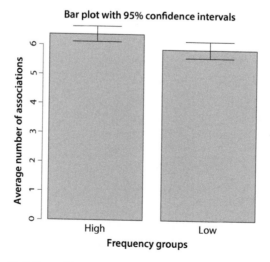

Figure 5.2. Bar plot with 95% confidence intervals around the means of the average number of associations triggered by high- and low-frequency nouns

How to create a bar plot with 95% confidence intervals with the help of `ggplot2`

To create a `ggplot2` version of a bar plot with 95% confidence intervals (Figure 5.2a), you should first create a small data frame that contains only the means, standard errors and group names for the high-frequency and low-frequency samples:

```
> assoc.df <- data.frame(group = c("High", "Low"), mean = means,
se = c(se.high, se.low))
> assoc.df
    group   mean        se
1   High    6.380000    0.1315214
2   Low     5.857451    0.1447616
```

To create the plot, you can use the following code:

```
> ggplot(assoc.df, aes(x = group, y = mean)) + geom_bar(stat =
"identity", fill = "lightblue", colour = "black") + xlab("Frequency
group")  +  ylab("Average  number  of  associations")  +  geom_
errorbar(aes(ymin = mean - 1.96*se, ymax = mean + 1.96*se), width
= 0.2)
```

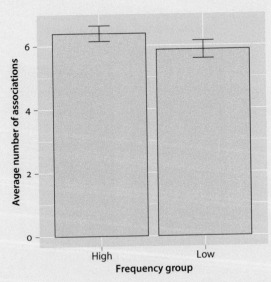

Figure 5.2a. A `ggplot2` version of the bar plot with 95% confidence intervals in Figure 5.2

Bar plots of sample means with 95% confidence intervals provide a lot of useful information. In addition to the average numbers of associations, they show how variable the data are and how much one can rely on the mean (or another statistic) as a measure of central tendency. The smaller the confidence interval, the less the error margin. Moreover, the overlap in 95% confidence intervals can provide an informal estimation of statistical significance. Non-overlapping 95% confidence intervals signal significant differences between samples at the significance level of 0.05. If the intervals overlap strongly, the difference is most probably not statistically significant. If there is a small overlap, as in our case, the means can still be significantly different. Recall that the *t*-test yielded a *p*-value of 0.004, so the difference is statistically significant. In case of overlap, only a statistical test can give a definite answer.

Note that confidence intervals around the mean are meaningful only if the mean is a good estimator of the central tendency, that is, your distribution is not skewed, there are no outliers, the samples are large, etc. If any of these conditions do not hold, you can either try to transform the data, as shown in Chapter 3, or use non-parametric bootstrap methods (see, for example, the package `simpleboot`).

Some common misconceptions about *p*-values, confidence intervals and hypothesis testing

Misconception 1: *p*-values show the probability that the null hypothesis is true.
Correction: *p*-values show the probability of observing the given and more extreme results if the null hypothesis were true.

Misconception 2: A 95% confidence interval means that the probability that this interval includes the population mean is 95%.
Correction: A 95% confidence interval means that this interval has a 95% probability of being one that contains the population mean.

Misconception 3: If your *p*-value is small, the difference is very large. If a *p*-value is large, the difference is very small.
Correction: If your *p*-value is small, this tells only about how confident you can be about the difference. Even a tiny difference can be statistically significant if the sample is very large. In other words, **statistical significance** does not tell you anything about the **effect size**.

(Continued)

> **Misconception 4:** If your *p*-value is smaller than the significance level, you have **proven** that the null hypothesis is wrong.
>
> **Correction:** If your *p*-value is smaller than the significance level, you can **reject** the null hypothesis (but you cannot **prove** that it is wrong!)
>
> You can find other wide-spread misconceptions in Huck (2009).

5.3   Comparing concreteness scores of high- and low-frequency nouns with the help of a two-tailed Wilcoxon test

5.3.1   Data and hypotheses

To be able to work with the data and functions discussed in this case study you will need the following add-on packages:

```
> install.packages("ggplot2")
> library(Rling); library(ggplot2)
```

You will need the same datasets that were presented in the previous case study: pym_high, with 50 high-frequency nouns, and pym_low, with 51 low-frequency nouns. Both datasets can be found in the Rling package.

```
> data(pym_high)
> data(pym_low)
```

See the description of the datasets in the previous section. This time the variable of interest is *conc* (concreteness). It shows the average scores on the concreteness – abstractness scale given by the subjects on the scale from 1 to 7. The higher the score, the more concrete the noun. One can hypothesize that the high- and low-frequency nouns will on average have different concreteness scores. This hypothesis is non-directional because we do not have expectations which group will have higher scores than the other.

5.3.2   Descriptive statistics and visualizations: Strip charts and rug plots

As usual, let us first look at the main descriptive statistics. They demonstrate that the high-frequency nouns tend to have greater concreteness values that the low-frequency ones.

```
> summary(pym_high$conc)
  Min.  1st Qu.  Median   Mean   3rd Qu.  Max.
 1.830   3.202    5.850   5.074   6.590   7.000
> summary(pym_low$conc)
  Min.  1st Qu.  Median   Mean   3rd Qu.  Max.
 1.730   2.740    4.850   4.728   6.620   7.000
```

It is also instructive to look at the overall distributions, as was done in Chapter 3. The code below creates a Q–Q plot and a density plot of the concreteness scores in the high-frequency dataset (you can also create a histogram on your own):

```
> qqnorm(pym_high$conc, main = "Q-Q plot of concreteness scores")
> qqline(pym_high$conc)
> plot(density(pym_high$conc), main = "Density plot of concreteness
scores", xlab = "Concreteness")
```

The graphs are shown in Figure 5.3. They demonstrate that the distribution is not normal and that it is actually bimodal, having two local peaks. You can repeat the procedure to see that low-frequency nouns behave in a similar way.

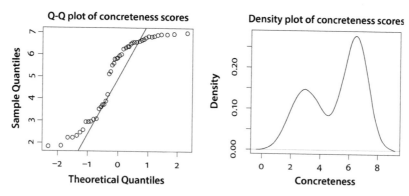

Figure 5.3. Concreteness scores of high-frequency nouns. Right: Q–Q plot; left: a density plot

Other useful alternatives to visualize distributions are a strip chart and a rug plot. The former can be created as follows:

```
> stripchart(list(pym_high$conc, pym_low$conc), main = "Distribution
of concreteness scores", group.names = c("high", "low"), method =
"jitter", xlim = c(1, 7))
```

The argument group.names = c("high", "low") provides labels for the two subplots, whereas method = "jitter" allows one to avoid overplotting of symbols. Adding some jitter is useful when your data contain many similar scores. Finally, xlim = c(1, 7) is added to display the full range of possible scores from 1 to 7.

It is also possible to add a 'rug' representation of each distribution to the plot. One has to specify the sides ('1' is bottom and '3' is top), where the rug representations should appear. You can see the result in Figure 5.4.

```
> rug(pym_high$conc, side = 1)
> rug(pym_low$conc, side = 3)
```

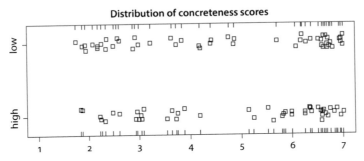

Figure 5.4. A strip chart with rug representations of concreteness scores of high- and low-frequency nouns

How to create a strip chart with the help of `ggplot2`

To represent two or more vectors with the help of a strip chart, you can use the following code (see the result in Figure 5.4a):

```
> pym_conc <- data.frame(conc = c(pym_high$conc, pym_low$conc),
freq = c(rep("high", 50), rep("low", 51)))
> ggplot(pym_conc, aes(x = freq, y = conc)) + geom_point(position
= position_jitter(width = 0.05), shape=0) + coord_flip() + labs(x
= "Frequency group", y = "Average concreteness score", ylim =
c(1, 7))
```

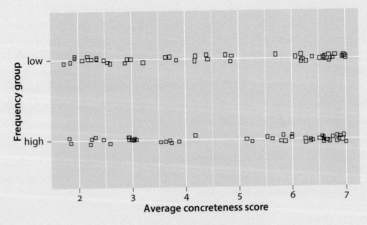

Figure 5.4a. A `ggplot2` version of the strip chart in Figure 5.4

What are the concrete and abstract nouns like? This is a good opportunity to practice in complex subsetting of data frames. Below is the code for retrieving all high-frequency nouns with concreteness scores greater than six, and their concreteness scores:

```
> pym_high[pym_high$conc > 6, 4, drop = FALSE]
             conc
home         6.25
church       6.59
door         7.00
college      6.38
girl         6.83
person       6.51
river        6.83
paper        6.89
earth        6.58
letter       6.94
poet         6.35
king         6.34
judge        6.25
bottle       6.94
valley       6.66
animal       6.75
forest       6.69
newspaper    6.56
cell         6.63
library      6.87
coast        6.59
stone        6.96
```

To perform this operation, one has to subset both rows and columns. The first expression in the square brackets specifies the rows to be selected. It tells R to select only the rows with *conc* scores greater than 6. The digit 4 after the first comma specifies the fourth column, *conc*. See Appendix 1 for more examples of subsetting. The final argument, drop = FALSE, is added in order to retain the row names. Without this argument, you will get only a sequence of numbers, as shown below.

```
> pym_high[pym_high$conc > 6, 4]
 [1] 6.25 6.59 7.00 6.38 6.83 6.51 6.83 6.89 6.58 6.94 6.35 6.34 6.25
6.94 6.66 6.75 6.69 6.56 6.63 6.87 6.59 6.96
```

The smaller peak in the high-frequency sample (approximately between the scores 2 and 4) is represented by abstract nouns shown below. To retrieve them, you can use the following expression with &, which means that the score should be greater than two AND smaller than four:

```
> pym_high[pym_high$conc > 2&pym_high$conc < 4, 4, drop = FALSE]
            conc
time        2.47
life        2.96
mind        2.60
pressure    3.63
effort      2.22
hour        2.93
trouble     2.25
science     3.05
series      3.88
length      3.75
health      3.54
event       3.72
dream       3.03
duty        2.32
victory     2.95
silence     3.09
```

The words that are located in the 'valley' between those two peaks are as follows:

```
> pym_high[pym_high$conc > 4&pym_high$conc < 6, 4, drop = FALSE]
              conc
university    5.87
property      5.99
volume        5.14
lord          4.18
product       5.80
leader        5.83
master        5.53
contract      5.24
disease       5.63
```

Some of them are polysemous or vague, e.g. *property* (an object that one owns and an abstract feature), *volume* (a book and an abstract characteristic), *product* (a material object or abstract result), *contract* (an agreement or a written document that represents it) and *university* (a social institution or a building, or people who work there). It is also interesting to find nouns related to social status (*lord*, *leader* and *master*). The noun *disease* is a state with salient physical manifestations, which probably explains the in-between status of the word.

5.3.3   Inferential statistics: The two-tailed Wilcoxon test

After we have explored the data, it is time to perform an appropriate test. We have independent observations, so the test will be independent. The alternative hypothesis is non-directional: we expect that the concreteness scores of the high-frequency nouns are different from the concreteness scores of the low-frequency nouns. Thus, the test should be two-tailed. Shall we use a parametric or non-parametric test? The previous section discussed the main assumptions of the parametric t-test for independent samples. There are some problems. First, the psychological scaling data are problematic. Even when numbers from 1 to 7 are used, subjects may treat the distances between the points at the ends of the scale differently than the distances between the points in the middle of the scale. Thus, the data are in fact quasi-interval, although it is quite common to treat them as interval, for instance, by computing averages, as it is done here.

It is also clear that the assumption of normality is not met: each group has two more or less distinct clusters that correspond to abstract and concrete nouns. The Shapiro-Wilk test supports this conclusion:

```
> shapiro.test(pym_high$conc)

        Shapiro-Wilk normality test

data: pym_high$conc
W = 0.8468, p-value = 1.269e-05

> shapiro.test(pym_low$conc)

        Shapiro-Wilk normality test

data: pym_low$conc
W = 0.8553, p-value = 1.827e-05
```

The very small p-values support our observation that both samples strongly depart from normality. Since the data are quasi-interval and markedly non-normal, with two clusters for abstract and concrete nouns, we will be cautious and use the non-parametric option, the Wilcoxon test, even though both sample sizes are greater than 30. The test is equivalent to the Mann-Whitney test, and the Mann-Whitney test is also sometimes called the U-test because of the name of the test statistic. The Mann-Whitney and Wilcoxon tests are called non-parametric because they do not assume a distribution of any particular shape. There is another important difference. Instead of actual scores, the Mann-Whitney and Wilcoxon tests use the ranks of the scores in each group. In the Mann-Whitney test, the test statistic U is computed by comparing all possible pairs of values, one from each group, and then giving these pairs the score 1 if the observation from the first group is greater than the one from the second group, and 0 is the first group observation is lower than that from the second group. The Wilcoxon test has a slightly different procedure: first, all observations from both groups are put together and ranked; next, the test statistic W is computed as the sum of the ranks in the smaller group. However, the results of the two tests are identical. Since these tests are based on ranks, they can be used with **ordinal** data. They are also regarded as tests of the difference in medians, rather than the difference in means.

As was mentioned in Section 5.1, the independent Wilcoxon and Mann-Whitney tests have a number of assumptions, as well:

- *Each sample has been drawn randomly from the population.*
- *The observations are independent, both between the two samples and within each sample.*
- *The measurement scale is at least ordinal.*
- *The underlying population distributions should be of a similar shape.*

Since all these assumptions are met, the Wilcoxon test can be performed. The two-tailed option and independent test are the default options, so they do not have to be specified. Instead, we will add `correct` = `FALSE` to cancel the continuity correction,[3] and `conf.int` = `TRUE` to obtain the 95% confidence intervals.

```
> wilcox.test(pym_high$conc, pym_low$conc, correct = FALSE, conf.
int = TRUE)

        Wilcoxon rank sum test

data: pym_high$conc and pym_low$conc
W = 1380, p-value = 0.4757
alternative hypothesis: true location shift is not equal to 0
95 percent confidence interval:
-0.2699598 0.7700643
sample estimates:
difference in location
              0.1599588
```

The W-statistic is 1380, and the p-value is much greater than 0.05. Therefore, we cannot reject the null hypothesis of no differences in the concreteness scores of the high- and low-frequency nouns. Even though the descriptive statistics were slightly greater for the former ones, these differences are not statistically significant.

5.4   Comparing associations produced by native and non-native speakers: The dependent one-tailed *t*-test

5.4.1   Creating simulation data

To reproduce the code in this case study, you will need only one add-on package, `Rling`.

---

3.   According to some statisticians, the correction for continuity should be applied when non-parametric tests for continuous variables are run on discrete data. The correction decreases the risk of Type I error. See Sheskin (2011: 252).

```
> library(Rling)
```

The previous case studies in this chapter were based on independent samples. Therefore, unpaired tests were performed. A different situation is observed when one has paired observations. Imagine that you want to compare the average number of associations per word produced by native and non-native speakers. In that case, you would have a pair of scores for each word. Another example is language proficiency scores of a group of students before and after some innovative teaching technology was used in the class. There would be two scores per student. All these are examples of paired data, which require a dependent, or paired test.

To provide an illustration, we will take the scores from the high-frequency nouns in the dataset pym_high, which was discussed in the previous sections, and will assume that these are native speakers' scores. See Section 5.2 for more details about the dataset and the variables.

```
> data(pym_high)
```

The scores for non-native speakers will be generated automatically. First, we will create a vector with 50 numbers that represent the differences between the native speakers and non-native speakers. The function rnorm() will generate normally distributed data with the given number of observations (50), the mean (−1.35) and the standard deviation (1.27). The mean and the standard deviation are completely arbitrary. A negative mean means that the average number of associations produced by non-native speakers should be smaller. Note that your vector will look different because the numbers are generated randomly.

```
> diff <- rnorm(50, -1.35, 1.27)
> head(diff)
[1] -1.8013467 -2.1152391 -1.6954642 -0.8052109 -1.2967283
[6] -0.5255384
```

Next, the fictitious scores of the non-native speakers are created, which are equal to the native speakers' scores plus the difference:

```
> nn <- pym_high$assoc + diff
> head(nn)
[1] 5.198653 4.664761 5.184536 6.714789 4.583272 7.434462
```

Next, the scores are rounded up to two decimal places:

```
> nn <- round(nn, 2)
> head(nn)
[1] 5.20 4.66 5.18 6.71 4.58 7.43
```

The data are ready for the demonstration of the paired test.

5.4.2   Performing the dependent *t*-test

The assumptions of the dependent *t*-test, which were listed in Section 5.1, are very similar to those of the independent *t*-test. One important difference is that instead of testing the samples for normality, we test the **differences** between the pairs of scores. We already have the vector with differences. They should be normally distributed because this is the way how we have created them. Not surprisingly, the Shapiro-Wilk test returns a high *p*-value.

```
> shapiro.test(diff)

        Shapiro-Wilk normality test

data: diff
W = 0.9922, p-value = 0.9832
```

If you have real observed scores, the vector with differences can be obtained by subtracting the scores of one group (imaginary vector groupA) from the scores of the other group (imaginary vector groupB):

```
> diff <- groupA - groupB # do not run; only given as an example
```

Since all other assumptions hold, as well, we can use the parametric *t*-test. To perform a dependent, or paired test, one should add `paired = TRUE` to the list of arguments. Because the alternative hypothesis is directional (that is, native speakers produce more associations than non-native speakers) and the test is one-tailed, it is also necessary to add `alternative = "greater"`:

```
> t.test(pym_high$assoc, nn, alternative = "greater", paired =
TRUE)

        Paired t-test

data: pym_high$assoc and nn
t = 8.4935, df = 49, p-value = 1.698e-11
alternative hypothesis: true difference in means is greater than 0
95 percent confidence interval:
1.330853      Inf
sample estimates:
mean of the differences
          1.658162
```

The *t*-statistic is 8.494 with 49 degrees of freedom. The *p*-value is very small. This means that the null hypothesis of no difference can be rejected and the difference between the average number of associations produced by native and non-native speakers is statistically significant.

In case of violations of the test assumptions, one can use the paired version of the Wilcoxon (Mann-Whitney) test. The default unpaired version of this test was presented in Section 5.3. To perform a paired test, add the argument `paired = TRUE`.

5.5   Summary

This chapter has presented dependent and independent, parametric and non-parametric, one-tailed and two-tailed tests for investigating differences between two group means. The choice of the appropriate test requires a careful check of numerous assumptions, but you will be rewarded by statistically reliable results. You have also learnt about standard errors and confidence intervals around the mean. All these fundamental notions and skills will be useful in the following case studies.

Reporting the *t*-test and the Wilcoxon/Mann-Whitney test

When you write up the results of your independent or dependent *t*-test or its non-parametric equivalent, you should mention the test statistic (*t* or *W*), the degrees of freedom and the *p*-value. It is crucial to mention whether you performed an independent or dependent test, one-tailed or two-tailed. For example, one could write up the results of the first case study as follows: "An independent one-tailed *t*-test with Welch's correction was performed to compare the average number of associations produced by native speakers for two lists of randomly selected high- and low-frequency words. On average, high-frequency words triggered a significantly higher number of associations ($M = 6.38$, $SE = 0.13$) than low-frequency words ($M = 5.86$, $SE = 0.14$), $t_{(98.281)} = 2.67$, $p = 0.004$."

Another application of the *t*-test

In addition to comparing two dependent or independent samples, the *t*-test can be used on one sample only when we know the population mean and want to find out whether the sample mean M is significantly different from the population mean μ (see Baayen 2008: Section 4.1.2; Gries 2013: 205–209).

CHAPTER 6

Relationships between two quantitative variables

correlation analysis with elements of linear regression modelling

What you will learn from this chapter:

Will your knowledge of statistics improve as you read more and more books on the subject? Is there a relationship between the length of a word and its frequency? Does grammatical proficiency of children depend on the number of lexical items which they have mastered? Does the number of phonemes in a language depend on the number of speakers? All these questions involve correlation between two variables. This chapter explains the principles of correlation analysis and demonstrates how it can be carried out using popular parametric and non-parametric tests. You will also learn how to produce correlograms and scatter plots with a regression line. Some fundamental notions of regression analysis, such as residuals, homo- and heteroscedasticity, will be introduced. The case studies investigate the relationship between word frequency and mean reaction time in a lexical decision task and the correlation between vocabulary size and grammatical proficiency in first language acquisition.

6.1   What is correlation?

The previous chapters dealt with descriptive and inferential statistics that describe a single variable (mean, median, standard deviation, etc.) or pinpoint the differences between scores of two groups on the same variable (the *t*-test and analogous non-parametric tests). In this chapter, you will learn how to investigate the relationship between two quantitative variables. More specifically, you will learn to measure and test **correlations**. A correlation is called **positive** if the values of both variable X and variable Y increase and decrease together: if X increases, Y increases, and if X decreases, Y decreases, as well. For instance, suppose you are interested whether there is a relationship between the size of a child's vocabulary and his or her grammatical proficiency (see Section 6.3). You will probably expect to find a positive correlation: the more words a child knows, the higher his or her grammatical proficiency will be. A **negative**, or inverse, correlation is observed when the values of X and Y change in opposite directions: if X increases, Y decreases, or if X decreases, Y increases. An example of a negative correlation would be the relationship between word frequency and word length: according to Zipf's Law of Abbreviation (see Chapter 5), the more frequent a word, the shorter it is, i.e. the fewer syllables or phonemes it contains.

The strength of such relationships is usually measured with the help of a **correlation coefficient**. It normally ranges from −1 (perfect negative correlation) to 1 (perfect positive correlation). 0 indicates a lack of relationship. In this chapter we will discuss three different correlation coefficients: Pearson's product-moment coefficient r, Spearman's ρ ('rho') and Kendall's τ ('tau'). The Pearson r is applied to interval- or ratio-scaled variables, whereas the Spearman and Kendall coefficients deal with ordinal data (ranks), as well as interval or ratio-scaled variables transformed into ranks.

After a researcher has computed a correlation coefficient, he or she also needs to know whether this relationship will be observed if one takes another sample from the same population. In other words, one has to test if the coefficient is statistically significant. As in the previous chapter, the choice of an appropriate correlation test depends on a number of conditions. While the significance test of the Pearson r is based on the assumption of normality, the Spearman ρ and Kendall τ are non-parametric tests, which do not assume a distribution of a particular shape.

The remaining part of the chapter is organized as follows. Section 6.2 discusses the Pearson product-moment correlation coefficient in a case study that investigates the relationship between word length and mean reaction times in a lexical decision task. Section 6.3 explores the relationship between vocabulary size and grammatical proficiency in first language acquisition using the Spearman ρ and Kendall τ. Section 6.4 shows how one can visualize correlations between more than two variables in a correlogram. Section 6.5 summarizes the main ideas of the chapter.

6.2   Word length and word recognition: The Pearson product-moment correlation coefficient

6.2.1   The data and hypothesis

For this case study you will need data and functions from the following add-on packages that should be installed and loaded, unless you have done so already:

```
> install.packages(c("ggplot2", "energy", "car"))
> library(Rling); library(ggplot2); library(energy); library(car)
```

This case study will investigate if there is a correlation between the length of a word, on the one hand, and how fast it is recognized by speakers in a lexical decision experiment, on the other hand. The data can be found in the data frame `ldt` in `Rling`. This dataset was introduced in Chapter 3. The variables of interest are *Length* (word length in letters) and *Mean_RT* (average reaction times in a lexical decision task). This time, the dataset will be attached, so that the variables can be easily accessed without specifying the name of the data frame.

```
> data(ldt)
> attach(ldt)
> summary(Length)
   Min.   1st Qu.   Median    Mean   3rd Qu.   Max.
   3.00     6.00     8.00     8.23    10.00   15.00
> summary(Mean_RT)
   Min.   1st Qu.   Median    Mean   3rd Qu.   Max.
  564.2    713.1    784.9    808.3   905.2   1459.0
```

The distributional characteristics of these variables should already be familiar to the reader from Chapter 3, where the variables were analysed in detail with the help of various descriptive statistics and graphs.

The alternative hypothesis of this case study is as follows: the longer a word, the longer the time that is needed to recognize it. The hypothesis is directional. The null hypothesis is that there is no correlation between word length and reaction time.

6.2.2   Descriptive statistics and visualizations

To visualize the relationship between two quantitative variables, one can create a scatter plot with the help of the `plot()` function. The first argument specifies the coordinates of the points on the horizontal axis, and the second argument provides the values on the vertical axis:

```
> plot(Length, Mean_RT, main = "Scatter plot of word length and mean
reaction times")
```

Alternatively, you can use an expression with a tilde. The variable on the left from the tilde will be plotted on the vertical axis, and the variable on the right will be plotted on the horizontal axis:

```
> plot(Mean_RT ~ Length, main = "Scatter plot of word length and
mean reaction times")
```

The plot is shown in Figure 6.1. The plot also displays a regression line. Roughly speaking, a regression line shows a general trend in the data. A more detailed explanation will be provided below. To add the line, use the following code:

```
> m <- lm(Mean_RT ~ Length)
> abline(m)
```

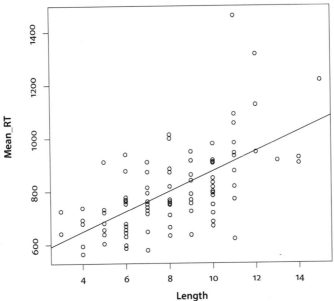

Scatter plot of word length and mean reaction times

Figure 6.1. Scatter plot of word length in letters and mean reaction times

How to create a scatter plot with a regression line the help of ggplot2

To create a ggplot2 scatter plot with a regression line, similar to the one shown in Figure 6.1, one can use the following code:

```
> ggplot(ldt, aes(x = Length, y = Mean_RT)) + geom_point(shape =
1, size = 3) + stat_smooth(method = lm)
```

Note that stat_smooth() also adds a 95% confidence region around the regression line. The result can be seen in Figure 6.1a.

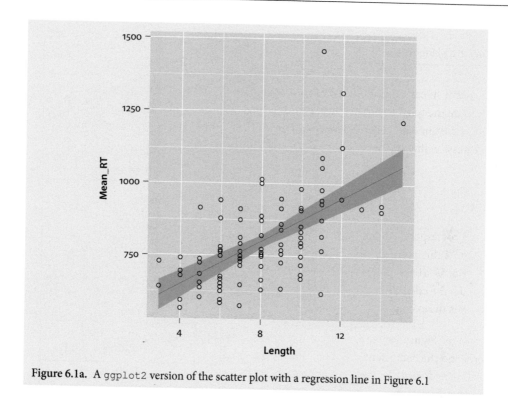

Figure 6.1a. A `ggplot2` version of the scatter plot with a regression line in Figure 6.1

The correlation seems to be positive. The longer a word, the more time it is needed to recognize it. But what is the strength of this correlation? To find this out, we need to compute the correlation coefficient. Let us begin with the Pearson product-moment correlation coefficient, which is probably the most widely used one. It can be computed as follows:

```
> cor(Mean_RT, Length) # equivalent to cor(…, use = "everything",
method = "pearson")
[1] 0.6147456
```

The coefficient is positive: $r = 0.615$. Some other possibilities are shown in Figure 6.2. When r is -1 or $+1$, all points fall on the regression line. The correlation is perfect. The closer r to zero, the more individual points deviate from the line and the weaker the correlation. As a very approximate rule of thumb, if r is equal to or greater than 0.7 or smaller than -0.7, the correlation is considered to be strong. If r is between 0.3 and 0.7 or between -0.3 and -0.7, it is considered to be moderate. If r is between 0 and 0.3 or 0 and -0.3, the correlation is considered to be weak. Note that a steep slope does not mean that the correlation is strong. It only shows the number of units by which y will change if x changes. The angle of the slope also depends on how R scales the axes.

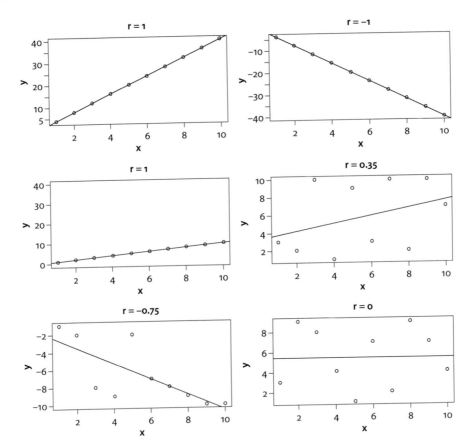

Figure 6.2. Several possible values of Pearson product-moment correlation coefficient r

Correlation can be discussed in terms of regression analysis, which models the relationship between one response (dependent) variable and one or several explanatory (independent) variables. In our case, we model the relationship between mean reaction time and word length. In regression analysis, it is crucial to distinguish between **observed** and **fitted values** of the response variable. The observed y-scores are as follows (only six first numbers are shown):

```
> head(Mean_RT)
[1] 819.19 977.63 908.22 766.30 1125.42 948.33
```

The corresponding fitted values are as follows:

```
> head(fitted(m))
       1         2         3         4         5         6
799.5952  874.8831  761.9512  724.3072  950.1711  950.1711
```

Another crucial concept is **residuals**, which are the differences between the observed and fitted values of the response variable:

```
> head(residuals(m))
1              2            3            4            5
19.594813    102.746875    146.268782    41.992751    175.248936
6
-1.841064
```

Consider the scatter plot in Figure 6.3. Observed values are the actual values of the points on the y-axis. Fitted values correspond to the y-values of the projections of the observed values on the regression line. Finally, the value of a residual is equal to the height of the vertical line that can be drawn from a point to the regression line. Most commonly, the regression line is drawn in such a way as to approach all points as closely as possible and thus to minimize the sum of squared residuals (this is called the least squares method). The smaller the residuals (relative to the total variation of y), the stronger the correlation. More on this will follow in the next chapter.

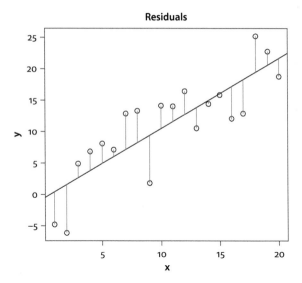

Figure 6.3. Plot with a cloud of points, a regression line (the diagonal) and residuals (vertical lines)

Correlation analysis and paired *t*-test: superficial similarity

Both correlation analysis and the paired *t*-test deal with paired observations represented by vectors X and Y. However, the similarity is only superficial. The paired *t*-test

(Continued)

tests the difference between the mean values of X and Y, whereas correlation analysis measures the strength of relationship between X and Y. Correlation analysis does not tell you whether the mean value of X is greater or smaller than the mean value of Y.

There are a few caveats to keep in mind when using the Pearson correlation coefficient. First, it makes sense only if the relationship between the variables is monotonic and linear. Second, it is very sensitive to the presence of outliers.

A relationship between variables X and Y is called **monotonic** when an increase in X is followed by an increase in Y, or a decrease in X is followed by a decrease in Y. Relationships are linear when Y decreases or increases at the same rate as X does, and vice versa. Consider the illustrations in Figure 6.4. The left graph shows a monotonic linear relationship. The central plot displays a monotonic, but non-linear relationship. Finally, a non-monotonic relationship is shown in the right graph. As an example, consider the relationship between age and weight. A baby's weight increases by three times during its first year, but then the growth slows down. Thus, the relationship between age and weight is non-linear: if one draws a graph with age as the x-axis, and weight as the y-axis, it will look like a curve, not like a straight line. Sometimes a person's weight even decreases in the old age, so the relationship can be described as both non-linear and non-monotonic.

It does not make sense to use the Pearson correlation coefficient if the relationship is non-monotonic and/or non-linear. Consider the right graph of Figure 6.4, which illustrates a non-monotonic relationship. The correlation coefficient computed by R is in fact almost zero: $r = -0.02$. However, this does not mean that there is no relationship: on the contrary, the relationship between x and y is quite strong, but it is a quadratic one, $y = x^2$. In such cases, the Pearson r gives a wrong idea of the relationship between the variables. However, if we transform the data by squaring x and measure the correlation between y and x^2, the correlation coefficient will be 0.61, which represents the relationship more correctly.

In the central plot of Figure 6.4, the underlying relationship is a logarithmic one: $y = log(x)$. The correlation is positive and strong, $r = 0.8$, if one measures the correlation between x and y, but it becomes somewhat higher, $r = 0.85$, if the logarithmic nature of the relationship is taken into account, $log(x)$ vs. y. These and other transformations will become very useful when you learn to fit linear regression models in the next chapter.

As one could see in the previous exploratory plots, the relationship between word length and mean reaction time seems to be linear. More precise diagnostic tools will follow in the next chapter.

The second potential problem is outliers. Consider two situations shown in Figure 6.5. The left graph (without the outlier) shows no relationship, $r = 0$. The right part shows a strong positive correlation between x and y when the outlier is present, $r = 0.87$. Obvi-

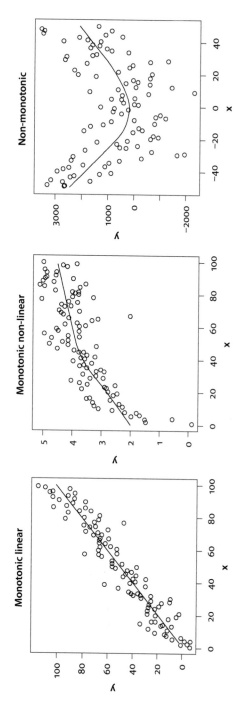

Figure 6.4. Monotonic and non-monotonic relationships between variables *x* and *y*

ously, $r = 0$ describes the general trend (or, rather, a lack of any trend) more correctly. Such observations are called **leverage** points because they can 'pull' the regression line in some direction.

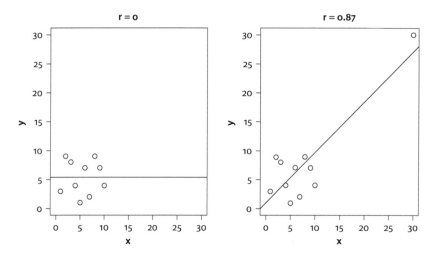

Figure 6.5. Impact of an outlier on the value of the Pearson r

Recall that we identified three outliers in the mean reaction times in Chapter 3 with the help of different diagnostic techniques. Those were unusually long reaction times. If you look at Figure 6.1 again, you will see a few points above $y = 1200$, which do not fit the pattern well, especially the one with the score above 1400. They are located in the top left corner. Let us try to exclude these points and see what happens:

```
> Mean_RT_1 <- Mean_RT[Mean_RT < 1200]
> length(Mean_RT_1)
[1] 97
```

The corresponding values in the frequency vector should be excluded, as well:

```
> Length_1 <- Length[Mean_RT < 1200]
> length(Length_1)
[1] 97
```

Now we are left with 97 observations out of the initial 100. What will change? Let us add a new regression line to the scatter plot in Figure 6.1. If you have already closed the graphics window with the plot, you will need to create the plot again before adding the line. This new line will be based on the data without these three points. The new trend is represented with a dashed line (`lty = 2`):

```
> m1 <- lm(Mean_RT_1 ~ Length_1)
> abline(m1, lty = 2)
```

The result is shown in Figure 6.6.

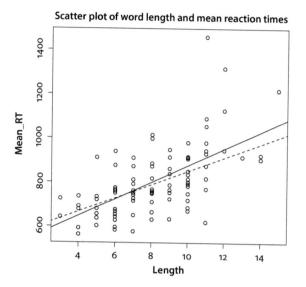

Figure 6.6. Scatter plot of word length and mean reaction time, with two regression lines. The solid line is based on the full dataset; the dashed line is based on the dataset without three outliers

The slope has changed slightly. This is because the line is no longer 'pulled' up by the outliers in the top right corner. Has the correlation coefficient changed?

```
> cor(Mean_RT_1, Length_1)
[1] 0.5886011
```

The correlation coefficient has become more moderate.

Handling missing data

If your data contain missing scores in at least one variable, R will return 'NA' instead of the correlation coefficient. Consider two vectors, x and y. The former contains no missing data, whereas the latter has one missing value:

```
> x <- 1:10
> x
[1] 1 2 3 4 5 6 7 8 9 10

> y <- x*2
> y[5] <- NA
```

(*Continued*)

```
> y
[1]  2 4 6 8 NA 12 14 16 18 20
```

If you try computing a correlation coefficient, R will return 'NA':

```
> cor(x, y)
[1] NA
```

You may want to tell R to consider only those cases where both scores are non-missing by adding use = "complete" or use = "pairwise":

```
> cor(x, y, use = "complete")
[1] 1
```

6.2.3 Testing the significance of the correlation coefficient

It is not enough to compute the correlation coefficient and interpret it. One should also test whether the observed correlation is statistically significant. That is, if one takes another sample and measures the correlation, will the results be similar?

If you want to test whether the Pearson correlation coefficient is statistically significant, a few assumptions should be met:

- *The sample is randomly selected from the population it represents.* In our case, this means that the words should have been selected randomly, which is the case.
- *Both variables are at least interval-scaled.*
- *Both variables come from a **bivariate** normal distribution* and/or the sample size is large (30 and more observations). A bivariate normal distribution means that both variables and their linear combination are normally distributed. In other words, for any given value of variable X, the scores on variable Y will be normally distributed, and vice versa.[1] We will discuss a test that can help you detect violations of this assumption.
- *The residual (error) variance is **homoscedastic*** (*homo* is 'same' and *scedastic* comes from 'scatter'). That is, the relationship between the variables should be of equal strength across the entire range of both variables.
- *The residuals are independent.* This means that there should be no **autocorrelation** between residuals. One speaks about autocorrelation when the value of a variable depends on its previous or next value. Consider temperature: it increases gradually in the summer and decreases in the winter. It is very unlikely to have $+35^0$ C one day and -20^0 next day. Another example is economic cycles. Economic indicators, such as GDP, in one year tend to depend on their values in the previous year. As linguistic examples one can mention within-subject priming and syntactic persistence in language production. Autocorrelation plays a central role in time series analysis.

1.　In practice, however, it is common to test only univariate normality of each variable.

Let us check whether the reaction times data without the outliers meet these assumptions. The observations were sampled randomly. Both variables are ratio-scaled. The sample size is large enough, so we do not have to worry about normality. To test the assumption of a bivariate normal distribution, one can use the function `mvnorm.etest()` from the package `energy`. The function requires a matrix or a data frame, so we will combine the vectors as columns in a matrix:

```
> mvnorm.etest(cbind(Length_1, Mean_RT_1))

  Energy test of multivariate normality: estimated parameters

data: x, sample size 97, dimension 2, replicates 999
E-statistic = 0.485, p-value = 0.8969
```

Since the test is implemented by bootstrap, which involves drawing random samples from the data (999 replicates by default) and re-computing the test statistic, your results will be slightly different from what is shown in the output. The p-value is much greater than 0.05. This means that we cannot reject the null hypothesis of normality. In other words, we can consider that the assumption of bivariate normality is met. This function can be used to test not only bivariate, but also multivariate and univariate normality (see examples on the help page of the function).

Now it is time to discuss the assumption of homoscedasticity. Consider Figure 6.7, where the left panel shows a homoscedastic pattern, and the right panel displays a violation of homoscedasticity (in other words, it displays heteroscedasticity).

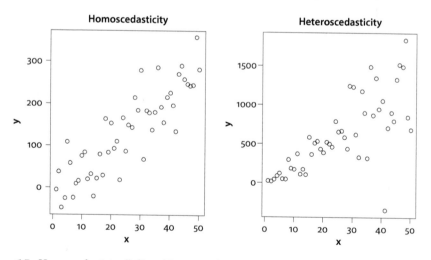

Figure 6.7. Homoscedasticity (left) and heteroscedasticity (right)

We do not find clear indications of heteroscedasticity in Figure 6.6 (three outliers should be disregarded). To perform a more formal test, one can use a function in the package `car` created by John Fox. It is called `ncvTest()`. The abbreviation stands for 'non-constant variance test'. The main argument is a fitted linear regression model.

```
> ncvTest(m1)
Non-constant Variance Score Test
Variance formula:  ~ fitted.values
Chisquare = 1.243717      Df = 1 p = 0.2647559
```

The null hypothesis of the test is that the error variance is homoscedastic. Since the p-value is greater than 0.05, the null hypothesis cannot be rejected. Thus, we do not have to worry about heteroscedasticity.

Finally, the residuals have to be tested for autocorrelation. We do not expect to find autocorrelation in the data, but it might be useful to show how one's data can be tested for the presence of autocorrelation. Again, we will use a function from the package `car`. The procedure is called the Durbin-Watson test.

```
> durbinWatsonTest(m1)
lag   Autocorrelation   D-W Statistic    p-value
1     0.03234626        1.923466         0.698
Alternative hypothesis: rho != 0
```

The test returns the $D-W$ test statistic, which ranges between 0 and 4. The closer it is to 2, the smaller the chance of positive or negative autocorrelation. The p-value is very high. This means that we cannot reject the null hypothesis of no autocorrelation. Note that the test provides bootstrapped p-values based on many random resamples from the data, so the results will differ every time you run the test (see more in Sections 7.2.8 and 7.2.9 of Chapter 7). They also depend on the order of observations (rows) in your data.

Since all assumptions have been met, we can now use `cor.test()`. As in the t-test, one has to decide in advance whether we need a one- or two-tailed test. Since the alternative hypothesis is directional, a one-tailed test should be preferred. We expect the correlation between the mean reaction times and the word lengths to be positive. In other words, the alternative hypothesis of the test is that the correlation coefficient is greater than zero. Therefore, one has to add `alternative = "greater"`. If one tests a negative correlation, the alternative hypothesis would be that the correlation coefficient is less than zero, and one should add `alternative = "less"`.

```
> cor.test(Length_1, Mean_RT_1, alternative = "greater")

    Pearson's product-moment correlation

data: Length_1 and Mean_RT_1
t = 7.0965, df = 95, p-value = 1.145e-10
alternative hypothesis: true correlation is greater than 0
95 percent confidence interval:
```

```
0.4667205 1.0000000
sample estimates:
cor
0.5886011
```

The function returns a lot of useful information, including the effect size (correlation coefficient 0.589), as well as the test statistic t, degrees of freedom, the p-value, and the 95% confidence interval. The p-value is very small, so the null hypothesis of no correlation can be rejected.

To summarize, the initial prediction has been borne out: the longer a word, the slower it is recognized by speakers. However, as was mentioned in Chapter 1, one should be careful with interpretation of correlations. In this situation, one can think of other factors that may influence the reaction times. For instance, longer words tend to be also less frequent, according to Zipf's Law of Abbreviation (see Chapter 5), and less frequent words are less familiar and therefore more difficult to recognize. Thus, one should take into account other potentially relevant explanatory variables, as well. This is a task for multiple linear regression, which will be introduced in the next chapter. For the present moment, we finish the case study and detach the dataset:

```
> detach(ldt)
```

Effect size versus statistical significance

It is crucial to understand the difference between effect size and statistical significance. Effect size shows how strongly different variables are related/associated, or how greatly groups of observations differ from one another. The correlation coefficient r is a good example of effect size. Statistical significance, which is associated with the p-value, does not show the strength of a relationship or the magnitude of a difference. It only shows how confident one can be that the observed relationship or difference are not due to chance alone. A strong effect does not automatically entail significance, and vice versa. Crucially, if the same effect size is observed in a smaller sample and a larger sample, the p-value will be smaller in the latter. Consider an example with two variables x and y and ten observations:

(Continued)

```
# do not run; the code in this box provided as an example
> x
[1]  1    2   3   4   5   6   7   8   9   10
> y
[1]  -10  5   14  4   6   7   7   9   4   10
```

The correlation coefficient is positive and moderate (r = 0.462), but not statistically significant (p = 0.179). Let us simply double the number of observations by repeating the values of x and y.

```
> x1
[1]  1    2  3   4  5  6  7  8  9  10 1   2  3   4  5  6  7  8  9  10
> y1
[1]  -10 5  14  4  6  7  7  9  4  10 -10 5  14  4  6
[16] 7    7  9   4  10
```

The correlation coefficient remains the same (r = 0.462), but the p-value becomes smaller: p = 0.04. If there is a correlation in the population, the chances of detecting it in the data increase with the sample size. Of course, one should not increase the number of observations just to be able to report some significant p-values. This would be similar to 'p-hacking', or manipulating the data or tests in order to achieve statistical signifi-cance, – an unethical but not uncommon practice in science. Moreover, it is important to remember that not every significant correlation is meaningful.

6.3   Emergence of grammar from lexicon: Spearman's ρ and Kendall's τ

6.3.1   The data and hypothesis

To perform this case study, you will need no additional packages. The R objects will be constructed from scratch as will be shown below.

Language acquisition has been a battleground for empiricists and nativists for a long time. Is grammar innate or is it learnt by children from the input? Is it autonomous or does it depend on the knowledge of lexicon? To answer these questions, Bates and Goodman (1997) investigated relationships between vocabulary size and grammatical development of young children during the period from 16 to 30 months. The vocabulary size was mea-sured as the number of words produced by the children, and grammatical development was operationalized as the total number of selected target constructions acquired by a child (from 0 to 37). Bates and Goodman found a very high correlation between the levels of lexical and grammatical development. Their results strongly support the empiricist view of language as one dynamic system, which does not consist of separate domain-specific neural modules.

This case study will reproduce their findings with some simulation data from ten imaginary children from 16 to 30 months old. Let us create two numeric vectors: `lex` with total numbers of lexical units acquired by each child, and `gram` with grammatical complexity scores.

```
> lex <- c(47, 89, 131, 186, 245, 284, 362, 444, 553, 627)
> gram <- c(0, 2, 1, 3, 5, 9, 7, 16, 25, 34)
```

The alternative hypothesis of this study is that there is a positive correlation between the size of productive vocabulary and the complexity of grammatical structures. The hypothesis is directional. The null hypothesis states that there is no correlation between these two variables.

6.3.2   Exploring the data and computing correlation coefficients

As in the previous case study, let us begin with plotting the variables one against the other. The vocabulary size will be plotted on the *x*-axis, and the grammatical complexity scores on the *y*-axis.

```
> plot(gram ~ lex, main = "Vocabulary size and grammatical complexity",
xlab = "Productive vocabulary size", ylab = "Grammatical complexity
score")
```

Obviously, the relationship is not linear. We will also add a curved (polynomial) regression line that describes the general trend:

```
> lines(lowess(gram ~ lex))
```

The result can be seen in Figure 6.8.

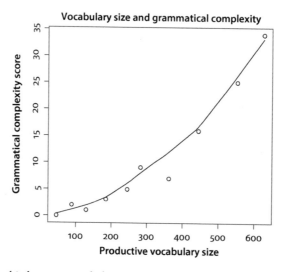

Figure 6.8. Relationship between vocabulary size and grammatical complexity scores

Although the relationship is not linear, it is clearly monotonic and positive: the more words a child uses, the more complex his or her grammatical structures are. The non-linear trend shows that one has to acquire quite a large vocabulary without any noticeable increase of complexity. However, after some critical amount of vocabulary has been learnt, complexity goes up very fast. Here we will perform a traditional correlation analysis, but see Chapter 7 on variable transformation in linear regression.

When the relationship is not linear but monotonic, one should use non-parametric correlation statistics, such as Spearman's ρ ('rho') and Kendall's τ ('tau'). To compute Spearman's ρ with the help of cor() or cor.test(), one should simply add method = "spearman":

```
> cor(gram, lex, method = "spearman")
[1] 0.9757576
```

Spearman's statistic is identical with Pearson's r, when one ranks the original scores and computes r on the ranked data:

```
> cor(rank(gram), rank(lex))
[1] 0.9757576
```

The results are identical. Kendall's τ is also based on ranks, but the algorithm is different. To compute τ, one takes all pairs of ranks on the X variable and all pairs of ranks on Y. For each pair of observations, one looks at the difference in their ranks (positive or negative) on the X variable and on the Y variable. If both differences are positive, the pair of ranks is said to be concordant. If both differences are negative, the pair is considered to be concordant, as well. A pair is said to be discordant if one of the rank differences is positive, and the other is negative. The greater the proportion of concordant pairs, the higher Kendall's τ. For the same data, Kendall's τ is as follows:

```
> cor(gram, lex, method = "kendall")
[1] 0.9111111
```

Similar to Pearson's r, Spearman's ρ and Kendall's τ range from –1 (perfect negative correlation) to + 1 (perfect positive correlation). However, the scores are not identical. Normally, Kendall's τ yields less extreme values than the Spearman ρ, but this should not be a cause of concerns because this difference does not affect the statistical power of the test. That is, one has the same chances of finding a significant correlation, if it is there, as with the Spearman ρ.

Now we should check whether the correlation is statistically significant. The non-parametric tests of significance have only two main assumptions:

- *The sample is randomly drawn from the population.* This means that the subjects were selected randomly.

   –   *Both variables are on the ordinal scale of measurement.* If they are interval- or ratio-scaled, they will be transformed to ranks by R automatically.

Note that, as in the previous case, the relationship between X and Y should be monotonic, that is, it should not change its sign in different regions of X or Y. For non-monotonic relationships, the correlation coefficients simply do not make sense, unless you transform the data and make the relationship monotonic.

     Since both assumptions are met, we can perform the significance tests. We will use the one-tailed version because our alternative hypothesis of positive correlation is directional:

```
> cor.test(gram, lex, method = "spearman", alternative = "greater")

  Spearman's rank correlation rho

data: gram and lex
S = 4, p-value < 2.2e-16
alternative hypothesis: true rho is greater than 0
sample estimates:
  rho
0.9757576

> cor.test(gram, lex, method = "kendall", alternative = "greater")

  Kendall's rank correlation tau

data: gram and lex
T = 43, p-value = 1.488e-05
alternative hypothesis: true tau is greater than 0
sample estimates:
  tau
0.9111111
```

Both tests yield statistically significant results, which is good for our research hypothesis, but which one should we report? This is often a matter of convention in a particular field of research. In addition, some statisticians say that the Kendall τ should be preferred if one has a small dataset and many ranks are tied (Field et al. 2012: 225). Ties are observed when two or more observations have identical scores and therefore identical ranks. If two scores are identical, they get an average of the ranks that they occupy. For example, 6.5 may correspond to two observations that share ranks 6 and 7.[2]

---

2.   Of course, since correlation does not imply causation, one can also say that the correlation can be explained by a third factor, such as the children's age. However, there is evidence that the correlation remains strong even when age is partialled out (Bates and Goodman 1997: 519).

Why bother with parametric tests?

Why not simply use non-parametric tests and statistics in all situations, e.g. the Wilcoxon test instead of the *t*-test, or Spearman's *ρ* instead of Pearson' *r*? If parametric tests have so many assumptions to meet, why not use their non-parametric equivalents all the time?

The main reason is as follows. When one moves down the scale of measurements from interval- or ratio-scaled to ordinal data, one loses information about the actual differences between scores with different ranks. In addition, there are some exceptions to the general rule of thumb, which is to use non-parametric tests with non-normally distributed data. This depends on statistical power, that is, the probability of rejecting the false null hypothesis. Parametric tests are more powerful than their non-parametric 'colleagues' when the distributions have light (short) tails, even when the data are not normally distributed, e.g. discrete scores on a scale from 1 to 5 in an acceptability rating task. In contrast, non-parametric tests are more powerful in the presence of heavy (long) tails and outliers (Conover 1999: 116–117).

6.4   Visualization of correlations between more than two variables with the help of correlograms

To be able to reproduce the code in this case study, you will need the following add-on packages:

```
> install.packages("corrgram")
> library(Rling); library(corrgram)
```

When you have more than two quantitative variables, one can use investigate the relationships between them with the help of a correlation matrix. This is easy to do by using the function cor(). For example, one can create a correlation matrix of three variables in the ldt dataset, which was introduced in Chapter 3 and discussed in Section 6.2 of this chapter. The dataset contains 100 observations (words), which were used as stimuli in a lexical decision task. The three variables are word length in characters, word frequency in a corpus and mean reaction time of lexical decision.

```
> data(ldt)
> cor(ldt, method = "spearman")
```

```
            Length       Freq           Mean_RT
Length    1.0000000    -0.5157536      0.6266207
Freq      -0.5157536    1.0000000     -0.6733258
Mean_RT   0.6266207    -0.6733258      1.0000000
```

The correlation of each variable with itself is one. We also observe a positive correlation between word length and mean reaction time, a negative correlation between frequency and length, and a negative correlation between frequency and mean reaction time. This means, the more frequent a word, the shorter it is, and the faster it is recognized.

For those who prefer visual ways of displaying information, an attractive option might be a correlogram,[3] which provides different colours or other intuitive symbols instead of numerical values in a correlation matrix. This may be particularly helpful for investigating a large set of variables. The relationships between different scores can be even more closely inspected with the help of the corrgram() function in the corrgram package. The corrgram() function can be applied to the original matrix with the scores (in that case, the Pearson correlation coefficient will be computed by default) or to a correlation matrix, which can contain any correlation coefficients.

For illustration, let us create a representation with shaded panels and pie charts based on the Spearman coefficient.

```
> corrgram(ldt, lower.panel = panel.shade, upper.panel = panel.pie,
cor.method = "spearman")
```

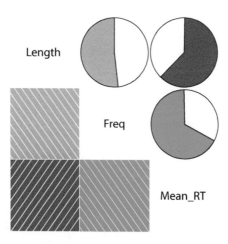

Figure 6.9. Correlogram of word length, corpus frequency and mean reaction times in a lexical decision task (ranked data): shaded panels and pies

---

3.   Note that the term "correlogram" is also used in time series analysis to visualize autocorrelations.

Figure 6.9 displays the result. The strength of correlation is represented by the intensity of shading and also by the size of the coloured segments of the pie charts. The direction is represented by colours (blue for positive correlations, red for negative correlations), direction of shading lines in the panels (bottom left to top right for positive correlations, top left to bottom right for negative correlations), and the orientation of the coloured segments in the pie charts (clockwise for positive correlations, anticlockwise for negative correlations). When the number of variables is large, you may wish to add the argument order = TRUE, which orders the variables in such a way that one can see the groups of strongly correlated variables.

For the purposes of more precise diagnostics of the relationships and detection of outliers, it is also possible to visualize the observations as points plotted against the values of each variable compared, and ellipses that show the direction and strength of association. This is possible, however, only if we have original data with individual observations, rather than a matrix with correlation coefficients. Let us first create a new data frame that is identical to ldt, but the word frequencies are log-transformed (cf. a discussion of the purpose of this transformation in Chapter 3):

```
> ldt1 <- data.frame(Length = ldt$Length, LogFreq = log1p(ldt$Freq),
Mean_RT = ldt$Mean_RT)
> head(ldt1)
    Length   LogFreq    Mean_RT
1    8       4.882802   819.19
2    10      4.418841   977.63
3    7       0.000000   908.22
4    6       6.385194   766.30
5    12      1.098612   1125.42
6    12      2.302585   948.33
```

Now we can create the correlogram:

```
> corrgram(ldt1, lower.panel = panel.ellipse, upper.panel = panel.
pts)
```

The lower part of Figure 6.10 shows ellipses. The rounder the ellipse, the weaker the correlation. There are also the so-called LOESS smoothed curves, which show the general direction of relationships (the technique is closely related to lowess(), which was used in the previous section). The straighter the line, the more linear the relationship. The plots with points in the upper part of the correlogram are simple scatter plots, which can help one detect outliers. This kind of representation is a useful exploratory tool in correlation analysis and regression.

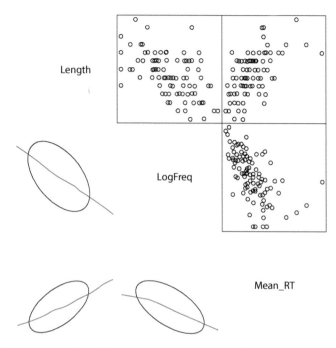

Figure 6.10. Correlogram of word length, log-transformed word frequency and mean reaction times in a lexical decision task: points (individual words) and ellipses with smoothed curves

6.5 Summary

This chapter has introduced parametric and non-parametric measures of correlation between two quantitative variables, as well as means of exploring relationships between more than two variables. Correlation analysis and linear regression are very closely related. This is why a few basic notions of linear regression modelling, such as residuals and homoscedasticity, have been discussed here, as well. The next chapter introduces linear regression analysis in greater depth. You will also learn how to perform multiple regression, which measures the relationships between a response variable and many explanatory variables simultaneously.

Writing up the results of a correlation analysis

To report the results of correlation analysis, you can use the following template, which describes the results of the first case study in this chapter: "The correlation between word length and average reaction time was positive, moderately strong and statistically significant, $r = 0.589$, $df = 95$, $p_{\text{one-tailed}} < 0.001$".

CHAPTER 7

More on frequencies and reaction times

Linear regression

What you will learn from this chapter

After the previous chapter has introduced some basic elements of regression analysis, this chapter will provide a more thorough discussion of linear regression. This method enables one to model and explain the relationships between one or more explanatory variables at any level of measurement, on the one hand, and one ratio- or interval-scaled response variable, on the other hand. In addition, one can investigate interactions between explanatory variables. You will learn how to fit a multiple linear regression model, to perform its diagnostics and to interpret the results. You will also learn how to carry out non-parametric linear regression with the help of bootstrap. The case study investigates the relationship between reaction times in a lexical decision task, and such factors as word length, corpus frequency and part of speech of lexical stimuli. In contrast with the previous case studies, all these factors are tested here simultaneously in a multiple linear regression model.

7.1 The basic principles of linear regression analysis

Regression analysis is a method that allows one to explain and model the relationship between the response (dependent) variable, on the one hand, and one or more explanatory (independent) variables, on the other hand. When a model contains one explanatory variable, one speaks about **simple regression** analysis. When the number of explanatory variables is two or more, that is a case of **multiple regression**. In linear regression analysis, which will be discussed in this chapter, explanatory variables can be on any scale of measurement, from categorical to ratio-scaled, while the response should be on the interval or ratio scale. For example, one can model the relationship between a test score in a language test, on the one hand, and the method of teaching, number of hours spent on preparation, level of motivation and other possible factors, on the other hand. Multiple regression enables one to measure the individual impact of each variable in the model while controlling for the other variables. It is also possible to model interactions between the explanatory variables.

The previous chapter discussed correlation analysis, which measures the relationship between two quantitative or ordinal variables x and y. If x is regarded as an explanatory variable and y as a response variable, correlation analysis can be thought of as an instance of simple linear regression. A regression line was added to the scatter plots in order to visualize the relationship between x and y (see Figure 6.1 in Chapter 6). However, we did not discuss in detail how this line was constructed. In fact, the position and orientation of a regression line can be described by the following formula:

$$\hat{y} = b_0 + bx$$

where

- $\hat{y}$ corresponds to the fitted values of the response variable y;
- b_0 is the intercept, i.e. the value of y when the line crosses the vertical axis. In other words, this is the predicted value of the response when x is equal to zero;
- b is the coefficient that determines the slope of the regression line;
- x is the explanatory variable;

Consider Figure 7.1 with different regression lines. In the top left graph, the intercept is zero, and the coefficient is 1. Thus, $y = 0 + 1x$, or simply $y = x$. The line crosses the y-axis at zero, and with every unit of x, y increases by one unit, as well. On the top right graph, the intercept is again zero, but the coefficient is 3. Again, the line crosses the y-axis at $y = 0$, but this time, y increases by three units as x increases by one unit. The slope of the regression line is therefore much steeper. On the bottom left plot, the intercept is 2, and the coefficient is 1. This means that the regression line crosses the y-axis at $y = 2$, and as x

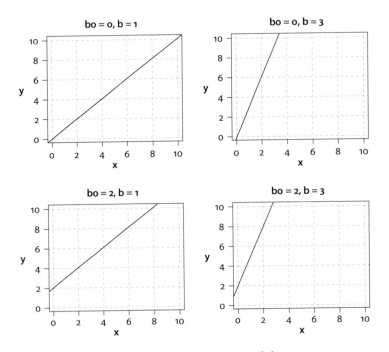

Figure 7.1. Simple regression: lines with different intercepts and slopes

increases by one unit, y increases by one unit, too. Finally, the bottom right plot displays a line with the intercept of 2 and the coefficient of 3. That is, the line crosses the y-axis at 2, and every increase of x by one unit leads to an increase of y by three units.

These plots show the relationships between two variables, an explanatory variable x and a response y. In case of two explanatory variables, one can visualize the relationships with the help of a regression plane in a three-dimensional space, and if the number of explanatory variables is large, one would have to create a hyperplane in a multidimensional space. The principle, however, and the form of the equation remain the same. The only difference is the presence of new terms in the equation:

$$\hat{y} = b_0 + b_1 x_1 + b_2 x_2 + b_3 x_3 + \dots$$

So far, we have focused on the regression line (or hyperplane), which describes the fitted values of the response variable. But this line should be drawn through a cloud of points that represent real observations with actual values of y. In fact, there is one more crucial element that should be added to the equation, the **error**. This is the difference between the fitted and observed values of y. Thus, the actual values of y can be described as follows:

$$y = \hat{y} + \varepsilon$$

or

$$y = b_0 + b_1 x_1 + b_2 x_2 + b_3 x_3 + \dots + \varepsilon$$

where y is the actual value of the response variable, and ε is the error, or residual term. The differences between the fitted and observed values of each individual observation are called **residuals**. This notion was introduced in the previous chapter. An observed value of y for a given observation is therefore the sum of its fitted value, which can be computed from the intercept, coefficients and the values of the explanatory variables, and the residual.

Why bother with multiple regression?

Why fit a multiple regression model instead of fitting a few simple ones? The main reason is that multiple regression allows one to estimate the effect of each individual independent variable in your model **while controlling for the other independent variables.** Imagine that you investigate the relationship between age and gender of young children (explanatory variables) and their vocabulary size (the response). Suppose you have two expectations. First, the vocabulary size grows with age. Second, you expect girls to have

(Continued)

a greater vocabulary than boys at the same age. However, if the boys in your sample are on average older that the girls, this may result in a smaller gender difference than there actually is. And the other way round: if the boys in the sample are on average younger than the girls, then the gender difference might be greater than it is in the reality. You need multiple regression to control for such confounding effects.

The aim of regression modelling is to fit the line in such a way that the residuals are as small as possible (this is called the least squares approach). The smaller the sum of squared residuals, the better the model fits the data. The goodness of fit of a linear regression model is usually measured with the help of the R^2 statistic, which ranges from 0 to 1. It is worth mentioning that in usual cases the R^2-value of a simple linear regression model with explanatory variable x and response y is in fact the squared Pearson correlation coefficient r that measures the relationships between x and y.

7.2   Putting several explanatory variables together: Predicting reaction times in a lexical decision task

7.2.1   Data and hypotheses

To reproduce the code in this case study, you will need quite a few add-on packages that should be installed and loaded before you begin.

```
> install.packages(c("leaps", "car", "rms", "visreg", "boot"))
>   library(Rling);   library(leaps);   library(car);   library(rms);
library(visreg); library(boot)
```

The data are available as the dataset ELP in Rling. This is a small sample of data from the English Lexicon Project (Balota et al. 2007).[1] The dataset contains several variables for 880 randomly selected English nouns, adjectives and verbs. The first factor, *Word*, specifies the lexical stimuli. The integer numeric vector *Length* displays the word lengths in letters. *POS* is the part of speech. It is a categorical variable represented by a factor with three levels: 'JJ' (adjectives), 'NN' (common and proper nouns) and 'VB' (verbs). The numeric vector SUBTLWF contains normalized word frequencies in a corpus of film subtitles (per million words). This type of data has been found to be a useful source of lexical norms in recent psycholinguistic studies (Keuleers et al. 2012). Finally, the quantitative variable Mean_RT shows the mean reaction times in the lexical decision task (in milliseconds). This variable

---

1.   The experimental data are freely available from http://elexicon.wustl.edu/WordStart.asp (last access 30.06.2014).

will be regarded as the response, and the previous ones (excluding *Word*) will be analysed as the explanatory variables.

```
> data(ELP)
> str(ELP)
'data.frame': 880 obs. of 5 variables:
$ Word: Factor w/ 880 levels "abbreviation",..: 631 747 200 773 821
134 845 140 94 354 …
$ Length: int 7 10 10 8 6 5 5 8 8 6 …
$ SUBTLWF: num 0.96 4.24 0.04 1.49 1.06 3.33 0.1 0.06 0.43 5.41 …
$ POS: Factor w/ 3 levels "JJ","NN","VB": 2 2 3 2 2 2 3 2 2 2 …
$ Mean_RT: num 791 693 960 771 882 …
```

Note that your data for linear regression should have the following format:

- the data are optimally a data frame object in R;
- the rows are individual items or subjects, and the columns are variables;
- the response variable should be a numeric vector;
- the explanatory variables can be numeric vectors (quantitative variables) or factors (categorical variables). The number of factor levels should not be too large: twenty different values are likely to result in data sparseness. If the dataset contains many correlated (associated) variables that present very similar information, try to choose the ones that are the most relevant, or reduce the number of variables by using different exploratory dimensionality reduction techniques, such as Principal Components Analysis (Chapter 18) and Multiple Correspondence Analysis (Chapter 19);
- if you prepare your data in a spreadsheet, make sure that there are no empty cells. It is possible to mark the missing data as 'NA', but you should be aware that the observations with at least one 'NA' value in the response or explanatory variables will be excluded automatically by most algorithms that fit regression models. There exist some solutions to this problem, e.g. one can impute the missing information, but this is beyond the scope of this textbook. For more information, see Harrell (2001: Ch. 3).

Is your sample large enough?

Having too few observations and too many explanatory variables can result in overfitting, which makes your model useless if you try it on a new dataset. However, opinions

(Continued)

vary with regard to the exact minimal number of observations. Many statisticians are skeptical about any rules of thumb because the amount of variance in the data, the number of outliers and the size of an effect that one wants to detect can vary greatly. Still, there is a popular formula, according to which the minimum sample size *n* equals 10–15 observations per each regression coefficient that you want to estimate (including the intercept). For example, if we have two quantitative variables and one categorical variable with three levels, we will have five coefficients in the model, including the intercept (see below for an explanation of how categorical explanatory variables can be dealt with in R). Therefore, we will need at least 50–75 observations to fit the model, ignoring possible interactions at the moment. With 880 observations, we are quite safe. Still, it is always useful to check if your model overfits the data with the help of the bootstrap test presented in Section 7.2.8.

As was shown in Chapter 3, corpus frequencies tend to be distributed in a very peculiar way that is known as the Zipfian distribution, which is to say such data contain very few high-frequency items, and very many low-frequency items. Frequency data are often log-transformed to overcome this skewness (see Section 3.3 in Chapter 3 on the effect of a log-transformation of frequencies). Thus, we will use the log-transformed version of the variable `log(SUBTLWF)` in the analyses presented below.

7.2.2 The `lm()` function and interpretation of its output

The main function for linear regression is `lm()`. Let us fit our first model with three explanatory variables. To specify the model, one should use the *formula* interface, where the response variable is on the left side from the tilde sign, and the explanatory variables are on the right. The explanatory variables are separated by the plus sign, which means that we are interested in the additive effect of all these variables on the response variable. To model non-additive effects of interacting variables, one has to make some changes in the formula, as will be shown below. The results can be accessed with the help of the `summary()` function.

```
> m <- lm(Mean_RT ~ Length + log(SUBTLWF) + POS, data = ELP)
> summary(m)

Call:
lm(formula = Mean_RT ~ Length + log(SUBTLWF) + POS, data = ELP)

Residuals:
Min        1Q      Median   3Q      Max
-213.70  -62.55   -9.71    53.87   389.00
```

```
Coefficients:
                Estimate Std.   Error    t value   Pr(>|t|)
(Intercept)     622.466         14.191   43.864    < 2e-16 ***
Length          19.555          1.433    13.645    < 2e-16 ***
log(SUBTLWF)    -29.288         1.784    -16.420   < 2e-16 ***
POSNN           -6.115          8.506    -0.719    0.47238
POSVB           -29.184         10.154   -2.874    0.00415 **
--
Signif. codes:  0 '***'  0.001 '**'   0.01 '*'   0.05 '.' 0.1 ' ' 1

Residual standard error: 93.29 on 875 degrees of freedom
Multiple R-squared: 0.4565,      Adjusted R-squared: 0.454
F-statistic: 183.7 on 4 and 875 DF, p-value: < 2.2e-16
```

The summary contains a lot of information. First, it repeats the formula. The next line shows the distribution of residuals. Ideally, those should be normally distributed and centre around zero. This assumption will be discussed in more detail in Section 7.2.5.

Under the information about the residuals, one can see a table of regression coefficients. The first column shows the estimates, which specify the intercept and the slopes of the regression line. The p-values in the rightmost column are based on the t-statistics (see the second column from the right) and show how confident we can be that the values are different from zero. A p-value less than 0.05 suggests that the null hypothesis of no effect can be rejected. In addition, the table displays the standard errors of estimated coefficients.

The estimated coefficients for quantitative and categorical explanatory variables are displayed differently and should be interpreted differently. The coefficient of *Length* is approximately 19.6. It means that for every additional letter in a lexical stimulus the average reaction time increases by 19.6 milliseconds. Thus, the longer a word, the slower the response. The estimate of *log(SUBTLWF)* is approximately –29.3. This means that the average reaction time decreases by 29.3 with every additional unit of *log(SUBTLWF)*. In other words, the more frequent a word, the faster the response. The categorical variable *POS*, however, is displayed twice, as POSNN and POSVB. The corresponding estimated coefficients show the change in mean reaction times in comparison with the reference level, *POS* = JJ. Both estimates are negative. Therefore, nouns and verbs are on average recognized faster than adjectives. Note, however, that only the second coefficient ('VB') has the p-value smaller than 0.05. This suggests a lack of statistically significant difference between mean reaction times of nouns and adjectives, other factors being controlled for.

Categorical explanatory variables in regression analysis

The default way of treating categorical variables in R is by using the so-called treatment contrasts. That is, the reference level serves as the basis of comparison for all other levels. If an explanatory variable *YourVar* is binary with levels 'A' and 'B', the algorithm will compare 'B' with 'A', i.e. the default reference level (unless you choose 'B' as the reference level). The corresponding estimated coefficient will show by how much the observations with value 'B' differ on average from those with value 'A'. If a categorical variable *X* contains levels 'A', 'B' and 'C', then the algorithm will compare 'B' and 'C' with the reference level 'A'. As a result, you will see only two terms in the model, *YourVar* = 'B' and *YourVar* = 'C', and their coefficients. Four levels will produce three terms, and so on. By default, R chooses the category that comes first alphabetically as the reference level, but you can choose another one by using `factor(YourVar, levels = c("C", "A", "B"))` or `relevel(YourVar, ref = "C")`, as was shown in Chapter 4.

Another popular option is sum contrasts, when the intercept is an unweighted average of the fitted values for all levels of *YourVar* ('A', 'B' and 'C'). The average is called unweighted because it does not take into account that the levels may have different frequencies. In that case, the coefficient of *YourVar* = 'A' shows how much one should add to the intercept to compute the estimated mean value for the observations in the category 'A', and the coefficient of *YourVar* = 'B' shows how much one should add to the intercept to compute the estimated mean value for the category 'B'. The last category, 'C', will be omitted. Its estimated average can be computed by subtracting both coefficients of 'A' and 'B' from the intercept. See a detailed discussion in Gries (2013: Sections 5.2.1 and 5.2.2).

Finally, you may want to consider using Helmert coding for ordinal variables, which compares the second level with the first, the third level with the average of the first and the second levels, and so on.

To use the alternative contrasts in your model, you can do the following (3 is given as an example of the number of levels):

```
# do not run; the code below is provided only as an example
> contrasts(YourVar) <- contr.sum(3) # for sum contrasts
> contrasts(YourVar) <- contr.helmert(3)# for Helmert contrasts
> contrasts(YourVar) <- contr.treatment(3)# to return to treatment
contrasts (the default)
```

As has been explained above, the intercept is the predicted value of *y* at the point where the regression line crosses the *y*-axis. In case of multiple regression, the intercept is the expected value of the response variable for a situation when all quantitative explanatory variables equal zero, and all categorical variables are at their reference levels (provided the default treatment coding is used). In our case, this is the reaction time for a word when its length is zero characters, the log-transformed frequency is zero (this corresponds to the untransformed frequency 1), and the word is an adjective. Although zero-length words do not exist, the algorithm simply extrapolates to the length of zero.

In practice, you will need the information about the intercept only when you want to compute the **fitted** or **predicted values** of the response variable for a specific observation.[2] This is the same as finding the *y*-value of a point on the regression line when you know the *x*-value. Let us illustrate the idea by computing the fitted reaction time for the first word in the list, *rackets*. To do so, one should simply insert the corresponding values of the independent variables to the regression equation and use the estimated coefficients from the `lm()` output above. For categorical variables, one should multiply a regression coefficient given in the table by 1 in case the value applies, or by zero if it does not apply:

$$\text{Mean\_RT}_1 = \text{Intercept} + 7 \times \text{Length} + \log(0.96) \times \log(\text{SUBTLWF}) + 1 \times \text{POSNN} + 0 \times \text{POSVB}$$
$$= 622.466 + 7 \times 19.555 + \log(0.96) \times (-29.288) + 1 \times (-6.115) + 0 \times (-29.184)$$
$$= 754.43$$

To compute the fitted values automatically, one can use `fitted(m)`, which will return a vector with fitted values of the response variable. For example, the first word has the following fitted mean reaction time:

```
> fitted(m)[1]
     1
754.4299
```

This number coincides with the result of the manual calculations above.

In previous chapters, we discussed the notion of confidence intervals around a statistic. One can obtain the 95% confidence intervals of estimates of regression coefficients as follows:

```
> confint(m)  # equivalent to confint(..., level = 0.95)
                   2.5 %       97.5 %
(Intercept)    594.61399    650.318207
Length          16.74194     22.367571
log(SUBTLWF)   -32.78872    -25.787038
POSNN          -22.80935     10.579145
POSVB          -49.11280     -9.254989
```

---

2.   There exist models without an intercept, but this topic is beyond the scope of this introductory chapter.

Only one 95% confidence interval, that of POSNN, contains the zero. Recall that this regression coefficient also had a p-value greater than 0.05. Thus, the confidence intervals corroborate the conclusions made on the basis of the p-values from the table of coefficients.

One- and two-tailed tests of regression coefficients

By default, regression analysis involves two-tailed tests. The alternative hypothesis is that the coefficients are different from zero. Whether the difference is positive or negative is not important. However, it is possible to use a one-tailed test if the consequences of missing an effect in the opposite direction are negligible, or if observing the opposite effect is impossible. For example, a pharmaceutical company might want to test if their new drug performs worse than some standard. Obviously, if this is the case and the drug goes into production, the company will face serious legal and economic problems. However, it may be irrelevant whether the new drug performs better than the standard. For example, if the new drug is considerably cheaper, this alone is a strong reason for producing it. In that case, one can simply divide the p-value by two to obtain a p-value of a one-tailed test. Of course, this method should not be used for 'p-hacking'.

The next line in the summary shows the standard error of the residuals, i.e. how much variation they display, and the degrees of freedom. These statistics are followed by R^2. As has been mentioned above, this is a standard measure of goodness of fit in linear regression. It shows the proportion of variation in the response variable that is due to variation in the explanatory variables. The coefficient ranges from 0 (a totally useless model; one could achieve the same success by always predicting the mean value of the response) to 1 (perfect fit; each individual value of the response is predicted with exact precision). In our case, the model explains 0.4565, or 45.65% of entire variance. This is not bad for a start, although there is still room for improvement. The adjusted R^2 (0.454) is a useful measure of the model's effectiveness because it penalizes the model for having too many variables that do not make a substantial contribution, as well as for having too few observations. A combination of those two factors is particularly dangerous. The adjusted R^2 provides a necessary correction. Note that the adjusted R^2 can be negative, unlike the original R^2 statistic.

The final line contains the F-ratio. It shows if the model is significant in general. In most cases, this means that at least one variable has an estimate that is significantly different from zero. The statistic is the ratio of the variance explained by the model and the residual variance. The F-ratio should be at least greater than 1. The p-value shows the probability of observing a given F-ratio if the null hypothesis were true (that is, the variables had no effect). Since the p-value is very low, we can conclude that the model is significant.

To summarize, the model yields interpretable results and has some explanatory power. But is this model good? Can we improve it? The remaining part of this chapter deals with these questions.

7.2.3   Selecting the explanatory variables

If one has more than one explanatory variable, a crucial question is which of them should enter the model, and which should not. According to the principle of parsimony, known as Occam's razor, a simpler model should be preferred to a more complex one if they have the same explanatory power. This is why an optimal model should contain only those variables that contribute substantially to explaining variance in the response variable. There exist different approaches to variable selection. One of them is stepwise selection, which adds or removes explanatory variables iteratively according to some criterion (p-values, R^2 scores, AIC values, etc.). Another approach is to try to retain all theoretically relevant factors in the model. Finally, a relatively new approach is the best subsets method. It simply tries all possible models with all variables, and then returns the best one according to some statistical criterion.

We have already fitted a model with all explanatory variables, and it has yielded interpretable results. For the purposes of illustration, however, we will do stepwise selection and use the best subsets method and compare the results. There are three ways of performing stepwise selection: forward, backward and bidirectional. To perform forward selection, one should begin with a null model without any explanatory variables. The program tries to add variables one by one, until no further improvement can be made. To perform backward selection, one begins with a model which contains all explanatory variables, and then the program tries to get rid of all irrelevant ones. Finally, the bidirectional approach begins like the forward approach, but every time a new variable is added to the model, the algorithm also tries to remove one redundant variable.

Let us begin with forward selection. First, we will create a null model with the intercept only by using the `step()` function in the forward direction. The statistical criterion is the Akaike Information Criterion (AIC), which penalizes a model if it has too many variables. It is similar in this respect to the adjusted R^2. Note that the smaller the AIC, the better the fit.

```
> m0 <- lm(Mean_RT ~ 1, data = ELP)
> m.fw <- step(m0, direction = "forward", scope = ~ Length +
log(SUBTLWF) + POS)
[output omitted]

> m.fw

Call:
lm(formula = Mean_RT ~ log(SUBTLWF) + Length + POS, data = ELP)

Coefficients:
(Intercept)  log(SUBTLWF)  Length  POSNN
622.466        -29.288      19.555  -6.115
POSVB
-29.184
```

The algorithm picks all three variables. For comparison, let us run backward stepwise selection. In that case, one starts with a maximal model and then uses the step() function in the backward direction.

```
> m.bw <- step(m, direction = "backward")
[output omitted]
> m.bw
Call:
lm(formula = Mean_RT ~ Length + log(SUBTLWF) + POS, data = ELP)

Coefficients:
(Intercept)  Length  log(SUBTLWF)  POSNN
622.466      19.555  -29.288        -6.115
POSVB
-29.184
```

Finally, we will run bidirectional selection. Since both is the default option, the argument that specifies the direction can be omitted:

```
> m.both <- step(m0, scope = ~ Length + log(SUBTLWF) + POS)  #
equivalent to step(…, direction = "both")
[output omitted]

> m.both

Call:
lm(formula = Mean_RT ~ log(SUBTLWF) + Length + POS, data = ELP)

Coefficients:
(Intercept)  log(SUBTLWF)  Length  POSNN
622.466        -29.288      19.555  -6.115
POSVB
-29.184
```

The results of the forward, backward and bidirectional methods converge. Every explanatory variable in the initial model contributes to explaining variation in the response.

Finally, let us try the best subsets method, which is implemented in the function regsubsets() from the package leaps.

```
> subsets <- regsubsets(Mean_RT ~ Length + log(SUBTLWF) + POS, data
= ELP, nbest = 4)
```

The function regubsets() finds the best subsets of explanatory variables. The argument nbest = 4 tells the algorithm to return up to four best models of each possible size (from one to four terms). It is the maximal number of estimates in the model, disregarding the intercept (recall that POS yields two estimates). One can obtain several goodness-of-fit statistics for each model, including the unadjusted and adjusted R^2:

```
> round(summary(subsets)$rsq, 3)
 [1]   0.328  0.278  0.018  0.000   0.450  0.339  0.330 0.286 0.456
[10]   0.451  0.341  0.289  0.456
> round(summary(subsets)$adjr2, 3)
 [1]   0.327  0.278  0.017  -0.001  0.449  0.338  0.328 0.284
 [9]   0.454  0.449  0.339  0.287   0.454
```

To interpret these results, one needs to know which variables are in which model. One can obtain a table with this information as follows:

```
> summary(subsets)$which
```

	(Intercept)	Length	log(SUBTLWF)	POSNN	POSVB
1	TRUE	FALSE	TRUE	FALSE	FALSE
1	TRUE	TRUE	FALSE	FALSE	FALSE
1	TRUE	FALSE	FALSE	FALSE	TRUE
1	TRUE	FALSE	FALSE	TRUE	FALSE
2	TRUE	TRUE	TRUE	FALSE	FALSE
2	TRUE	FALSE	TRUE	FALSE	TRUE
2	TRUE	FALSE	TRUE	TRUE	FALSE
2	TRUE	TRUE	FALSE	FALSE	TRUE
3	TRUE	TRUE	TRUE	FALSE	TRUE
3	TRUE	TRUE	TRUE	TRUE	FALSE
3	TRUE	FALSE	TRUE	TRUE	TRUE
3	TRUE	TRUE	FALSE	TRUE	TRUE
4	TRUE	TRUE	TRUE	TRUE	TRUE

If the value is TRUE, the term is in the model. If the value is FALSE, it is omitted. The last model with all three variables and four terms has the highest scores ($R^2 = 0.456$, adjusted $R^2 = 0.454$), although the ninth model without the term POSNN performs equally well. This means that one could conflate POS = 'NN' and POS = 'Adj' without a loss in the explanatory power of the model. Since there are no obvious theoretical reasons for such conflation, we will keep both levels as they are.

Do not be surprised when you hear different opinions about the optimal strategy of regression modelling. For instance, some people use stepwise variable selection, when one adds new variables to the model sequentially (Hosmer & Lemeshow 2000), whereas others recommend beginning with a model which contains all variables of interest (Harrell 2001). The main problem with stepwise selection is that the usefulness of one variable is assessed on the basis of other variables that have been selected. This may be dangerous when potential explanatory variables are correlated. Field et al. (2012) draw the following humorous analogy between stepwise selection and getting dressed:

> If a stepwise regression method was selecting your clothes, it would decide what clothes you should wear, based on the clothes it has already selected. If, for example, it is a cold day, a stepwise selection method might choose a pair of trousers to put on first. But if you are wearing trousers already, it is difficult to get your underwear on: stepwise methods will decide that underwear does not fit, and you will therefore go without.
> (Field et al. 2012: 265)

However, if you really need to do stepwise selection, backward selection poses less risk of missing out important variables than forward selection. In any case, one should not rely blindly on automatic approaches. Your choice of variables should be informed by theory and previous research.

Other useful functions that help one estimate whether a variable is useful are `anova()` for model comparison, which will be introduced in the section about testing of interactions, and `drop1()`, which removes one variable from the model at a time and tests the difference. To test explanatory variables in a linear regression model, you should specify that you want to carry out the *F*-test.

```
> drop1(m, test = "F")
Single term deletions

Model:
Mean_RT ~ Length + log(SUBTLWF) + POS
             Df Sum of Sq   RSS      AIC  F value    Pr(>F)
(none)                    7614993  7987.8
Length        1  1620252  9235246  8155.6  186.1749  < 2e-16 ***
log(SUBTLWF)  1  2346341  9961335  8222.2  269.6061  < 2e-16 ***
POS           2    92194  7707187  7994.4    5.2968  0.00517 **
--
Signif. codes: 0 '***' 0.001 '**' 0.01 '*' 0.05 '.' 0.1 ' ' 1
```

The results show, not surprisingly, that all variables contribute significantly to the explanatory power of the model. This method is particularly useful when you have categorical variables with more than two values. In that case, it may not be obvious from the table of coefficients and the *p*-values whether the variable has any significant effect on the response, since not all possible pairwise comparisons are shown.

7.2.4   Checking for outliers and overly influential observations

As you already know from Chapter 3, outliers are observations that behave in a different way from the rest of the data. In regression analysis, these are observations with large discrepancies between the observed and fitted values of the response variable. They have unusually large residuals and lie far above or below the regression line. Their presence indicates a lack of fit. Another class of potentially problematic data is so-called influential observations. These points have unusually small or large values on an explanatory variable. They can – but not necessarily do – have a significant effect on the regression slopes, i.e. the estimates of regression coefficients. To identify both types of problematic cases, one can use the function `influencePlot()` in the `car` package. The argument `id.method = "identify"` will start an interactive session. In this session, you can identify the points on the plot by clicking on them. After you have identified all points of interest, press *Esc* or press the *Finish* button (in RStudio).[3] The IDs (the row numbers in our data frame) will be displayed on the plot (see Figure 7.2).

```
> influencePlot(m, id.method = "identify")
```

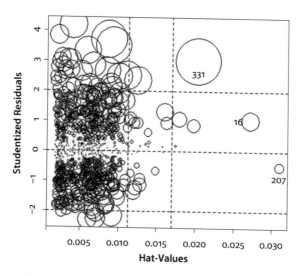

Figure 7.2. Influence plot with several identified points

The bubble plot in Figure 7.2 is based on three values for each observation in the corpus: hat-values, studentized residuals and Cook's distances. The meaning of the values is as follows:

---

3.   There seems to be a problem with identification of points in the current version of the package. If you receive an error message after finishing an interaction session, ignore it.

– Studentized residuals (the *y*-axis) are normalized residuals, adjusted by their expected variability. They represent the discrepancy between the actual and fitted values. It is recommended to check observations with the values greater than 2 or smaller than –2 on the vertical axis.

– Hat-values, or leverage (the *x*-axis), indicate how much influence the observation can potentially have on the fitted values. The influence of a given observation is determined by the difference between the observation's value on an explanatory variable and the mean value of the variable. For leverage, there is no absolute threshold that needs to be controlled. The vertical lines are drawn through the points which correspond to two and three times the average hat-values.

– Cook's distances show the effect of removing an observation on the coefficients and fitted values. They are represented by the size of the bubbles.

As one can see in Figure 7.2, there is one point that has a relatively high leverage, a large residual and a very high Cook's distance score. The ID number of this observation is 331. The word is 'interdepartmental':

```
> ELP[331, ]
Word                     Length  SUBTLWF POS  Mean_RT
331 interdepartmental  17       0.04    JJ   1324.57
```

This 17-letter word is the second longest stimulus with the longest reaction time in the dataset. If we fit a model without this observation, the coefficients of *Length*, POS = 'NN' and POS = 'VB' now have slightly smaller values:

```
> m1 <- lm(Mean_RT ~ Length + log(SUBTLWF) + POS, data = ELP[-331,])
> summary(m1)

Call:
lm(formula = Mean_RT ~ Length + log(SUBTLWF) + POS, data = ELP[-
331, ])

Residuals:
Min        1Q       Median   3Q      Max
-213.32   -63.04   -10.42   53.09   388.42

Coefficients:
               Estimate Std.  Error    t value   Pr(>|t|)
(Intercept)    624.932        14.151   44.163    < 2e-16  ***
Length         19.073         1.436    13.285    < 2e-16  ***
log(SUBTLWF)   -29.288        1.776    -16.495   < 2e-16  ***
POSNN          -4.629         8.482    -0.546    0.58540
POSVB          -27.891        10.117   -2.757    0.00596  **
--
```

```
Signif. codes: 0 '***' 0.001 '**' 0.01 '*' 0.05 '.' 0.1 ' ' 1
Residual standard error: 92.87 on 874 degrees of freedom
Multiple R-squared: 0.4506, Adjusted R-squared: 0.4481
F-statistic: 179.2 on 4 and 874 DF, p-value: < 2.2e-16
```

What should one do in such cases? Outliers and influential observations should be removed or recoded when they arise as a result of coding or sampling errors. If this is not the case and unusual points represent inherent variability in the data, as in this case, opinions differ. Some statisticians consider that removal of 'legitimate' outliers will make the data less representative of the whole population, while others believe it would be best to remove such points for statistical reasons. It is worth mentioning here that today, with the advance of non-parametric methods, such as bootstrap and permutation, the need for 'brushing up' the data in order to meet all assumptions has become less pressing. In case there are legitimate outliers and influential points it is worthwhile to perform non-parametric regression with bootstrap, which will be discussed in Section 7.2.8.

7.2.5 Checking the regression assumptions

Similar to all previously discussed tests, linear regression has a number of assumptions that should be met if one wants to obtain reliable and meaningful results:

Assumption 1. *The observations are independent from one another.*
Assumption 2. *The response variable is at least interval-scaled.*
Assumption 3. *The relationship between the dependent and independent variables is linear.* If not, a power transformation of the response or explanatory variables should be applied.
Assumption 4. *The errors vary constantly.* This is also called homoscedasticity of variance. In other words, the variability of the residuals does not increase or decrease with the explanatory variables or the response.
Assumption 5. *There is no strong linear dependence between explanatory variables.* Such dependence is also known as **multicollinearity**.
Assumption 6. *The residuals are not autocorrelated.*
Assumption 7. *The residuals are normally distributed, with a mean of 0.* This assumption becomes less important when the sample is large.

Let us examine whether our model meets these assumptions one by one.

Assumption 1. *The observations are independent from one another.*
This means that each value of the response variable should be independent from the values of other observations. In our case, this means that the reaction time needed for recognition of one lexical stimulus should not depend on the reaction time of another word in the dataset. This might happen, for example, if the data contained only words with the same small set of roots. This is clearly not the case. If this assumption is violated, one should use a mixed model with fixed and random effects (see Chapter 8).

Assumption 2. *The response variable is measured at least on the interval scale.*
The reaction time is a ratio-scaled variable. Although it would be unusual to observe reaction times of zero milliseconds, this number is still meaningful. One can also apply multiplication and say that 500 ms is twice as fast as 1000 ms.

Assumption 3. *The relationship between the dependent and independent quantitative variables is linear.*
The assumption of linearity was mentioned in Chapter 6, when the Pearson correlation coefficient was discussed. To detect non-linearity in a simple regression model with one explanatory variable *x*, a simple scatter plot of *x* and *y* should suffice (see Chapter 6). A convenient tool for detection of non-linearity in multiple regression analysis is the so-called component-residual, or partial-residual plot. It is available as `crPlot()` in the package `car`. The model contains two quantitative explanatory variables, *Length* and *log(SUBTLWF)*. We will create two plots with these two variables side by side.

```
> par(mfrow = c(1, 2))
> crPlot(m, var = "Length")
> crPlot(m, var = "log(SUBTLWF)")
> par(mfrow = c(1, 1))
```

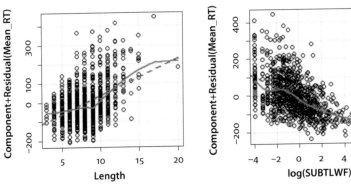

Figure 7.3. Component-residual plot with *Length* (left) and *log(SUBTLWF)* (right)

Both plots are displayed in Figure 7.3. The component-residual plot shows how the residuals plus the corresponding regression coefficient (the vertical axis) change depending on an explanatory variable (the horizontal axis), after taking into account the effect of all other explanatory variables. The dashed red lines represent the slopes of the explanatory variables based on the regression estimates, and the solid green lines reflect the main tendency in the cloud of data points. The solid lines deviate from the dashed lines, indicating some non-linearity. There is, however, a more serious problem, which is evident in the right-hand plot. Namely, the variance is not homogeneous: the dispersion of points seems to be decreasing with *x*. That brings us to the next assumption.

Assumption 4. *The errors vary constantly. There is no heteroscedasticity.*
Visual diagnostics of homoscedasticity is possible with the help of the plot of the residuals against fitted values. It is easily performed with the help of `plot.lm()`, which can be simply invoked by `plot()` when the first argument is an `lm` object. This function offers in fact several different plots, which can be selected by using `which`.

```
> plot(m, which = 1)
```

The result is displayed in Figure 7.4. The plot indicates that the greatest spread of residuals is observed where the fitted values ranges approximately from 800 to 950 milliseconds, and the smallest variability is when the words are recognized very quickly, with the predicted mean reaction times from 400 to 600 milliseconds. The pattern is not homoscedastic.

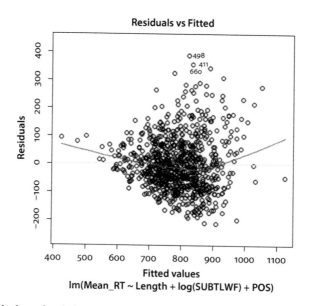

Figure 7.4. Residuals vs. fitted plot

One can also perform the non-constant variance test from the package `car`:

```
> ncvTest(m)
Non-constant Variance Score Test
Variance formula:  ~ fitted.values
Chisquare = 79.67363        Df = 1 p = 4.41657e-19
```

This test has the null hypothesis that the error has constant variance with the response (fitted values). The *p*-value smaller than 0.05 tells us that we can reject the null hypothesis of constant error variance. All this signals a problem.

It is also necessary to test whether the error has constant variance depending on the values of quantitative explanatory variables. To test that, one can use the component-residual plots shown above, as well as the non-constant variance test, where you should specify the name of the explanatory variable:

```
> ncvTest(m, ~ Length)
Non-constant Variance Score Test
Variance formula: ~ Length
Chisquare = 42.39826        Df = 1 p = 7.445615e-11
> ncvTest(m, ~ log(SUBTLWF))
Non-constant Variance Score Test
Variance formula: ~ log(SUBTLWF)
Chisquare = 59.12633 Df = 1       p = 1.478672e-14
```

The small p-values in both tests are a clear indication of heteroscedasticity in the residuals, depending on the values of both variables.

In such situations, one can try power transformations of the response variable. Some popular power transformations, such as squaring (raising to the power of 2) or unsquaring (raising to the power of 0.5), were discussed in Section 3.3 of Chapter 3. Power transformations are often done by trial and error, and require some experience. Alternatively, one can find the optimal transformation with the help of the Box-Cox plot, which is based on the approach developed by George Box and Sir David Cox and implemented as boxCox() in the package car. The resulting plot is shown in Figure 7.5.

```
> boxCox(m)
```

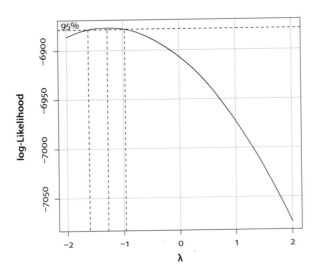

Figure 7.5. A Box–Cox plot

The plot displays two values. The horizontal axis represents the transformation power of the response variable. Note that 0 does not correspond to raising a number to the power of 0 (which will result in 1 for any number). Instead, it means taking the natural logarithm. The vertical axis represents the log-likelihood of the corresponding power transformation. The optimal transformation is the one with the highest y-value. The dashed lines mark the 95% confidence region. If necessary, the range of possible transformations can be extended, for example, from −3 to 3:

```
> boxCox(m, lambda = seq(-3, 3, 1/10)) # output not shown
```

Figure 7.5 shows that the optimal transformation is approximately $y^{-1.3}$. It is equal to 1 divided by $y^{1.3}$.[4]

```
> m.trans <- lm(Mean_RT^-1.3 ~ Length + log(SUBTLWF) + POS, data = ELP)
> ncvTest(m.trans)
Non-constant Variance Score Test
Variance formula: ~ fitted.values
Chisquare = 0.9711398     Df = 1 p = 0.3243961
```

The high p-value allows us to believe that the problem of heteroscedastic error variance is resolved. The readers are encouraged to repeat the tests with the two quantitative explanatory variables and see that there is no evidence of heteroscedasticity in those cases, as well. One can also re-create the component-residual plots and the residuals vs. fitted values plot to see that adding the transformation improves the model.

As was mentioned in Section 3.3 of Chapter 3, transformation gives neater data at the cost of interpretability of results. An alternative is to use non-parametric regression, which is described in Section 7.2.8.

Assumption 5. *There is no multicollinearity.*

Multicollinearity is a phenomenon that can be observed when some variables relate to the same underlying causal effect. Imagine that you want to predict whether a postgraduate student will obtain a Ph.D. or not on the basis of such factors as the university grades, the number of books read per month and the difficulty level of the courses that he or she has taken at college. All these variables might reflect one underlying factor, namely, learning motivation. When combined in one model, very strongly correlated variables tend to have unstable estimates and large standard errors. This means that the estimates of correlated variables are no longer reliable, even if the model has sufficient predictive power (i.e. a high R^2). Multicollinearity can be detected with the help of vif() in the car package.[5]

---

4.   When applying transformations to predictors, you should use the function I(), which tells R to interpret the operator in its arithmetical sense, rather as a regression formula expression. An example is $y \sim I(x^2)$. However, expressions like $y \sim log(x)$ or $y \sim sqrt(x)$ are perfectly legal.

5.   A function under the same name can be found in the rms package (see an example in Chapter 12). It does not matter which one you use. If two functions from different loaded add-on packages

The function returns the Variance Inflation Factors (VIF-scores), which help us estimate how much collinearity is associated with each regression term. The generalized VIF-scores are shown in the first column, whereas the third column displays the same scores corrected for the degrees of freedom.

```
> car::vif(m.trans)
                GVIF        Df   GVIF^(1/(2*Df))
Length          1.151054    1    1.072872
log(SUBTLWF)    1.150140    1    1.072446
POS             1.026925    2    1.006664
```

There exist various rules of thumb, some of them stricter (VIF-scores should not exceed 5) and others less so (VIF-scores should not be greater than 10). In our case, both uncorrected and corrected VIF-scores are very small. Thus, multicollinearity is not a matter of concern.

To illustrate the effects of multicollinearity, let us create a vector of word length that is identical to *Length*, with the exception of the first three values, which will be changed to 8 letters with the help of the function rep(), i.e. repeat.

```
> Length1 <- ELP$Length
> Length1[1:3] <- rep(8, 3)
> head(ELP$Length)
[1] 7 10 10 8 6 5
> head(Length1)
[1] 8 8 8 8 6 5
```

The vectors differ only in the first three values. The remaining scores are absolutely identical. Let us now add the new term *Length1* to the model:

```
> m.test <- lm(Mean_RT^-1.3 ~ Length + log(SUBTLWF) + POS + Length1,
data = ELP)
```

```
> car:: vif(m.test)
                GVIF        Df   GVIF^(1/(2*Df))
Length          543.443758  1    23.311880
log(SUBTLWF)    1.150140    1    1.072446
POS             1.028782    2    1.007119
Length1         543.518917  1    23.313492
```

The VIF-scores of both *Length* and *Length1* are huge. This is an indication that something is really wrong. Let us examine the table of coefficients of the new model:

---

have the same name, e.g. vif() in car and rms, one of them will be masked, and R will give a warning message. To use a masked function, you should specify the package where it comes from, e.g. car::vif(m).

```
> summary(m.test)

Call:
lm(formula = Mean_RT^-1.3 ~ Length + log(SUBTLWF) + POS + Length1,
data = ELP)

Residuals:
Min             1Q           Median       3Q          Max
-7.313e-05   -1.681e-05   -2.530e-07   1.646e-05   6.679e-05

Coefficients:
               Estimate     Std. Error   t value   Pr(>|t|)
(Intercept)    2.200e-04    3.724e-06    59.081    < 2e-16 ***
Length        -3.031e-06    8.166e-06    -0.371    0.71066
log(SUBTLWF)   9.059e-06    4.678e-07    19.367    < 2e-16 ***
POSNN          1.017e-06    2.231e-06    0.456     0.64871
POSVB          7.614e-06    2.665e-06    2.857     0.00437 **
Length1       -1.835e-06    8.173e-06    -0.225    0.82239
--

Signif. codes: 0 '***' 0.001 '**' 0.01 '*' 0.05 '.' 0.1 ' ' 1

Residual standard error: 2.446e-05 on 874 degrees of freedom
Multiple R-squared: 0.4951, Adjusted R-squared: 0.4922
F-statistic: 171.4 on 5 and 874 DF, p-value: < 2.2e-16
```

The table of coefficients shows that the *p*-values of the estimates of *Length* and *Length1* are very large. The estimates of the correlated variables are not reliable any more. In situations of multicollinearity, one can either try to get rid of one of the correlated variables, or, if all correlated variables are equally theoretically important, try to use a dimensionality-reduction technique, such as Principal Components Analysis (for quantitative variables) or Multiple Correspondence Analysis (for categorical variables). See more information in Chapters 18 and 19, respectively.

Assumption 6. *There should be no autocorrelation between the residuals.*
As was discussed in the previous chapter, autocorrelated residuals tend to emerge when we have time series. We would not expect them here. The test is performed solely for illustration:

```
> durbinWatsonTest(m.trans)
lag Autocorrelation D-W Statistic  p-value
1     -0.001031322     2.000717     0.932
Alternative  hypothesis: rho != 0
```

Since the *p*-value is greater than 0.05, and the *D–W* statistic is very close to 2, we can conclude that there is no autocorrelation.

Assumption 7. *The residuals should be normally distributed, with the mean of 0.*
One can use the Shapiro-Wilk normality test to check is there are any violations of
normality:

```
> shapiro.test(residuals(m.trans))
   Shapiro-Wilk normality test
data: residuals(m.trans)
W = 0.9983, p-value = 0.5434
```

Since the *p*-value is greater than 0.05, the null hypothesis of normality cannot be rejected.
One can also inspect a Q–Q plot shown in Figure 7.6, which is one of the plots produced by
`plot.lm()`. The Q–Q plot (`which = 2`) does not display deviations from non-normality.

```
> plot(m.trans, which = 2)
```

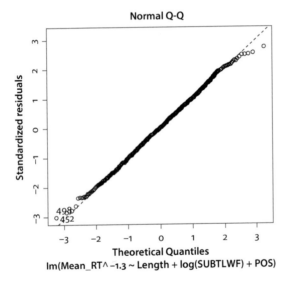

Figure 7.6. Q–Q plot of residuals

7.2.6 Testing and interpreting interactions

Interactions are observed when the effect of one explanatory variable on the outcome
depends on the value of another variable. The effect can be reinforced, weakened, or even
reversed. For instance, consider caviar and vanilla ice-cream. As separate courses, they are
delicious, but to put them together would be a culinary blunder. One can also say that the
joint effect is not additive.

R supports two ways of designating an interaction between two or more variables,
which are equivalent:

(1)   Response ~ Var1*Var2

(2)   Response ~ Var1 + Var2 + Var1:Var2

Let us test whether the effect of word length varies for different parts of speech. To do so, we will fit a model with an interaction between *Length* and *POS*, using the first type of notation:

```
> m.int <- lm(Mean_RT^-1.3 ~ Length*POS + log(SUBTLWF), data = ELP)
```

One can use ANOVA (Analysis of Variance) to compare two models, one with main effects only, and the other with the interaction term:

```
> anova(m.trans, m.int) # equivalent to anova(…, test = "F")
Analysis of Variance Table
Model 1: Mean_RT^-1.3 ~ Length + log(SUBTLWF) + POS
Model 2: Mean_RT^-1.3 ~ Length *POS + log(SUBTLWF)
Res.Df  RSS Df  Sum of Sq  F Pr(>F)
1  875  5.2314e-07
2  873  5.1931e-07 2 3.8336e-09 3.2223 0.04034 *
--
Signif. codes: 0 '***' 0.001 '**' 0.01 '*' 0.05 '.' 0.1 ' ' 1
```

More on different kinds of ANOVA will follow in Chapter 8, but this particular use of ANOVA allows one to test the null hypothesis that the models are not significantly different. Since the *p*-value smaller than 0.05, the interaction term is significant. Note that the second model should contain all explanatory variables in the first model.

How can this interaction be interpreted? The best option is to make a visual representation. The package `visreg` offers many useful options for visualization of interactions. To explore the interaction between *Length* and *POS*, one can use the following code:

```
> visreg(m.int, xvar = "Length", by = "POS")
```

where the first argument is the model that contains the interaction, `xvar` specifies the explanatory variable that will be represented by the *x*-axis of the interaction plot, and `by` introduces the variable that will be used to divide the plot into cross-sections. The resulting plot is shown in Figure 7.7. It is crucial that the lines are not exactly parallel. The length of nouns has a smaller effect on the reaction times than the length of verbs and adjectives. Although short verbs and adjectives have a slightly higher *y*-value than nouns of the same length, very long verbs and adjectives have a lower *y*-value than very long nouns. Note that the transformed *Mean_RT* is close to the inverse of the original scores. That is, the smaller the original reaction times, the greater the transformed ones, and vice versa. Thus, the greater the *y*-value on the plot, the faster the word is recognized.

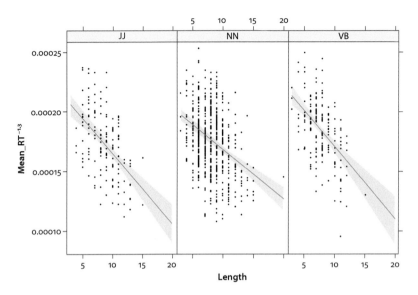

Figure 7.7. Interaction of *POS* and *Length*

The interaction is mild. For all parts of speech, the effect of word length is similar. To show what a very strong interaction may look like, consider Figure 7.8. It shows two interacting explanatory variables: a binary variable with values 'A' and 'B' and *numVar*, a numerical variable ranging from 1 to 50. The dependent variable is called *response*. The interaction is very strong because the effect of *numVar* is opposite for different levels of the nominal variable, 'A' and 'B'. As *numVar* increases, the response variable increases when the binary variable has value 'A', and decreases with it has value 'B'. Such interactions are called cross-over.

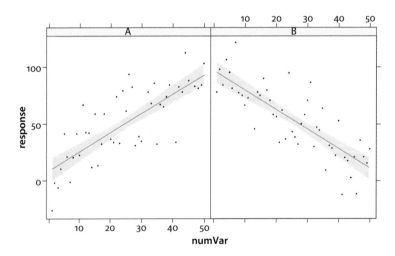

Figure 7.8. Interaction plot of a binary and continuous independent variables, which displays a cross-over interaction

If you have a look at the summary of the model with the interaction, you will find two new terms in the table of coefficients: `Length:POSNN` and `Length:POSVB`.

```
> summary(m.int)
Call:
lm(formula = Mean_RT^-1.3 ~ Length + log(SUBTLWF) + POS +
  Length:POS, data = ELP)
Residuals:
Min           1Q          Median       3Q          Max
-6.901e-05   -1.643e-05   -1.510e-07   1.650e-05   6.835e-05

Coefficients:
                Estimate Std.   Error       t value   Pr(>|t|)
(Intercept)     2.285e-04       7.046e-06   32.423    < 2e-16  ***
Length          -5.825e-06      7.770e-07   -7.497    1.6e-13  ***
log(SUBTLWF)    9.061e-06       4.665e-07   19.424    < 2e-16  ***
POSNN           -1.324e-05      8.014e-06   -1.652    0.0989  .
POSVB           9.297e-06       9.758e-06   0.953     0.3410
Length:POSNN    1.670e-06       8.909e-07   1.875     0.0612  .
Length:POSVB    -3.348e-07      1.136e-06   -0.295    0.7683
--

Signif. codes:  0 '***' 0.001 '**' 0.01 '*' 0.05 '.' 0.1 ' ' 1
Residual standard error: 2.439e-05 on 873 degrees of freedom
Multiple R-squared: 0.4987,    Adjusted R-squared: 0.4953
F-statistic: 144.8 on 6 and 873 DF, p-value: < 2.2e-16
```

It is important to understand that the interpretation of all terms involved in the interaction is now different. The coefficient of *Length* does not correspond to the effect of length for all data, but only for the observations with the reference level of the interacting term *POS* = 'JJ'. The coefficient of POSNN is now the effect of *Length* for *POS* = 'NN' for words with the length of 0 ms, which exists only hypothetically. The same holds for POSVB. The interaction term `Length:POSNN` shows the difference between the change in the transformed reaction times of nouns and the change in the transformed reaction times of the reference level, adjectives, for every additional unit of word length. For `Length:POSVB` the interpretation is analogous.

More about interactions

Examples of interactions between categorical variables will be discussed in the next chapter. See also Chapter 12. If you have multiple or high-order interactions, you might

(Continued)

wish to use additional techniques to disentangle such complex relationships, e.g. conditional inference trees and random forests (see Chapter 14).

7.2.7   Checking for overfitting

Overfitting is a serious problem in regression modelling. If you take another sample, an overfitted model will perform poorly on the new data. Such models have little, if any, scientific value. Overfitting usually occurs in situations 'small n, large p', where n is the number of cases, and p is the number of explanatory variables. Ideally, every fitted model should be tested on new data (this is called cross-validation). However, this is not always possible because new data are costly. Instead, one can use resampling methods, such as bootstrapping. In a nutshell, bootstrapping means that we use one sample to both carry out an analysis and validate its results, as if one tried to pull him- or herself up by bootstraps, similar to Baron Munchhausen, who pulled himself out of a swamp by his pigtail. Although such deeds may sound like impossible tasks, bootstrapping is a very popular procedure in statistics. Its basic principle is simple: a new dataset is sampled from the original data randomly with replacement (that is, the same observation can be used more than once), and then the statistical analysis is performed again. One usually logs some statistics of how similar the new result is to the original one. When one repeats the procedure many times, one can obtain reliable estimates of the accuracy of a model.

To perform bootstrap validation, we will use the `validate()` function in the `rms` package. To be able to use this function, one has to refit the model first with the help of the `ols()` function, which is equivalent to `lm()`. It is also necessary to add `x = TRUE` and `y = TRUE`.

```
> m.val <- ols(Mean_RT^-1.3 ~ Length*POS + log(SUBTLWF), data = ELP,
x = TRUE, y = TRUE)
> validate(m.val, bw = TRUE, B = 200)
             Backwards Step-down - Original Model

No Factors Deleted

Factors in Final Model

[1] Length    POS    SUBTLWF      Length *POS
Loading required package: tcltk
            index.orig training test    optimism index.corrected  n
R-square    0.4987     0.4996    0.4943 0.0054   0.4934           200
MSE         0.0000     0.0000    0.0000 0.0000   0.0000           200
g           0.0000     0.0000    0.0000 0.0000   0.0000           200
Intercept   0.0000     0.0000    0.0000 0.0000   0.0000           200
Slope       1.0000     1.0000    0.9966 0.0034   0.9966           200
```

```
Factors Retained in Backwards Elimination

Length   POS   SUBTLWF   Length * POS
  *       *       *           *

  *       *       *           *

  *       *       *           *

[output omitted]

Frequencies of Numbers of Factors Retained

 2   3    4
 4  49  147
```

The algorithm does a resampling validation of the regression model. The procedure is repeated many times. In our case, B = 200 tells R to make 200 bootstrap runs. The argument bw = TRUE chooses backward stepwise variable elimination. The output shows how many times the variables were retained in the model. In our case, all variables were retained in 147 resamplings from 200. Note that your results will be slightly different every time you run the procedure.

However, the most important information about potential overfitting is contained in the column named Optimism. It displays the differences between the training and test statistics shown in the corresponding columns. The training statistics are averaged over all regression models based on bootstrapped data, whereas the test statistics are obtained when the bootstrap models are used to predict the transformed reaction times on the full dataset. See Baayen (2008: 212–214) for more details. Large optimism values indicate overfitting. As a rule of thumb, the slope optimism (i.e. the optimism in the estimation of the regression coefficients of the explanatory variables) should not exceed 0.05. In case of overfitting, a possible solution is adding a penalty to the model, which will make the estimates shrink (see Baayen 2008: 224–227). Overfitting may also result from ignoring dependence between observations, such as individual variation between subjects. In this case, fitting a mixed model with fixed and random effects may help. This method will be briefly introduced in the next chapter. In our example, the optimism in the slopes is less than 0.01, and the optimism in R^2 is around 1%: 0.0054/0.4987 = 0.01. Thus, there are no signs of overfitting.

7.2.8   Non-parametric regression: Bootstrap

When one or more assumptions of linear regression have been violated, one can use regression based on bootstrapping, which was introduced in the previous subsection. Its advantage is that it does not require all those assumptions to be met in order to return results that can be trusted. We have already used bootstrapping to check whether there is evidence that the model overfits the data. In this section, you will learn how to obtain non-parametric confidence intervals with the help of bootstrap to see whether the explanatory variables will have similar effect sizes if you take another sample. The procedure we will follow is described in Field et al. (2012: 299–300). We will use the function boot () from the package boot. The first step is to create a function that will return regression coefficients after each bootstrap:

```
> bootcoef <- function(formula, data, indices)
{

   d <- data[indices,]
   model <- lm(formula, data=d)
   return(coef(model))

}
```

Next, we will test the model where the assumption of homoscedasticity was violated. Recall that we had to use a power transformation of the response variable. This improved the model, but the results are much more difficult to interpret now. For better comparability with the model discussed in detail previously, we will perform the bootstrap procedure for the model without the interaction. The bootstrap will involve 2000 resamplings.

```
> m.boot <- boot(formula = Mean_RT ~ Length + log(SUBTLWF) + POS,
data = ELP, statistic = bootcoef, R = 2000)
```

Now we can compute the 95% confidence intervals for each of our estimates. The confidence intervals for the intercept, *Length*, *POS*, *log(SUBTLWF)*, *POS* = 'NN' and *POS* = 'VB' can be retrieved as follows:

```
> boot.ci(m.boot, type = "bca", index = 1) # Intercept
BOOTSTRAP CONFIDENCE INTERVAL CALCULATIONS
Based on 2000 bootstrap replicates

CALL:
boot.ci(boot.out = m.boot, type = "bca", index = 1)

Intervals:
Level   BCa
95%     (596.1, 649.3)
Calculations and Intervals on Original Scale
> boot.ci(m.boot, type = "bca", index = 2) # Length
BOOTSTRAP CONFIDENCE INTERVAL CALCULATIONS
Based on 2000 bootstrap replicates

CALL:
boot.ci(boot.out = m.boot, type = "bca", index = 2)

Intervals:
Level   BCa
95%     (16.72, 22.58)
Calculations and Intervals on Original Scale
```

The reader is encouraged to repeat the procedure for the three remaining terms. Note that the results will be slightly different every time you run the procedure. The output is quite verbose, but the confidence intervals can be easily found on the second line from the bottom, in parentheses. The confidence intervals are very similar to the confidence intervals that were computed in Section 7.2.2.

The bootstrap method also allows for computation of the 95% confidence interval of any other statistic in the model. For instance, one can compute the interval of the model's R^2 as follows:

```
> bootR2 <- function(formula, data, indices)
{
  d <- data[indices,]
  model <- lm(formula, data=d)
  return(summary(model)$r.squared)
}

> m.boot.R2 <- boot(formula = Mean_RT ~ Length + log(SUBTLWF) + POS,
data = ELP, statistic = bootR2,  R = 2000)
> boot.ci(m.boot.R2, type = "bca")
BOOTSTRAP CONFIDENCE INTERVAL CALCULATIONS
Based on 2000 bootstrap replicates

CALL:
boot.ci(boot.out = m.boot.R2, type = "bca")

Intervals:
Level   BCa
95%     (0.4096, 0.5033)
Calculations and Intervals on Original Scale
```

The original statistic lies in the middle of the confidence interval based on the bootstrap. Therefore, the results of our initial model are stable and reliable.

7.3 Summary

In this chapter we have discussed linear regression, including modelling strategies, diagnostics, assumptions, interactions and non-parametric tests with the help of bootstrapping. We have found significant effects of frequency, word length and part of speech on the time needed by speakers to recognize a word. Of course, many other factors may be relevant, as well (cf. Balota et al. 2007), although even the current small model has a reasonable predictive power. There is one caveat, however. The model, which is based on average reaction times, does not take into account individual variation between the subjects, which may have considerable effects on the results. See Chapter 8, Section 8.3 for more information about mixed Generalized Linear Models.

How to report your linear regression model

There are no strict rules for reporting the results, but you should provide the following information: (a) the table with estimated regression coefficients (including the intercept), their standard errors and p-values; (b) the goodness-of-fit statistic (R^2). Additionally, you can also report the 95% confidence intervals for your estimates. You can also use the asterisk system to indicate the significance of coefficients in the table (*** for $p < 0.001$, ** for $0.001 \leq p < 0.01$, * for $0.01 \leq p < 0.05$, "." for $0.5 \leq p < 0.1$), e.g. 12.17*** or −5.49*.

More about regression

Regression modelling is a very complex and broad topic. This chapter only provides the basic strategies of fitting and interpreting linear regression models. For more detailed information, see, for example, Faraway (2009) and Fox (2008). Regression can also be performed on non-numeric response variables. Such extensions are called Generalized Linear Models. For example, logistic regression is an extension that deals with binary, multinomial and ordinal response variables. Logistic regression will be discussed in Chapters 12 and 13. Another popular extension is the Poisson regression, where one regresses on count data. It is also known as log-linear regression, especially when the counts are represented in contingency tables. See Gries (2013: 324–327) for a brief illustration of Poisson regression models and Field et al. (2012: 829–852) for a discussion of log-linear analysis.

CHAPTER 8

Finding differences between several groups

Sign language, linguistic relativity and ANOVA

What you will learn from this chapter:

> This chapter introduces ANOVA (analysis of variance), a special case of linear regression with binary or categorical independent variables. This method is widely used in experimental linguistics, when the researcher compares several groups of experimental objects that undergo different treatments. In this chapter you will learn several types of ANOVA: one-way ANOVA with one factor as an independent variable, factorial ANOVA with two or more categorical independent variables, and repeated-measures and mixed ANOVA. The methods are illustrated by three case studies. The first two focus on grammatical features of an emergent sign language. The third case study deals with cross-linguistic differences in time conceptualization, which are interpreted as evidence in favour of the linguistic relativity hypothesis.

8.1 What is ANOVA?

In Chapter 5, we discussed the *t*-test and its non-parametric equivalents, which can be used for comparison of two groups. ANOVA (analysis of variance) is a family of methods that enable one to investigate the differences between any number of groups, which can be specified by one or more categorical variables. Although some researchers are not aware of this fact, ANOVA can be regarded as a special case of regression analysis. Due to historical reasons, ANOVA has been used mostly in experimental research, whereas regression has been mostly employed in correlational research based on observations (e.g. corpus data), surveys or questionnaires.

A typical application of ANOVA is when the researcher wants to find if there are differences between several groups, which undergo different experimental treatments. For example, imagine that you want to test the usefulness of video subtitles for learning English as a foreign language. In that case, you might compare three different conditions. In one group, subtitles are in English. In a second group, subtitles are in the students' native language. A third group is the control group where no subtitles are used at all.

In this chapter you will learn how to perform three major types of ANOVA:

- **independent one-way ANOVA**, which is used for comparison of three and more groups, as in the example above. The situations when it can be used are similar to the ones when the independent *t*-test is applied. However, as has been said already, the latter is limited to two groups only.
- **independent factorial ANOVA**, which involves two or more categorical independent variables. Imagine that native speakers of two different languages are exposed to two different experimental conditions, e.g. two types of stimuli, and their reaction times are measured. Factorial ANOVA allows one to measure the individual effects of the variables, as well as their possible interactions. In this example, an interaction may emerge, for instance, if the speakers of one language react to the different types of stimuli differently, and the speakers of the other language react to all stimuli in the same way.
- **repeated-measures and mixed ANOVA**, which are used for the same purposes as the above-mentioned types of ANOVA in situations when observations are not independent, e.g. when every subject is tested more than once, or every stimulus is presented more than once. These types of ANOVA test the differences between groups while taking into account individual variation.

There are two important concepts related to ANOVA, namely, **within-subject** and **between-group design**. In between-group design, which is also called between-subject design, different groups of subjects are assigned to different experimental conditions. For example, one group may be the one where the subjects are administered a new drug. The other group may be the control group, which receives a placebo. In this example, the type of medical treatment is a between-group variable. Independent one-way and factorial ANOVAs contain only between-group variables.

In within-subject design, the same subjects are tested in several experimental conditions. Imagine you conduct a lexical decision experiment. You ask your subjects to decide whether a word does or does not exist in the language. The stimuli are a mixture of real and nonce words. Every subject reacts to both types of stimuli. The type of stimuli is considered then a within-subject variable. One can also say that this variable is tested within one subject. If all subjects are tested in all possible conditions, this means that all variables are within-subject variables. In that case, you will need **repeated-measures ANOVA**. If your design contains both within-subject and between-group variables, you will have to perform **mixed ANOVA**. ANOVA with within-subject variables can also be one-way, two-way (factorial), and so on, depending on the number of independent variables in the model.

8.2   Motion events in Nicaraguan Sign Language: Independent one-way ANOVA

8.2.1   Theoretical background and data

For this case study you will need a number of add-on packages, which should be first installed, if they have not been installed previously, and then loaded.

```
> install.packages(c("car", "coin", "nparcomp"))
> library(Rling); library(car); library(coin); library(nparcomp)
```

This case study focuses on Nicaraguan Sign Language (NSL). It is a very young language, which has been developing over the last thirty years. Many of its originators are still around today, and researchers can observe how the language has changed since its earliest days. In a series of studies, e.g. Senghas & Coppola (2001) and Senghas et al. (2004), Ann Senghas and her collaborators have demonstrated that NSL has been developing 'from analog to digital', that is, from holistic continuous expressions to discrete elements, which resemble words and morphemes. For example, the early expressions of motion in NSL were holistic movements, which express the path and manner simultaneously. As an illustration, consider a rolling event. One can express it gesturally in a single holistic movement, which combines the manner and the path. The manner can be expressed as a wiggling movement, and the path as a movement to the speaker's right or left. Senghas and her colleagues, however, observed that younger NSL speakers prefer to express the manner and the path sequentially, in two separate signs. For a rolling event, the manner would be expressed by circling, and the path would be indicated as a sign that shows the trajectory to the signer's side. This finding is not surprising. According to Talmy's well-known theory (1985), languages typically represent motion events by separate linguistic elements that correspond to path and manner (e.g. *roll [MANNER] down [PATH] the hill*).

For illustration, we will explore a fictitious dataset that resembles the data in Senghas et al. (2004). The data are available in the data frame `NSL` in the `Rling` package. The data frame contains two columns. The first one, *MannerPath*, displays the proportions of separate expressions of manner and path by NSL signers when they were asked to describe a set of different motion events. Each participant was shown an animated cartoon that included those events, and was asked to narrate this story to a peer. The proportions range from 0 (no separate expressions, only holistic analog expressions) to 1 (only separate expressions, no holistic analog expression). The second column, *Cohort*, shows one of the three generational groups to which each signer belongs: Cohort 1 includes the very first NSL signers, who joined the community and learnt to sign in the late 1970s – early 1980s; Cohort 2, which arrived in the mid- to late 1980s; and Cohort 3, which arrived from 1990 to the moment of data collection. Each cohort is represented by nine participants. Although the cohorts are represented by numbers, this variable is a factor.

```
> data(NSL)
> head(NSL)
Manner  Path    Cohort
1        0.44    1
2        0.24    1
3        0.41    1
4        0.03    1
5        0.32    1
6        0.18    1
> str(NSL)
'data.frame': 27 obs. of 2 variables:
$ MannerPath: num 0.44 0.24 0.41 0.03 0.32 0.18 0.25 0.42 0.17 0.77
...
$ Cohort: Factor w/ 3 levels "1","2","3": 1 1 1 1 1 1 1 1 1 2 ...
```

The earlier a signer joined the community, the more 'ancient' level of NSL he or she represents. We expect thus that the mean proportion of separate expressions of manner and path will be higher for the more recent Cohorts than for the earlier ones. We will use ANOVA to test this hypothesis. *MannerPath* will be the response variable, and *Cohort* will be a between-group exploratory variable. Since each subject was tested only once, the design is independent.

8.2.2 Exploring the data

We will begin with a graphical exploration and will create a box plot that represents the distribution of scores in each cohort:

```
> boxplot(NSL$MannerPath ~ NSL$Cohort, xlab = "Cohort", ylab =
"Proportion of separate expressions", main = "Path and motion in
NSL")
```

Figure 8.1 displays the graph (for information about how to make a ggplot2 version, see Chapter 3; see also Chapter 5 about how to create a bar plot with 95% confidence intervals). The box plot shows clearly that the first cohort of NSL signers use separate expressions of manner and path much less frequently than the second and the third cohorts. However, we do not see a clear difference between the second and third cohorts.

Next, we will compute the mean proportions of separate expressions in each cohort with the help of tapply(). This useful function can compute a statistic of interest for several groups at the same time:

```
> tapply(NSL$MannerPath, NSL$Cohort, mean)
1          2          3
0.2733333  0.7555556  0.7344444
```

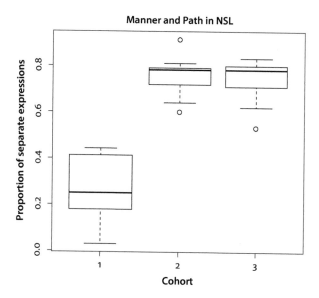

Figure 8.1. Box plots of proportions of separate expression of manner and path in three cohorts of Nicaraguan Sign Language

The first argument of `tapply()` is the quantitative variable, `NSL$MannerPath`. It is followed by the grouping variable, `NSL$Cohort`. Finally, we specify the function that computes the statistic, `mean`. The result is a one-dimensional table with three means. Again, we see that the mean proportion of separate expressions in the first cohort is much smaller than those in the second and third cohorts. Interestingly, there is even a small decrease in the third cohort. To see whether these differences are statistically significant, one needs one-way ANOVA.

Why bother with ANOVA?

Indeed, why not perform several *t*-tests instead? The answer to this question lies in the expression 'inflation of surprise' (Baayen 2008: 114). To put it simply, when one performs multiple comparisons on the same data, the probability that he or she finds some surprising results goes up. As the number of hypotheses to test increases, the chances to commit a Type I error (i.e. reject the null hypothesis when it is in fact true) increase, as well. This is the main reason for using ANOVA instead of multiple *t*-tests.

8.2.3   Assumptions of one-way parametric ANOVA

The alternative hypothesis of one-way ANOVA is that at least two group means are differ-ent from one another. The test is therefore non-directional. To obtain reliable results with the help of traditional parametric ANOVA, the following assumptions should be met:

–   *The observations in the samples are independent from one another.*
–   *The response variable is at least interval-scaled.*
–   *Each sample is drawn from a normally distributed population and/or the sample sizes are equal* (Field et al. 2012: 413).
–   *The variance is homogeneous, or homoscedastic* (cf. Chapter 6). In other words, the variances of the populations represented by the groups should be equal. The opposite of homogeneity is heterogeneity, or heteroscedasticity.

If any of these assumptions is saliently violated, other versions of ANOVA should be used. They will be discussed in the next subsection.

Are these assumptions met in the data? There are no reasons to assume that the obser-vations are dependent. The response variable is ratio-scaled. It is difficult to evaluate the normality, since the samples are very small. However, the sample sizes are equal. For didac-tic purposes, we provide the code that enables one to run the Shapiro test three times simultaneously and obtain the p-value for each of the three groups:

```
> aggregate(MannerPath ~ Cohort, data = NSL, function(x) shapiro.
test(x)$p.value)
Cohort  MannerPath
1          1 0.5614787
2          2 0.5210358
3          3 0.1266828
```

None of the p-values, which are shown in the right-hand column, is smaller than 0.05. Therefore, we do not have reasons to believe that the assumption of normality is not met. However, these results should be taken with caution because the chances that the Shapiro test will detect non-normality depend on the sample size.

Finally, homogeneity of variance, or homoscedasticity, can be tested with the help of the Levene test, which is available as leveneTest() in the package car.

```
> leveneTest(MannerPath ~ Cohort, data = NSL) # equivalent to
leveneTest(…, center = median), which provides a more robust test
than the original Levene test with mean as the center.

Levene's Test for Homogeneity of Variance (center = median)
          Df  F value  Pr(>F)
group   2    0.9207   0.4118
         24
```

The null hypothesis of the Levene test is that the groups have equal variances. Since the p-value is greater than 0.05, the null hypothesis of equal variances cannot be rejected.

There exist many alternatives to the Levene test. One of them is the Fligner – Killeen median test, which is robust to departures from normality (Conover et al. 1981). The test can be carried out as follows:

```
> fligner.test(MannerPath ~ Cohort, data = NSL)

        Fligner-Killeen test of homogeneity of variances

data: MannerPath by Cohort
Fligner-Killeen:med chi-squared = 2.3505, df = 2, p-value = 0.3087
```

The large p-value again suggests that we cannot discard the null hypothesis that the variance is homogeneous across the groups.

8.2.4 Performing parametric one-way ANOVA

Since we have not found any violations of the test assumptions, we can perform the parametric one-way ANOVA. There are two options. First, we can use the general lm() function for linear regression:

```
> NSL.lm <- lm(MannerPath ~ Cohort, data = NSL)
> summary(NSL.lm)

Call:
lm(formula = MannerPath ~ Cohort, data = NSL)

Residuals:
Min         1Q        Median    3Q        Max
-0.24333   -0.06444   0.02444   0.06000   0.16667

Coefficients:
              Estimate  Std. Error  t value   Pr(>|t|)
(Intercept)   0.27333   0.03727     7.334     1.42e-07 ***
Cohort2       0.48222   0.05271     9.149     2.71e-09 ***
Cohort3       0.46111   0.05271     8.748     6.26e-09 ***
--
Signif. codes: 0 '***' 0.001 '**' 0.01 '*' 0.05 '.' 0.1 ' ' 1

Residual standard error: 0.1118 on 24 degrees of freedom
Multiple R-squared: 0.8167,      Adjusted R-squared: 0.8014
F-statistic: 53.46 on 2 and 24 DF, p-value: 1.439e-09
```

The second option is to use aov(), which produces the traditional ANOVA output:

```
> NSL.aov <- aov(MannerPath ~ Cohort, data = NSL)
> summary(NSL.aov)
             Df   Sum Sq   Mean Sq   F value   Pr(>F)
Cohort        2   1.337    0.6684    53.47     1.44e-09 ***
Residuals    24   0.300    0.0125
--
Signif. codes: 0 '***' 0.001 '**' 0.01 '*' 0.05 '.' 0.1 ' ' 1
```

The main test statistic in both versions is the *F*-ratio. In ANOVA, it is usually interpreted as the ratio of the average between-group variability and the average within-group variability. Between-group variability measures variance of group means. In the aov() output, you can find it in the Cohort row, in the column Mean Sq, which represents the mean between-group variability. This value is 0.6684, and it is equal to the sum of squares (Sum Sq) 1.337 divided by two degrees of freedom (DF). Within-group variability is variability that can be attributed to chance factors. It is also called error or residual variability. The mean residual variability in our example is 0.0125 (0.3 divided by 24), as one can see in the Residuals row. The greater the average between-group variability in comparison with the average within-group variability, the greater the *F*-ratio. In this example, it is 0.6684/0.0125 ≈ 53.47, with 2 and 24 degrees of freedom. The alternative hypothesis of the test is that there is at least one pair of groups with different means, or, in other words, that at least one difference between groups means is different from zero. Since $p < 0.001$, we can conclude that at least one pair of groups has different means.

8.2.5   Alternative tests

There exist a number of alternative tests, which can be used when one or more assumptions are violated. There is still controversy about the use of some tests, but the following guidelines seem to represent the consensus:

-   oneway.test() can be used when the variance is not homogeneous, but the other assumptions hold. To perform the test, one can follow the example:

    ```
    > oneway.test(MannerPath ~ Cohort, data = NSL)

    One-way analysis of means (not assuming equal
    variances)

    data: MannerPath and Cohort
    F = 41.2291, num df = 2.000, denom df = 15.648,
    p-value = 5.787e-07
    ```

-   The Kruskal-Wallis one-way ANOVA by ranks can be used when the response variable is on the ordinal scale or when the samples come from markedly non-normal distributions. However, at least one of the two assumptions should still be met: homogeneous variances of the ranks and/or equal sample sizes (Sheskin 2011: 1002). The test is an extension of the Mann-Whitney test (U-test), which was introduced in Chapter 5. It can also be used on interval- or ratio-scaled data when one needs to reduce the impact of outliers. Consider an example:

```
> kruskal.test(MannerPath ~ Cohort, data = NSL)

Kruskal-Wallis rank sum test

data: MannerPath by Cohort
Kruskal-Wallis chi-squared = 17.4208, df = 2, p-value
= 0.0001649
```

- Non-parametric ANOVA based on bootstrapping or permutation (see Chapters 7 and 14) can be used when all assumptions concerning the distribution are violated, except for the assumption of independence. There are many packages that offer this option. For example, one can use ANOVA based on permutation that is implemented in `oneway_test()` from the package `coin`:

```
> oneway_test(MannerPath ~ Cohort, data = NSL, distribution =
approximate(B = 9999))

Approximative K-Sample Permutation Test

data: MannerPath by Cohort (1, 2, 3)
maxT = 4.6046, p-value < 2.2e-16
```

One can also use Wilcox' (2005) functions based on the comparison of medians and trimmed means with bootstrap (Field et al. 2012: 441–443).

- repeated-measures and mixed ANOVA should be used when observations are dependent (see Section 8.4).

8.2.6   Post hoc tests

The F-ratio test is an omnibus test. That is, it can tell us that there is some significant difference somewhere, but it does not say where exactly. To find out which groups differ significantly, one can perform a post hoc test. There is a variety of post hoc tests for one-way ANOVA. In this section, we will consider only two, the parametric Tukey Honest Significant Differences test and a non-parametric multiple comparison test.

The Tukey Honest Significant Differences (HSD) test is available as `TukeyHSD()`. This function requires an `aov` object. The function returns the adjusted 'honest' p-values, hence the name of the test, 'Honest Significant Differences'. The test is quite robust to violations of the normality assumption. However, there are two assumptions that should be met: homogeneous variances and independence of observations. The test can be performed as follows:

```
> TukeyHSD(NSL.aov)
Tukey multiple comparisons of means
95% family-wise confidence level

Fit: aov(formula = MannerPath ~ Cohort, data = NSL)

$Cohort
          diff          lwr          upr       p adj
2-1    0.48222222    0.3505939    0.6138506   0.00000
3-1    0.46111111    0.3294828    0.5927394   0.00000
3-2   -0.02111111   -0.1527394    0.1105172   0.91568
```

The function returns the differences between the group means for three pairs of groups. The greatest difference is between Cohorts 2 and 1. It is positive because the mean response in Cohort 2 is greater than that in Cohort 1. It is also statistically significant, judging from a very small p-value, which can be found in the rightmost column. The results for Cohorts 3 and 1 are very similar. The negative difference between Cohorts 3 and 2 indicates that the mean response in Cohort 3 is smaller than that in Cohort 2. However, this difference is not statistically significant.

In addition, the function returns the 95% confidence intervals of the differences between the groups. The column lwr gives us the lower end points of the intervals, whereas the upr column tells about the upper boundary. If a confidence interval includes 0, we cannot be sure that the groups are truly different. The differences and their confidence intervals can be visualized as follows: (see the result in Figure 8.2)

```
> plot(TukeyHSD(NSL.aov))
```

If the assumption of equal variances is violated, one can use a non-parametric test. Here we will discuss nparcomp() from the eponymous package:

```
> npar <- nparcomp(MannerPath ~ Cohort, data = NSL, type = "Tukey")
#---Nonparametric  Multiple  Comparisons  for  relative  contrast
effects---#
[output omitted]

> npar$Analysis
Comparison    Estimator    Lower   Upper   Statistic    p.Value
1 p(1, 2)      0.999        0.996   1.000   11.3376072   0.0000000
2 p(1, 3)      0.999        0.996   1.000   11.3376072   0.0000000
3 p(2, 3)      0.463        0.176   0.776   -0.2546148   0.9918819
```

The output provides a lot of details, most importantly, which groups are compared (the leftmost column) and the p-value (the rightmost column). The results confirm that

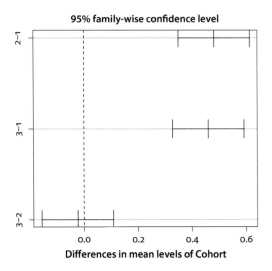

Figure 8.2. Confidence intervals of differences between group means

the first Cohort is different from the second and third ones, but the difference between the second and third Cohorts is not statistically significant.

More on post hoc tests

Other useful functions include `pairwise.t.test()`, which offers a range of corrections for inflation of surprise, such as the famous Bonferroni correction, which is, however, less widely used now in comparison with more modern corrections, such as the Holm method. See also `glht()` in the package `multcomp`. The statistical details for different correction methods can be found in Sheskin (2011: 903–924), and a more concise and practical overview is provided in Larson-Hall (2010: 282).

8.3 Development of spatial modulations in Nicaraguan Sign Language: Independent factorial (two-way) ANOVA

8.3.1 The data and hypothesis

In this case study we will use two add-on packages, which should be installed (unless you have already done so) and then loaded:

```
> install.packages("car")
> library(Rling); library(car)
```

As the previous case study, this section focuses on Nicaraguan Sign Language (NSL). See the background information about this language in Section 8.2. The research question comes from the paper by Senghas & Coppola (2001), who compared newly emerging spatial devices in two different cohorts of NSL learners: those who joined the community before and after 1983 (the median year). The cohort served thus as a between-group variable. The other factor was the age group of the signer when he or she joined the community. The dependent variable is the average number of spatial modulations per verb for every signer. This is a particular type of spatial modulation that indicates 'shared reference'. Most signs are produced neutrally in the central position in front of the signer's chest. However, sign languages also include spatial modulations, when signs are produced in a non-neutral location, e.g. on the right or left from the signer. In developed sign languages, such spatial modulations convey deictic, locative or temporal information. In particular, one can use non-neutral locations to show that different actions were related to one and the same referent, e.g. the verbs in *he came, saw and conquered* describe actions of the same agent.

In the experiment, the signers watched a short cartoon and then signed the story to a peer. Their use of spatial modulation was videotaped and later analysed by the researchers. The hypothesis of the study is that shared reference modulations have been emerging as a grammatical device in the new generation of NSL signers. This is why shared reference modulations (per verb) are expected to be higher in the output of the second cohort signers. One can also expect differences depending on the age of exposure.

The imitation dataset is called `sharedref` and is available in `Rling`. The data frame contains 48 observations, which correspond to individual subjects. The first variable, *mod*, represents the average number of shared reference modulations per verb. The second variable, *age*, indicates the age when the signer joined the community. There were three age groups: 'early' (before 6 years and a half), 'middle' (between 6 years and a half and 10 years old), and 'late' (after 10). Finally, the variable *cohort* indicates which cohort each signer belongs to. Note that the variable is a factor, although its levels are represented by the numbers 1 and 2.

```
> data(sharedref)
> head(sharedref)
    mod     age    cohort
1   0.75    early  1
2   0.85    early  1
3   0.93    early  1
4   0.80    early  1
5   1.24    early  2
6   1.38    early  2
```

Since both predictors are between-group variables and there are no within-subject variables because every person was tested once, the appropriate choice is independent factorial ANOVA.

8.3.2   Descriptive statistics for different groups and interaction plot

One can compute average means of shared reference expressions in age group by cohort with the help of `aggregate()`:

```
> ref <- aggregate(mod ~ age + cohort, data = sharedref, FUN = mean)
> ref
    age      cohort   mod
1   early    1        0.8325
2   middle   1        0.6800
3   late     1        0.3700
4   early    2        1.3550
5   middle   2        1.2200
6   late     2        0.4400
```

The group means suggest that the earlier a signer joined the community, the higher the average frequency of shared reference expressions. In addition, the means of each age group in the second cohort are higher than the corresponding means in the first cohort. These results meet our expectations. However, it is difficult to say using the numbers alone whether there is an interaction between age and cohort. To investigate that, we will create an interaction plot:

```
> interaction.plot(ref$age, ref$cohort, ref$mod)
```

The result is shown in Figure 8.3. There is an interaction. Namely, the difference between the cohorts almost disappears for those who joined the community relatively late. Are the differences between the cohorts and age groups, as well as their interaction statistically significant? This is a question for factorial ANOVA.

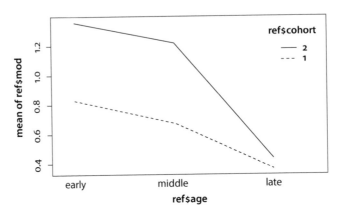

Figure 8.3. Interaction plot of use of shared reference expressions across age groups and cohorts of NSL

8.3.3   Assumptions of parametric factorial ANOVA

The assumptions of parametric factorial ANOVA are the same as those of one-way ANOVA (see Section 8.2.3). Since the design is balanced, one does not have to be very strict about the normality. However, it is useful to know how to perform the Shapiro test simultaneously on several groups created by cross-tabulated factors. Again, a convenient option is to use the function `aggregate()`:

```
> aggregate(mod ~ age + cohort, data = sharedref, function(x)
shapiro.test(x)$p.value)
    age      cohort   mod
1   early    1        0.305382517
2   middle   1        0.611790881
3   late     1        0.975408765
4   early    2        0.710437680
5   middle   2        0.424433620
6   late     2        0.002067517
```

The *p*-values in the last column are greater than 0.05, except for the last group (late learners, Cohort 2). However, ANOVA is quite robust with regard to some non-normality, especially if the design is balanced and the other assumptions are met.

To test the assumption of homogeneity of variance, one can use again the Fligner – Killeen median test, which is robust with regard to non-normal data:

```
> fligner.test(mod ~ interaction(age, cohort), data = sharedref)

    Fligner-Killeen test of homogeneity of variances

data: mod by interaction(age, cohort)
Fligner-Killeen:med chi-squared = 6.1292, df = 5, p-value =
0.2939
```

The Levene test, which was described in the previous case study, returns a similar result. Again, there are no indications that this assumption is violated, so we can move on to performing a parametric factorial ANOVA.

8.3.4 ANOVA and orthogonal contrasts

In order to evaluate the contribution of each variable and interaction term(s), one has to compute sums of squares, which are required for computing the F-score (see Section 8.2.4). There are different types of sums of squares: Type I, Type II, Type III and Type IV. The most important thing for this discussion is that Type III sums of squares evaluate all effects in the model taking into account all other effects in the model. This means that the effect of *age* will be evaluated after the effects of *cohort* and the interaction between *cohort* and *age*, and so on. Type III sums of squares are also the most reliable when the sample sizes are not equal.

Type III sums of squares can only be used when the predictors are coded with orthogonal contrasts. As the reader may remember from Chapter 7, there exist different contrasts: treatment, sum, Helmert, etc. For example, the default treatment contrasts involve comparison of all levels of a categorical variable with the reference level. What was not mentioned explicitly in the previous chapter, however, is the fact that all contrasts can be represented as numerical values, or weights. For example, if a binary variable has the treatment coding, the reference level by default has the weight of 0, and the other level has the weight of 1. The variable is then represented as the contrast, or dummy variable with the weights (0, 1). If there are three levels, then we have two dummy variables, or contrasts, with the weights (0, 1, 0) for the first contrast and (0, 0, 1) for the second contrast , and so on.

Contrasts are considered **orthogonal** if the products of their coefficients sum up to zero. For two levels, this can be done by coding one level as –1 and the other one as 1. The sum is –1 + 1 = 0. If a variable has three levels, the orthogonal contrasts can be (–2, 1, 1) and (0, –1, 1). The sum of products is –2 × 0 + 1 × (–1) + 1 × 1 = 0 – 1 + 1 = 0. For four levels, there are different options, e.g. (3, –1, –1, –1), (0, 2, –1, –1) and (0, 0, 1, –1). The sum of products is 3 × 0 × 0 + (–1) × 2 × 0 + (–1) × (–1) × 1 + (–1) × (–1) × (–1) = 0 + 0 + 1 – 1 = 0. See a summary in Table 8.1.

Now let us assign orthogonal contrasts to the factors. First, *age* with three levels can be represented by two contrasts with three weights in each:

```
> contrasts(sharedref$age) <- cbind(c(-2, 1, 1), c(0, -1, 1))
> sharedref$age
[output omitted]
attr(,"contrasts")
          [,1]  [,2]
early    -2    0
middle    1   -1
late      1    1
Levels: early middle late
```

Table 8.1 Orthogonal contrasts for factors with two, three and four levels

A factor with two levels

Group	Contrast weights	Product
1	−1	−1
2	1	1
Total	0	0

A factor with three levels

Group	Weights of Contrast 1	Weights of Contrast 2	Product
1	−2	0	0
2	1	−1	−1
3	1	1	1
Total	0	0	0

A factor with four levels

Group	Weights of Contrast1	Weights of Contrast 2	Weights of Contrast 3	Product
A	3	0	0	0
B	−1	2	0	0
C	−1	−1	1	1
D	−1	−1	−1	−1
Total	0	0	0	0

Orthogonal contrasts for *cohort*, which has two levels, look as follows (note that in this case the coding is identical with sum contrasts, except for the order of weights):

```
> contrasts(sharedref$cohort) <- c(-1, 1)
> sharedref$cohort
[output omitted]
attr(,"contrasts")
     [,1]
1   -1
2    1
Levels: 1 2
```

After these preparations, we can perform ANOVA with the help of aov(). The formula below specifies two main effects *age* and *cohort*, and their interaction. Alternatively, you can write mod ~ age + cohort + age:cohort.

```
> sharedref.aov <- aov(mod ~ age*cohort, data = sharedref)
```

Next, the ANOVA table based on Type III sums of squares can be obtained by using `Anova()` – mind the capital letter! – from the package `car`:

```
> Anova(sharedref.aov, type = "III")
Anova Table (Type III tests)

Response: mod
              Sum Sq   Df   F value    Pr(>F)
(Intercept)   31.981    1   7447.676   < 2.2e-16 ***
age            4.224    2    491.884   < 2.2e-16 ***
cohort         1.710    1    398.243   < 2.2e-16 ***
age:cohort     0.568    2     66.132   1.054e-13 ***
Residuals      0.180   42
--
Signif. codes: 0 '***' 0.001 '**' 0.01 '*' 0.05 '.' 0.1 ' ' 1
```

The p-values in the rightmost column show that both independent variables and the interaction term have highly significant effects.

8.3.5 Alternative tests

If some of the assumptions are not met, there are a few options:

- Similar to `oneway.test()` in one-way ANOVA, which provides a correction for heterogeneous variance, one can use White's adjustment for factorial ANOVA when the assumption of homogeneity of variance is violated. This option is available in `Anova()` in the package `car`, for example:

  ```
  > Anova(sharedref.aov, type = "III", white.adjust = TRUE)
  Analysis of Deviance Table (Type III tests)

  Response: mod
              Df   F          Pr(>F)
  (Intercept)  1   6516.716   < 2.2e-16 ***
  age          2    401.274   < 2.2e-16 ***
  cohort       1    348.463   < 2.2e-16 ***
  age:cohort   2     60.725   4.047e-13 ***
  Residuals   42
  --
  Signif. codes: 0 '***' 0.001 '**' 0.01 '*' 0.05 '.' 0.1 ' ' 1
  ```

- In all situations when the normality and homogeneity assumptions are violated, one can fit a linear regression model and perform bootstrap validation of the confidence intervals around the estimated coefficients (see Section 7.2.8 in Chapter 7).
- Again, if the observations are not independent, one should use repeated-measures or mixed ANOVA (see Section 8.4).

8.3.6 Post hoc tests

As in one-way ANOVA, one can use post hoc tests for factors with more than two levels to find out which groups are different and which are not. Although it is does not make much sense to perform post hoc tests on the main effects of a model in the presence of a significant interaction, we will demonstrate how one can compare the group means of *age*. For example, one could perform the Tukey Honest Significant Differences test of this predictor as follows:

```
> TukeyHSD(sharedref.aov, "age")
Tukey multiple comparisons of means
    95% family-wise confidence level

Fit: aov(formula = mod ~ age *cohort, data = sharedref)

$age
                diff        lwr        upr        p adj
middle-early    -0.14375    -0.2000365    -0.0874635    6e-07
late-early      -0.68875    -0.7450365    -0.6324635    0e+00
late-middle     -0.54500    -0.6012865    -0.4887135    0e+00
```

The confidence intervals and the adjusted *p*-values tell us that all differences between the age groups are significant. Of course, since the independent variable interacts with the other one, this example serves only as an illustration.

When reporting the results of a factorial ANOVA, it is convenient to summarize the data with the help of model.tables(). If you add type = "means", the function will return the means of the response for all groups and their intersections, including the grand mean for the entire dataset. By default, the function returns 'effects', or coefficients, which are more difficult to interpret. You can also compute standard errors for differences of means by adding se = TRUE.

```
> model.tables(sharedref.aov, type = "means")
Tables of means
Grand mean

0.81625

age
age
early middle late
1.0938 0.9500 0.4050

cohort
cohort
1       2
0.6275  1.0050

age:cohort
```

```
     cohort
        age      1   2
early   0.8325  1.3550
middle  0.6800  1.2200
late    0.3700  0.4400
```

To summarize, the case study has demonstrated that language can be created by sequences of child learners who are not exposed to a developed language. The second cohort of NSL signers did not reproduce the language; rather, it changed the language in the process, making it more grammaticized. The difference between the cohorts is present, however, only for children who joined the community relatively early (before the age of 10). These findings are important for our understanding of language dynamics in general, from transformation of pidgins into creoles, to different processes of slow incremental language change.

8.4 Do native English and native Mandarin Chinese speakers conceptualize time differently? Repeated-measures and mixed ANOVA (mixed GLM method)

8.4.1 The data and hypothesis

To reproduce the code from this case study, you will need several add-on packages, which should be installed and loaded.

```
> install.packages(c("gplots", "ggplot2", "nlme"))
> library(Rling); library(gplots); library(ggplot2); library(nlme)
```

This case study deals with metaphoric conceptualization of time. In English, as in many other languages, time is construed as FUTURE IS IN FRONT OF EGO and PAST IS IN BACK OF EGO, as in the examples *The exam is three weeks ahead* and *The worst is behind us*. In Aymara language, the pattern is reverse: the past is in front, and the future is behind. Consider the following expressions (examples from Núñez & Sweetser 2006):

(1) *nayra*   *mara*
     eye/sight/front year
     'last year'

(2) *qhipa*   *mara* -na
     back/behind   year   at
     'in the next year'

Aymara speakers also produce frontward gestures when they speak about the past and backward gestures when they speak about the future. Núñez & Sweetser (2006) argue that Aymara speakers conceptualize time in a static way. When one stands, the objects in front are visible and therefore known, and the objects behind are invisible and therefore unknown. The future is unknown and unseen, as if it were located behind the speaker.

The past is known and 'observable', so it is 'located' in front. In contrast, English and other Western languages use a dynamic mapping. When a person walks, the past is what is left behind and known, and the future is the unknown in front. However, in spite of these differences, both Aymara and English share the underlying metaphor KNOWLEDGE IS SEEING, which represents the future as unseen, and the past as seen.

Such observations rekindle the old debate about the hypothesis of linguistic relativity that goes back to Benjamin Whorf. Does language shape the way we think and, if yes, to what extent? Although only few linguists nowadays would support the original (strong) version of the hypothesis, according to which language fully determines thought, many researchers would agree with a weak version: language determines thinking because we get used to pay more attention to the distinctions coded in language, and less attention to other possible distinctions. Such differences are sociocultural, and are acquired gradually. Consider English and Korean. The languages exhibit substantial differences in the spatial domain. For instance, in Korean, containment events are subdivided into putting things into containers that fit tightly (*kkita*), e.g. putting a book in a book cover, and putting objects into containers that fit loosely (*nehta*), e.g. putting a book in a large box. Bowerman & Choi (2003) studied spatial distinctions made by English and Korean infants. In the prelinguistic stage, both English and Korean infants were sensitive to this distinction. However, this sensitivity diminishes over time, as children master their mother tongue. Trying to fit the expressions they hear to the referential situations they observe, they gradually acquire the relevant distinctions that are specific to their language, like the tight vs. loose fit distinction. Potentially, we are capable to make the distinctions that are not salient in our language, but we normally do not have to worry about them.

In this case study we will use simulation data to reproduce Boroditsky's (2001) findings with regard to conceptualization of time by native English and native Chinese speakers. Boroditsky used a priming experiment to test if conceptualization of time depends on mother tongue. As was mentioned above, English has predominantly horizontal conceptualization of time, where the past is behind, and the future is in front. In Mandarin Chinese, however, the dominant metaphor seems to be vertical: future events are *xià* 'down' and past events are *shàng* 'up'. An experiment showed that native English speakers processed time expressions faster when they were primed by a horizontal array of objects, whereas native Chinese speakers processed time expressions in English faster when the primes contained vertically arranged objects.

The dataset, which contains simulation data of Boroditsky's experiment, is called time_exper. It can be found in the package Rling. There are four variables: the subject ID, language (English or Chinese), type of prime (horizontal or vertical) and reaction times in milliseconds:

```
> data(time_exper)
> str(time_exper)
'data.frame': 200 obs. of 4 variables:
```

```
$ Subj: Factor w/ 20 levels "1","2","3","4",..: 1 1 1 1 1 1 1 1 1 1 …
$ Lang: Factor w/ 2 levels "CH","EN": 1 1 1 1 1 1 1 1 1 1 …
$ Prime: Factor w/ 2 levels "Horiz","Vert": 1 1 2 1 2 1 2 1 2 2 …
$ rt: num 3221 2079 1940 2655 1913 …
```

The question is whether there is difference between native English and native Mandarin speakers in their reaction times depending on the type of prime. One can expect native English speakers to react to a stimulus (an English non-metaphoric time expression) faster after horizontal primes, and native Mandarin speakers to react faster after vertical primes. However, we should also take into consideration that the observations in the dataset are not independent. Each subject participated in ten trials and gave ten responses. This situation is common in experimental studies because it would be impractical to collect only one observation per subject. As a result, reaction times may be influenced by speakers' individual characteristics. Some subjects may be faster to respond to the stimuli, and some may be slower. This study is thus an example of mixed design, with *Lang* as a between-group variable, and *Prime* as a within-subject variable nested within the *Subj* factor. In other words, scores for the type of prime can be found within each subject.

Individual variation between the subjects can be examined with the help of a box plot with different colours. Since the first ten subjects are Mandarin Chinese speakers, and the last ten are English speakers, we can use the following code:

```
> boxplot(rt ~ Subj, data = time_exper, xlab = "Subjects", ylab =
"Reaction times, in ms", col = c(rep("grey", 10), rep("white", 10)))
> legend("topright", c("Chinese", "English"), fill = c("grey", "white"))
```

The resulting plot is displayed in Figure 8.4. One can see that there is substantial individual variation among the native speakers of each language. Will the independent variables and their interaction be still significant after this individual variation has been taken into account? To answer this question, one needs to perform a mixed ANOVA.

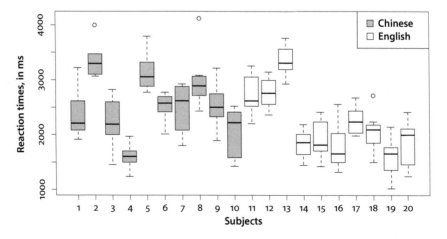

Fugure 8.4. Box plot with different colours representing different groups

How to make a box plot with different colours for different groups with `ggplot2`

The code below allows one to reproduce the plot in Figure 8.4a.

```
> ggplot(time_exper, aes(x = Subj, y = rt, fill = Lang)) + geom_
boxplot() + labs(x = "Subjects", y = "Reaction times, in ms") +
scale_fill_grey(start = 0.5, end = 1)
```

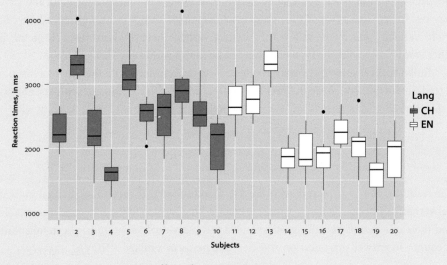

Figure 8.4a. A `ggplot2` version of box plot in Figure 8.4

8.4.2 Fitting a mixed ANOVA with the help of mixed GLM

The method that will be introduced below is essentially the same for repeated-measures and mixed designs. It involves mixed Generalized Linear Models (GLM), which are often called mixed models. The main characteristic of these models is that they contain both **fixed** effects and **random** effects. Fixed effects are 'normal' explanatory variables, whose effect should be measured. Random effects are sampled randomly from the population, for example, individuals in an experiment, lexical stimuli in a lexical decision task, etc. In a way, this is 'noise' that should be filtered out.

Mixed GLM models are superior to the traditional repeated-measures and mixed ANOVA approaches. One of the main advantages is the fact that mixed models, unlike ANOVA, do not require that all measurements should be present for all subjects. One does not have to discard all measurements related to one subject if one value is missing. In experimental research, this represents a serious advantage. Second, mixed models are part of a larger framework, which provides numerous other extensions based on the same principles, such as non-linear mixed models, complex multilevel models with several hierarchical levels, etc. Finally, mixed models, unlike repeated-measures and mixed ANOVA, do not require the assumption of sphericity to be met, which may be a challenging task (cf. Field et al. 2012: 551–554).

In this case study we will use the function `lme()` from the package `nlme`. To add a random effect, one should specify `random = ~1|YourRandomEffect`. Such effects are called **random intercepts**. This means that individual adjustments are made to the intercept for each individual (subject, stimulus, place where the experiment was performed, and other randomly selected items). Such individual adjustments are also called Best Linear Unbiased Predictors (BLUPs). In mixed ANOVA, one has to specify both the subjects and the nested variable: `random = ~1|Subj/Prime`. Another type of random effects is **random slopes**, which are added when the effect of one or more predictors varies across the individuals. Random slopes are not discussed here, but see numerous examples in Baayen (2008: Ch. 7).

This section introduces the procedure which was proposed in Field et al. (2012) for both repeated-measures and mixed designs. First, one fits a baseline model with the intercept only, which contains no predictors. The baseline model can be fit as follows:

```
> m0 <- lme(rt ~ 1, random = ~ 1|Subj/Prime, data = time_exper,
method = "ML")
```

It is important to remember is that there are two available methods of fitting a mixed model, maximum likelihood (ML) and restricted maximum likelihood (REML). When one wants to compare different models with different number of parameters, as will be demonstrated below, it is recommended to use maximum likelihood estimation. The default method is REML, so it is necessary to add `method = "ML"`.[1]

Next, we add more and more parameters and compare the models with the help of ANOVA. For example, the following code can be used to add *Lang*:

```
> m1 <- lme(rt ~ Lang, random = ~ 1|Subj/Prime, data = time_exper,
method = "ML")
```

---

1.   The ML method of estimation is also considered preferable when one is more interested in obtaining accurate estimates of fixed effect parameters than in estimation of random variation (Field et al. 2012: 879).

However, it is more convenient to use the function `update()` for adding new parameters to the model, including the interaction term:

```
> m1 <- update(m0,.~. + Lang)
> m2 <- update(m1,.~. + Prime)
> m3 <- update(m2,.~. + Lang:Prime)
```

Finally, ANOVA can be used to establish which terms have been useful when added sequentially:

```
> anova(m0, m1, m2, m3)
     Model df AIC      BIC      logLik    Test    L.Ratio    p-value
m0   1     4  2967.152 2980.346 -1479.576
m1   2     5  2967.434 2983.926 -1478.717 1 vs 2  1.717997   0.1900
m2   3     6  2968.936 2988.726 -1478.468 2 vs 3  0.498424   0.4802
m3   4     7  2945.424 2968.512 -1465.712 3 vs 4  25.512348  <.0001
```

The p-values are based on the difference in the log-likelihoods (`L.Ratio`) in the adjacent models. The log-likelihoods are shown in the column `logLik` (more exactly, each log-likelihood value is multiplied by –2). Other useful statistics are AIC (Akaike Information Criterion) and BIC (Bayesian Information Criterion). As the reader may remember from Chapter 7, AIC is a goodness-of-fit measure for comparison of models with different number of parameters. It penalizes a model for having too many predictors. BIC is similar to AIC, but it is considered to be more efficient when the sample is large and the number of parameters is small (Field et al. 2012: 868). The smaller AIC and BIC, the better. Interestingly, neither the language (`m1`) nor the type of prime (`m2`) brought a significant improvement individually. However, their interaction in the final model is highly significant, as can be seen from a very low p-value.

The final model with all predictors and the interactions looks as follows:

```
> summary(m3)
Linear mixed-effects model fit by maximum likelihood
Data: time_exper
AIC        BIC        logLik
2945.424   2968.512   -1465.712

Random effects:
Formula: ~1 | Subj
        (Intercept)
StdDev: 496.187

Formula: ~1 | Prime %in% Subj
        (Intercept) Residual
StdDev: 0.0297535 313.0908
```

```
Fixed effects: rt ~ Lang *Prime
                    Value    Std.Error  DF   t-value    p-value
(Intercept)         2674.48  164.69104  160  16.239378  0.0000
LangEN              -568.20  232.90830  18   -2.439587  0.0253
PrimeVert           -313.54  63.25390   18   -4.956849  0.0001
LangEN:PrimeVert    530.26   89.45452   18   5.927705   0.0000
Correlation:
               (Intr)   LangEN   PrmVrt
LangEN         -0.707
PrimeVert      -0.192   0.136
LangEN:PrimeVert 0.136  -0.192   -0.707

Standardized Within-Group Residuals:
Min           Q1            Med          Q3           Max
-2.06200493   -0.67236516   0.01431141   0.62678708   3.28816200

Number of Observations: 200
Number of Groups:
    Subj Prime    %in% Subj
    20            40
```

The summary shows that all coefficients in the model are significant, although we have just seen that the individual contributions of *Lang* and *Prime* added sequentially were not significant. There is a simple explanation. As you may remember from Chapter 7, in the presence of an interaction, the interacting terms shown in the table are no longer main effects. They represent the estimates for the combinations of the specified level with the reference level of the interacting variable (note that we use the default treatment contrasts). The coefficient of LangEN thus shows the difference between the reaction times of the English native speakers and those of the Chinese native speakers after a horizontal prime (the reference level). This difference is significant. Similarly, the coefficient of PrimeVertical represents the significant difference between the reaction times after the vertical and horizontal primes, but only for the native speakers of Chinese.

To obtain the 95% confidence intervals of the coefficients, one can use intervals() from the package nlme. It also returns the confidence intervals of the standard deviations of the random effects provided in the summary above.

```
> intervals(m3) # equivalent to intervals(…, level = 0.95)
Approximate 95% confidence intervals

Fixed effects:
                    lower       est.     upper
(Intercept)         2352.5003   2674.48  2996.45968
LangEN              -1052.6042  -568.20  -83.79575
PrimeVert           -445.0959   -313.54  -181.98412
LangEN:PrimeVert    344.2119    530.26   716.30811
```

```
attr(,"label")
[1] "Fixed effects:"

Random Effects:
Level: Subj
                   lower      est.       upper
sd((Intercept))   359.492   496.187   684.8597
Level: Prime
                   lower          est.          upper
sd((Intercept))   2.997266e-21   0.0297535   2.953595e+17
Within-group standard error:
lower       est.        upper
282.3632   313.0908   347.1623
```

8.4.3   Post hoc tests

One normally does not perform traditional post hoc tests when fitting a GLM. Instead, one can use the estimates in the model and their confidence intervals to see which group means are different. Of course, if a factor has more than two levels, one cannot estimate the differences between all pairs of values. In that case, one can use planned contrasts, as shown in Field et al. (2012: 617–618) to focus only on the comparisons that are theoretically relevant. Needless to say, it does not make sense to report the global differences between the group means in the presence of a significant interaction, as in this case.

8.5   Summary

This chapter has introduced one-way, two-way (factorial), as well as repeated-measures and mixed ANOVAs. One-way ANOVA is used to compare the means of three and more groups. It can be regarded as an extension of the *t*-test. Factorial ANOVA measures the effect of two and more categorical variables on the response, as well as their possible interactions. Finally, repeated-measures and mixed ANOVAs are used for the same purposes as one-way and factorial ANOVA in the situations when the assumption of independence is not met and the model contains within-subject variables. Note that you can use linear regression, which was described in Chapter 7, to carry out independent one-way and factorial ANOVA, as well.

Writing up the results of ANOVA

When reporting the results of a one-way ANOVA with independent observations, one has to report the F-ratio, the degrees of freedom and the corresponding p-value. For example, you could write: "We observe a significant effect of cohort in our model, $F(2, 24) = 53.47$, $p < 0.001$". Note that the second number of the degrees of freedom (24) comes from the residual component of variance (see the last line of the `aov()` or `Anova()` output). In case of independent factorial ANOVA, you should describe all effects in the model, including the interaction, e.g. for *age* in the factorial ANOVA, the numbers would look as follows: $F(2, 18) = 214.353$, $p < 0.001$.

The results of a post hoc test should be reported, as well. It is crucial to be very specific about the type of the post hoc test and report the p-value and the difference d (if available), as well as the mean and the standard deviation (or standard error) for each group compared. For example, one can write about the one-way ANOVA case study: "the second cohort of the NSL users ($M = 0.756$, $SD = 0.09$) produced significantly more separate expressions of manner and path than the first cohort ($M = 0.273$, $SD = 0.137$), $d = 0.482$, $p < 0.001$, according to the post hoc Tukey Honest Significant Differences test".

Reporting the results of repeated-measurements or mixed ANOVA, which was fitted with the help of `lme()`, one should mention the statistic from the `L.ratio` column, which is distributed like the χ^2 statistic, the degrees of freedom and the p-value. For example, one could write, "We found a significant interaction of language and the type of prime, $\chi^2(1) = 25.5$, $p < 0.001$". The number of degrees of freedom is 1, which can be computed as a product of the degrees of freedom of each interacting factor minus one: $(2 - 1) \times (2 - 1) = 1$.

More on ANOVA

There exist many other varieties of ANOVA, e.g. analysis of covariance (ANCOVA), when a model contains one or more quantitative variables, which are called covariates. Another member of the ANOVA family is MANOVA, multivariate analysis of variance, which can deal with several response variables, for example, in a situation when experimental subjects are administered different tests of language proficiency after experimental training. A combination of ANCOVA and MANOVA is called MANCOVA. A well-known method of performing one-way repeated-measures ANOVA is Friedman's test (see `?friedman.test` for more details). A discussion of all these methods is far beyond the scope of this introductory textbook. If you would like to learn more about mixed models, see numerous linguistic examples in Chapter 7 of Baayen (2008). To incorporate crossed (non-nested) random effects (e.g. subjects and items) in repeated-measures and mixed ANOVA, check the package `lme4`.

CHAPTER 9

Measuring associations between two categorical variables
Conceptual metaphors and tests of independence

What you will learn from this chapter:

> This chapter focuses on associations between two categorical variables. You will learn how to measure the association strength using odds ratios, Cramér's V and the φ-coefficient. You will also learn how to test whether the association is statistically significant with the help of the χ^2-test and the Fisher exact test. Bar plots, mosaic plots and association plots are used as visualization tools for cross-tabulated data. All these concepts and tools will be illustrated by case studies of metaphoric and non-metaphoric uses of the preposition *over* and the verb *see* in different registers.

9.1 Testing independence

Imagine you want to compare frequencies of two near synonymous constructions in two language varieties. An example might be constructions *going to* + V and *will* + V that express the future, and the British and American varieties of English. The frequencies are obtained from two comparable corpora. In this case, you will have four frequencies:

- *a*: frequency of construction *X* in variety *A*;
- *b*: frequency of construction *Y* in variety *A*;
- *c*: frequency of construction *X* in variety *B*;
- *d*: frequency of construction *Y* in variety *B*.

It is common to represent these frequencies in a table, as shown in Table 9.1. Such tables, which cross-tabulate the levels of two or more categorical variables, are called **contingency tables**. They play a very important role in analysis of categorical data.

Table 9.1 A contingency table

	Variety A	Variety B	Total
Construction X	a	c	a + c
Construction Y	b	d	b + d
Total	a + b	c + d	a + b + c + d

The rows represent one binary variable, which can be called *Construction*. The columns represent another binary variable, which describes the language variety. The row and column totals are called **marginal frequencies**. The question is whether the variables *Variety* and *Construction* are **independent** or **dependent** (**associated**). In other words, is the use of construction X and construction Y independent from the language variety? Or does variety A 'prefer' construction X over construction Y more strongly than variety B, or vice versa?

In this chapter, we will consider the most popular test of independence, the χ^2 ('chi-square', or 'chi-squared') test, as well as the Fisher exact test. The latter is more appropriate when the frequencies are low (see more details in the additional information box in Section 9.2.3). While these well-known tests can tell us if the association is statistically significant, one should also measure the effect size. The effect size measures for categorical variables, such as the odds ratio, Cramér's *V* and the ϕ-coefficient, indicate the strength of association. These measures are analogous to the correlation coefficient, which measures the strength of correlation between two quantitative variables (see Chapter 6). As in correlation analysis, it is important to distinguish between effect size and statistical significance and report both.

9.2 The story of *over* is not over: Metaphoric and non-metaphoric uses in two registers (analysis of a 2-by-2 contingency table)

9.2.1 The data and hypothesis

To be able to reproduce the code in this case study, make sure that you have the following packages installed:

```
> install.packages(c("ggplot2", "reshape", "vcd"))
```

These packages should also be loaded in the beginning of your R session:

```
> library(ggplot2); library(reshape); library(vcd)
```

The case studies in this chapter focus on metaphoric and non-metaphoric uses of words in different registers. In their seminal work, *Metaphors we live by*, Lakoff and Johnson (1980) made a very significant contribution to our understanding how metaphors organize the conceptual system and shape up the language. In metaphors, we normally map a more embodied, concrete source domain onto a more abstract, less directly accessible target domain. For instance, the basic image schemata UP and DOWN are frequently used to speak about emotions (*That boosted my spirits* vs. *I'm feeling down*), quantity (*The prices soar* vs. *The prices plummet*), social status (*She's made it to the top* vs. *He's an underdog*), morality (*She's got high standards* vs. *This is a low thing to do*), etc. (Lakoff & Johnson 1980).

Another influential work in Cognitive Linguistics was Brugman's (1988 [1981]) study of *over*, where she showed, among other things, how more abstract meanings of the preposition, such as *agonize over a problem* and *take over the responsibilities*, emerge as metaphorical extensions from the more physical ones, e.g. *fly over a city* or *walk over a field*. This case study will investigate how the metaphorical and non-metaphorical meanings of *over* are distributed in the academic and spoken registers of English. The data for this study come from the VU Amsterdam Metaphor Corpus (Steen et al. 2010).[1] This is a small (190,000 words at the moment of writing) corpus that represents four registers of British English: academic texts, conversations, fiction and news. The corpus has been manually annotated by several researchers for metaphoric use according to a metaphor identification protocol and has an online search interface.

Measuring (dis)agreement: Cohen's κ

When one has to decide whether a word in a corpus is used metaphorically or not, or to perform any other kind of semantic annotation, it is useful to collect opinions of different annotators and check if they tend to agree or disagree. A well-known measure of inter-rater agreement is Cohen's κ ('kappa'). It is based on the observed proportions of inter-rater agreement and disagreement compared to the expected proportions. The expected values are used in order to take into account possible biases towards some answers. To compute Cohen's κ for two vectors `Rater1` and `Rater 2`, which contain imaginary raters' scores, one can use the function `ckappa()` in the `psy` package:

```
> install.packages("psy")
> library(psy)
> ckappa(cbind(Rater1, Rater2)) # do not run; only provided as
an example
```

For more than two raters, you can use the `lkappa()` function in the same package:

```
> lkappa(cbind(Rater1, Rater2, Rater3)) #do not run
```

Similar to correlation coefficients, the scores range from to –1 (complete disagreement) to 1 (full agreement).

---

1.   Available online at http://www2.let.vu.nl/oz/metaphorlab/metcor/search/index.html (last access 11.06.2015).

The hypothesis of this case study is that the subcorpora with spoken data and academic prose have different distributions of metaphorical and non-metaphorical uses of the preposition. The four corresponding numbers, which are shown in Table 9.2, were obtained by using the online interface. Rare ambiguous cases were discarded.

Table 9.2 Frequencies of metaphoric and non-metaphoric uses of *over* in academic and conversational registers of the VU Amsterdam Metaphor Corpus

	Academic	*Conversations*
Metaphoric use	22	5
Non-metaphoric use	4	12

To create a similar contingency table in R, you can use the `cbind()` command, which can create a matrix from two or more vectors joined as columns:

```
> over <- cbind(c(22, 4), c(5, 12))
> over
       [,1]  [,2]
[1,]   22    5
[2,]   4     12
```

Alternatively, you can use `rbind()`, which combines vectors as rows:

```
> over <- rbind(c(22, 5), c(4, 12))
```

Next, the names of the rows and columns are added:

```
> rownames(over) <- c("met", "nonmet")
> colnames(over) <- c("acad", "conv")
```

The result looks as follows:

```
> over
         acad   conv
met       22     5
nonmet    4     12
```

How to cross-tabulate data in two (or more) factors

In this example, the four frequencies in the contingency table were already available. However, in many cases you will need to cross-tabulate the levels in two (or more) factors. To demonstrate how this can be done, let us create two factors, `f1` and `f2`:

```
> f1 <- factor(c(rep("A", 10), rep("B", 20)))
> f1
[1] A A A A A A A A A A B B B B B B B B B B B B B B B B B B B B
Levels: A B
> f2 <- factor(c(rep("X", 15), rep("Y", 15)))
> f2
[1] X X X X X X X X X X X X X X X Y Y Y Y Y Y Y Y Y Y Y Y Y Y Y
Levels: X Y
```

The first option is to use the familiar `table()` function:

```
> yourTable <- table(f1, f2)
> yourTable
      f2
f1    X    Y
A     10   0
B     5    15
```

Alternatively, you can use `xtabs()` with the formula interface. Note that the place of the response variable on the left of the tilde sign is empty:

```
> yourTable <- xtabs(~ f1 + f2)
> yourTable
      f2
f1    X    Y
A     10   0
B     5    15
```

9.2.2 Visualizations, proportions and measures of effect size: Odds ratios, Cramér's V and the φ-coefficient

It is always instructive to begin with visual inspection of the data. There are many ways of visualizing counts for two or more categories. One of the most popular options is the bar plot, which shows the numbers in columns as bars of different heights. We discussed how one can create a bar plot for a one-dimensional table of counts in Chapter 4. A bar plot that represents a two-dimensional table can be created easily as follows:

```
> barplot(over, col = c("grey20", "grey80"), main = "Bar plot
of (non-)metaphoric uses of over", xlab = "Register", ylab =
"Frequency")
> legend("topright", fill = c("grey20", "grey80"), c("metaphoric",
"non-metaphoric"))
```

The result is displayed in Figure 9.1. The plot shows clearly that the proportion of metaphoric uses is greater in the academic register than in the spoken data.

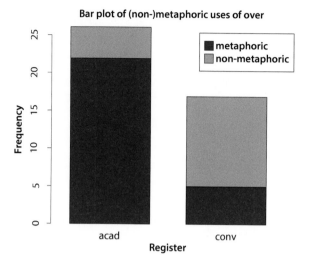

Figure 9.1. Bar plot of metaphoric and non-metaphoric uses of *over* with stacked bars

How to create a bar plot based on a contingency table with the help of `ggplot2`

First, you need to transform your contingency table into a data frame with two factors that specify the register and (non-)metaphoricity, and the third column that contains the counts of all combinations of the first two factors. For this purpose, you can use the function `melt()` from the package `reshape`.

```
> over.df <- melt(over)
> colnames(over.df) <- c("Metaphoricity", "Register", "Frequency")
> over.df
  Metaphoricity  Register  Frequency
1 met            acad      22
2 nonmet         acad      4
3 met            conv      5
4 nonmet         conv      12
```

Now we can create a bar plot of counts with stacked bars shown in Figure 9.1a:

```
> ggplot(over.df, aes(x = Register, y = Frequency, fill =
Metaphoricity)) + geom_bar(stat = "identity", colour = "black")
+ scale_fill_grey()
```

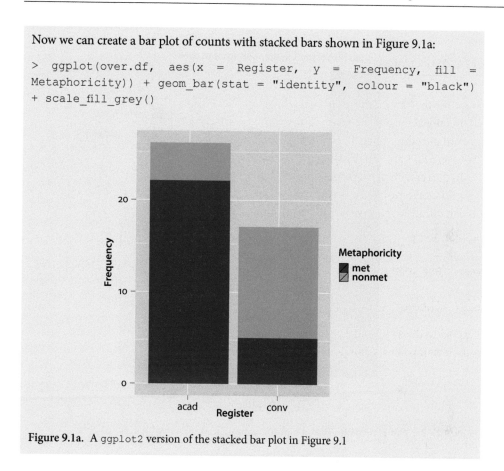

Figure 9.1a. A `ggplot2` version of the stacked bar plot in Figure 9.1

The bars that represent the metaphoric and non-metaphoric uses are stacked. Another option is to create a bar plot where these bars are placed next to one another. To do so, simply add the argument `beside = TRUE`. The result is shown in Figure 9.2.

```
> barplot(over, beside = TRUE, col = c("grey20", "grey80"), main
= "Bar plot of (non-)metaphoric uses of over", xlab = "Register",
ylab = "Frequency")
> legend("topright", fill=c("grey20", "grey80"), c("metaphoric",
"non-metaphoric"))
```

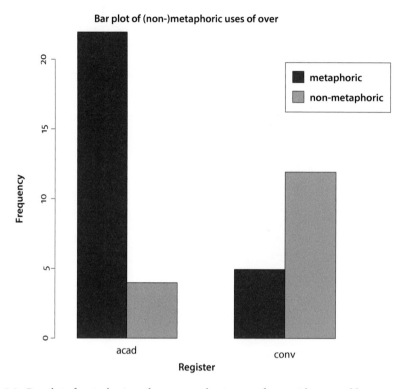

Figure 9.2. Bar plot of metaphoric and non-metaphoric uses of *over* with grouped bars

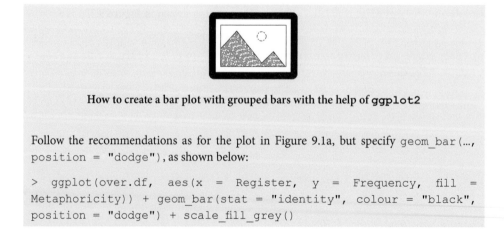

How to create a bar plot with grouped bars with the help of **ggplot2**

Follow the recommendations as for the plot in Figure 9.1a, but specify `geom_bar(...,` `position = "dodge")`, as shown below:

```
> ggplot(over.df, aes(x = Register, y = Frequency, fill =
Metaphoricity)) + geom_bar(stat = "identity", colour = "black",
position = "dodge") + scale_fill_grey()
```

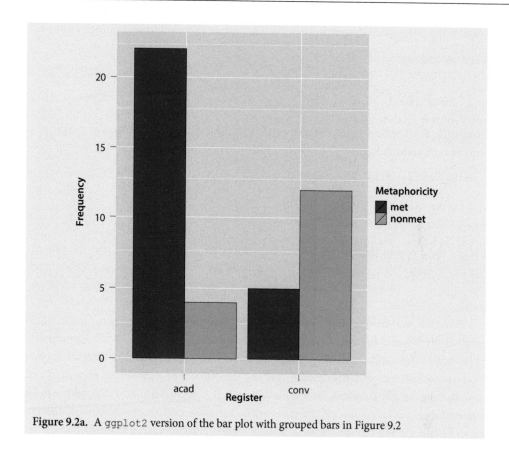

Figure 9.2a. A `ggplot2` version of the bar plot with grouped bars in Figure 9.2

It could be useful to count the proportions of metaphoric and non-metaphoric uses instead of representing the raw frequencies. Chapter 4 showed how one can transform a vector of frequencies into proportions with the help of `prop.table()`. For two-dimensional tables, there exist several opportunities:

- It is possible to compute proportions of the total number of observations in the table (the sum of all cells in the table is regarded as 1). This is the default option;
- One can also compute proportions of each cell in a row (for every row, the sum of cells is 1). To do so, add '1';
- A third option is to compute proportions of every cell in a column (for every column, the sum of cells is 1). To use this option, add '2'.

The first (default) option yields the following table:

```
> prop.table(over)
           acad         conv
met      0.51162791   0.1162791
nonmet   0.09302326   0.2790698
```

Below is the outcome of the second option. The sum of the proportions in each row is 1.

```
> prop.table(over, 1)
           acad         conv
met      0.8148148   0.1851852
nonmet   0.2500000   0.7500000
```

Finally, the third option yields the proportions shown below. Now the sum of the proportions in each column is 1.

```
> prop.table(over, 2)
           acad         conv
met      0.8461538   0.2941176
nonmet   0.1538462   0.7058824
```

It is the third option that we are particularly interested in. One can see that the proportion of the metaphoric uses of *over* in the academic register (almost 0.85, or 85%) is much greater than the proportion of metaphoric uses in the conversational register (approximately 0.29, or 29%).

Thus, the proportions are clearly different. But how big is this difference? In statistical terminology, what is the effect size? The simplest measure of effect size for contingency tables is the **odds ratio**. It is a simple ratio of odds. As was mentioned in Chapter 4, odds are the ratio that compares the chances of X and the chances of Y (or simply non-X). If two outcomes are equally frequent, their odds will be 1. If X is greater than Y, the odds will be greater than 1. If X is less than Y, the odds will be less than 1. What are the odds of observing a metaphoric use of *over* versus a non-metaphoric use in each given register? Let us begin with the academic subcorpus:

```
> 22/4
[1] 5.5
```

The odds are greater than 1. The odds of metaphoric vs. non-metaphoric uses of *over* in the conversational register are smaller than one:

```
> 5/12
[1] 0.4166667
```

To compute the odds ratio (OR), one should divide the first odds by the second odds:

$$OR = \frac{Odds1}{Odds2}$$

```
> (22/4)/(5/12)
[1] 13.2
```

An odds ratio greater than 1 means that the first odds are greater than the second odds. If an odds ratio is less than 1, then the first odds are less than the second odds. In our case, the odds ratio is 13.2. That means that the odds of the metaphoric uses of *over* in the academic register are 13.2 times greater than those in the conversational register.

Some other measures of effect size are Cramér's *V* and the ϕ ('phi') coefficient, which are identical for 2-by-2 tables. To compute them, one can use the `assocstats()` function in the `vcd` package:

```
> assocstats(over)
      X^2 df  P(> X^2)
Likelihood Ratio 13.843 1 0.00019871
Pearson 13.407 1 0.00025064

Phi-Coefficient    : 0.558
Contingency Coeff. :0.488
Cramer's V         : 0.558
```

For 2-by-2 tables, the absolute values of the ϕ-coefficient and Cramér's *V* range from 0 (no association) to 1 (perfect association). Some statisticians suggest the following guidelines for interpretation of effect size: $0.1 \leq \phi < 0.3$ indicates small effect size; $0.3 \leq \phi < 0.5$ shows a moderate effect; $\phi \geq 0.5$ indicates a strong effect (Sheskin 2011: 535). The value 0.558 shows a strong association. The third score is the Pearson contingency coefficient, but it is less widely used than the other two.

For illustration, let us consider an example of a very strong association. If the proportion of metaphoric uses of *over* were very high in the academic register, and there were very few in the conversational register, the coefficients would be close to 1. That is, if one takes a table `test` with the following values:

```
> test # do not run
      [,1]    [,2]
[1,]   99     1
[2,]   1      99
```

and computes the coefficients, the latter would be very close to the maximum value:

```
> assocstats(test) # do not run
                  X^2 df P(> X^2)
Likelihood Ratio 254.86 1  0
Pearson              192.08 1   0

Phi-Coefficient    : 0.98
Contingency Coeff. :0.7
Cramer's V         : 0.98
```

The main advantage of the ϕ-coefficient or Cramér's *V* in comparison with the OR is that they give an idea of association strength within the range from 0 to 1 (at least, for 2-by-2 tables). However, the OR shows the direction of association. That is, if an OR is greater than 1, the first odds are greater than the second ones, and if an OR is less than 1, the first odds are smaller than the second ones. Unfortunately, the ϕ-coefficient in `assocstats()` ignores this information. That is, if you swap the columns, the results will be the same, although the direction of association will change:

```
> over1 <- over[, c(2,1)]
> over1
          conv  acad
met        5     22
nonmet     12    4

> assocstats(over1)
                      X^2 df        P(> X^2)
Likelihood Ratio      13.843        1 0.00019871
Pearson               13.407        1 0.00025064

Phi-Coefficient    : 0.558
Contingency Coeff. :0.488
Cramer's V         : 0.558
```

The OR will be, however, different:

```
> (5/12)/(22/4)
[1] 0.07575758
```

In fact, the new OR is the inverse of the old value:

```
> 1/13.2
[1] 0.07575758
```

If you want to use the ϕ-coefficient and retain the information about the direction of association, you can add a minus sign to the coefficient in case the odds ratio is smaller than 1. Negative values of Cramér's V, however, are not reported. This measure is used predominantly for larger than 2-by-2 tables, where the direction of association is not specified.

9.2.3   Testing statistical significance: The χ^2-test of independence

The previous analyses show clearly that the proportion of metaphoric uses of *over* is much greater in the academic register, but is the difference statistically significant? To answer this question, we will carry out the χ^2-test. The null hypothesis of the test is that there is no association between the variables, i.e. between the rows and columns in the contingency table. In other words, the event "an observation is in row i" is independent of the event that the same observation is in column j (Conover 1999: 205). This is why the χ^2-test is regarded as a test of independence.

The χ^2-test is based on the comparison of **observed** and **expected frequencies**. Observed frequencies are the frequencies that you observe in the data, i.e. the actual numbers in the table. Expected frequencies are the frequencies that one can expect if the variables are independent, that is, if the null hypothesis were true and there were no differences in the proportions of metaphoric and non-metaphoric uses of the preposition in the two registers. The generic formula for computing the expected frequency in row i and column j is as follows:

$$E_{ij} = \frac{S_i \, S_j}{n}$$

where S_i is the marginal frequency of row i, S_j is the marginal frequency of column j and n is the total number of observations. For example, the expected frequency of metaphoric uses of *over* in the academic register can be computed as follows:

```
> ((22 + 4)*(22 + 5))/(22 + 4 + 5 + 12)
[1] 16.32558
```

A more convenient way to retrieve all expected frequencies in a contingency table is as follows:

```
> chisq.test(over)$expected
           acad          conv
met    16.325581    10.674419
nonmet  9.674419     6.325581
```

If one transforms the expected frequencies to a table of proportions of metaphoric and non-metaphoric uses in both registers, the proportions in both registers will be equal:

```
> prop.table(chisq.test(over)$expected, 2)
          acad       conv
met    0.627907   0.627907
nonmet 0.372093   0.372093
```

Similarly, it is possible to make another table of proportions, with 1 as the sum for each row (recall that one has to use '1' instead of '2'). The proportions of the registers in the total number of metaphoric uses of the preposition are then identical to those in the total number of non-metaphoric uses, since the proportions in each row are the same:

```
> prop.table(chisq.test(over)$expected, 1)
           acad          conv
met    0.6046512    0.3953488
nonmet 0.6046512    0.3953488
```

To summarize, the expected values are the values that one could observe if there were no difference in the proportions between rows and no difference in the proportions between columns, in accordance with the null hypothesis. The expected values are influenced only by the marginal frequencies of non-metaphoric and metaphoric uses of *over* in the two registers taken together, on the one hand, and by the marginal frequencies of *over* in each register, on the other hand.

There exist only two assumptions of the χ^2-test that should be met:

- The sample is randomly selected from the population of interest and the observations are independent.
- Every observation can be classified into exactly one category according to the criterion represented by each variable (Conover 1999: 204–205).

There are no reasons to suspect that the assumptions are violated.[2] The function for performing the test is chisq.test().[3] Its use is straightforward:

```
> chisq.test(over) #equivalent to chisq.test(…, correct = TRUE)

        Pearson's Chi-squared test with Yates' continuity correction

data: over
X-squared = 11.1487, df = 1, p-value = 0.0008409
```

As in all previous tests, the *p*-value below the level of significance, which is conventionally 0.05, allows one to discard the null hypothesis of no association. Note that due to some conceptual reasons one cannot choose between a one-tailed and two-tailed versions of the test.[4] The alternative hypothesis is always bidirectional, saying that the variables are associated, without specifying the direction of this association.

The bottom row also contains two other important statistics: the X-squared (the main statistic), and df (degrees of freedom). The χ^2-statistic is the sum of all squared deviations of the observed values in the table from the corresponding expected values divided by the expected values:

$$\chi^2 = \sum_{i=1}^{r} \sum_{j=1}^{c} \frac{\left(O_{ij} - E_{ij}\right)^2}{E_{ij}}$$

where O_{ij} is the observed frequency in a table cell and E_{ij} is the expected frequency for that cell. The deviations are squared in order to get rid of the minus sign if the observed frequency

---

2. It may happen that several occurrences of the preposition come from a text written by the same author. In that case, the corresponding observations would be dependent. However, this assumption is often relaxed in corpus linguistics (e.g. in collostructional analysis).

3. By default, the algorithm uses Yates' continuity correction. There is a lot of controversy about it in the statistical literature. One can run the test without the correction by adding correct = FALSE. In practice, this will not result in much difference.

4. Although there are ways of testing a directional hypothesis in case of 2-by-2 tables (e.g. Gries [2013: 171–172] recommends simply dividing the resulting *p*-value by two), this is seldom done in practice and may create an impression of trying to obtain a significant result at all costs.

is smaller than the expected frequency. This also gives more weight to large deviations. The larger the sum of differences between the observed and expected frequencies, the greater the χ^2-statistic. In addition to the test statistic, the result of the test also depends on the size of the table. The more cells, the higher the chance of finding divergences. This is taken into account in the notion of degrees of freedom, which was introduced in Chapter 1. To calculate the number of degrees of freedom for a contingency table, one should subtract 1 from the number of rows and the number of columns and multiply the results. In the case of a 2-by-2 table, the number of degrees of freedom is determined as follows: $(2 - 1) \times (2 - 1) = 1$. The p-values, as usual, are computed on the basis of both the χ^2-statistic and the degrees of freedom.

When the χ^2-test is not appropriate

There are situations when it is not correct to use the χ^2-test. Consider the following contingency table:

```
> test <- cbind(c(12, 2), c(4, 6))
> test
     [,1]  [,2]
[1,]  12    4
[2,]   2    6
```

If one runs the test, one will receive a warning from R:

```
> chisq.test(test)

        Pearson's Chi-squared test with Yates' continuity correction

data: test
X-squared = 3.6214, df = 1, p-value = 0.05704

Warning message:
In chisq.test(test): Chi-squared approximation may be incorrect
```

If one checks the expected values, one can see that two of them are smaller than 5:

```
> chisq.test(test)$expected
        [,1]        [,2]
[1,]  9.333333   6.666667
[2,]  4.666667   3.333333
```

(Continued)

In such situations, one is advised to use the Fisher exact test instead:

```
> fisher.test(test)

        Fisher's Exact Test for Count Data

data: test
p-value = 0.03241
alternative hypothesis: true odds ratio is not equal to 1
95 percent confidence interval:
        0.9560338 114.1109502
sample estimates:
odds ratio
8.055902
```

As one can see, the p-value returned by the χ^2-test is greater than 0.05, whereas the one returned by the Fisher exact test is smaller than the significance level. The result retuned by the Fisher test should be preferred because it is exact. Therefore, the association is statistically significant.

Some statisticians suggest more complex rules of thumb. According to these rules, the Fisher exact test should be preferred always when the total number of observations in all cells is smaller than 20. If the total number of observations is from 20 to 40, the Fisher exact test should be preferred if at least one expected frequency is smaller than 5. If the total number of observations is above 40, the Fisher exact test should be preferred if at least one of expected frequencies is smaller than 1 (Sheskin 2011: 646).

To conclude, the analyses have shown that the proportion of metaphoric uses of *over* is greater in the academic register than in the spoken register, and this difference is statistically significant. How can we interpret these results? Let us have a look at the data. In the conversational subcorpus, one sees mostly spatial uses of *over*:

(1)   *Forgive me smiling but does everybody do that fall **over** the step there…*

Compare this with the following concordance lines from the academic subcorpus:

(2)   *This session allows for an in depth examination of the drinking diaries **over** the last five weeks identifying the risky circumstances or situations…*

(3)   *In the long debates **over** Marconi in 1913 and **over** the Curragh mutiny in 1914 Law was able to nail Asquith 's evasions where a more polished stylist might have…*

These examples demonstrate the temporal use of *over* and the sense 'concerning, referring to', where *over* introduces the object of discussion. Since the academic prose usually relates to abstract things, such as theories, concepts, ideas, facts, etc., it is natural that the non-physical metaphorical senses of *over* are preferred.

9.3   Metaphorical and non-metaphorical uses of *see* in four registers (analysis of a 4-by-2 table)

9.3.1   The data and hypothesis

For this case study you will need use only one add-on package, `vcd`. If you have not installed it previously, you should do so. Next, load the package:

```
> install.packages("vcd")
> library(vcd)
```

This case study focuses on the verb *see*. Verbs of perception are experientially basic. This is why they play an important role in metaphorical mapping of more abstract events. For instance, the KNOWLEDGE IS SEEING metaphor is pervasive across different languages (Sweetser 1990). Consider the word *idea*, which originates from the Greek *eidon* 'see'. In contemporary English, as in many other languages, verbs of seeing have sense extensions related to knowledge, understanding, opinion and other mental states, e.g. *I see your point; She views the situation differently; This project looks fishy.* Below are examples from the VU Amsterdam metaphor corpus. The example in (4) contains a literal use of the verb see, whereas (5) contains a metaphorical one.

(4)   *He **saw** a tall handsome woman dressed with careful and expensive informality in a black cashmere sweater with a silk scarf at the throat and fawn trousers.*

(5)   *Maslow (1966) and Hudson (1966 and 1968) **saw** science as providing undemanding emotional activity appealing to boys moving from the calm of latency to the turbulence of adolescence.*

This case study explores frequencies of metaphorical and non-metaphorical uses of *see* in four registers of communication available in the corpus. A query about the total number of metaphoric or non-metaphoric uses of the verb *see* in different registers yields the counts shown in Table 9.3.

Table 9.3 The frequencies of metaphoric and non-metaphoric uses of *see* in four registers

	Academic	Conversations	Fiction	News
Metaphoric	44	48	27	17
Non-metaphoric	26	135	98	19

To create a table with the counts in R, one needs two vectors which contain the frequencies shown in the rows of Table 9.3. Vector `see.m` represents the frequencies of metaphoric uses of *see* in different registers, whereas `see.m` contains the frequencies of *see* used non-metaphorically:

```
> see.m <- c(44, 48, 27, 17)
> see.nm <- c(26, 135, 98, 19)
```

Next, the vectors are combined as rows in a matrix with the help of `rbind()`:

```
> see.reg <- rbind(see.m, see.nm)
```

The final step is to add the column names:

```
> colnames(see.reg) <- c("aca", "conv", "fic", "news")
> see.reg
       aca  conv  fic  news
see.m   44    48   27    17
see.nm  26   135   98    19
```

9.3.2 Descriptive statistics and visualizations

The frequencies are visualized in a bar plot with a legend (Figure 9.3):

```
> barplot(see.reg, beside = TRUE, main = "Barplot of (non-)metaphoric
uses of see", xlab = "Registers", ylab = "Frequencies")
> legend("topright", fill = c("grey30", "grey90"), c("metaphoric",
"non-metaphoric"))
```

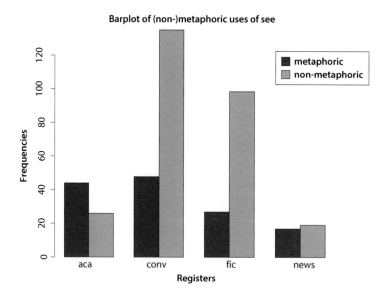

Figure 9.3. Bar plot of metaphoric and non-metaphoric uses of *see* in four registers with grouped bars

The heights of the dark grey and light grey bars represent the frequencies of the meta-phoric and metaphoric uses, respectively. The bar plot demonstrates that the proportion of metaphoric uses is the greatest in the academic register, but it is not very clear whether the smallest proportion is found in fiction or conversations. Let us look at the proportions:

```
> prop.table(see.reg, 2)
           aca         conv        fic     news
see.m    0.6285714   0.2622951   0.216   0.4722222
see.nm   0.3714286   0.7377049   0.784   0.5277778
```

The table of proportions tells us that the lowest proportion of metaphoric uses (0.216) is found in fiction. This is somewhat counterintuitive, since fiction is the register where meta-phoric language is expected to be used the most frequently. To measure the effect size, we can again use `assocstats()` from the vcd package:

```
> assocstats(see.reg)
                        X^2     df   P(> X^2)
Likelihood Ratio     41.000   3    6.5378e-09
Pearson              42.753   3    2.7773e-09
Phi-Coefficient        : 0.321
Contingency Coeff.   : 0.306
Cramer's V             : 0.321
```

Although the function again returns three effect size measures, it is only Cramér's V that is traditionally reported as the effect size measure for larger than 2-by-2 tables. The main disadvantage of the ϕ-coefficient is that it can have values greater than 1 in case of larger than 2-by-2 tables, which is not desirable. The effect size (0.32) is moderate.[5]

9.3.3 Testing the statistical significance and analysing the residuals: The χ^2-test and mosaic and association plots

The χ^2-test will be used again to test if the register differences in the frequencies of meta-phoric and non-metaphoric *see* are statistically significant:

```
> chisq.test(see.reg)

        Pearson's Chi-squared test

data: see.reg
X-squared = 42.7527, df = 3, p-value = 2.777e-09
```

The *p*-value is very small. The null hypothesis, which says that the proportions of meta-phoric uses are equal in all registers, can thus be discarded. In other words, the categorical variables 'metaphoric/non-metaphoric use' and 'register' are not independent.

---

5. In principle, odds ratios can be computed, as well, but only for pairwise comparisons between different registers, not for the entire table.

When analysing medium and large contingency tables, it is often interesting to know which frequencies in the contingency table are greater than what can be expected by chance, and which are smaller. To do so, one can compare the observed and expected frequencies:

```
> chisq.test(see.reg)$observed
          aca  conv  fic news
see.m      44    48   27 17
see.nm     26   135   98 19
> chisq.test(see.reg)$expected
         aca      conv     fic      news
met     22.99517 60.11594  41.0628  11.82609
nonmet  47.00483 122.88406 83.9372  24.17391
```

For instance, the expected frequency of metaphoric *see* in the academic texts is approximately 23. It is much smaller than the observed frequency 44. Therefore, the metaphoric *see* is overrepresented in the academic register. But which differences are more important, and which are less so? To answer this question, one can check the residuals:

```
> chisq.test(see.reg)$residuals
          aca         conv       fic        news
see.m     4.380270   -1.562652  -2.194561  1.504522
see.nm   -3.063712    1.092973   1.534951 -1.052315
```

The notion of residuals was discussed in Chapters 6 and 7. In a contingency table, the residuals (they are also called Pearson residuals) are the differences between the observed and expected frequencies divided by the squared root of the expected value. For a given cell in a row i and a column j, the Pearson residual can be computed as follows:

$$e_{ij} = \frac{O_{ij} - E_{ij}}{\sqrt{E_{ij}}}$$

where O_{ij} is the observed frequency in the given cell and E_{ij} is the expected frequency. For example, the Pearson residual of the frequency of the metaphoric *see* in the academic register can be computed as follows:

```
> (44 - 22.99517)/sqrt(22.99517)
[1] 4.38027
```

If the observed frequency is greater than expected, the residual is positive. If the observed frequency is smaller than expected, the residual is negative. The greater the absolute value of a residual, the greater the discrepancy between the observed and expected frequencies, and the more it contributes to the test statistic. In fact, the χ^2-statistic is the sum of squared Pearson residuals. Therefore, the metaphoric uses of *see* are strongly overrepresented in the academic register, and underrepresented in fiction. The non-metaphoric uses are strongly underrepresented in the academic texts.

The observed frequencies and the corresponding Pearson residuals can be visually represented in a mosaic plot with shading. To create a mosaic plot, one can use the mosaic() function from the package vcd. The result is displayed in Figure 9.4.

```
> mosaic(see.reg, shade = TRUE, varnames = FALSE)
```

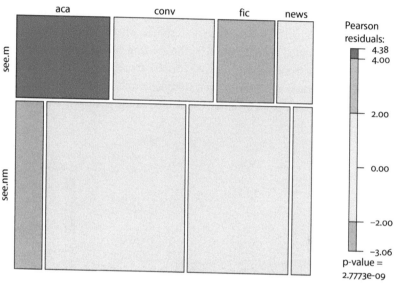

Figure 9.4. Mosaic plot of metaphorical and non-metaphorical uses of *see* in four registers. The colour of shading corresponds to the sign of a residual, and the intensity shows its relative importance

The colour of shading corresponds to the sign of a residual, and the intensity shows its relative importance: the more intensive, the greater the deviation. Unfortunately, the default colour scheme is lost in the black-and-white version, but when you reproduce the plot in R, you should be able to see the colours. Large positive residuals are indicated by blue rectangles if Pearson residuals range between 2 and 4, and by dark blue ones if the residuals are above 4. As for negative residuals, red rectangles indicate values between −2 and −4, whereas dark red ones (not shown in this plot) have residuals below −4.

The plot also reflects the total proportions of the cells, rows and columns in the contingency table. For example, the total area occupied by the metaphoric *see* is smaller than the total area occupied by the non-metaphoric uses because the total number of non-metaphoric occurrences of *see* is larger. On the other hand, the conversations occupy the largest areas both in the metaphoric and non-metaphoric rows, since this register contains the greatest number of instances of *see* in general. In contrast, the smallest total area is occupied by the news.

Another way of visualizing residuals is with the help of a so-called association plot. To create it, you can use another function from the vcd package, which is called assoc():

```
> assoc(see.reg, shade = TRUE, varnames = FALSE)
```

The result is shown in Figure 9.5. The plot displays bars that either 'grow' or 'fall'. If a bar 'grows' above the baseline, like a stalagmite, the residual is positive, i.e. the observed frequency is greater than expected. If it 'falls' below the baseline, like a stalactite, the residual is negative, i.e. the observed frequency is smaller than expected. The height of a bar represents the value of the corresponding Pearson residual, whereas the width stands for the squared root of the expected value in the cell. The shading colour and intensity represent the same information as in the mosaic plot. Again, the graph shows that the metaphorical *see* is strongly overrepresented in the academic register and underrepresented in fiction, whereas the non-metaphorical *see* is underrepresented in the academic register.

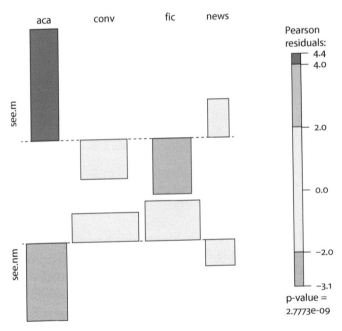

Figure 9.5. Metaphorical and non-metaphorical uses of *see* in four registers: association plot of residuals. The colour of shading and its orientation up- or downward corresponds to the sign of a residual, and the intensity of shading shows its relative importance

One can also determine which residuals represent significant deviations from the expected values at a given level of statistical significance. For this purpose, Agresti (2002: 81) recommends using standardized Pearson residuals, that is, Pearson residuals divided by their standard error, which can be computed as follows:

$$e_{sij} = \frac{O_{ij} - E_{ij}}{\sqrt{E_{ij}\left(1 - p_{i+}\right)\left(1 - p_{+j}\right)}}$$

where O_{ij} is the observed frequency in the given cell, E_{ij} is the expected frequency, p_{i+} is the proportion of the marginal frequency of row i with regard to the total number of observations, and p_{+j} is the proportion of the marginal frequency of column j. To obtain standardized residuals for a contingency table, you can use the following code:

```
> chisq.test(see.reg)$stdres
            aca         conv        fic         news
see.m     5.864076   -2.552903  -3.205358    1.921457
see.nm   -5.864076    2.552903   3.205358   -1.921457
```

If a standardized residual value is greater than 1.96 or smaller than –1.96, the cell makes a statistically significant contribution to the obtained χ^2-statistic value at the significance level of 0.05. For the significance level of 0.01, the numbers are 2.58 and –2.58, respectively. We find that all cells, except for the ones in the news column, make statistically significant contributions at the significance level of 0.05.

To summarize, the analyses reveal differences in the use of metaphoric and non-metaphoric *see* in different registers. These differences are highly significant ($p < 0.001$), which allows one to discard the null hypothesis of no association between metaphoricity of *see*, on the one hand, and the register, on the other hand. Most importantly, the metaphoric *see* is used more frequently than expected in the academic register, and less frequently than expected in fiction. Since seeing is an important metaphor for thinking, understanding and other mental processes, its highly frequent use in the academic texts is in fact not so surprising. Still, the relative scarcity of metaphors with *see* in fiction may seem counterintuitive at first. After all, fiction should be considered the most appropriate register for figurative language. A possible explanation is that narratives are often written from the point of view of a character who observes the events. A character's literal, perceptual seeing, like hearing, smelling, etc. provides a window to the world of the narrative.

9.4   Summary

This chapter has demonstrated how one can measure and test associations between two categorical variables. You have learnt how to compute such popular measures of effect size as the odds ratio, Cramér's V and the ϕ-coefficient. The concepts of odds and odds ratios will be central in Chapter 12 on logistic regression. Note that only Cramér's V is used when the table contains more than two rows and/or columns. The best-known significance test is the χ^2-test, although the Fisher exact test should be used in cases of low expected frequencies. A further discussion of the Fisher exact test and a variety of association measures follows in Chapter 10 and Chapter 11. You have also learnt how to create and interpret mosaic plots and association plots.

When your table has more than two dimensions, it is recommended to use log-linear analysis. This topic is beyond the scope of this introductory book, but see Field et al. (2012: Ch. 18). If one of the categorical variables can be regarded as the dependent one, then logistic regression may be appropriate (see Chapters 12 and 13).

How to write up the results of an independence test

One can report the results of an independence test using the following template: "We have found a significant association between metaphorical use of the preposition *over* and the register: $\chi^2(1) = 11.15$, $p < 0.001$. The odds of metaphorical use were 13.2 times higher in the academic register than in the conversational register, $\phi = 0.558$". Note that (1) designates the degrees of freedom. It is also important to report the effect size. When reporting effect sizes for larger tables, it is recommended to use Cramér's V. For 2-by-2 tables you can choose between ϕ, Cramér's V and the odds ratio.

CHAPTER 10

Association measures

Collocations and collostructions

What will you learn from this chapter:

Collocations, as well as colligations and other co-occurrence patterns, play an important role in corpus linguistics, psycholinguistics and usage-based grammar and lexicology. To measure the degree of attraction between words and other units, one can use diverse association measures, such as collostructional strength, Pointwise Mutual Information or ΔP. From this chapter you will learn how to compute a variety of association measures using a small set of different co-occurrence frequencies. The case study is based on co-occurrence frequencies of different verbs in the Russian ditransitive construction.

10.1 Measures of association: A brief typology

10.1.1 Frequencies that you will need in order to compute association measures

There are dozens of possible measures of association proposed in the literature (e.g. Evert 2004). All of them require all or at least some values from a 2-by-2 contingency table shown in Table 10.1. For two words (or any other units) X and Y, these frequencies can be defined as follows:

- a corresponds to the number of co-occurrences of X and Y;
- b is the number of occurrences of X without Y (in all other contexts), i.e. the total number of occurrences of X minus a;
- c corresponds to the sum frequency of all other target words that co-occur with Y, i.e. the total frequency of Y minus a;
- d is the frequency of all units except X that occur with all units except Y. In practice, this is the total number of words, sentences or other units in the corpus minus a, b and c. A more specific definition of this total number depends on the research question.

Table 10.1 The main co-occurrence frequencies that are needed for measuring association between X and Y

	Unit Y	$\neg$ Y (all other units)
Unit X	a	b
$\neg X$ (all other units)	c	d

If you know these four frequencies, you can compute any popular association measure between words (lexical collocations), or words and constructions, as in collostructional analysis. These measures can be subdivided into different classes, which are presented in the following subsection.

10.1.2 Unidirectional (asymmetric) vs. bidirectional (symmetric) measures

The main difference between unidirectional (asymmetric) and bidirectional (symmetric) measures is that the former will change if the rows and columns in Table 10.1 are swapped, whereas the latter will remain the same. The most important unidirectional measures are the conditional probability of X given Y ($X|Y$) and, conversely, the conditional probability of Y given X ($Y|X$). Clearly, these probabilities may be very different, and relationships between different parts of collocations need not be symmetric (Michelbacher et al. 2011). For instance, the first component *bonsai* in *bonsai tree* suggests, or predicts, the second component *tree* better than the other way round. Consider the data in Table 10.2.

Table 10.2 Co-occurrence frequencies of word forms *bonsai* and *tree* (based on the British National Corpus)

	bonsai	$\neg$ *bonsai*
tree	5	6131
$\neg$ *tree*	50	96980521

The conditional probability of *tree* given *bonsai* can be computed as the co-occurrence frequency of *bonsai* and *tree* divided by the total frequency of *bonsai*: $5/(50 + 5) = 0.09$, or about 9%. The conditional probability of *bonsai* given *tree* is equal to their co-occurrence frequency divided by the total frequency of *tree*: $5/(6131 + 5) = 0.0008$, or less than 0.1%. Thus, *bonsai* should be a much stronger clue for *tree* than the other way round. If one swaps the rows and columns in Table 10.1, the numbers will be reversed.

Unidirectional measures are also known in corpus-based Construction Grammar studies, where X is a word and Y is a construction. They are called Attraction (the conditional probability of the lexeme given the construction, i.e. collexeme|construction), and Reliance, or Faith (the conditional probability of the construction given the lexeme, i.e. construction|collexeme) (Schmid 2000; Gries et al. 2005). Again, high Attraction does not imply high Reliance. Consider the verb *make*. One can expect it to be frequent in the *way*-construction, as in *She made her way to the bar*, but in comparison with all other uses of *make* its appearance in the *way*-construction should be very modest. That means that it will have a high Attraction score and a low Reliance score with regard to the *way*-construction.

An example of a bidirectional measure is the collostructional strength based on an independence test (Stefanowitsch & Gries 2003). The relationships between a construction and a collexeme (e.g. the verb *give* and the English ditransitive construction) are most commonly measured with the help of statistical independence tests (e.g. the Fisher exact test), which show whether the co-occurrence frequency is significantly different from what one could expect under the assumption of no association (the null hypothesis). Regardless of what serves as a cue, the construction or the collexeme, the attraction score is the same. For all bidirectional association measures, all four frequencies in the table are needed, and the outcome will remain the same if one swaps the rows and columns.

10.1.3 Contingency-based vs. non-contingency-based measures

Let us begin with a conceptual question. If a unit A, e.g. the word *apple*, is a cue that triggers a unit B, e.g. the word *orange*, does the frequency of A as a cue for other units C, D, E, etc. (e.g. *pear*, *cider*, *cinnamon*) influence its role as a trigger of B? Psychologists would argue that this information is important in category learning.

> Consider how, in the learning of the category of birds, while eyes and wings are equally frequently experienced features in the exemplars, it is wings which are distinctive in differentiating birds from other animals. Wings are important features to learning the category of birds because they are reliably associated with class membership, eyes are neither. Raw frequency of occurrence is less important than the contingency between the cue and interpretation.
> (Ellis & Ferreira-Junior 2009: 194)

For example, if the verb *make* is frequently used in the transitive construction *X makes Y*, but it is also frequently used in other contexts, e.g. *X makes Y Z*, as in *make me a cup of tea*, or in the periphrastic causative *X makes Y do Z*, as in *he made me do it*, does this cognitively 'devalue' in any way the strength of association between *make* and the transitive construction? Does this have an effect on learning of the transitive construction? Are speakers sensitive to such contingency information and to what extent? These are questions that are still open.

There is a vast inventory of measures that take into account contingency information (they will be referred here as contingency-based measures). All bidirectional measures except for the simple co-occurrence of *X* and *Y* include contingency information. Some unidirectional measures contain it, as well, e.g. *ΔP* ('delta *P*'), a psychological cue-response measure introduced by Allan (1980) and recently used in constructionist studies by Ellis (2006) and Ellis and Ferreira-Junior (2009). See the next section for details.

In the remaining part of the chapter, you will learn how to compute different measures of association between constructions and collexemes. The object of the case study is the Russian ditransitive construction and its collexemes.

10.2   Case study: The Russian ditransitive construction and its collexemes

10.2.1   Theoretical background and data

To perform this case study, you will need several add-on packages. You should install and load them, if you have not done so yet.

```
> install.packages(c("ggplot2", "corrgram"))
> library(Rling); library(ggplot2); library(corrgram)
```

Ditransitive constructions exist in many languages. They normally denote transfer and consist of a verb of transfer and three arguments: the Agent (giver), the Recipient and the Theme (the object of transfer). The semantics of the construction can be very diverse. For example, transfer can be literal (e.g. *pass me the salt*) or metaphorical (*he told me a story, she gave him a punch*), actual (*he gave her a diamond ring*) or future (*he promised her a diamond ring*), positive (*she gave him an apple*) or negative (*it cost me a fortune*).

The Russian ditransitive construction has two objects, which correspond to the Recipient and Theme, which are marked with the Dative and Accusative case, respectively. It is very similar semantically to its English counterpart. The construction expresses events of transfer, and also has various semantic extensions that relate to transfer of information, future giving, and so on. Some of the unique extensions are malefactive events with external possession (*slomat' komu-to nogu*, lit. 'break somebody a leg') and what might be called 'causing to undergo' (*podvergat' kogo-to nakazaniju*, lit.: 'subject somebody to punishment'). Unlike the English ditransitive, the Russian construction is not used in some functions of negative transfer (e.g. cost or deny somebody something).

This case study will demonstrate how to compute some popular measures of association between the Russian ditransitive construction and its collexemes (e.g. *davat'* 'to give', *posylat'* 'to send', *darit'* 'to give as a gift'). The data come from a larger-scale study (Levshina, In preparation). The sample is available as the `ditr` data frame in the `Rling` package. It contains 47 verb lemmata, which constitute the rows of a data frame. The variables (columns) are *Freq_VC*, which shows the frequency of a verb in the ditransitive construction in the syntactically parsed segment of the Russian National Corpus, and *Freq_V*, which represents the total frequency of a verb in the corpus.

```
> data(ditr)
> head(ditr)
                Freq_VC    Freq_V
brat            1          443
darit           10         28
davat           131        682
demonstrirovat  5          73
govorit         6          1160
nahodit         1          333
```

10.2.2   Computation of some popular association measures

To compute association measures, one first has to derive the co-occurrence frequencies that are shown in Table 10.3, which is a customized version of Table 10.1 for this case study.

Table 10.3 Main types of co-occurrence frequencies of the ditransitive construction and its collexemes

	Ditransitive construction	¬ Ditransitive construction (all other verbal constructions)
Collexeme X	a	b
¬ Collexeme X (all other collexemes of the ditransitive construction)	c	d

Let us begin by creating four vectors that contain a, b, c and d counts for all verbs in the dataset. Some additional information is needed. First, the total frequency of the ditransitive construction in the corpus is 667. Second, the total number of verbs (104162) will be used as an approximation of the total frequency of all verbal constructions. This number is needed in order to obtain the frequencies d.

Note that the frequencies from the table should be computed for each of 47 collexemes. Computing them individually would be very time-consuming. Fortunately, one can easily apply arithmetic operations to all values in a vector:

```
> a <- ditr$Freq_VC
> b <- ditr$Freq_V - a
> c <- 667 - a
> d <- 104162 - (a + b + c)
```

For instance, the expression 667 – a means that the algorithm subtracts each value in a (the corpus frequencies of each verb in the construction) from 667. The result is a vector of numbers:[1]

```
> head(c)
[1] 666 657 536 662 661 666
```

Some other useful measures can be derived from these four. The most important is the expected frequency of a verb in the construction. The expected frequency, which was discussed in the previous chapter, is the frequency that would be observed if the proportion of the verb in the construction were equal to the proportion of the verb in all other constructions. The vector of expected frequencies for all 47 verbs can be obtained as follows:

```
> aExp <- (a + b)*(a + c)/(a + b + c + d)
> head(aExp)
[1] 2.8367447 0.1792976 4.3671780 0.4674545 7.4280448 2.1323611
```

Now we are ready to compute a few popular association scores. The R code for them is given in Table 10.4. The measures vary with regard to the directionality of the relationships between words and constructions (unidirectional vs. bidirectional) and with regard to the use of contingency information (contingency-based vs. contingency-free). The simplest measures are Attraction and Reliance (Schmid 2000). In this case, Attraction is the relative frequency of a verb in the ditransitive construction based on all uses of the construction in the corpus. Reliance, in contrast, is the relative frequency of a verb in the ditransitive construction with regard to all uses of the given verb. Both measures are unidirectional and do not include contingency information. Using the frequencies from Table 10.3, one can compute Attraction and Reliance as follows:

$$Attraction = \frac{a}{a+c}$$

$$Reliance = \frac{a}{a+b}$$

For convenience, the measures can be expressed as percentages by multiplying the result by 100:

```
> Attr <- 100*a/(a+c)
> Rel <- 100*a/(a+b)
```

---

1. Note that there is a built-in function c() in R, which concatenates objects. However, R can disambiguate overlapping names of the user's objects and functions.

Let us look at the top five verbs, which are the most attracted to the construction. Since the created vectors only contain numbers, let us add the names (individual verbs) to the vector elements in order to facilitate interpretation:

```
> names(Attr) <- rownames(ditr)
> head(Attr)
  brat         darit       davat         demonstrirovat
  0.1499250    1.4992504   19.6401799    0.7496252
  govorit      nahodit
  0.8995502    0.1499250
> sort(Attr, decreasing = TRUE)[1:5]
  davat       pridavat  predlagat  otdavat     peredavat
  19.640180   3.598201  3.448276   3.298351    3.298351
```

The top verbs are the generic *davat'* 'to give', followed at a distance by the prefixal verbs meaning 'to attach', 'to offer', 'to give away' and 'to pass, transfer', respectively. Three of them contain the same root as *davat'* and represent a specification of the generic meaning.

The verb *davat'* 'to give' is clearly the leader. There is evidence that high-frequency collexemes play a special role in constructional acquisition. For example, Goldberg et al. (2004) have shown that the presence of one high-frequency collexeme in the input facilitates learning of a construction. According to Goldberg and her colleagues, high-frequency collexemes help language learners note a correlation between the meaning of the word and the construction itself. Presumably, *davat'* plays such a role in acquisition of the Russian ditransitive construction.

The top five Reliance scores look as follows:

```
> names(Rel) <- rownames(ditr)
> sort(Rel, decreasing = TRUE)[1:5]
podkidyvat  pridavat  odalzhivat  navjazyvat  prepodnosit
100.00000   68.57143  66.66667    53.33333    40.00000
```

The first verb has 100% Reliance because the only time it occurs in the corpus, it is used in the ditransitive construction. The translations of the five verbs are, respectively, 'to put, plant (often secretly)', 'to attach (importance), to give (taste)', 'to lend', 'to impose' and 'to present' (e.g. a gift or, metaphorically, a surprise). Only one verb, *pridavat'* 'to attach (importance), to give (taste)', is also in the top five Attraction scores. On the other hand, *davat'* 'to give', the verb with the highest Attraction score, has only the top eleventh Reliance score. This means that these measures represent very different kinds of information. Figure 10.1 demonstrates how the verbs are distributed with regard to Attraction and Reliance, with *davat'* being an outlier with its high Attraction score, and most verbs having low Attraction and Reliance scores. To create a plot with text labels, you first have to create an empty plot (`type = "n"`) and then add text. The argument `cex = 0.7` specifies the font size.

```
> plot(Attr, Rel, type = "n", main = "Attraction and Reliance scores
of verbs in Russian Ditransitive Cx")
> text(Attr, Rel, rownames(ditr), cex = 0.7)
```

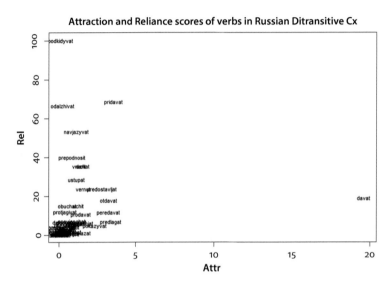

Attraction and Reliance scores of verbs in Russian Ditransitive Cx

Figure 10.1. Attraction and Reliance scores

How to create a scatter plot with text labels using `ggplot2`

If you want to make a `ggplot2` version of the plot in Figure 10.1, you can use the code below. The result is shown in Figure 10.1a.

```
> ggplot(data.frame(Attr, Rel), aes(x = Attr, y = Rel)) + geom_
text(label = names(Attr), size = 3)
```

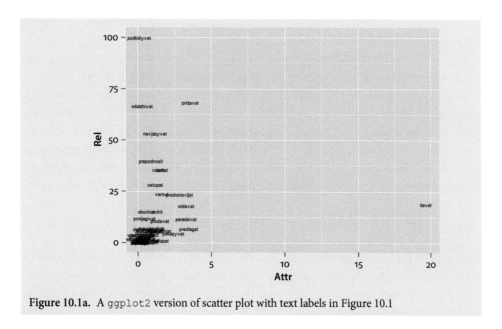

Figure 10.1a. A `ggplot2` version of scatter plot with text labels in Figure 10.1

In fact, if the Attraction and Reliance scores are sorted in decreasing order and plotted, the distributions closely resemble the Zipfian curve (see Chapter 3), as Figure 10.2 demonstrates. The plots can be created with the help of the following code:

```
> plot(sort(Attr, decreasing = TRUE), type = "l", main = "Attraction",
ylab = "Attraction, in %")
> plot(sort(Rel, decreasing = TRUE), type = "l", main = "Reliance",
ylab = "Reliance, in %")
```

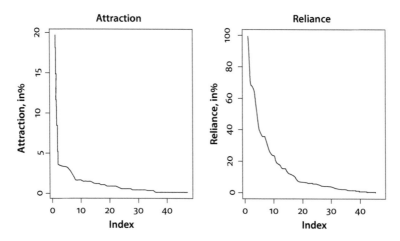

Figure 10.2. Distribution of Attraction and Reliance scores

This result corroborates previous findings about constructional collexemes in English (Ellis & Ferreira-Junior 2009).

The next measures are slightly more complex. Consider ΔP, recently used in constructionist studies by Ellis (2006) and Ellis & Ferreira-Junior (2009). It is a unidirectional contingency-based measure, which requires all four frequencies and comes in two 'flavours'. In one of them, the construction is the cue, and the collexeme is the response. The scores show the difference between the probability of the verb in the ditransitive construction and in all other contexts. The other version, conversely, treats the collexeme as the cue, and the construction as the response. It corresponds then to the difference between the probability of the ditransitive construction for a given verb, and that for all other verbs.

```
> dP.cueVerb <- a/(a + b) - c/(c + d)
> dP.cueCx <- a/(a + c) - b/(b + d)
```

If you explore the verbs with the top dP.cueVerb and dP.cueCx scores the way we did it above, you will see that the results are very similar to Reliance and Attraction, respectively.

So far, we have computed only unidirectional, or asymmetric measures. Let us now compute several popular bidirectional, or symmetric measures. All of them take into account contingency information. An example is the log-transformed Fisher exact test p-value (Stefanowitsch & Gries 2005). One could create for each set of frequencies a 2-by-2 table and use the Fisher exact test implemented in fisher.test() to obtain the p-values (see Chapter 9), but, to save time, you can use the function pv.Fisher. collostr() in the Rling package, which immediately returns a vector with p-values for all verbs:

```
> pvF <- pv.Fisher.collostr(a, b, c, d)
> round(head(pvF), 3)
[1] 0.539 0.000 0.000 0.000 0.852 0.729
```

To make the interpretation more intuitive, it is common in collostructionist studies to log-transform the p-values, so that they range from – infinity (mutual repulsion) to + infinity (mutual attraction), with the zero showing the lack of any association, either positive or negative. This is achieved by taking the negative logarithm of the p-value, and changing the sign to minus when the observed frequency is smaller than the expected one. Normally, the logarithm with the base 10 is used:

```
> logpvF <- ifelse(a < aExp, log10(pvF), -log10(pvF))
```

The function ifelse() takes three arguments: the condition ("if the observed frequency is smaller than the expected frequency"), the instruction what to do when the condition is met ("take a logarithm", which will result in a negative value because all numbers between 0 and 1 produce negative logarithms), and, finally, the instruction what to do when the condition is NOT met, i.e. the observed frequency is greater than expected ("take a negative logarithm of the *p*-value", which will result in a positive number, since two minuses give a plus).

Now, compare the simple *p*-values and the log-transformed ones:

```
> round(head(pvF), 3)
[1] 0.539 0.000 0.000 0.000 0.852 0.729
> round(head(logpvF), 3)
[1] -0.268 14.892 151.008  3.954 -0.070 -0.137
```

One can see that large and insignificant *p*-values have become small values somewhere around zero. In contrast, very small and significant *p*-values have turned into large absolute numbers after the log-transformation. Note also that the sign has appeared. The negative log-values show that the verb occurs in the construction less frequently than one could expect. In other words, the collexeme is 'repelled'. The positive log-values, in contrast, indicate a very strong mutual attraction between a collexeme and the construction. The greatest score (151.008) belongs to *davat'* 'to give'.

Since minus log_{10} of 0.05 is approximately 1.3, this threshold can be used as a cut-off point to identify significantly attracted and repelled collexemes:

```
> -log10(0.05)
[1] 1.30103
```

Thus, the collexemes with the log-value greater than 1.3 are significantly attracted to the ditransitive construction, whereas the collexemes with the scores smaller than –1.3 are significantly repelled from it. However, this cut-off value should be taken with a grain of salt. The distinction between central and marginal collexemes is not clear-cut. Rather, it represents a continuum, and any cut-off point is arbitrary. One should also remember that *p*-values depend on the sample size. That is, a larger corpus will yield normally lower *p*-values and larger log-transformed scores than a smaller one.

Another popular measure is the log-likelihood ratio score (e.g. Dunning 1993), although the Fisher exact test is considered to be more powerful in case of low frequencies. To compute the log-likelihood scores, you can use another ready-made function from the `Rling` package:

```
> LL <- LL.collostr(a, b, c, d)
> LL1 <- ifelse(a < aExp, -LL, LL)
```

A list of these and other popular association measures and the R code is provided in Table 10.4.

How similar are these measures? This question can be answered with the help of correlation analysis (see Chapter 6). For contrastive purposes, one can also add a random score with replacement. That is, the algorithm picks up a random number from a pool, e.g. all integers from 0 to 100, *n* times (here, *n* is the total number of verbs, or the length of the frequency vector *a*). Imagine drawing lotto balls with numbers from a box *n* times.

Table 10.4 Association measures, based on Evert (2004) with some additions

Measure	Characteristic	R code
Attraction	unidirectional, non-contingency-based	`Attr <- 100*a/(a + c)`
Reliance	unidirectional, non-contingency-based	`Rel <- 100*a/(a + b)`
ΔP, construction as cue, collexeme as response	unidirectional, contingency-based	`dP.cueCx <- a/(a + c) - b/(b + d)`
ΔP, verb as cue, construction as response	unidirectional, contingency-based	`dP.cueVerb <- a/(a + b) - c/(c + d)`

Log-transformed Fisher's Exact Test p-value	bidirectional, contingency-based	`pvF <- pv.Fisher.collostr(a, b, c, d)`
		`logpvF <- ifelse(a < aExp, log10(pvF),`
		`-log10(pvF))`

Log-likelihood ratio	bidirectional, contingency-based	`LL <- LL.collostr(a, b, c, d)` `LL1 <- ifelse(a < aExp, -LL, LL)`
Pointwise Mutual Information	bidirectional, contingency-based	`PMI <- log(a/aExp)`^{2}
MI2	bidirectional, contingency-based	`MI2 <- log(a^2/aExp)`
MI3	bidirectional, contingency-based	`MI3 <- log(a^3/aExp)`
local MI	bidirectional, contingency-based	`MIloc <- a*log(a/aExp)`
normalized PMI	bidirectional, contingency-based	`nPMI <- PMI/(-log(a/(a + b + c + d)))`
z-score	bidirectional, contingency-based	`z.score <- (a - aExp)/sqrt(aExp)`
t-score	bidirectional, contingency-based	`t.score <- (a - aExp)/sqrt(a)`

Pearson's χ^2-test statistic	bidirectional, contingency-based	`dExp <- (d + b)*(d + c)/(a + b + c + d)`
		`chisq <- (a + b + c + d)*(a - aExp)^2/`
		`(aExp*dExp)`

(*Continued*)

---

2. Different authors use different logarithmic bases, which can be specified in R as `log()` (natural logarithm to base $e \approx 2.718$), `log2()` (logarithm to base 2) or `log10()` (logarithm to base 10). Changing the base will change the magnitude of association scores, but the ranking of collexemes will remain the same.

Table 10.4 (Continued)

Measure	Characteristic	R code
Minimum sensitivity	bidirectional, contingency-based	`MS <- apply(cbind(Attr, Rel), 1, min)`
Jaccard coefficient	bidirectional, contingency-based	`Jaccard <- a/(a + b + c)`
Dice coefficient	bidirectional, contingency-based	`Dice <- 2*a/(2*a + b + c)`
Log odds ratio	bidirectional, contingency-based	`logOR <- log(a*d/(b*c))`
Discounted log odds ratio	bidirectional, contingency-based	`logOR.disc <-log((a + 0.5)*(d + 0.5)/` `((b + 0.5)*(c + 0.5)))`
Geometric mean	bidirectional, contingency-based	`gmean <- a/sqrt((a + b)*(a + c))`
Liddell's difference of proportions	unidirectional, contingency-based	`Liddell <- (a*d - b*c)/((a + c)*` `(b + d))`

The phrase 'with replacement' means that each number can be drawn from the total pool any number of times, as if you put a ball that you have drawn back into the box. Since the procedure is random, your scores will diverge from the ones below:

```
> random <- sample(0:100, length(a), replace = TRUE)
> head(random)
[1] 77 7 80 100    1 59
```

To obtain the correlations between all pairs of measures simultaneously, all association scores will be combined as columns in a matrix:

```
> assoc <- cbind(Attr, Rel, dP.cueCx, dP.cueVerb, logpvF, LL1, random)
```

Next, the function `cor()` can be used to compute all pairwise correlation coefficients. The Pearson product-moment correlation coefficient is computed as the default option. For convenience, the coefficients are rounded up to three decimal points in order to get a more compact representation:

```
> assoc.cor <- cor(assoc)
> round(assoc.cor, 3)
            Attr   Rel    dP.cueCx dP.cueVerb logpvF LL1    random
Attr        1.000 0.111  0.997    0.112      0.983  0.983  0.054
Rel         0.111 1.000  0.140    1.000      0.220  0.220  -0.253
dP.cueCx    0.997 0.140  1.000    0.141      0.988  0.988  0.070
dP.cueVerb  0.112 1.000  0.141    1.000      0.221  0.221  -0.253
logpvF      0.983 0.220  0.988    0.221      1.000  1.000  0.041
LL1         0.983 0.220  0.988    0.221      1.000  1.000  0.040
random      0.054 -0.253 0.070    -0.253     0.041  0.040  1.000
```

The correlation matrix tells us that there are two very strongly correlated groups of scores. The first one includes Attraction, ΔP with the construction as the cue, the log-transformed Fisher exact test p-value and the log-likelihood measure. The second group is formed by Reliance and ΔP with the verb as the cue. The random variable, as one might have expected, is not strongly correlated with any parameters, although there is a weak negative correlation with Reliance and ΔP with the verb as the cue.

For those who prefer visual ways of displaying information, an attractive option might be a correlogram, which was introduced in Chapter 6. Figure 10.3 displays one of the graphical options. The strength of correlation is represented by the intensity of shading and also by the size of the coloured segments of the pie charts. The direction is represented by colours and the orientation of the coloured segments in the pie charts. The argument `order = TRUE` orders the variables in such a way that one can see the groups of strongly correlated variables.

```
> corrgram(assoc, order = TRUE, lower.panel = panel.shade, upper.
panel = panel.pie)
```

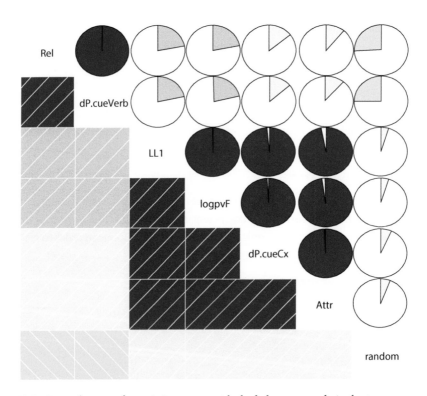

Figure 10.3. A correlogram of association scores with shaded squares and pie charts

For the purposes of more precise diagnostics of the relationships, it is also possible to visualize the observations as points plotted against the values of each variable compared, and ellipses that show the direction and strength of association. The rounder the ellipse, the weaker the correlation. One can also see smoothed curves, which show the direction of the relationship. The result is shown in Figure 10.4.

```
> corrgram(assoc, order = TRUE, lower.panel = panel.ellipse, upper.
panel = panel.pts)
```

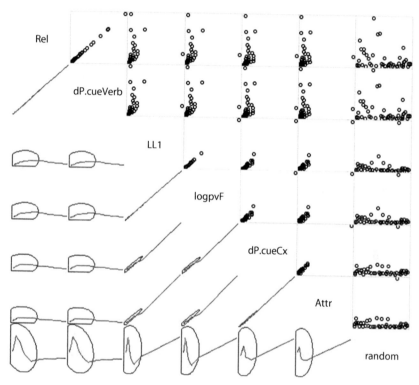

Figure 10.4. Correlogram of association measures: points (individual verbs) and ellipses with smoothed lines

Consider the nearly perfectly linear relationships between *Rel* and *dP.cueVerb*, or between *Attr*, *dP.cueCx*, *logpvF* and *LL1*. One can also detect the presence of outliers with the help of the scatter plots in the upper panel. Notably, all plots with *Attr*, *dP.cueCx*, *logpvF* and *LL1*, show the presence of a powerful outlier. A quick examination of the initial scores reveals that the outlier is again *davat'* 'to give'. In such situations, it is more correct to use a non-parametric correlation test, such as Kendall's τ. The latter gives somewhat different results:

```
> assoc.cor1 <- cor(assoc, method = "kendall")
> round(assoc.cor1, 3)
               Attr   Rel    dP.cueCx dP.cueVerb  logpvF LL1    random
Attr          1.000 0.442 0.864       0.442        0.738  0.724  0.076
Rel           0.442 1.000 0.591       1.000        0.716  0.731  0.045
dP.cueCx      0.864 0.591 1.000       0.591        0.870  0.859  0.007
dP.cueVerb    0.442 1.000 0.591       1.000        0.716  0.731  0.045
logpvF        0.738 0.716 0.870       0.716        1.000  0.985  0.014
LL1           0.724 0.731 0.859       0.731        0.985  1.000  0.019
random        0.076 0.045 0.007       0.045        0.014  0.019  1.000
```

According to the ranks method, Attraction is less strongly correlated with ΔP with the construction as the cue, the log-transformed Fisher exact test p-value and the log-likelihood measure than when the Pearson correlation coefficients were used. On the other hand, Attraction and Reliance are now correlated more strongly than before. These differences in the results demonstrate the importance of diagnostics and visualization of data, and show how the choice of a statistic may change the picture.

10.3 Summary

This chapter has introduced a few popular measures of collocational and collostructional strength. The reader may wonder which ones he or she should use. There is no easy and definite answer to this question. It is still unclear which measures represent the information that the speakers store in their minds more adequately than the others, since recent empirical studies based on corpus-based and experimental evidence have yielded divergent results. Yet, it is possible to give some general recommendations. For low-frequency data, such measures as t-scores and z-scores are less reliable than the log-likelihood values and especially the log-transformed Fisher exact p-values. Log-odd ratios are not sensitive to frequency information, unlike the hypothesis-testing statistics based on p-values or log-likelihood ratios. As a consequence, it would make more sense to use odds ratios if you want to compare results based on datasets of different sizes. The PMI measure gives more weight to co-occurrences of low-frequency elements, and has been widely used in computational studies with very many target words and contextual features (see Chapter 16). In addition, as the correlogram plots have shown, most measures are highly correlated, so another recommendation is to be cautious when reporting the 'best' measures. The next chapter will demonstrate how collostructional strength can be applied in quantitative models of semantics and language variation.

How to report association measures

There are no general rules for reporting association measures. The format depends on the specific task. For example, collostructional studies often present the results in tables with ranked collexemes, their observed and expected frequencies, as well as the association measure scores.

More on association measures

To find out more on different association measures, one can refer to Evert (2004). For applications in collostructional analysis, see numerous publications by Gries, Stefanowitsch and their colleagues, beginning from Stefanowitsch & Gries (2003). A comparison of different measures of association between collexemes and constructions can be found in Wiechmann (2008). See also Barnbrook et al. (2013) for a broader background and applications of collocational analysis.

CHAPTER 11

Geographic variation of *quite*

Distinctive collexeme analysis

What you will learn from this chapter:

> This chapter introduces distinctive collexeme analysis, which employs bidirectional
> association measures discussed in the previous chapter. This method is based
> on the co-occurrence frequencies of words that occur in two near-synonymous
> constructions, or in two or more dialectal or diachronic variants of the same
> construction. Here we will compare the variants of *quite* + ADJ construction in
> different national varieties of English. We will first present a canonical distinctive
> collexeme analysis with only two varieties, British and American English, and then
> will show how this approach can be extended to more lects, presenting a unified
> approach to multiple distinctive collexeme analysis.

11.1 Introduction to distinctive collexeme analysis

The method of distinctive collexeme analysis (Gries & Stefanowitsch 2004; Wulff 2006;
Wulff et al. 2007), henceforth DCA, belongs to the family of corpus-based collostructional methods developed by Stefan Th. Gries and Anatol Stefanowitsch (Stefanowitsch &
Gries 2003 and later works). DCA is a technique designed specifically to compare two or
more constructions by finding the distinctive slot fillers (collexemes) that are significantly
attracted to one construction and repelled by the other. One can examine two (or more)
near-synonymous constructions in one variety, e.g. *go*-V vs. *go-and*-V in Wulff (2006) or
English analytic causatives (Gilquin 2006). Another option, which is demonstrated here,
is comparison of formally identical constructions in two varieties, e.g. the *into*-causative
in British and American English (Wulff et al. 2007). The result of the statistical procedure
is two lists of distinctive collexemes, which are typical of each lectal variant. For instance,
Wulff et al. (2007) found out that many verbs that are distinctive of the British variant
of the *into*-causative designate negative emotions (e.g. *She terrified me into doing it*) and
threatening (*He blackmailed me into doing it*). These semantic classes are not typical of
collexemes in the American English variant of the same construction. On the other hand,
many distinctive American collexemes refer to communication (e.g. *She talked me into
doing it*). Wulff et al. (2007) hypothesize that these and other differences may reflect the

varying degrees of prominence of specific semantic scenarios in the two cultures. These scenarios are expressed in the title of their paper, 'Brutal Brits and Persuasive Americans'.

A similar analysis was carried out in Levshina at al. (2011), where the Netherlandic and Belgian variants of the causative construction with *doen* were compared. An inspection of the constructional slots reveals that the Netherlandic causative *doen* seems to be specialized in the so-called affective causation, i.e. situations when a stimulus produces a mental reaction, e.g. *Zijn kapsel doet me denken aan een vogelnest* 'His hairstyle reminds me of (lit. makes me think) of a bird's nest'. Since Netherlandic Dutch is considered to be the leader in language change, and Belgian Dutch is believed to be more conservative, the more limited semantic repertoire of Netherlandic *doen* ties in well with the previous observations of the ongoing qualitative and quantitative shrinking of the auxiliary *doen* in Dutch (e.g. Speelman & Geeraerts 2009).

There exists special software (Gries 2004) that can help you perform this and other types of collostructional analysis. The aim of this chapter, however, is to demonstrate the basic principles of DCA in a sequence of simple steps. In DCA it is common to apply a significance test (traditionally, the Fisher exact test is used) to find out which collexemes are over- and underrepresented in each variety at a statistically significant level. The log-transformed *p*-value is frequently used as a measure of distinctiveness. The results are symmetric: if one collexeme is significantly overrepresented in Construction/Variety A, then it is significantly underrepresented in Construction/Variety B, and vice versa. The next section will discuss simple DCA, whereas a unified approach to multiple DCA will be introduced in Section 11.3.

11.2 Distinctive collexeme analysis of *quite* + ADJ in different varieties of English: A unified approach

11.2.1 Theoretical background and data

To reproduce the code in this case study, you will need two datasets from the add-on companion package `Rling`.

```
> library(Rling)
```

The method will be illustrated with a case study of the construction *quite* + ADJ in British and American English. A few examples of the construction are below:

(1)   a.   *The restaurant is quite good.*
       b.   *All art is quite useless.* (Oscar Wilde)
       c.   *The result is quite extraordinary.*

Quite has complex semantics. It can function both as a maximizer ('entirely'), and a moderator, similar to *fairly* or *rather*. Often, these functions can be disambiguated only in context. However, there are also distributional cues, most importantly, semantic classes of modified adjectives (Paradis 1997). With scalar adjectives (e.g. *good, nice, interesting, difficult, rich*), as in (1a), *quite* can function as a moderator. With limit adjectives, which imply a clear boundary (e.g. *useless, sure, cooked, clear, different, wrong, dead*), and extreme adjectives, which describe a high degree of some quality (e.g. *extraordinary, huge, scorching, marvellous, astounding*), *quite* tends to be a maximizer, as in (1b) and (1c).

These properties are characteristic of contemporary British English. However, there is evidence that the moderating function emerged not earlier than the 18th century. Thus, there are reasons to expect that this function would not be so prominent in American English. In fact, some lexicographic sources observe that this is indeed so. First, *quite* is not used as a moderator in American English. Instead, American *quite* serves as a booster with scalar adjectives, similar to *very* or *extremely*. The sentence (1a) could therefore only mean in American English that the restaurant is very good. Second, American *quite* is not used with extreme adjectives.

On the basis of the second observation, we can formulate the hypothesis that American *quite* will contain fewer adjectives with extreme semantics than its British counterpart. Another prediction can be made based on the history of *quite* as a degree modifier: since the maximizer function with limit adjectives seems to be the only one fully developed before English was exported to America, we will expect more limit adjectives among the collexemes of American *quite*.

To test the hypotheses, we will use adjectives that occur immediately after *quite* in the Corpus of Global Web-based English (GloWbE), which represents geographic varieties of English in twenty countries (Davies 2013). The lists can be found in the `quite_Br` and `quite_Am` datasets.

```
> data(quite_Br)
> data(quite_Am)
> head(quite_Br)
    Adj        BrE
1 DIFFERENT   2313
2 SURE        1916
3 HAPPY       1710
4 GOOD        1614
5 CLEAR       1470
6 RIGHT       1162
```

The datasets have similar structure. The rows correspond to the adjectives (lemmas). The column `BrE` displays the frequencies in the British variant of the construction, and `AmE` in the dataset `quite_Am` corresponds to the American data. The number of unique adjectives is different: the British dataset contains 3702 collexemes, and its American counterpart has 3046 adjectives.

```
> nrow(quite_Br)
[1] 3702
> nrow(quite_Am)
[1] 3049
```

The frequencies of the constructional variants differ, as well: the British variant has almost twice as many instances as the American one (61722 vs. 37699), although the subcorpora are of almost equal size:

```
> sum(quite_Br$BrE)
[1] 61722
> sum(quite_Am$AmE)
[1] 37699
```

Are there any qualitative differences between the variants? This is a question for simple DCA, which will be performed in the next subsection. After that, the Canadian variant of the construction will be added to illustrate a unified approach to multiple DCA.

11.2.2　Simple distinctive collexeme analysis of *quite* + ADJ in British and American English

To perform the analysis, one needs a 2-by-2 table of co-occurrence frequencies shown in Table 11.1 (cf. Table 10.1 in the previous chapter).

Table 11.1　Frequencies required for simple distinctive collexeme analysis

	Construction/Variety A	Construction/Variety B
Collexeme *X*	*a*	*b*
¬ *X* all other collexemes	*c*	*d*

To perform the analysis, one needs to create the vectors that contain the frequencies *a*, *b*, *c* and *d* for each adjective, following the approach introduced in Chapter 10. The first step is to create a data frame which will contain all adjectives and will have two columns, with the British and American frequencies:

```
> quite <- merge(quite_Br, quite_Am, by = "Adj", all = TRUE)
> head(quite)
       Adj         BrE AmE
1 ABASHED       1   NA
2 ABBREVIATED   1   1
3 ABLE          91  46
4 ABNORMAL      2   2
5 ABOMINABLE    1   NA
6 ABRASIVE      6   3
```

The 'NA' values in the table show that the corresponding adjective is missing in one of the lists. The missing values should be replaced with zeroes:

```
> quite[is.na(quite)] <- 0
```

The next step is to obtain four frequencies from Table 11.1. The columns in `quite` are in fact vectors with the frequencies *a* and *b*. The vector with frequencies *c* can be obtained as the sum of all instances of the construction in the British data minus *a*, and the vector with *d* is the sum of all instances of the American variant of *quite* + ADJ minus *b*:

```
> a <- quite$BrE
> b <- quite$AmE
> c <- sum(quite$BrE) - quite$BrE
> d <- sum(quite$AmE) - quite$AmE
```

You will also need the expected frequency in the British variety:

```
> aExp <- (a + b)*(a + c)/(a + b + c + d)
```

Now you are ready to run the statistical tests and compare the geographical variants of *quite*. Since the relationships between the varieties are symmetric, it suffices to compute attraction/repulsion scores for British English. You can use the `pv.fisher.collostr()` function, which was presented in the previous chapter, to compute the Fisher exact test *p*-values for all adjectives. This function is available in the `Rling` package.

```
> pvF <- pv.Fisher.collostr(a, b, c, d)
```

For better interpretability, it is common to take a negative logarithm with base 10 of the *p*-values. It is also necessary to add information about the direction of association, i.e. whether a given adjective is overrepresented or underrepresented in the British variant of the construction. If the observed frequency in the British data is smaller than the expected frequency, then the log-transformed score will remain negative. If the observed frequency in the British construction is greater than the expected frequency, the log-transformed score will become positive (see more details in Chapter 10):

```
> logpvF <- ifelse(a < aExp, log10(pvF), -log10(pvF))
```

The greater the `logpvF` score, the more overrepresented the collexeme in the British data and the more underrepresented in the American data. Now the scores can be added to the data as a new column, and the data frame can be sorted according to the scores. The function `order()` can be used to sort a data frame in ascending and descending order. In the latter case, one can use the minus sign before the name of the variable by which the data are sorted. The collexemes that are the most distinctive of the British variant can be found at the top of the list.

```
> quite$logp <- logpvF
> quite <- quite[order(-quite$logp),]
```

```
> quite[1:20,]
        Adj              BrE  AmE   logp
1424    HAPPY            1710 545   44.054249
1426    HARD             659  160   29.375670
1111    EXTRAORDINARY    217  46    12.160975
281     BIG              224  53    10.761473
2586    RELAXED          82   7     9.762904
698     DAUNTING         103  17    7.869958
798     DIFFICULT        848  366   7.836994
2516    QUICK            87   12    7.782684
2517    QUIET            61   5     7.543155
2651    RIGHT            1162 537   7.309045
2969    STAGGERING       67   7     7.308632
1808    KEEN             105  20    6.856004
2115    NICE             557  229   6.570673
991     EMOTIONAL        119  26    6.545695
1073    EXCITING         161  44    6.280060
3236    TRICKY           146  38    6.228315
3689    WORRYING         56   6     5.969637
1630    INCREDIBLE       119  29    5.633430
2412    PREPARED         166  49    5.546736
1922    LUCKY            132  35    5.523337
```

To obtain the top twenty collexemes that are distinctive of the American variant, one can simply remove the minus sign before the name of the variable, so that the scores are ordered from the smallest to the largest one:

```
> quite <- quite[order(quite$logp),]
> quite[1:20,]
        Adj            BrE   AmE    logp
413     CERTAIN        175   281    -23.787625
2390    POSSIBLE       791   791    -22.028837
793     DIFFERENT      2313  1872   -19.421232
1131    FAMILIAR       87    168    -18.763244
228     AWARE          97    173    -17.416095
3070    SURE           1916  1492   -11.916458
3558    VALUABLE       23    64     -10.727512
2547    REAL           52    97     -10.615434
3046    SUCCESSFUL     124   161    -9.558394
2546    READY          301   307    -9.473267
1238    FOND           65    104    -9.112043
2837    SIMILAR        420   393    -8.831172
958     EFFECTIVE      108   140    -8.431429
```

2851	SKEPTICAL	8	36	-8.415016
26	ACCURATE	113	143	-8.179308
3119	TASTY	20	51	-8.025411
3665	WILLING	123	149	-7.721011
1465	HELPFUL	94	122	-7.347363
2913	SOMETIME	47	74	-6.580660
3969	FAVORABLE	0	15	-6.317976

It is a popular practice in distinctive collexeme analysis to classify all distinctive collexemes (i.e. those whose absolute scores are above the cut-off point) into some semantic classes and then sum up the scores for the classes. Because of space limitations, we will only look at the top twenty collexemes in each variety.

An informal inspection of the top collexemes seems to support the theoretical expectations. First, about a half of the top twenty collexemes in the British list can be considered scalar (e.g. *big*, *nice*, *difficult*). The exceptions are extreme adjectives *extraordinary*, *daunting*, *staggering* and *incredible*, and limit adjectives *right* and *prepared*. In contrast, the American top twenty list contains mostly limit adjectives (*certain*, *possible*, *different*, *aware*, *sure*, etc.),[1] and no extreme adjectives.

It is also surprising that the American top collexemes are in general more positive than the British ones, which may have negative connotations (*difficult*, *hard*, *tricky*, *worrying*). This observation will also hold if the lists beyond the top 20 limit are inspected. This finding suggests interesting differences in the semantic prosody of *quite*.

The absolute standard cut-off value, which corresponds to the p-value of 0.05 is approximately 1.3 for log-transformed values (with 10 as the logarithm base). Only 182 adjectives from the entire list are distinctive of the British variant, and 185 are distinctive of the American variant at the significance level 0.05.

```
> nrow(quite[quite$logp > 1.3,])
[1] 182
> nrow(quite[quite$logp < (-1.3),])
[1] 185
```

The overwhelming majority of the collexemes are therefore not distinctive of either variety at the significance level of 0.05. Most of them are simply not sufficiently frequent, but some of them are nearly equally distributed in the two varieties.

To summarize, British *quite* seems to be more frequently used with scalar adjectives where the attenuation function is the most natural (*quite nice*, *quite big*). It also tends to attract extreme adjectives (*quite extraordinary*) more strongly than its American

---

1.   The word *sometime* ended up in the list due to a parsing error in the corpus.

counterpart, which, in its turn, more frequently functions as an intensifier of non-gradable limit adjectives (*quite sure, quite different*). This means that the British modifier is more polysemous than American *quite*, which has to do with the relatively recent development of the new functions of *quite* in addition to its oldest meaning 'absolutely, entirely'. These changes happened in British English in the second part of the 18th–19th centuries, after English was exported to America (see Levshina 2014 for more information).

11.2.3 Multiple distinctive collexeme analysis: *Quite* + ADJ in the British, American and Canadian varieties of English

This subsection shows how to extend simple DCA to cases with more than two varieties or near-synonymous constructions. This time, the Canadian variant of *quite* + ADJ will be added. Canadian English is known to have retained some properties of British English, but at the same time it has been strongly influenced by American English as a part of North American English. The list of adjectives from the GloWbE corpus can be found in the dataset `quite_Ca` in `Rling`. To compare all three lists, one should add the adjectives from `quite_Ca` to the list of the British and American collexemes stored in the data frame `quite`. To do so, we will use again the `merge()` function. The `logp` column from `quite` can be discarded because the old distinctiveness scores are no longer needed:

```
> data(quite_Ca)
> quite1 <- merge(quite[, -4], quite_Ca, by = "Adj", all = TRUE)
> quite1[is.na(quite1)] <- 0
> str(quite1)
'data.frame': 4856 obs. of 4 variables:
$ Adj: Factor w/ 4856 levels "ABASHED","ABBREVIATED",..: 1 2 3 4 5
6 7 8 9 10 …
$ BrE: num 1 1 91 2 1 6 1 7 4 1 …
$ AmE: num 0 1 46 2 0 3 1 6 1 0 …
$ CE: num 0 0 17 3 1 0 0 1 2 0 …
```

The main principle of multiple DCA is the same as in the simple DCA. One compares the proportions of every collexeme in different constructions or variants of the same construction. The main difference is that multiple DCA, as implemented in our unified approach, compares each construction/variant against all others.

This case study will focus only on the distinctive collexemes of the Canadian *quite* + ADJ construction against the British and American variants taken together. We will need the frequencies shown in Table 11.2. Variety *A* in the table is then Canadian English, and the 'other' varieties are British and American.

Table 11.2 Frequencies required for multiple distinctive collexeme analysis

	Construction/Variety A	Other constructions/varieties
Collexeme X	a	b
$\neg X$ (all other collexemes)	c	d

To obtain the frequencies, one can use a procedure that is very similar to the one described in the previous subsection. The only difference is that one should sum up the frequencies of collexemes in both British and American data to obtain the count b

```
> a <- quite1$CE
> b <- quite1$BrE + quite1$AmE
> c <- sum(a) - a
> d <- sum(b) - b
```

You will also need the expected frequency of every collexeme in Canadian English.

```
> aExp <-(a + b)*(a + c)/(a + b + c + d)
```

Gries (2004) uses the binomial test to compute distinctiveness scores for multiple distinctive collexeme analysis, but we will use the Fisher exact test, as before, for the sake of consistency, presenting a unified approach. The correlation between the original Gries' method scores and ours is nearly perfect ($r = 0.98$). The R code is the same as above:

```
> pvF <- pv.Fisher.collostr(a, b, c, d)
> logpvF <- ifelse(a < aExp, log10(pvF), -log10(pvF))
> quite1$logpCE <- logpvF
```

The top twenty most distinctive collexemes in the Canadian variant of the construction can be obtained as follows:

```
> quite1 <- quite1[order(-quite1$logpCE),]
> quite1[1:20,]
        Adj              BrE   AmE   CE    logpCE
1833    LARGE            334   247   128   4.894402
870     DISTINGUISHABLE  1     0     6     4.646948
4642    GOOD-NATURED     0     0     5     4.536043
374     BUSY             134   75    57    4.468647
2546    READY            301   307   128   4.095098
793     DIFFERENT        2313  1872  690   3.802790
1061    EVIDENT          94    101   51    3.688441
638     CRAPPY           2     1     6     3.664810
1592    IMPRESSIVE       198   141   78    3.616966
```

978	ELITE	2	0	5	3.308234
3119	TASTY	20	51	24	3.298938
508	COMFORTABLE	178	175	78	3.254352
1909	LOW	328	202	109	3.240176
1744	INTRIGUED	28	10	16	3.215085
415	CHALLENGING	111	75	47	3.176938
2837	SIMILAR	420	393	155	3.071796
1186	FILLING	4	4	7	2.937432
816	DISAPPOINTED	88	60	38	2.770482
4535	APPRECIATIVE	0	0	3	2.721544
4550	BOOKISH	0	0	3	2.721544

The list bears more resemblance to the top distinctive American collexemes than to the British ones, containing *different* (and its synonym *distinguishable*), *similar*, *ready* and *tasty*. We can also examine the collexemes that are significantly underrepresented in the Canadian variant:

```
> quite1 <- quite1[order(quite1$logpCE),]
> quite1[1:20,]
```

	Adj	BrE	AmE	CE	logpCA
1424	HAPPY	1710	545	208	-9.422766
2651	RIGHT	1162	537	151	-8.223901
1426	HARD	659	160	62	-6.595266
2724	SCARY	175	58	8	-5.756694
348	BRILLIANT	131	39	6	-4.297981
281	BIG	224	53	15	-4.277109
3694	WRONG	282	103	26	-4.186445
3236	TRICKY	146	38	9	-3.380667
1922	LUCKY	132	35	8	-3.117908
1304	FUNNY	413	179	53	-3.025242
132	ANNOYING	122	75	11	-3.006459
3689	WORRYING	56	6	1	-2.428485
617	CORRECT	244	220	42	-2.357467
2920	SORRY	31	15	0	-2.271914
1283	FRIGHTENING	82	27	5	-2.197128
1343	GLAD	74	36	5	-2.190326
3070	SURE	1916	1492	421	-2.121099
3062	SUPERB	37	4	0	-2.119141
117	AMUSING	165	86	20	-2.015827
2179	ODD	104	62	11	-1.943230

Some of the repelled collexemes were in the British top list (*happy, right, hard, big, tricky, lucky, worrying*). Only one of them (*sure*) was ranked high on the American list. There are also extreme adjectives, which are typical of the British construction: *superb* and *brilliant*.

So, Canadian *quite* + ADJ seems to be more similar to the American variant than to the British one. This is not surprising, considering the history of the North American varieties and the diachronic development of *quite* (see the previous subsection). To obtain the distinctive collexemes for the British and American varieties, one can repeat the procedure by comparing each variety against the rest.

11.3 Summary

This chapter has introduced the basic principles of distinctive collexeme analysis. They were illustrated by a case study of *quite* as a pre-adjectival modifier in British, American and Canadian English. The approach is based on the computation of association measures for 2-by-2 tables, which were introduced in the previous chapter. Although log-transformed Fisher exact test *p*-values are usually computed due to their robustness to low frequencies, in principle, any bidirectional measure that was mentioned in Chapter 10 can be used. Since the *p*-value is a hypothesis-testing statistic, which is influenced by the overall sample size, it may be more appropriate to use a measure of effect size, such as the odds ratio, especially if one wants to compare results based on corpora of different sizes. From this also follows that the length of a list of distinctive collexemes depends on the sample size.

How to write up the results of distinctive collexeme analysis

To report the results of DCA, you can make a table with top distinctive collexemes (or all, if the space permits) for each constructional or lectal variant and provide their distinctiveness scores. It is also recommended that you classify the distinctive collexemes into several theoretically interpretable classes, and add up their distinctiveness scores. These scores can then be compared across the varieties and presented in a table.

CHAPTER 12

Probabilistic multifactorial grammar and lexicology

Binomial logistic regression

What you will learn from this chapter:

> In this chapter you will learn how to model the speaker's choice between two near synonymous words or constructions on the basis of contextual features. The most popular statistical tool that is used to create such models is logistic regression. The approach is illustrated by a case study of two Dutch causative auxiliaries. As in the case of linear regression, you will learn how to create, test and interpret a logistic model with the help of different R tools.

12.1   Introduction to logistic regression

Logistic regression models the relationships between a categorical response variable with two or more possible values and one or more explanatory variables, or predictors. This technique is particularly popular in probabilistic multifactorial models that explain and predict the speaker's choice between two or more near synonyms or variants on the basis of conceptual, geographic, social, pragmatic and other factors. If there are two possible outcomes (i.e. near synonyms), the logistic model is called **binomial**, or **dichotomous**. In case of three and more outcomes, we deal with **multinomial**, or **polytomous** regression. This chapter will discuss binomial models. Multinomial models will be introduced in the next chapter.

The structure of a logistic regression model is very similar to that of a linear regression model. It can be represented by the following equation:

$$g(x) = b_0 + b_1 x_1 + b_2 x_2 + \ldots$$

where $g(x)$ is called the logit (or log odds) of the outcome (i.e. construction A or B). It is a value that reflects the chances of one outcome compared with the other outcome for a given configuration of values of the predictors. In multifactorial grammar, the logit represents the chances of construction A to be chosen in a particular type of context compared with the chances of construction B to be used in the same type of context. These chances depend on the predictors shown in the right part of the equation. For example, one can expect that the chances that the speaker will choose the modal verb *may* as opposed to *might* to express probability depend on the degree of (un)certainty. The chances of choosing the word *gown* as opposed to *dress* may depend on the degree of formality of the event and length of the clothing item. The chances of *windshield* compared with *windscreen* may depend on the variety of English used by the speaker.

The remaining components of the formula are identical to the basic components of linear regression discussed in Chapter 7. The first term, b_0, is the intercept. It is the value that determines the chances of an outcome when all predictors are equal to zero (for quantitative variables) or the reference value (for categorical variables).[1] The terms b_1, b_2, and so on, are the estimates of the effect of x_1, x_2, etc. They show by how much the chances of a particular outcome will increase or decrease when the value of the predictor (e.g. certainty, formality, language variety, etc.) changes.

Fitting a model means finding the values of all coefficients b_0, b_1, b_2, etc. The main method for fitting regression models is called maximum likelihood. When fitting a logistic regression model, the algorithm tries again and again different sets of values of the model parameters and returns the combination which maximally closely models the actual outcomes.

However, after R returns you a fitted model with specific values of the coefficients, this is only a beginning of your analysis. As in linear regression, one has to carry out model diagnostics and evaluation. These steps will be considered in the remaining part of the chapter and illustrated in a case study of the Dutch causative constructions with *doen* 'do' and *laten* 'let'.

12.2   Logistic regression model of Dutch causative auxiliaries *doen* and *laten*

12.2.1   Theoretical background and data

To reproduce the code in this case study, you will need the following add-on packages that should be installed (if you have not installed them yet) and loaded:

```
> install.packages(c("rms", "visreg", "car"))
> library(Rling); library(rms); library(visreg); library(car)
```

Causative constructions with *doen* and *laten* in Dutch, similar to the English constructions *make/have/get/cause X (to) do Y*, refer to complex causative events, which normally involve

---

1.   This holds for the treatment coding, when one level is chosen as the reference level (see Chapter 7). This is the default coding of categorical and binary variables in R, and also the most convenient one for fitting and interpreting logistic regression models.

the causing event, the effected event, the Causer (the entity that initiates the causation) and the Causee (the entity that actually carries out the effected event). Consider the following example:

(1)   *Hij   deed   me   denken   aan   mijn   vader.*
      He   did   me   think   at   my   father
      "He reminded me of my father."

In this example, *hij* 'he' is the Causer and *me* 'me' is the Causee. The auxiliary *deed* (the past form of *doen*) relates to the causing event, and the infinitive *denken* 'think' designates the effected event, i.e. what happened as the result of the causing event. As in all analytic causatives, the causing event (what the Causer actually did to bring about the effected event) is left unspecified.

The differences between the constructions with *doen* and *laten* have been explored extensively (e.g. Verhagen & Kemmer 1997; Levshina 2011). Most researchers agree that the construction with *doen* denotes direct causation, whereas the *laten*-construction refers to indirect causation. Direct causation means that "there is no intervening energy source 'downstream' from the initiator: if the energy is put in, the effect is the inevitable result" (Verhagen & Kemmer 1997: 70). Indirect causation, which also includes the situations of enablement and permission, emerges when the situation "can be conceptualized in such a way that it is recognized that some other force besides the initiator is the most immediate source of energy in the effected event" (Verhagen & Kemmer 1997: 67).

Compare (1) with (2). While in (1) the causation is construed as involuntary, not controlled by the Causee, who is the affected entity, in (2) the main source of energy is the Causee, who acts deliberately. Thus, in (2) the causation is less direct than in (1):

(2)   *Ik   liet   hem   mijn   huis   schilderen.*
      I   let   him   my   house   paint
      "I had him paint my house."

One could think of several ways of operationalizing this difference in a corpus-based quantitative study. First, as Verhagen & Kemmer (1997) show, (in)directness is closely related to the semantic characteristics of the main participants. Four types of causation are distinguished:

- inducive: a mental Causer acts upon a mental Causee
- volitional: a mental Causer acts upon an non-mental Causee
- affective: a non-mental Causer acts upon a mental Causee
- physical: a non-mental Causer acts upon a non-mental Causee

Verhagen & Kemmer (1997) demonstrate that inducive causation 'favours' *laten*, since a human entity normally does not act upon another human mind directly (except for telepathy). In contrast, affective and physical causation 'prefer' *doen* because an inanimate

Causer usually produces direct effect, as in (1). There are no theory-driven expectations about volitional causation; it can be both direct and indirect.

Another operationalization of directness and indirectness is (in)transitivity of the effected predicate (*denken* 'think' in the first example, and *schilderen* 'paint' in the second one). If the effected predicate is intransitive, the causation chain is short, and the causation can be seen as more direct. If the predicate is transitive, and there is a third entity, which is affected by the causation, like the house in (2), the causation chain is longer and the causation is less direct.

In addition to the conceptual factors related to (in)directness of causation, we should take into account a geographic factor, namely, Netherlandic or Belgian (Flemish) variety of Dutch. As was mentioned in the previous chapter, the decrease in the use of causative *doen* has been especially dramatic in Netherlandic Dutch.

The dataset that will be used to test the conceptual and variational hypotheses is collected from Netherlandic and Flemish newspapers. It is available as the data frame doenLaten in Rling. It contains a random sample of observations with the causative auxiliaries coded for the variables mentioned above. Every row in the data frame is an observation (case), i.e. a unique context where one of the auxiliaries was used. The columns are manually coded variables. From str() one can see that the data frame contains 455 observations and 5 variables. All of them are categorical. The response variable *Aux* has two levels, 'doen' or 'laten'. *Country* stands for Belgium ('BE') or the Netherlands ('NL'). *Causation* specifies one of the four causation types: 'Affective', 'Inducive', 'Physical' or 'Volitional'. *EPTrans* shows whether the effected predicate is transitive ('Tr') or intransitive ('Intr'). The last variable (*EPTrans1*) will be introduced later.

```
> data(doenLaten)
> head(doenLaten)
    Aux    Country   Causation    EPTrans    EPTrans1
1   laten  NL         Inducive     Intr       Intr
2   laten  NL         Physical     Intr       Intr
3   laten  NL         Inducive     Tr         Tr
4   doen   BE         Affective    Intr       Intr
5   laten  NL         Inducive     Tr         Tr
6   laten  NL         Volitional   Intr       Intr

> str(doenLaten)
'data.frame': 455 obs. of 5 variables:
$ Aux: Factor w/ 2 levels "laten","doen": 1 1 1 2 1 1 2 2 2 1 …
$ Country: Factor w/ 2 levels "NL","BE": 1 1 1 2 1 1 1 1 1 2 …
$ Causation: Factor w/ 4 levels "Affective","Inducive",..: 2 3 2 1
2 4 3 1 2 2 …
$ EPTrans: Factor w/ 2 levels "Intr","Tr": 1 1 2 1 2 1 1 2 1 1 …
$ EPTrans1: Factor w/ 2 levels "Intr","Tr": 1 1 2 1 2 1 1 2 1 1 …
```

The frequencies of *doen* and *laten* are as follows:

```
> summary(doenLaten$Aux)
laten doen
277   178
```

How many observations are needed for logistic regression?

There exist different rules of thumb for logistic regression. According to one of them, the maximal number of parameters (i.e. all *b*-values in the formula) in a logistic regression model is approximately equal to the frequency of the *less* frequent outcome divided by 10 (Hosmer & Lemeshow 2000: 346–347). In our case, the less frequent auxiliary is *doen*. It occurs 178 times. Therefore, the maximum number of regression parameters is 178/10 ≈ 18. As you can see from the tables of regression coefficients presented below, the number of parameters in different models tested in this chapter is much lower.

12.2.2   Fitting a binary logistic regression model: Main functions

The main function in this analysis is `lrm()` from the add-on package `rms`. We will be using `lrm()` most of the time because it returns many useful statistics. However, for some purposes you will also need `glm()` for generalized linear models from the base package. The use of these functions is similar but not identical. The main arguments of the functions are the formula and the data. In the formula, the response variable should be on the left side of the tilde sign, and all the predictors of interest should be on the right. An important difference between the functions is that the `glm()` function requires that you specify the type of the model (i.e. binomial logistic) by adding the argument `family = binomial`.

To fit a logistic regression model with `lrm()`, you can use the following template:

```
> yourModel1 <- lrm(Outcome ~ PredictorX + PredictorY + ..., data = yourData)
```

To create a logistic model with `glm()`, use the following:

```
> yourModel2 <- glm(Outcome ~ PredictorX + PredictorY + ..., family = binomial, data = yourData)
```

To see the coefficients and other statistics of the model fitted with `lrm()`, you can simply type in the name of the model:

```
> yourModel1
```

To do the same with `glm()`, you should use the `summary()` function:

```
> summary(yourModel2)
```

Let us illustrate this by fitting a model with *Aux* as the response and three predictors with the help of `lrm()`:

```
> m.lrm <- lrm(Aux ~ Causation + EPTrans + Country, data = doenLaten)
> m.lrm

Logistic Regression Model

lrm(formula = Aux ~ Causation + EPTrans + Country, data = doenLaten)
                     Model Likelihood   Discrimination   Rank Discrim.
                       Ratio Test          Indexes           Indexes
Obs            455   LR chi2    271.35   R2      0.609     C      0.894
laten          277   d.f.       5        g       2.296     Dxy    0.787
doen           178   Pr(>chi2)  <0.0001  gr      9.935     gamma  0.817
max |deriv|  1e-07   gp                0.378     tau-a   0.376     Brier  0.112
                     Coef       S.E.      Wald Z  Pr(>|Z|)
Intercept            1.8631     0.3771    4.94    <0.0001
Causation=Inducive   -3.3725    0.3741    -9.01   <0.0001
Causation=Physical   0.4661     0.6275    0.74    0.4576
Causation=Volitional -3.7373    0.4278    -8.74   <0.0001
EPTrans=Tr           -1.2952    0.3394    -3.82   0.0001
Country=BE           0.7085     0.2841    2.49    0.0126
```

After the line with the formula, the output contains several columns with different statistics. The column on the left reports the total number of observations and the frequency of each outcome.

The column 'Model Likelihood Ratio Test' says whether the model is significant in general. This is an omnibus test, similar to the *F*-test in linear regression and ANOVA. In this column, one can find the Likelihood Ratio test statistic, the number of degrees of freedom and the *p*-value. The null hypothesis of the test is that the **deviance** (a term for unexplained variation in logistic regression) of the current model does not differ from the deviance of a model without any predictors. In such a model, which is called the intercept-only model, the probability of each outcome is kept constant for all observations. Since the *p*-value is smaller than 0.05, our model is significant, i.e. at least one predictor significantly deviates from zero.

The two columns on the right contain various goodness-of-fit statistics. The most frequently reported statistics for logistic regression are the concordance index C, also known as the area under the ROC-curve, and the Nagelkerke pseudo-R^2. If you take all possible pairs that contain a sentence with *doen* and a sentence with *laten*, and try all combinations, the statistic C will be the proportion of the times when the model predicts a higher probability of *doen* for the sentence with *doen*, and a higher probability of *laten* for the sentence with *laten* (see below on how these probabilities are computed). For this model, $C = 0.894$. This means that for 89.4% of the pairs of *doen* and *laten* examples, the predicted probability of *doen* is higher for the sentence where the speaker actually used *doen* than for the example where *laten* occurred. How good is this result? Hosmer & Lemeshow (2000: 162) propose the following scale:

$C = 0.5$ no discrimination
$0.7 \le C < 0.8$ acceptable discrimination
$0.8 \le C < 0.9$ excellent discrimination
$C \ge 0.9$ outstanding discrimination

It seems that our model discriminates well.

The second important measure is the Nagelkerke pseudo-R^2 (R2). It ranges from 0 (no predictive power) to 1 (perfect prediction). However, in logistic regression R^2 tends to be lower than in linear regression models, where this statistic originates from, even if the quality of models is comparable. This is why Hosmer & Lemeshow (2000: 167) do not recommend reporting the statistic. Another reason is that it is less conceptually clear than its linear regression counterpart, which shows the proportion of total variance in the response explained by the model (see Chapter 7).

Next, let us have a look at the table of coefficients. The first estimate belongs to the intercept. This value (1.8631) is the estimated **log odds** of the outcome when all predictors are at their reference levels (for categorical variables) or are equal to zero (for quantitative variables). The reference levels of each variable correspond to affective causation, intransitive Effected Predicate and Netherlandic Dutch. Note that this holds only for the treatment coding of categorical variables, which is the default in R. But which outcome is meant here, *doen* or *laten*? The algorithm compares the second level of the factor that represents the outcome with the first, or reference level. To check the order of levels, you can type in the following:

```
> levels(doenLaten$Aux)
[1] "laten" "doen"
```

Thus, the algorithm compares the second level ('doen') with the reference level ('laten'). To obtain simple odds, one should exponentiate the coefficient with the help of `exp()`, which is the opposite of `log()`:

```
> exp(1.8631)
[1] 6.443681
```

Compare:

```
> log(6.443681)
[1] 1.8631
```

This means that the odds of *doen* vs. *laten* in affective causation contexts with intransitive Effected Predicates and in the Netherlandic variety are approximately 6.44. Recall that odds greater than 1 mean that the probability of the first outcome is greater than the probability of the second outcome (see Chapter 9). If odds are between 0 and 1, the probability of the first outcome is smaller than that of the second outcome. The odds of 6.44 mean that the chances of *doen* are 6.44 times greater than those of *laten* for this type of context (affective causation, intransitive verb, Netherlandic newspapers).

Next, let us interpret the coefficients of the predictors, which are represented as **log odds ratios**. What do they indicate? A log odds ratio compares the odds of the outcome for each level of a predictor with the reference level (the default option). The *Causation* variable has four levels, but only three are shown in the table of coefficient. 'Affective' is the reference level. *EPTrans* has two levels, but only *EPTrans* = 'Tr' is shown. The *Country* variable has two levels ('NL' and 'BE'), but the table shows only the coefficient of *Country* = 'BE'. If the reference value is not specified by the user, the program selects the one that comes first alphabetically: *EPTrans* = 'Intr' and *Causation* = 'Affective'. As for *Country* with the values 'BE' and 'NL', the reference level 'NL' has been selected manually. Which value of a predictor is selected as the reference level, is not important statistically. However, for the purposes of interpretation you might wish to choose the reference level manually (see Chapter 4).

After this introduction, let us interpret the coefficients. Unlike simple odds and odds ratios, where equal probabilities correspond to 1, log odds and log odds ratios are centred around zero. If the coefficient is positive, the level specified in the table boosts the chances of *doen* (and therefore decreases the odds of *laten*). If the coefficient is negative, the specified level decreases the odds of *doen* (and boosts the chances of *laten*). For *Causation*, the reference level is 'Affective'. We see that inducive and volitional causation types have negative coefficients. That means that they decrease the odds of *doen* (and, conversely, boost the chances of *laten*) in comparison with affective causation. Physical causation has a positive estimate, so it seems to boost the chances of *doen* in comparison with the reference level. Transitive Effected Predicates seem to 'disfavour' *doen* (or 'favour' *laten*) when compared with intransitives. The odds of *doen* in the Belgian variety of Dutch are higher than those in the Netherlandic variety.

The log odds ratios, like odds ratios, represent the effect size. To transform log odds ratios into simple odds ratios, one can use exponentiation. For example, if the log odds ratio of *doen* in the Belgian variety vs. the Netherlandic variety is 0.7085, the simple odds ratio is computed as follows:

```
> exp(0.7085)
[1] 2.030943
```

Therefore, the odds of *doen* vs. *laten* in the Belgian variety of Dutch are approximately 2.03 times higher than those in the Netherlandic variety, other variables being controlled for.

This model contains only categorical predictors. In case of quantitative independent variables, their coefficients will show the change in the probability of a given outcome per measure unit (per word, per second, etc.).

Odds, log odds, odds ratios and log odds ratios

These notions are very important for understanding of logistic regression and interpretation of its results. Although odds and odds ratios have been already introduced (see Chapter 9), this box provides an overview of the old and new terms together.

Odds are a simple ratio of the probability of one event to the probability of another event, which can be expressed in a simplified form as a ratio of the frequency of outcome X to the frequency of non-X. The odds of *doen* vs. *laten* can be calculated as the ratio of occurrences of the causative *doen* to the frequency of *laten*, 178/277 ≈ 0.64. If odds equal 1, the probabilities of the outcomes are equal. If odds are greater than 1, the chances of the first event to happen are greater. If odds are between 0 and 1, as the odds of *doen* in this case study, the other outcome (*laten*) is expected to be used more frequently.

Odds should not be confused with **probabilities**, which are normally expressed as proportions or percentages. The proportion of *doen* in our data is equal to the number of occurrences of *doen* divided by the *total* number of observations: 178/455 ≈ 0.39, or 39%. If the chances of two events are equal, the probability of either outcome is 0.5, or 50%. Probabilities range from 0 to 1 (or from 0% to 100%).

Log odds are logarithmically transformed odds. We will be speaking about the natural logarithm (*ln*, or `log()` in R) everywhere in this chapter. Log odds have a nice property of being centred around 0 because the natural logarithm of 1 (when the odds of two outcomes are equal) is 0. The log odds of *doen* in our data are then *ln*(0.64) ≈ −0.45. The negative log odds show that this outcome is less probable than the other one (*laten*). The value of log odds can range from -Infinity (the natural logarithm of 0) to Infinity. Another name for log odds is **logit**.

(Continued)

Odds ratio is the ratio of two odds. Consider the odds of *doen* in the Belgian and Netherlandic varieties of newspaper Dutch. The odds ratio will look as follows:

$$OR = \frac{\dfrac{doen\,in\,BE}{laten\,in\,BE}}{\dfrac{doen\,in\,NL}{laten\,in\,NL}}$$

Similar to simple odds, an OR of 1 would mean that there is no difference between the odds of *doen* in the two varieties. If an OR is greater than 1, the odds of *doen* vs. *laten* in Belgian Dutch are higher than those in Netherlandic Dutch. If an OR is between 0 and 1, the odds of *doen* vs. *laten* in Belgian Dutch is smaller than in Netherlandic Dutch. To compute the actual odds ratio, one needs the frequencies of the auxiliaries in both varieties of Dutch:

```
> table(doenLaten$Aux, doenLaten$Country)

        NL    BE
laten   162   115
doen    71    107
```

The odds of *doen* vs. *laten* in the Belgian data are $107/115 \approx 0.93$. The value is close to 1 because *doen* is almost as frequent as *laten* in the Belgian sample. The odds of *doen* vs. *laten* in the Netherlandic newspapers are much lower: $71/162 \approx 0.44$. The odds ratio is then $0.93/0.44 \approx 2.12$. This means that the odds of *doen* in the Belgian newspapers are about twice as high as those in the Netherlandic newspapers.

Finally, a logarithm of an odds ratio is called the **log odds ratio**. In our case, $ln(2.12) \approx 0.75$. In fact, this is the coefficient of *Country* = 'BE' in a model with *Country* as the only predictor:

```
> m.Country <- lrm(Aux ~ Country, data = doenLaten)
> m.Country
[output omitted]
            Coef      S.E.     Wald    Z      Pr(>|Z|)
Intercept   -0.8249   0.1423   -5.80          <0.0001
Country=BE  0.7528    0.1957   3.85           0.0001
```

Thus, the coefficients of predictors are log odds ratios. Recall that the log odds ratio will be close to 0 if there is no difference between the levels of the predictor with regard to the choice between the synonyms. If a log odds ratio is positive, the specified level (e.g. *Country* = 'BE' in the model) boosts the chances of the selected outcome (*doen*) in comparison with the reference level (*Country* = 'NL'). If a log odds ratio is negative, the chances of the specified outcome decrease in comparison with the reference level.

One can easily obtain a simple odds ratio from a logistic regression coefficient (i.e. the log odds ratio) by using `exp()`.

```
> exp(0.7528)
[1] 2.122936
```

Let us now have a look at the remaining columns in the table of coefficients. The column S.E. shows the standard errors. Unusually high standard errors may signal data sparseness or multicollinearity (see Section 12.2.6). Wald is the Wald test statistic, a ratio of the estimate and the standard error. It is used to obtain the p-values. The latter can be found in the last column. Note that some other packages may use other tests to compute p-values, such as the likelihood ratio test or the Score test. The p-values of coefficients show how confident one can be about the estimate and whether the null hypothesis of no difference between the given value and the reference value of the predictors (e.g. *Country* = 'BE' and *Country* = 'NL') can be rejected. If the p-value is smaller than 0.05, the null hypothesis of no difference can be rejected.

All p-values in this example are smaller than the conventional level of significance 0.05, except for *Causation* = 'Physical'. This means that there is no significant difference between physical causation and affective causation (the reference level) with regard to the odds of *doen* vs. *laten*. This result ties in with the previous hypotheses, where affective and physical causation were regarded as two manifestations of direct causation.

As in linear regression, it is useful to compute the 95% confidence intervals of the estimated coefficients. This can be done with a `glm` object:

```
> m.glm <- glm(Aux ~ Causation + EPTrans + Country, data = doenLaten,
family = binomial)
> confint(m.glm)
Waiting for profiling to be done...
                      2.5%         97.5%
(Intercept)           1.1596659    2.6449674
CausationInducive    -4.1408874   -2.6683830
CausationPhysical    -0.7012840    1.8170992
CausationVolitional  -4.6187118   -2.9362799
EPTransTr            -1.9819904   -0.6446563
CountryBE             0.1566746    1.2746268
```

If a 95% confidence interval contains zero, this indicates that the corresponding effect is not significant. To obtain simple odds ratios, you can use exponentiation:

```
> exp(confint(m.glm))
Waiting for profiling to be done...
```

	2.5%	97.5%
(Intercept)	3.188867846	14.08298573
CausationInducive	0.015908728	0.06936430
CausationPhysical	0.495948081	6.15398090
CausationVolitional	0.009865497	0.05306276
EPTransTr	0.137794692	0.52484288
CountryBE	1.169615002	3.57736608

In case of simple odds ratios, the confidence interval of a significant effect should not include 1.

Similar to linear regression, the coefficients of the predictors and the intercept can be used to compute the fitted values, or the probabilities of the outcomes as predicted by the model. They can be obtained from the logit value, which is calculated by multiplying the regression coefficients by the actual values of the variables according to the logistic regression formula and summing up the results. To illustrate the procedure, let us take one of the observations from the dataset:

(3)   *Dit   doet   denken   aan   de   onzalige   tijden   van   de   junta   van*
      This   does   think   at   the wretched times   of   the junta of

      de   partijvoorzitters.
      the   party chairmen.

      'This reminds of the wretched times of the junta of party chairmen.'

This context is an example of affective causation with intransitive effected predicate *denken* 'think'. It comes from a Belgian newspaper. To calculate the predicted probability of *doen* for this context, we will need all coefficients in the model, including the intercept. Recall the structure of the logistic regression model:

$$g(x) = b_0 + b_1x_1 + b_2x_2 + \dots$$

To compute the logit of *doen*, one needs to sum up all coefficients in m.lrm multiplied by the values of the relevant predictors. If a value of a categorical variable is not true in this context (e.g. *Causation* = 'Inducive'), the corresponding coefficient is multiplied by 0. If it is true (e.g. *Causation* = 'Affective' in this example), the coefficient is multiplied by 1. The result looks as follows:

$$g(x) = 1.8631 + (-3.3725) \times 0 + 0.4661 \times 0 + (-3.7373) \times 0 + (-1.2952) \times 0 \\ + 0.7085 \times 1 = 2.5716$$

The sum 2.57 is the logit, or the log odds of the outcome (*doen*). The value is positive, so the chances of *doen* are estimated higher than those of *laten* in this context. In simple odds, it can be expressed as follows:

```
> exp(2.5716)
[1] 13.08675
```

This means that *doen* has approximately 13.09 times more chances to occur in this context than *laten*, according to the model. Predicted values are usually reported as probabilities. One can transform logits (log odds) into probabilities by using the following formula:

$$p = \frac{e^{g(x)}}{1 + e^{g(x)}}$$

where *P* is the probability of a given outcome, and *g(x)* is the logit value. In our case, the probability of *doen* can be computed as follows:

```
> exp(2.5716)/(1 + exp(2.5716))
[1] 0.9290113
```

The predicted probability of *doen* in this context is around 0.929, or 92.9%. Conversely, one can get the logit from probability *P* as follows:

$$g = log\,(odds)\; = log\frac{P}{1-P}$$

In this example, this would look as follows:

```
> log(0.9290113/(1 - 0.9290113))
[1] 2.5716
```

Some probabilities and the corresponding odds and logits are shown in Table 12.1. One can see that the probabilities are symmetrically distributed around 0.5, and logits are symmetric around 0. The simple odds scale is not symmetric: it is 'shrunk' in the range from 0 to 1 and 'stretched' in the range from 1 to Infinity. This is why it is more convenient to use log-transformed odds.

Table 12.1 Probabilities, corresponding odds and logits (rounded). The shaded row corresponds to the equal chances of either outcome, e.g. *doen* or *laten*

Probability	Odds	Logit (log odds)
0.001	0.001	−6.91
0.01	0.01	−4.6
0.05	0.05	−2.94
0.1	0.11	−2.2
0.25	0.33	−1.1
0.5	1	0
0.75	3	1.1
0.9	9	2.2
0.95	19	2.94
0.99	99	4.6
0.999	999	6.91

To obtain the predicted probabilities for all or one observation automatically, you can use `predict(model.lrm, type = "fitted")` for `lrm` models or `predict(model.glm, type = "response")` for `glm` models. The row number of the observation in our data was 27:

```
> predict(m.lrm, type = "fitted")[27]
        27
0.9290074
```

Since the probability is close to 1, this context is highly typical of *doen*.

Why not use linear regression instead of logistic regression?

Indeed, one could simply compute probabilities (proportions) of *doen* and *laten* for all possible combinations of predictors and run a linear regression with the probabilities as the response variable. However, this is not a very good idea. First, if you use linear regression, the regression line will be an endless straight line. As a result, the probability of an outcome may become greater than 1 or smaller than 0, which is impossible. The logit transformation of probabilities solves this problem. Second, such use of linear regression may result in violations of linear regression assumptions, such as homoscedasticity and normally distributed residuals.

12.2.3 Selection of variables

There are two strategies of variable selection available for logistic regression: fitting a model with all predictors of interest and stepwise selection (see Chapter 7). You will need to use a `glm()` object for stepwise selection. For example, to run forward selection, you can do the following:

```
> m0.glm <- glm(Aux ~ 1, data = doenLaten, family = binomial)
> m.fw <- step(m0.glm, direction = "forward", scope = ~ Causation
+ EPTrans + Country)
[output omitted]
```

Backward stepwise selection is the safest option if you really need a stepwise solution. To run it, you should enter the model with all predictors and add `direction = "backward"`:

```
> m.bw <- step(m.glm, direction = "backward")
Start: AIC=349.7
Aux ~ Causation + EPTrans + Country
```

```
              Df        Deviance   AIC
⟨none⟩        337.70    349.70
- Country     1         344.05     354.05
- EPTrans     1         353.36     363.36
- Causation   3         550.58     556.58
```

Finally, one can use the default bidirectional selection (`direction = "both"`). In all three cases, the stepwise algorithm picks all three variables that were in the first model.

In case you fit a model and find out that some *p*-values are above the 0.05 threshold, this is not a sufficient reason to discard the variable. When a predictor has more than two values, not all comparisons are shown in the table. In the model presented above, for example, the difference between inducive and volitional causation is not shown in the table of coefficients. This is why it is useful to perform an ANOVA to test if the model that includes this variable tells us more about the outcome than the model without this variable. For illustration, one can check if the variable *Causation* is worth including in the final model as follows:

```
> m.glm1 <- glm(Aux ~ EPTrans + Country, data = doenLaten, family
= binomial)
> anova(m.glm1, m.glm, test = "Chisq")
Analysis of Deviance Table

Model 1: Aux ~ EPTrans + Country
Model 2: Aux ~ Causation + EPTrans + Country
Resid. Df   Resid. Dev   Df Deviance   Pr(>Chi)
1           452          550.58
2           449          337.70 3      212.88 < 2.2e-16 ***
```

If the greater model reduces the deviance significantly in comparison with the model without a predictor, this is a sign that the predictor is worth keeping in the model. A useful function is `drop1()`, which removes each term from the model, one at a time, and tests the changes in the model's fit:

```
> drop1(m.glm, test = "Chisq")
Single term deletions

Model:
Aux ~ Causation + EPTrans + Country
            Df      Deviance   AIC      LRT       Pr(>Chi)
⟨none⟩              337.70 349.70
Causation   3       550.58     556.58   212.878   < 2.2e-16 ***
EPTrans     1       353.36     363.36   15.661    7.579e-05 ***
Country     1       344.05     354.05   6.348     0.01175 *
--
Signif. codes: 0 '***' 0.001 '**' 0.01 '*' 0.05 '.' 0.1 ' ' 1
```

The results indicate that all predictors are useful.

12.2.4   Testing possible interactions

As has been already explained in connection with linear regression and ANOVA, interactions are observed when the effect of one predictor on the outcome depends on the value of another variable. A commonly observed type of interactions in multifactorial models of grammar and lexicon is different effect of contextual variables on the choice between the constructions in different language varieties. An example is the loosening of the animacy constraint on the semantics of the possessor/recipient in the genitive and dative alternations from late Modern English on (Wolk et al. 2013). Such differences may also be detected in geographic varieties and registers (e.g. Bresnan & Hay 2008; Szmrecsanyi 2010).

Let us test if there are interactions between the variable *Country* and the other predictors.

```
> m.glm.int <- glm(Aux ~ Causation + EPTrans*Country, data =
doenLaten, family = binomial)
```

The significance of the interaction can be estimated with the help of ANOVA:

```
> anova(m.glm, m.glm.int, test = "Chisq")

Analysis of Deviance Table

Model 1: Aux ~ Causation + EPTrans + Country
Model 2: Aux ~ Causation + EPTrans *Country
  Resid. Df   Resid. Dev   Df        Deviance   Pr(>Chi)
1       449       337.70
2       448       334.58 1   3.1151      0.07757.
--
Signif. codes: 0 '***' 0.001 '**' 0.01 '*' 0.05 '.' 0.1 ' ' 1
```

The model with the interaction is not significantly better than the model with the main effects only ($p = 0.078$). Still, it is worth considering for didactic purposes. There are three terms in the table of coefficients that need interpretation:

```
> summary(m.glm.int)
[output omitted]
EPTransTr              -1.8825   0.4919   -3.827   0.00013 ***
CountryBE              0.3693    0.3416    1.081   0.27966
EPTransTr:CountryBE    1.0827    0.6215    1.742   0.08149.
[output omitted]
```

As you may remember from previous discussions of interactions in Chapters 7 and 8, the coefficient of *EPTrans* no longer corresponds to the independent effect of *EPTrans* as it was in the initial model. Instead, it shows the conditional effect of transitive Effected Predicates only if *Country* = 'NL' (the reference level). This effect is significant and negative. Likewise,

`CountryBE` is not an independent effect of *Country* any more. It is the effect of *Country* when the Effected Predicate is intransitive (again, this is the reference level). It is positive but not significant. Finally, `EPTransTr: CountryBE` is the interaction term. It reflects the difference in the effect of transitive Effected Predicates in the Belgian and Netherlandic data. The estimate is positive. This means that transitive Effected Predicates increase the chances of *doen* in Belgian Dutch in comparison with the Netherlandic variety, although this effect is only marginally significant.

These relationships can be visualized with the help of `visreg()` in the package under the same name. The arguments of `visreg()` are the `glm` model, the name of the variable whose effect we are interested in (*EPTrans*), and the variable that defines the conditions (`by = "Country"`)

```
> visreg(m.glm.int, "EPTrans", by = "Country")
```

The resulting plot is shown in Figure 12.1.

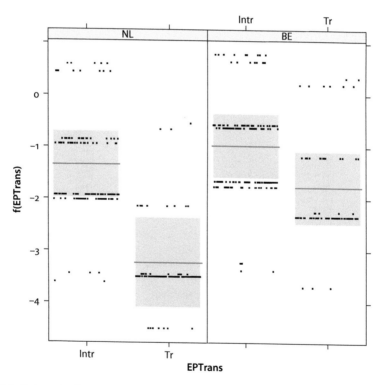

Figure 12.1. Interaction between *EPTrans* and *Country*

One can see that the effect of *EPTrans* is stronger in the Netherlands than in Belgium because the distance between the horizontal lines that correspond to transitive and intransitive Effected Predicates is greater in the Netherlandic data, even though the effect, essentially, remains the same: intransitive predicates are more pro-*doen* than transitive ones. As additional research in Levshina at al. (2013) has demonstrated, there seems to be lexical factors at play: in the Netherlandic data, there are very many observations with constructions *laten zien* 'show, let see', *laten weten* 'let know' and *laten horen* 'let hear'. All of them contain transitive Effected Predicates. Why these expressions are preponderant in the Dutch newspapers and much less frequent in the Belgian data requires further investigation.

12.2.5 Identifying outliers and overly influential observations

As was shown in Chapter 7, one can use the function `influencePlot()` in the car package to identify outliers and overly influential observations. The function requires a `glm` model. The argument `id.method = "identify"` will start an interactive session. You can identify the points by clicking on them. After you have finished, press *Esc*. Figure 12.2 shows the plot with a few identified points.

```
> influencePlot(m.glm, id.method = "identify")
```

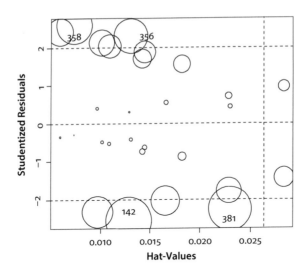

Figure 12.2. Plot with outliers and influential points

The plot allows one to examine discrepancy values (the vertical axis), leverage values (the horizontal axis) and Cook's distances (the size of bubbles) for every observation (see Chapter 7, Section 7.2.4 for more details). There are no points in the dangerous region with both high leverage (outliers with regard to the horizontal axis) and discrepancy values (below –2 or above 2 on the vertical axis). However, there are a few observations with large discrepancies and large Cook's distance values (according to the size of the bubbles). Let us have a closer look at the observations in the data:

```
> doenLaten[c(142, 356, 358, 381),]
      Aux      Country   Causation     EPTrans    EPTrans1
142   laten    BE        Physical      Intr       Intr
356   doen     BE        Volitional    Tr         Tr
358   doen     NL        Volitional    Tr         Tr
381   laten    NL        Physical      Intr       Intr
```

These contexts are not very typical of *doen* or *laten*. For example, observation 142, which was found in the Belgian subcorpus, contains an intransitive Effected Predicate and describes physical causation. Although these features are typical of *doen*, the auxiliary *laten* is used. This demonstrates that our corpus operationalization of causation types may be too coarse-grained for subtle conceptual differences, but this is a common problem for corpus-based semantic studies.

12.2.6   Checking the regression assumptions

Logistic regression has fewer assumptions than linear regression. These assumptions are as follows:

- Assumption 1. *The observations are independent (of one another).*
- Assumption 2. *The relationships between the logit and the quantitative predictors are linear.*
- Assumption 3. *No multicollinearity is observed between the predictors.*

Assumption 1. *The observations are independent.*
Similar to linear regression, observations should be independent of one another. In our case, observations might be dependent if, for example, we had several data points per speaker (the journalist) or per newspaper article. One could hypothesize that one's idiolect or syntactic priming effects might have influence on the choice between the auxiliaries. Since the sample was created on the basis of a wide selection of newspaper texts over several years, such effects are highly unlikely. Another possible problem is that the choice of the auxiliary might be affected by the fact that they can form set expressions with particular Effected Predicates, e.g. *doen denken aan X* 'remind of X, lit. make think of X' or *laten zien* 'show, lit. let see'. In that case, a mixed GLM with Effected Predicates as random effects may be a preferable option, although previous research suggests that the conceptual and lectal factors retain their influence when these and other lexical combinations are taken into account (Levshina 2011).

Assumption 2. *The relationships between the logit and the quantitative predictors are linear.*
Since the model does not contain quantitative predictors, this assumption does not have to be tested. If necessary, the relevant diagnostic tests can be found in Chapter 7 on linear regression (use the `glm()` object).

Assumption 3. *No multicollinearity is observed between the predictors.*

As in linear regression diagnostics (see Section 7.2.5 in Chapter 7), one can use the function `vif()` in the `rms` package, which computes VIF (Variance Inflation Factor) scores for each term in the `lrm()` object. The package `car` also contains such a function, which can be used with a `glm()` object, if necessary.

```
> rms::vif(m.lrm)
Causation=Inducive    Causation=Physical    Causation=Volitional
1.699064              1.356411              1.959948
EPTrans=Tr            Country=BE
1.270669              1.017354
```

As was already mentioned in Chapter 7, there exist different rules of thumb to detect the scores that are too high and therefore indicate the presence of multicollinearity. The thresholds of 5 or 10 are the most commonly used. Overall, logistic regression is quite robust with regard to some correlation between predictors.

The presence of multicollinearity is accompanied by large standard errors and *p*-values. The original model seems to contain no traces of serious multicollinearity, but we can model a situation when multicollinearity is obvious for illustration purposes, similar to what we did in Chapter 7 to illustrate multicollinearity in linear regression. Let us add another variable to the model, named *EPTrans1*, which is very similar to *EPTrans*, with the exception of a few values. See what happens with the coefficients, *p*-values and VIF-scores for *EPTrans* and *EPTrans1*:

```
> m.test <- lrm(Aux~Causation + EPTrans + EPTrans1 + Country, data
= doenLaten)
> m.test
[output omitted]
```

	Coef	S.E.	Wald	Z Pr(>|Z|)
Intercept	1.8749	0.3780	4.96	<0.0001
Causation=Inducive	-3.3661	0.3742	-9.00	<0.0001
Causation=Physical	0.5027	0.6336	0.79	0.4275
Causation=Volitional	-3.7178	0.4282	-8.68	<0.0001
EPTrans=Tr	-0.0889	1.6257	-0.05	0.9564
EPTrans1=Tr	-1.2153	1.5972	-0.76	0.4467
Country=BE	0.6936	0.2848	2.44	0.0149

```
> rms::vif(m.test)
Causation=Inducive    Causation=Physical    Causation=Volitional
1.697379              1.373455              1.959740
EPTrans=Tr            EPTrans1=Tr           Country=BE
29.170101             28.516853             1.021357
```

The VIF-scores of *EPTrans* and *EPTrans1* are almost 30. This is a sign of strong multi-collinearity. The estimates of these two predictors in the model are unreliable, and the *p*-values are now much greater than 0.05. However, the predictive power of the model does not suffer: the *C*-index is even slightly higher than in the previous model (0.895 compared to 0.894).

Most traditional linguistic categories, like transitivity or animacy, with their prototyp-ically organized structure and fuzzy boundaries allow for many different operationaliza-tions in a corpus-linguistic study. Although logistic regression is quite robust with regard to small amounts of multicollinearity, in situations of very similar operationalizations it is advisable to select one variable that is the most justified theoretically. Alternatively, one can use dimensionality-reduction techniques presented in Chapters 17 to 19.

Complete and quasi-complete separation

Complete and quasi-complete separation occurs when some values of a predictor or a combination of several predictors can perfectly predict the outcome. Imagine you want to predict the use of the definite and indefinite article in English and include the gram-matical number of the head noun as a predictor. If you cross-tabulate the predictor and the response, the table will contain a zero in the cell that corresponds to plural nouns and the indefinite article, as shown below. This is called **quasi-complete separation**. If the frequency of the definite article in the singular were zero, that would be an example of **complete separation.**

	Definite	Indefinite
Singular	18	15
Plural	12	0

Complete and quasi-complete separation should be avoided because the model either becomes unreliable (one can usually tell that from huge standard errors), or it simply may not converge and you will receive an error message. To solve the problem, you can recode the predictor (e.g. by conflating its levels) or use a model with a correction, such as the Firth penalized regression (see, for instance, the package `logistf` and the function under the same name). It is always useful to do cross-tabulation of all categorical predictors and the response before beginning your analysis in order to detect configura-tions with zero frequencies or a large number of cells with very low frequencies.

12.2.7 Testing for overfitting

Overfitting can be a serious problem in logistic regression, similar to linear regression. It seriously undermines the value of a model. Even if the sample size is sufficient, as in this case study, it is necessary to check how well the model will perform on new data. To do so, you can use validation with bootstrapping (see Chapter 7, Sections 7.2.7 and 7.2.8). To validate a logistic model, you will need a lrm() object. It is important to add two new arguments x = T and y = T.

```
> m.lrm1 <- lrm(Aux ~ Causation + EPTrans + Country, data = doenLaten,
x = T, y = T)
```

The function that performs bootstrapping is validate() in rms. The model will be refitted 200 times.

```
> validate(m.lrm1, B = 200)
          index.orig training test    optimism index.corrected  n
Dxy        0.7873     0.7946    0.7831  0.0115   0.7758          200
R2         0.6088     0.6183    0.6000  0.0182   0.5906          200
Intercept  0.0000     0.0000   -0.0139  0.0139  -0.0139          200
Slope      1.0000     1.0000    0.9614  0.0386   0.9614          200
Emax       0.0000     0.0000    0.0110  0.0110   0.0110          200
D          0.5942     0.6081    0.5825  0.0255   0.5687          200
U         -0.0044    -0.0044    0.0010 -0.0054   0.0010          200
Q          0.5986     0.6124    0.5815  0.0309   0.5677          200
B          0.1116     0.1095    0.1133 -0.0038   0.1154          200
g          2.2961     2.4163    2.2971  0.1192   2.1769          200
gp         0.3782     0.3801    0.3746  0.0055   0.3727          200
```

As was discussed in Chapter 7, the main indication of overfitting is high 'optimism' of the estimates and goodness-of-fit statistics. The optimism scores are displayed in the column optimism. The statistic Dxy, which is closely related to the concordance index C, and R2 are goodness-of-fit measures. The optimism values are relatively small. As one can see in the line with Slope, the estimates of the regression coefficients of the predictor variables are by 0.0386 too optimistic. This is not very dangerous. Your scores will be slightly different because the procedure is based on random resampling.

Let us carry out a small experiment for the purpose of illustration and fit our model on a smaller dataset of only 100 observations randomly sampled from the original dataset.

```
> s <- sample(455, 100)
> d.small <- doenLaten[s,]
> m.lrm1.small <- lrm(Aux ~ Causation + EPTrans + Country, data =
d.small, x = T, y = T)
> validate(m.lrm1.small, B = 200)
```

	index.orig	training	test	optimism	index.corrected	n
Dxy	0.7630	0.7826	0.7261	0.0565	0.7065	200
R2	0.5479	0.5989	0.4978	0.1011	0.4468	200
Intercept	0.0000	0.0000	-0.0861	0.0861	-0.0861	200
Slope	1.0000	1.0000	0.7753	0.2247	0.7753	200
Emax	0.0000	0.0000	0.0717	0.0717	0.0717	200
D	0.5001	0.5722	0.4422	0.1300	0.3701	200
U	-0.0200	-0.0200	0.0805	-0.1005	0.0805	200
Q	0.5201	0.5922	0.3618	0.2305	0.2896	200
B	0.1172	0.1075	0.1259	-0.0184	0.1356	200
g	2.0908	2.9614	1.9648	0.9966	1.0942	200
gp	0.3536	0.3644	0.3308	0.0336	0.3200	200

Now the optimism for the slope coefficients is 0.2247. The model strongly overfits the data.

What can one do if there is evidence of overfitting? If possible, you can try and add more data. A more viable solution, probably, is to use penalization to make the model more realistic (see Baayen 2008: 225–226; see also `help(pentrace)`). Alternatively, you can use random forests and conditional inference trees (see Chapter 14) which are particularly helpful in the situation of too few observations and too many predictors.

12.2.8 Interpretation of the model

Our analyses demonstrate that both the conceptual and geographical sources of variation are important in predicting the use of the Dutch causative constructions with *doen* and *laten*. The behaviour of the variables that are used to operationalize the (in)direct causation hypothesis is in accordance with the theory-driven expectations: the probability of *doen* is higher in the affective and physical causation situations, and in short causation chains, where the Causee is the final affected entity. All these features can be interpreted as manifestations of the (more) direct causation construal. The probability of *laten* is thus greater in the situations that indicate a less direct causation. In addition to these conceptual differences, there is also a significant effect of the language variety. The causative *doen* is more frequently used in Belgian Dutch, other factors being controlled for.

12.3 Summary

This chapter has discussed logistic regression with a binary outcome. This method is particularly useful for creation of multifactorial models of language variation. Although the procedure is very similar to linear regression analysis, there are some theoretical and practical differences that concern the goodness-of-fit measures, regression assumptions, interpretation of the results, etc. Of course, near synonyms do not come only in pairs. In the next chapter, you will learn how to fit a logistic model with more than two possible outcomes.

How to write up the results of logistic regression analysis

Logistic regression is reported similarly to linear regression. For a model with one predictor, you can provide the intercept b_0, the estimate b, standard error SE and p-value. To report the results of multiple logistic regression, you can make a table with these statistics. The asterisk system (***, **, *) can be used to indicate the significance of p-values. In both cases, it is necessary to provide some general goodness-of-fit statistic, preferably the concordance index C. Interactions are best represented visually. Although not strictly necessary, it is also useful to provide 95% confidence intervals, as well as to convert log odds ratios into simple odds ratios.

CHAPTER 13

Multinomial (polytomous) logistic regression models of three and more near synonyms

What you will learn from this chapter:

> This chapter continues the discussion of logistic regression models, which can be used to predict the speaker's choice between different near synonyms or variants. This time you will learn to model situations when the number of possible outcomes is greater than two. Such models are called multinomial, or polytomous. The method will be illustrated with a case study of three near synonyms: *let, allow* and *permit*.

13.1   What is multinomial regression?

A quick check in any dictionary of synonyms is sufficient to see that a pair of semantically similar words is rather an exception than a rule. Mostly, synonyms come in larger groups. For more than two possible outcomes you will need a special type of logistic regression, which is called multinomial, or polytomous. Multinomial models can be classified into two types. One type involves fitting two or more binary models, which compare each outcome against some reference level. Consider three near synonyms *let, allow* and *permit*. It is possible to model the choice between *permit* and *let*, and that between *allow* and *let*, with *let* as the base for comparison. The other approach models the odds of each outcome against all other outcomes ('one vs. rest'). For example, it can tell us which factors increase the chances of *let* against both *allow* and *permit*, the chances of *allow* against both *let* and *permit*, and the chances of *permit* against both *allow* and *let*. In this chapter, both approaches will be discussed and their results will be compared.

13.2   Multinomial models of English permissive constructions

13.2.1   Data and hypotheses

You will need several add-on packages, which contain the data and functions that are required for this case study. These packaged should be installed and then loaded.

```
> install.packages(c("mlogit", "polytomous"))
> library(Rling); library(mlogit); library(polytomous)
```

This case study will investigate the differences between three English permissive constructions *let*, *allow* and *permit* + (*to*) Infinitive. The data represent a random sample of the three constructions from COCA (Davies 2008 –). Since *let* is not used in passive contexts (*She was let leave*), only active forms will be considered. The sample is drawn from two registers of COCA: spontaneous conversations (transcripts from diverse TV and radio programmes) and popular magazines.

The variables reflect the following information:

-   *Verb* is the response variable with three values: 'allow', 'let' and 'permit'.
-   *Permitter* is the semantic class of the matrix clause subject: 'Anim' for animate, 'Inanim' for inanimate and 'Undef' for undefined.
-   *Imper* reflects the mood of *let*, *allow* or *permit*: 'Yes' (imperative) or 'No' (all other forms).
-   *Reg* is the register: 'Spok' for conversations and 'Mag' for magazine articles.
-   *Year* is the year when the source text was published or broadcast, from 1990 to 2012.

The dataset with over 500 examples is available as the data frame `let`.

```
> data(let)
> str(let)
'data.frame': 518 obs. of 5 variables:
$ Year: int 2003 2005 1990 2007 1997 1996 1995 2007 2005 1992 ...
$ Reg: Factor w/ 2 levels "MAG","SPOK": 1 2 2 2 1 1 1 2 1 2 ...
$ Verb: Factor w/ 3 levels "allow","let",..: 1 1 2 1 3 1 1 2 3 1 ...
$ Permitter: Factor w/ 3 levels "Anim","Inanim",..: 2 2 1 2 1 1 2
1 1 2 ...
$ Imper: Factor w/ 2 levels "No","Yes": 1 1 1 1 2 1 1 2 1 1 ...
```

The constructions and the corresponding permissive verbs have similar conceptual contents that can be described as non-occurrence or cessation of impingement. However, they are not identical. As noted by Wierzbicka (2006), *let* is used in many situations of cooperative interaction, as in *let me help you*, *let me know* or *let me see*, which involve the imperative use. This is why one can expect that *let* will have higher chances to be used in the imperative than the other verbs. Second, *permit* and *allow* can be used in the meaning 'to provide an opportunity, make possible', as in (1) and (2), whereas *let* would not be appropriate in such contexts. Therefore, we can expect *permit* and *allow* to be used with non-human Permitters more frequently than *let*.

(1)   *GEEK TRIVIA. Tesla Originally Believed His Radio **Allowed** Him To Communicate With Whom? The Dead. Astronauts. Sailors. Martians. Answer: Martians.* (http://www.howtogeek.com, accessed 3.03.2014)

(2)   *Not seeing people **permits** us to imagine them with every perfection.* (Victor Hugo)

In addition, *let* sounds the least formal of these three alternatives, whereas *permit* is the most formal verb, which can be used to denote official authorization. This is why *permit* is expected to have the highest odds of occurrence in the texts from magazines, and *let* to have the lowest ones.

13.2.2 Contrasting *allow* and *permit* with *let*

This subsection demonstrates how a multinomial model which contrasts each outcome with the reference level can be fitted and interpreted. For fitting the model, we will use the package `mlogit`. This function requires a special 'long' data format. In this format, every observation is repeated several times for every possible outcome. To transform a data frame in the original wide format, where each outcome is represented only once, into the long format, one can use the function `mlogit.data()` from the same package. It requires the following arguments: the original data frame, its current shape (`shape = "wide"`) and the outcome variable (`choice = "Verb"`). The resulting object contains three times more rows than the original data frame because every observation is repeated three times, for each of the possible three outcomes:

```
> let1 <- mlogit.data(let, shape = "wide", choice = "Verb")
> head(let1)
          Year  Reg   Verb   Permitter  Imper  chid  alt
1.allow   2003  MAG   TRUE   Inanim     No     1     allow
1.let     2003  MAG   FALSE  Inanim     No     1     let
1.permit  2003  MAG   FALSE  Inanim     No     1     permit
2.allow   2005  SPOK  TRUE   Inanim     No     2     allow
2.let     2005  SPOK  FALSE  Inanim     No     2     let
2.permit  2005  SPOK  FALSE  Inanim     No     2     permit
> nrow(let1)
[1] 1554
```

Let us begin with fitting a model that contains all predictors. The syntax is very similar to other regression functions, with two exceptions. First, one has to add `1|` to create a multinomial model. Second, one can specify the reference level of the response variable. That is the construction that every other synonym will be compared with. By default, the algorithm will select 'allow'. Instead, let us compare *allow* and *permit* with *let*, the second level.

```
> m.let <- mlogit(Verb ~ 1 | Year + Reg + Permitter + Imper, data
= let1, reflevel = 2)
```

One can access the fitted model by using `summary()`:

```
> summary(m.let)
```

```
Call:
mlogit(formula = Verb ~ 1 | Year + Reg + Permitter + Imper, data =
let1, reflevel = 2, method = "nr", print.level = 0)

Frequencies of alternatives:
     let    allow permit
0.36100 0.32239 0.31660

nr method
6 iterations, 0h:0m:0s
g'(-H)^-1g = 1.39E-05
successive function values within tolerance limits.

Coefficients:
                          Estimate    Std.Error  t-value  Pr(>|t|)
allow:(intercept)         0.8184551   47.1686986 0.0174   0.986156
permit:(intercept)        241.1632221 49.3786220 4.8840   1.040e-06 ***
allow:Year                -0.0004914  0.0235595  -0.0209  0.983359
permit:Year               -0.1206881  0.0246883  -4.8885  1.016e-06 ***
allow:RegSPOK             -0.0060516  0.2865426  -0.0211  0.983150
permit:RegSPOK            0.0871446   0.2958475  0.2946   0.768331
allow:PermitterInanim     2.5991669   0.4108197  6.3268   2.503e-10 ***
permit:PermitterInanim    2.6433057   0.4215179  6.2709   3.589e-10 ***
allow:PermitterUndef      1.2653550   0.6067334  2.0855   0.037022 *
permit:PermitterUndef     1.6024125   0.6027837  2.6584   0.007852 **
allow:ImperYes            -3.0887042  0.5453765  -5.6634  1.484e-08 ***
permit:ImperYes           -3.5291867  0.6287956  -5.6126  1.993e-08 ***
--
Signif. codes: 0 '***' 0.001 '**' 0.01 '*' 0.05 '.' 0.1 ' ' 1

Log-Likelihood: -401.94
McFadden R^2: 0.2926
Likelihood ratio test: chisq = 332.5 (p.value = < 2.22e-16)
```

The summary provides a lot of information. The goodness-of-fit statistics are at the bottom. The log-likelihood shows the amount of deviance still left. The smaller the absolute value, the better the fit. McFadden's R^2 is analogous to R^2 in linear regression. Values from 0.2 to 0.4 are considered to indicate a very good fit, which corresponds to 0.7 to 0.9 in linear models (Louviere et al. 2000: 55). With $R^2 = 0.29$ the model fits well. As in binary logistic regression, the likelihood ratio test statistic is used to test the overall significance of the model with the null hypothesis that none of the coefficients is different from zero. A very small p-value tells us that the model is significant.

The most unusual part, however, is the table of coefficients. Each predictor appears twice: first, with *allow*, and then with *permit*. Each line compares one of these verbs with the reference level, *let*. As in binary logistic regression, the coefficients are log odds ratios. A positive coefficient tells us that the given value of the predictor (or every additional unit of measurement, in case of quantitative variables) increases the chances of the given verb in comparison with *let*. A negative coefficient means that the predictor decreases the chances the given verb. For example, the verb *permit* seems to become less frequent with time than *let* (`permit:Year` = `-0.1206881`). One can get rid of the logarithm and obtain the corresponding simple odds ratio by using `exp()`:

```
> exp(-0.1206881)
[1] 0.8863104
```

Since *Year* is a quantitative variable, the odds of *permit* vs. *let* decrease by the factor of 0.886 with every additional unit of the numerical predictor, that is, with every additional year. Conversely, the odds of *let* against *permit* increase by the factor of $1/0.886 \approx 1.128$ every year. The low *p*-value suggests that this effect is significant.

The table also indicates that inanimate and undefined Permitters significantly increase the odds of *allow* and *permit* against *let*. This means that *let* is a verb that tends to 'prefer' animate semantic subjects, as expected. At the same time, the negative coefficients show that *allow* and especially *permit* are less frequently used in imperative constructions than *let*. Again, this finding is in accordance with the predictions.

Interestingly, the effect of register is not significant at all. It may be that the perceived informality of *let* comes from its association with cooperative interaction and imperative forms, because refitting a model without *Imper* yields significant or marginally significant coefficients of *Reg* (the readers are invited to test this themselves). On the other hand, the spoken conversations found in COCA are in fact quite formal, representing news broadcasts and on-air interviews.

As usual, the 95% confidence intervals of the coefficients can be obtained as follows:

```
> confint(m.let)
                          2.5 %        97.5 %
allow:(intercept)       -91.63049530   93.26740551
permit:(intercept)      144.38290150  337.94354279
allow:Year               -0.04666719    0.04568438
permit:Year              -0.16907626   -0.07229997
allow:RegSPOK            -0.56766482    0.55556163
permit:RegSPOK           -0.49270585    0.66699505
allow:PermitterInanim     1.79397509    3.40435869
permit:PermitterInanim    1.81714593    3.46946552
allow:PermitterUndef      0.07617940    2.45453054
permit:PermitterUndef     0.42097814    2.78384687
allow:ImperYes           -4.15762241   -2.01978601
permit:ImperYes          -4.76160340   -2.29677005
```

It is also possible to obtain fitted values for the actually observed outcomes with the help of fitted():

```
> head(fitted(m.let))
1.let          2.let          3.let          4.let          5.let
0.56121053     0.59260191     0.20854471     0.64121412     0.03173396

6.let
0.26904521
```

The values are the probabilities of the following observed choices:

```
> head(let$Verb)
[1] allow allow let allow permit allow
Levels: allow let permit
```

Relatively small fitted probabilities suggest that the predictive power of the model regarding the individual observations is not so fantastic. Ideally, all fitted probabilities should be close to 1.

It is also possible to obtain fitted values for all three outcomes:

```
> head(fitted(m.let, outcome = FALSE))
         let            allow          permit
[1,]     0.04924250     0.56121053     0.38954697
[2,]     0.05236395     0.59260191     0.35503415
[3,]     0.20854471     0.17673678     0.61471852
[4,]     0.05671517     0.64121412     0.30207071
[5,]     0.93217877     0.03608727     0.03173396
[6,]     0.31648259     0.26904521     0.41447221
```

Note that the probabilities in each row sum up to 1.

Recall that the variable *Reg* did not have any significant effect. Is it redundant? As in the previous regression models, you can use ANOVA to compare two models and see whether adding or deleting one variable has a significant effect. In mlogit, one has several options to perform such a comparison. We will use the Wald test here (see the help page of waldtest() in the mlogit package for two other options).

```
> m.let1 <- mlogit(Verb ~ 1 | Year + Permitter + Imper, data = let1,
reflevel = 2)
```

Next, we compare the less constrained model without *Reg* with the previous one:

```
> waldtest(m.let1, m.let)
Wald test

Model 1: Verb ~ 1 | Year + Permitter + Imper
Model 2: Verb ~ 1 | Year + Reg + Permitter + Imper
```

```
Res.Df Df Chisq Pr(>Chisq)
1     508
2     506 2 0.1658    0.9205
```

The high *p*-value indicates that the variable *Reg* does not improve the fit of the model. This method can be also used for testing potential interactions. There seems to be no significant two-way interactions, as the reader can test him- or herself.[1]

13.2.3   'One vs. rest' approach

The second approach is 'one vs. rest', when each possible outcome is compared with all other possibilities. To fit the model, you will need the package `polytomous`. The possibilities offered by this package are different from `mlogit`. For instance, one can use 'wide' data frames. In addition, the summary returns a variety of goodness-of-fit statistics. To fit a first model with all predictors, you can use the function `polytomous()`:

```
> m.let2 <- polytomous(Verb ~ Permitter + Imper + Year + Reg, data
= let)
```

Let us begin with the goodness-of-fit measures:

```
> summary(m.let2)$statistics
$df.null
[1] 1554

$df.model
[1] 1536

$AIC.model
[1] 845.5114

$BIC.model
[1] 922.011

$loglikelihood.null
[1] -568.1868

$loglikelihood.model
[1] -404.7557

$deviance.null
[1] 1136.374

$deviance.model
```

---

1. In some cases, the models with interactions did not converge due to a few zeros in the cells of the table of cross-tabulated categorical predictors. Try: `table(let$Permitter, let$Imper, let$Reg)`.

```
[1]  809.5114

$R2.likelihood
[1]  0.2876362

$R2.nagelkerke
[1]  0.5266656

$crosstable
           allow    let    permit
allow      71       42     54
let        8        152    27
permit     34       29     101

$accuracy
[1]  0.6254826

$recall.predicted
allow          let            permit
0.4251497    0.8128342      0.6158537
$precision.predicted
allow          let            permit
0.6283186    0.6816143      0.5549451
[output omitted]
```

The pseudo-R^2 measures are different approximations of the corresponding measure in linear regression. The first R^2 is the McFadden statistic, which was discussed in the previous section. Its value is similar to the one in the previous model. In addition to the measures that you should be already familiar with, there are measures of accuracy, recall and precision. The accuracy measure shows how correctly the model predicts the use of the verbs. To understand what this measure means, consider the numbers in $crosstable. The rows display the observed permissive verbs, and the columns show how many times the model would predict each outcome. The numbers in the diagonal show the correct predictions (e.g. the cases when *allow* was both predicted and observed). The statistic accuracy then shows the total number of correct predictions divided by the number of observations (71 + 152 + 101)/518 ≈ 0.625. The measure recall shows the proportion of instances of each verb, which were predicted by the algorithm. One can see that over 80% of instances of *let* would be predicted as instances of *let* by the model. *Allow*, unfortunately, has a relatively low recall value, only approximately 43%. The measure precision, in contrast, shows how many times the predictions of *allow*, *let* or *permit* made by the model were correct. Again, *let* has the highest value over 68%, but now *permit* is predicted the least accurately (about 55%).

Let us now examine the table of regression coefficients. To access it, one can use the code below. Note that by default the function summary() will return simple odds and odds ratios. For the sake of compatibility with our previous models, we will represent the estimated coefficients as log odds (ratios).

```
> print(summary(m.let2), parameter = "logodds")
Formula:
Verb ~ Permitter + Imper + Year + Reg
Heuristic:
one.vs.rest

Log-odds:
                    let         allow         permit
(Intercept)        -Inf         -Inf          Inf
ImperYes           3.292        -2.559        -2.954
PermitterInanim    -2.622       0.7804        0.7399
PermitterUndef     -1.411       (0.3325)      0.8294
RegSPOK            (-0.0443)    (-0.05829)    (0.09126)
Year               0.05592      0.07814       -0.1203

Null              deviance:   1136.0  on  1554   degrees  of freedom
Residual (model)  deviance:   809.5   on  1536   degrees  of freedom
R2.likelihood:    0.2876
AIC:              845.5
BIC:              922
```

The table of coefficients shows the log odds ratios of the linguistic and extralinguistic features. Note that if the estimates are in brackets, the coefficients are not statistically significant at the level of 0.05. The actual *p*-values (rounded up to 3 digits after the decimal separator for convenience) can be obtained as follows:

```
> round(m.let2$p.values, 3)
                    let      allow    permit
(Intercept)        0.008    0.000    0.000
ImperYes           0.000    0.000    0.000
PermitterInanim    0.000    0.000    0.001
PermitterUndef     0.012    0.415    0.043
RegSPOK            0.867    0.787    0.684
Year               0.009    0.000    0.000
```

Again, there is evidence that *let* is 'disfavoured' by inanimate Permitters at a significant level $(-2.622, p < 0.001)$ in comparison with the two other verbs, whereas both *allow* (0.7804, $p < 0.001$) and *permit* (0.7399, $p = 0.001$) have, in contrast, higher chances to occur when the Permitter is inanimate. These results are similar to the ones discussed in the previous subsection. As for undefined Permitters, they boost the chances of *permit* and decrease the odds of *let*. The estimated coefficient of *allow* is not significant.

The variable *Year* shows how much the log odds of a verb change with every year. The coefficients reveal a significant increase in the use of *allow* with time, followed by *let*, and a decrease in the use of *permit*. With every year, the odds of *permit* seem to decrease by –0.1203 log odds, which makes it 0.886 in simple odds (recall that odds smaller than 1 indicate a decrease).

```
> exp(-0.1203)
[1] 0.8866544
```

This coefficient is nearly identical to the coefficient of `permit:Year` in the `mlogit` model, which compared *permit* with *let*. It seems that *permit* is becoming a rarer verb in this construction in comparison with both *let* and *allow*, since the contrast between *allow* and *let* was not significant in the previous model. This gradual decrease of *permit* with time is somewhat unexpected. Whether this tendency can be traced within a longer period and in other registers is a question for further research.

The effect of register is again not significant, whereas the estimate of *Imper* supports the previous conclusion about *let* as the most 'interactive' verb. However, if all pairwise interactions are added to the model one by one and tested with the help of ANOVA, one can find a significant interaction between *Reg* and *Imper*.[2] The ANOVA results are below:

```
> m.let3 <- polytomous(Verb ~ Permitter + Imper*Reg + Year, data =
let)
> anova(m.let2, m.let3)
Analysis of deviance Table

Model 1: Verb ~ Permitter + Imper + Year + Reg
Model 2: Verb ~ Permitter + Imper *Reg + Year
        Resid. Df Resid. Dev. Df Deviance P(>|Chi|)
Model 1   1536    809.51
Model 2   1533    793.49 3   16.023 0.001122 **
--
Signif. codes: 0 '***' 0.001 '**' 0.01 '*' 0.05 '.' 0.1 ' ' 1
```

Adding the interaction has changed the goodness-of-fit statistics:

```
> summary(m.let3)$statistics
[output omitted]

$R2.likelihood
[1] 0.3017362

$R2.nagelkerke
[1] 0.544905

$crosstable
        allow   let   permit
allow    80     31    56
let      26    134    27
```

---

2.   Another significant interaction is observed between *Permitter* and *Imper*, but adding it results in data sparseness and 'NA' values due to the fact that some levels of the variables have zero co-occurrence frequency (see the previous footnote).

```
permit    37        23      104

$accuracy
[1] 0.6138996

$recall.predicted
allow         let           permit
0.4790419   0.7165775    0.6341463

$precision.predicted
allow         let           permit
0.5594406   0.7127660    0.5561497
[output omitted]
```

On the one hand, both versions of R^2 have slightly increased. At the same time, the overall accuracy has become slightly poorer. As one can see from the diagonal numbers in the cross-table, the prediction of *allow* and *permit* has in general improved, but the prediction of *let* has become worse (due to the drop in the recall of *let*).

Let us now examine the interaction.

```
> print(summary(m.let3), parameter = "logodds")

Formula:
Verb ~ Permitter + Imper *Reg + Year

Heuristic:
one.vs.rest

Log-odds:
                        allow        let        permit
(Intercept)             -Inf         -Inf       Inf
ImperYes                (-1.058)     1.665      -1.765
ImperYes:RegSPOK        (-16.77)     3.546      (-2.094)
PermitterInanim         0.8013       -2.684     0.7516
PermitterUndef          (0.3611)     -1.486     0.8452
RegSPOK                 (0.08194)    (-0.3801)  (0.1598)
Year                    0.07736      0.05865    -0.1209

Null deviance:              1136.0  on  1554   degrees of freedom
Residual (model) deviance:  793.5   on  1533   degrees of freedom

R2.likelihood:  0.3017
AIC:            835.5
BIC:            924.7
```

The term `ImperYes` does not show the general effect of *Imper*, but rather the effect of *Imper* when a context comes from a magazine (the reference level). In that case, there is a significant increase of the probability of *let* and a significant decrease of the probability of *permit*, compared to the reference level `ImperNo`. However, in the spoken data the chances of *let* in imperative constructions are much greater (see the positive interaction term 3.546), and this effect is significant. For non-imperative constructions (the reference level) and the spoken register (the term `RegSPOK`), there seems to be no significant difference between the verbs.

To summarize, the register effect is observed only in imperative contexts. Imperative constructions in the spoken data greatly increase the chances of *let*. What is so special about these constructions? It seems that such structures are very important pragmatically, for example, for argumentation management, which allows to introduce new turns in the topic within one speaker's discourse:

> (3)   Dr-VENTER: *So Congress is waiting to pass such legislation. But* **let** *me give you the other side of this.* (COCA SPOK NPR_Science 2003)

In TV and radio programmes, participants normally have to communicate under time pressure. This is why they have to negotiate, justify or even fight for a chance to say what they have to say, as in the examples below.

> (4)   SCHIEFFER: *Well,* **let** *me just say – and I want to make sure everyone understands this.* (COCA SPOK CBS_FaceNation 1997)

> (5)   Mr-QUINN: *No,* **let** *me –* **let** *me finish, Jonathan* (COCA SPOK CBS_FaceNation 1998)

As was mentioned above, such cases can be classified as *let* of cooperative dialogue, following Wierzbicka (2006). They are highly distinctive of *let*, not only in comparison with other verbs in English, but also with the similar verbs in other languages. However, this effect is observed only when *let* is contrasted with **both** *allow* and *permit*. When it is compared to *allow* and *permit* separately, we observe only a borderline significance of the interaction term ($p = 0.053$) for `permit:RegSPOK:ImperYes`, $b = -2.51$.

13.3   Summary

This chapter has introduced multinomial logistic regression analysis. Two approaches to multinomial regression has been discussed: (a) each outcome vs. the reference level and (b) one vs. rest. Although the model interpretation may be quite challenging, the case study demonstrates that the two approaches are complementary and enable one to fine-tune the interpretation of each model.

Writing up the results of multinomial regression

One can use the same approach as in binary logistic regression, but it is recommended to provide two or more tables for each comparison made. It is crucial that you present the estimates and the p-values, as well as a goodness-of-fit statistic, such as the McFadden R^2, which is a popular goodness-of-fit statistic for multinomial models.

More on multinomial models

Another linguistic case study where the package `polytomous` is used can be found in Arppe et al. (2013). The R code is provided, as well. The file can be accessed from R by typing in `vignette("shanghainese")`. An example of a `mlogit()` model with interactions is given in Field et al. (2012: Section 8.9). See also Gries (2013: 322–323), who uses another function, `multinom()`.

CHAPTER 14

Conditional inference trees and random forests

What you will learn from this chapter:

> This chapter discusses conditional inference trees and random forests. These are non-parametric tree-structure models of regression and classification that can serve as an alternative to multiple regression. They are especially useful in the presence of many high-order interactions and in situations when the sample size is small, but the number of predictors is large. You will learn how to fit such models, interpret their results and evaluate their quality. The case study that illustrates the techniques deals with three English causative constructions *make + V*, *cause + to V* and *have + V* and identifies the set of independent semantic variables that are important for distinguishing between the constructions.

14.1 Conditional inference trees and random forests

Conditional inference trees and random forests were introduced to linguistic analysis in a paper by Tagliamonte & Baayen (2012). **Conditional inference trees** are a method for regression and classification based on binary recursive partitioning. The latter involves several steps:

(1) the algorithm tests if any independent variables are associated with the given response variable, and chooses the variable that has the strongest association with the response.

(2) the algorithm makes a binary split in this variable, dividing the dataset into two subsets. In case of a binary predictor with values *A* and *B*, one subset will contain all observations with value *A,* and the other will contain all cases with value *B*. If a variable has more levels, one group may have values *A* and *B*, and the other may contain observations with *C*. If the variable is quantitative, the range of its values can be split into two, e.g. values from 0 to 100 can be split into two subsets: from 0 to 50 and from 51 to 100.

(3) the first two steps are repeated for each subset until there are no variables that are associated with the outcome at the pre-defined level of statistical significance. This is why the algorithm is called recursive. The result of this process can be visualized as a tree structure with binary splits forming 'branches' and 'leaves'.

Conditional inference trees offer several advantages over traditional approaches, such as the one implemented in `rpart()` in the package under the same name. First, variable selection is unbiased (the traditional method is biased towards variables with many possible splits). Second, one does not have to 'prune' (i.e. simplify) the resulting tree to avoid overfitting. Third, the algorithm also returns the *p*-values that show how confident one can be about every split.

To obtain the *p*-values, the algorithm uses **permutation**. Permutation means that the labels on the observed data points are rearranged many times, and for each rearrangement the relevant test statistic is computed. This is a way of obtaining the distribution of the test statistic under the null hypothesis of no difference, no association, etc. Next, one determines the proportion of the permutations that provide a test statistic greater than or equal to the one observed in the original data. If that proportion is smaller than some significance level, then the result is significant at that level. Permutation is similar to bootstrapping in that they both are non-parametric resampling methods, which use the same data for validation of results. However, they are not identical, since the former involves reshuffling of the labels, whereas the latter draws numerous random samples from the original sample. More details about the algorithm and available options can be found in Hothorn et al. (2006).

From many conditional trees one can grow a **random forest**. Random forests can yield the importance measure for every variable in the model averaged over many conditional trees. This measure reflects the impact of each predictor given all other independent variables.

Conditional inference trees and random forests can be particularly useful in situations of data sparseness ('small *n* large *p*', where *n* is the number of observations and *p* is the number of predictors), high-order interactions, and highly correlated predictors (Tagliamonte & Baayen 2012). In addition, recursive partitioning is non-parametric because it does not require distributional assumptions to be met. It is also considered to be robust in the presence of outliers.

14.2   Conditional inference trees and random forests of three English causative constructions

14.2.1   The data and hypotheses

To reproduce the code in this case study, you will need the following packages, which should be installed and loaded:

```
> install.packages("party")
> library(Rling); library(party)
```

The methods described in the first section will be illustrated by a case study of three causative constructions in English: *make + V* (e.g. *He made me believe he was an aristocrat*), *have + V* (e.g. *The professor had the students read Tolstoy in the original*) and *cause + to V* (e.g. *The crisis caused the demand for gold to grow*). According to previous research, *make + V* is the default causative in English with the widest scope of uses, whereas *cause + to V* denotes mostly physical causation, and *have + V* is typically used in inducive interpersonal causation (e.g. Levshina et al. 2013). These three constructions are only a part of the rich inventory of English causative constructions (see Chapter 15).

The dataset `caus` can be found in the package `Rling`. It is a data frame that contains nine causative constructions, each represented by fifty observations randomly sampled from the newspaper segment of the British National Corpus. For this case study, it is convenient to create a subset with three constructions of interest:

```
> data(caus)
> mhc <- caus[caus$Cx == "make_V"|caus$Cx == "have_V"|caus$Cx ==
"cause_toV", ]
> summary(mhc)
Cx              CrSem       CeSem       CdEv     Neg      Coref     Poss
cause_toV:50 Anim:88    Anim:105   Ment:34  No:143  No:148   No:142
have_V:50    Inanim:62 Inanim: 45 Phys:52  Yes: 7  Yes: 2   Yes: 8
make_V:50                          Soc:64
be_made_toV: 0
get_toV: 0
get_Ved: 0
(Other): 0
```

To get rid of the levels of *Cx* that have zero frequencies in the new data frame, one can use factor():

```
> mhc$Cx <- factor(mhc$Cx)
> summary(mhc$Cx)
cause_toV     have_V make_V
     50        50      50
```

Finally, the level names can be simplified:

```
> levels(mhc$Cx) <- c("cause", "have", "make")
> summary(mhc$Cx)
cause   have   make
50      50     50
```

The six other variables are explained in Table 14.1. They will be tested as predictors in conditional inference tree and random forest models, which predict the use of one of the three causative constructions specified in *Cx*.

Table 14.1 Semantic and syntactic variables

Variable	Values	Examples
CrSem (semantics of the Causer)	Animate	*He made me laugh.*
	Inanimate	*His joke made me laugh.*
CeSem (semantics of the Causee)	Animate	*She made him leave.*
	Inanimate	*The crisis caused the demand for gold to grow.*
CdEv (semantics of the caused event)	Mental	*She made him believe her.*
	Physical	*She made him leave.*
	Social	*The teacher had the students play a game.*
Neg (negation)	Yes	*She didn't make him leave.*
	No	*She made him leave.*
Coref (coreferentiality between the Causer and other participants)	Yes	*He made himself think more clearly.*
	No	*She made him leave.*
Poss (markers of possession between the Causer and other participants)	Yes	*She had her house elves do the dishes.*
	No	*She made him leave.*

14.2.2   Fitting a conditional inference tree model

Conditional inference trees are implemented as the `ctree()` algorithm in the `party` package. Although the dataset contains only categorical predictors, note that any kind of variables can be used. Before fitting a model, one should specify any random number for random number generation. The function `set.seed()` allows one to obtain a reproducible random result if one specifies the same number.

```
> set.seed(129)
> mhc.ctree <- ctree(Cx ~ CrSem + CeSem + CdEv + Neg + Coref + Poss,
data = mhc)
> plot(mhc.ctree)
```

Figure 14.1 presents the tree with all possible splits that are significant at the level of 0.05. The ovals contain the names of the variables selected for the best split, as well as the corresponding *p*-values. The levels of the variables are specified on the 'branches'. The bar plots at the bottom ('leaves') show the proportions of *make*, *have* and *cause* in each end node ('bin'), which contains all observations with a given combination of features. The number of observations in each bin is shown in parentheses above the boxes.

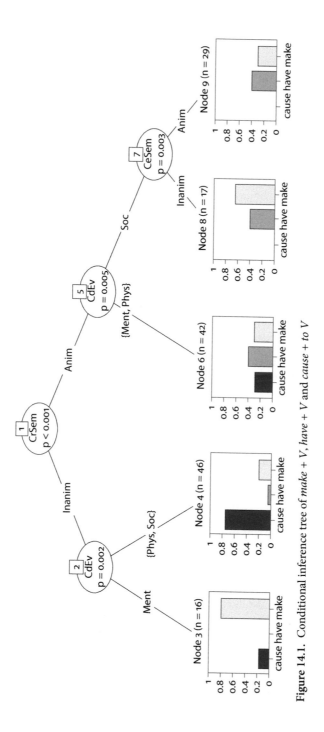

Figure 14.1. Conditional inference tree of *make + V*, *have + V* and *cause + to V*

Control parameters in conditional inference trees

It is possible to change the parameters of the algorithm, such as the level of significance, the minimum number of observations in a bin and other things. For example, if you wish to run a Monte-Carlo simulation with the significance level of 0.01 and 15 as the minimum number of observations in the bin, you can use the following code:

```
> mhc.ctree1 <- ctree(Cx ~ CrSem + CeSem + CdEv + Neg + Coref +
Poss, data = mhc, controls = ctree_control(testtype = "MonteCarlo",
mincriterion = 0.99, minbucket = 15))
```

See more information in `help(ctree_control)`.

The first split at the top divides animate and inanimate Causers (Node 1). The left branch with inanimate Causers is split into two branches (Node 2): contexts with mental caused events (Node 3) and physical or social caused events (Node 4). Node 3 contains 16 observations. Such contexts can be characterized as affective causation (see Chapter 12 on this and other types of causative situations). Most of them contain *make*, for example:

(1)   *Great course … I learned a lot and it really **made** me think about the way I communicate with people.*

Node 4, which contains 46 observations, has many instances of physical causation, which explains why *cause* is the most frequent verb in this group. Consider an example:

(2)   *It causes the plant to rot.*

Let us now explore the right branch. The next split is found at Node 5, which separates the observations with mental and physical caused events (Node 6) from those with social caused events on the right. The latter are then split at Node 7 into those with inanimate Causees (Node 8) and animate Causees (Node 9). The bin at Node 9 contains 29 observations. It represents inducive interpersonal causation, coded predominantly with the *have*-construction, such as in (3):

(3)   *She **had** us use the lecture room for an in-class discussion.*

Node 8, in contrast, contains mostly volitional causation represented by 17 observations. In this group, *make* is the predominant causative auxiliary:

(4)   *Everyone **made** it happen.*

Finally, Node 6 is a mixed category with different causation types represented nearly equally by all three verbs, for instance:

(5)   *I have sometimes **made** him laugh heartily.*

The results corroborate previous findings. One can conclude that *cause + to V* is associated with physical causation, whereas *have + V* typically expresses inducive causation. The default construction *make + V* is represented in every bin, although it seems to be particularly 'favoured' in situations of volitional and affective causation. In general, only those variables that reflect the semantics of the participants and that of the caused event seem to be useful for discriminating between the three constructions.

Does the tree represent the data well? To answer this question, one can cross-tabulate the predicted probabilities with the observed outcomes:

```
> table(predict(mhc.ctree), mhc$Cx)

             cause       have      make
cause         35          2         9
have          12         42        17
make           3          6        24
> (35 + 42 + 24)/150
[1] 0.6733333
```

If the numbers on the table diagonal are added up, the resulting number is the number of correct predictions. Here the correct predictions are made for 0.673, or 67.3% of the total 150 observations. If the algorithm simply assigned the verbs randomly, it would be correct in 33.3% of the cases. So, the model offers some improvement beyond that baseline.

To ensure that the results are stable, it is recommended to run the analysis several times with different random number seeds and compare the resulting models.

14.2.3   Random forests

To create a random forest, one can use the function `cforest()` from the same package:

```
> set.seed(35)
> mhc.rf <- cforest(Cx ~ CrSem + CeSem + CdEv + Neg + Coref + Poss,
data = mhc, controls = cforest_unbiased(ntree = 1000, mtry = 2))
```

The argument `ntree = 1000` tells R to grow a large forest with 1000 trees. It is recommended to define `mtry` (i.e. the number of randomly preselected predictors at each split) as the square root of the number of predictors, but one should try several different values.

Next, the measures of variable importance are computed. Note that this procedure is computationally intensive and you may have to wait for some time. Since the algorithm is based on permutation, your results will be slightly different every time you execute the code, unless you use set.seed() with the same number every time you compute the measures.

```
> mhc.varimp <- varimp(mhc.rf, conditional = TRUE)
> round(mhc.varimp, 3)
CrSem  CeSem  CdEv   Neg    Coref  Poss
0.098  0.043  0.045  0.000  0.000  0.000
```

The variable importance scores demonstrate that the semantics of the Causer is the most important predictor (0.098), followed by the semantic class of the caused event (0.045) and that of the Causee (0.043). Your results may slightly differ because the procedure is based on random reshuffling of the data. These are also the variables that were responsible for the splits in the conditional inference tree. Negation, coreferentiality and possession relations do not seem to have any discriminatory power. The impact of variables can be visualized in a dot chart, as shown in Figure 14.2:

```
> dotchart(sort(mhc.varimp), main = "Conditional importance of
variables")
```

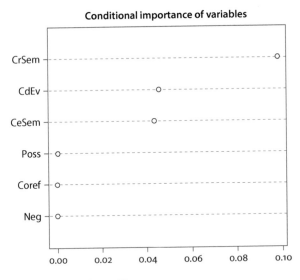

Figure 14.2. Dotchart of conditional variable importance

If a variable is irrelevant, its importance values will vary around the zero. Sometimes it is difficult to say which variable is relevant and which is not. According to a rule of thumb, the cut-off value is the absolute importance value of the variable with the smallest score.

To obtain an idea of how well the model fits the data, one can again compute the accuracy measure:

```
> table(predict(mhc.rf), mhc$Cx)

        cause   have   make
cause   39      2      9
have    8       48     28
make    3       0      13
> (39 + 48 + 13)/150
[1] 0.6666667
```

The accuracy is twice as large as the one that one could expect by chance. Note, however, that the model predicts *have* far too often (8 + 48 + 28 = 84 times), and 'underpredicts' *make* (3 + 13 = 16 times). There is definitely room for improvement, e.g. by trying larger values of mtry.

How to compute *C-index* for binary response

If your response variable is binary, you can obtain the *C-index* to evaluate the goodness of fit of your conditional inference tree or random forest model (see Chapter 12). It can be computed with the help of the function somers2() from the package Hmisc. For a conditional inference tree model, this can be done as follows:

```
# do not run; provided only as an example
> your.ctree.pred <- unlist(treeresponse(your.ctree))[c(FALSE,
TRUE)]
> somers2(your.ctree.pred, as.numeric(yourdata$Outcome) - 1)
```

To compute the *C-index* for a random forest model, replace the argument your.ctree with your random forest object.

Similar to conditional inference trees, it is recommended to rerun random forests several times with different random number seeds and compare the results.

14.3 Summary

This chapter has introduced conditional inference trees and random forests, two recent non-parametric techniques that can be used when regression modelling is problematic (complex interactions, too few observations in comparison with the number of variables, etc.). You have learnt how to fit, evaluate and interpret such models. This chapter concludes the large section on statistics for hypothesis testing. The final large part of this book will discuss exploratory methods that can be used for detecting structure in multivariate data.

Writing up your results

Since the techniques are relatively novel, there seem to be no rules for reporting the results. It is recommended to use a graphical representation and report the goodness-of-fit statistics.

More on trees and forests

See another example of conditional inference trees and random forests in Tagliamonte & Baayen (2012). For more information about traditional binary recursive partitioning methods, see Crawley (2007: Ch. 21).

CHAPTER 15

Behavioural profiles, distance metrics and cluster analysis

What you will learn from this chapter:

This chapter presents the Behavioural Profiles approach, which involves the comparison of contextual features of words or constructions in a corpus. The chapter also discusses several clustering algorithms, which are based on different distance metrics. Cluster analysis is a family of techniques that can help you discover groups of similar objects in the data. Several popular methods of cluster validation and diagnostics are discussed, which involve the computation of average silhouette widths and multiscale bootstrap resampling. The chapter also demonstrates how to interpret clusters with the help of the snake plot and effect size measures. In addition, you will learn to create and interpret scree plots, which are useful for determining the optimal number of clusters.

15.1 What are Behavioural Profiles?

The method of Behavioural Profiles (BP) is based on the ideas of Atkins (1987) and Hanks (1996), which have been more recently elaborated by Dagmar Divjak, Stefan Th. Gries and other linguists in a series of studies (e.g. Divjak 2003; Divjak & Gries 2006; Gries 2006). The approach is especially revealing for sets of near synonyms or different senses of one word. It is also particularly convenient for analysis of verb semantics because it can be used to incorporate the semantic and syntactic properties of verb arguments (e.g. the giver, the recipient and the object of transfer in the ditransitive construction, as in *I gave him the book*). For instance, Divjak & Gries (2006) compared the BP vectors of verbs of trying in Russian. The same approach can be applied to word senses, as Gries (2006) did in his study of the polysemous verb *run* (see Gries [2012] for more examples). The BP method typically requires many instances of a construction or a word coded for a number of semantic, syntactic and other categorical variables that characterize the local context, which is usually defined at the level of the sentence where the word occurs. Next, the data are represented as vectors of proportions of each value in a variable. These are BP vectors. The numerical differences between the vectors can be transformed into distances between the objects (words or word senses). Next, one can investigate semantic relationships between the objects by clustering them and exploring the common and distinctive features of clusters and individual words.

15.2 Behavioural Profiles of English analytic causatives

15.2.1 Data and theoretical background

To perform this case study, you will need the data and functions from several add-on packages. These packages should be first installed and then loaded.

```
> install.packages(c("cluster", "pvclust", "vcd"))
> library(Rling); library(cluster); library(pvclust); library(vcd)
```

Causation is a basic concept in human cognition and language (e.g. Talmy 2000). Languages have a wide range of strategies for expressing causal relationships, from mono-lexical verbs (e.g. *kill*, which expresses 'cause to die') to causal connectives (P *because* Q; Q, *therefore*, P). In this case study, we will examine English analytic causatives (see Chapter 12 for a description of this construction type). The English analytic causatives have received much attention in the literature (e.g. Stefanowitsch 2001; Wierzbicka 2006; Gilquin 2010; Levshina et al. 2013). The constructions that we address in this study contain the causative verbs *make*, *have*, *get* and *cause*. These verbs combine with different forms of the Effected Predicates, which include the active or passive infinitive and past or present participles. Table 15.1 shows the constructional patterns that will be considered in this study.

Table 15.1 Constructional patterns of English analytic causatives

Constructional Pattern	Example
make_V	She made him leave.
be_made_toV	He was made to resign (by the opposition).
cause_toV	The high interest rates caused the currency to collapse.
have_V	They had a draughtsman prepare the plans.
have_Ved	He had his hair cut (by a hairdresser).
have_Ving	The band will have you rocking in your seat.
get_toV	She got the minister to sign the papers.
get_Ved	They tried to get their plan accepted (by the community).
get_Ving	The new government got the economy going.

For this case study, a random sample of 450 observations was collected from the BNC. Each of the nine constructional patterns was represented by 50 observations. The observations were manually coded for six categorical variables shown in Table 14.1 (see Chapter 14). These data are available as the data frame `caus` in the `Rling` package

```
> data(caus)
> str(caus)
```

```
'data.frame': 450 obs. of 7 variables:
$ Cx: Factor w/ 9 levels "be_made_toV",..: 1 1 1 1 1 1 1 1 1 …
$ CrSem: Factor w/ 2 levels "Anim","Inanim": 1 1 1 1 1 1 1 1 1 …
$ CeSem: Factor w/ 2 levels "Anim","Inanim": 1 1 1 1 1 1 1 1 1 …
$ CdEv: Factor w/ 3 levels "Ment","Phys",..: 3 3 3 1 2 3 3 1 2…
$ Neg: Factor w/ 2 levels "No","Yes": 1 1 1 1 1 1 1 1 1 1 …
$ Coref: Factor w/ 2 levels "No","Yes": 1 1 1 1 1 1 1 1 1 1 …
$ Poss: Factor w/ 2 levels "No","Yes": 1 1 1 1 1 1 1 1 1 1 …
```

The main question of this case study is whether the distributional properties of the constructional patterns with the same causative auxiliaries are highly similar, or such patterns exhibit idiosyncratic properties.

To construct and analyse BP vectors, one can also use a ready-made package BehavioralProfiles written by Stefan Th. Gries (available upon request), but, since the primary goal of this textbook is to teach how one can use freely available R functions, the analyses will be performed and explained stepwise. The main steps are as follows:

Step 1. Creation of numeric BP vectors from categorical data.
Step 2. Computation of the matrix of distances between the BP vectors.
Step 3. Cluster analysis and identification of the optimal number of clusters.
Step 4. Interpretation of the cluster solution in terms of the distinctive features of clusters.
Step 5. Validation of the cluster solution.

In the remaining part of the chapter, these steps will be addressed one by one.

15.2.2 Computation of numeric BP vectors from the categorical data

To create BP vectors of nine causative constructions, one can first make subsets of the data frame, which correspond to the individual constructional patterns. The patterns are the levels of the factor in the first column:

```
> levels(caus$Cx)
[1] "be_made_toV" "cause_toV"    "get_toV"      "get_Ved"      "get_
Ving" "have_V" "have_Ved"     "have_Ving"    "make_V"
```

To create a subset with all observations that correspond to one pattern, we will use the following code:

```
> be_made_toV <- caus[caus$Cx == "be_made_toV", -1]
> cause_toV <- caus[caus$Cx == "cause_toV", -1]
> get_toV <- caus[caus$Cx == "get_toV", -1]
> get_Ved <- caus[caus$Cx == "get_Ved", -1]
> get_Ving <- caus[caus$Cx == "get_Ving", -1]
> have_V <- caus[caus$Cx == "have_V", -1]
```

```
> have_Ved <- caus[caus$Cx == "have_Ved", -1]
> have_Ving <- caus[caus$Cx == "have_Ving", -1]
> make_V <- caus[caus$Cx == "make_V", -1]
```

Note that we also discard the first column with the constructional types, since it becomes redundant. After having repeated the procedure for all patterns, we have nine separate small data frames. Now we are ready to create BP vectors. A BP vector contains the proportions of each value of every variable. To transform the frequencies into proportions, one can use prop.table(), which was introduced in Chapter 4. For instance, the proportions of animate and inanimate Causers for *make_V* can be obtained as follows:

```
> prop.table(table(make_V$CrSem))
Anim  Inanim
0.56  0.44
```

For the next variable, *CeSem*, the proportions are as follows:

```
> prop.table(table(make_V$CeSem))
Anim  Inanim
0.7   0.3
```

We could combine these proportions in one vector manually. However, to save the time, you can use the special function bp() in the Rling package. It also adds the names of variables to the levels:

```
> make_V.bp <- bp(make_V)
> make_V.bp
CrSem.Anim   CrSem.Inanim   CeSem.Anim   CeSem.Inanim   CdEv.Ment
0.56         0.44           0.70         0.30           0.34
CdEv.Phys    CdEv.Soc       Neg.No       Neg.Yes        Coref.No
0.32         0.34           0.98         0.02           1.00
Coref.Yes    Poss.No        Poss.Yes
0.00         1.00           0.00
```

The resulting numeric vector consists of 13 elements. The procedure should be repeated for the remaining constructions:

```
> be_made_toV.bp <- bp(be_made_toV)
> cause_toV.bp <- bp(cause_toV)
> get_toV.bp <- bp(get_toV)
> get_Ved.bp <- bp(get_Ved)
> get_Ving.bp <- bp(get_Ving)
> have_V.bp <- bp(have_V)
> have_Ved.bp <- bp(have_Ved)
> have_Ving.bp <- bp(have_Ving)
```

Finally, we can combine these vectors as rows in a matrix.

```
> caus.bp <- rbind(be_made_toV.bp, cause_toV.bp, get_toV.bp, get_
Ved.bp, get_Ving.bp, have_V.bp, have_Ved.bp, have_Ving.bp, make_V.
bp)
```

The matrix has nine rows and thirteen columns:

```
> dim(caus.bp)
[1] 9 13
```

Finally, we will replace the row names of the matrix with the original level names from caus$Cx. Short and clear labels are preferable when we explore clustering solutions.

```
> rownames(caus.bp) <- levels(caus$Cx)
```

A faster way of building BP vectors

A more efficient method with slightly more advanced code would take the following three steps. First, we split the data frame caus into a list of nine data frames that correspond to the values of *Cx*:

```
> caus.split <- split(caus, caus$Cx)
> str(caus.split)
List of 9
$ be_made_toV:'data.frame': 50 obs. of 7 variables:
..$ Cx: Factor w/ 9 levels "be_made_toV",..: 1 1 1 1 1 1 1 1 1 1 …
..$ CrSem: Factor w/ 2 levels "Anim","Inanim": 1 1 1 1 1 1 1 1
1 1 …
..$ CeSem: Factor w/ 2 levels "Anim","Inanim": 1 1 1 1 1 1 1 1
1 1 …
..$ CdEv: Factor w/ 3 levels "Ment","Phys",..: 3 3 3 1 2 3 3 1
2 1 …
..$ Neg: Factor w/ 2 levels "No","Yes": 1 1 1 1 1 1 1 1 1 1 …
..$ Coref: Factor w/ 2 levels "No","Yes": 1 1 1 1 1 1 1 1 1 1 …
..$ Poss: Factor w/ 2 levels "No","Yes": 1 1 1 1 1 1 1 1 1 1 …
[output omitted]
> length(caus.split)
[1] 9
```

(Continued)

Next, we remove the first column *Cx* in each data frame, since this column is no longer needed:

```
> caus.split <- lapply(caus.split, function(x) x = x[, -1])
```

Finally, we apply the `bp` function from `Rling` to each data frame with the help of `lapply()`:

```
> caus.split.bp <- lapply(caus.split, bp)
> caus.split.bp[1] # to check the first element
$be_made_toV
CrSem.Anim   CrSem.Inanim   CeSem.Anim   CeSem.Inanim
0.96         0.04           0.90         0.10
CdEv.Ment    CdEv.Phys      CdEv.Soc     Neg.No
0.14         0.18           0.68         0.94
Neg.Yes      Coref.No       Coref.Yes    Poss.No
0.06         1.00           0.00         1.00
Poss.Yes
0.00
```

and combine the vectors from the list as rows in a matrix by using `do.call()`. The resulting matrix is identical to the previously created `caus.bp`:

```
> caus.bp1 <- do.call(rbind, caus.split.bp)
> identical(caus.bp, caus.bp1) #to demonstrate that the resulting
matrices are identical
[1] TRUE
```

This approach may be particularly useful when the number of BP vectors is large.

15.2.3　Distance matrix

One way to explore the similarities and differences between the constructions is to eyeball the proportions in the matrix and compare the values for different constructions. Of course, this does not sound like a very reliable method. When dealing with multivariate data, it is often best to aggregate the information over many variables and try to find structure in the data. One can do so by computing a matrix of distances between the BP vectors and performing a cluster analysis.

　　The distances will reflect how (dis)similar the constructions are with regard to the proportions of values of the contextual variables that their BP vectors contain. The more similar their vectors, the smaller the distances. Conversely, the more dissimilar the vectors, the greater the distances. Computation of distances in R is very easy. The main function is `dist()`. Distances can be computed in several ways. The default method is the Euclidean distance, which is similar to our everyday idea of the distance between two objects. The distance between two vectors is the square root of the summed squared differences between all pairs of numbers in the vectors. Another popular measure is the Manhattan distance. In BP studies, Canberra distance has been used, because BP vectors often contain values around zero for rare categories. The differences between these small values are treated proportionally, not absolutely, which increases their contribution to the distance metric. See more information about various distances in the box 'Distance metrics'. The reader would be well-advised to experiment with several distances in order to obtain the most interpretable solution.

Distance metrics

When we think of the distance between two points A and B, we usually imagine the shortest route, 'as the crow flies'. This distance is called **Euclidean**. Imagine that you ask a taxi driver to bring you from A to B, as shown in Figure 15.1. The driver who uses the Euclidean distance will take the direct route. Another popular measure is the **Manhattan**, or city-block distance. A Manhattan distance taxi driver will choose a route that takes you first down the street and then continue on the avenue orthogonal to the street, and so on, until you finally reach B. Yet another metric is called the **maximum** distance. In that case, the taxi driver will take you only by the longest side of the triangle, and you will have to walk the remaining part yourself.

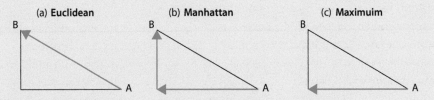

Figure 15.1. Distance metrics: (a) Euclidean, (b) Manhattan, (c) maximum

Finally, there is the Canberra distance, which is slightly more complex to interpret. It zooms in on the differences between small values, and zooms out from the differences

(Continued)

between large values. Therefore, it is very sensitive to small changes near zero, and less influenced by variables with large values.

In R, the Euclidean metric is set by default:

```
> dist(data) # do not run
```

To compute Manhattan distances, use the following code:

```
> dist(data, method = "manhattan") # do not run
```

To compute the maximum or Canberra distance, use `method = "maximum"` or `method = "canberra"`, respectively.

These distances can only be applied to numeric vectors. However, it is possible to compute distances between rows in a dataset with categorical variables by counting the proportion of non-overlapping values in two factors. This measure is called the **Gower** distance. It is available in the `daisy()` function in the `cluster` package. See Chapter 17 for an example. Another useful measure is the **Levenshtein** distance, which measures the number of editing operations that are needed to get one string from another string. For example, to turn *water* into *wine*, one needs three operations: replace *a* with *i*, *t* with *n*, and remove *r*. This measure is widely used in dialectometry and typology for comparison and identification of cognates. To compute it, you can use the function `adist()`, as in the following example:

```
> adist("water", "wine")
     [,1]
[1,]  3
```

Finally, one should mention the **cosine** as a measure of (dis)similarity. It is employed in vector space models of distributional semantics, which are discussed in the next chapter.

```
> caus.dist <- dist(caus.bp, method = "canberra")
> round(caus.dist, 2)
           be_made_toV   cause_toV   get_toV   get_Ved   get_Ving.
cause_toV  4.93
get_toV    3.13          5.07
get_Ved    5.93          6.24        4.41
get_Ving   5.02          4.62        5.27      6.63
[output omitted]
```

The distance matrix shows the pairwise distances between the BP vectors. For convenience, the `round()` function limits the desired number of decimal places after the point by only two. The distances between a vector and itself are not shown because they equal zero. The repeated values above the diagonal are not displayed, either (in the default settings).

One can examine the matrix and compare the distances. For example, the maximum distance is between *get_Ving* and *get_Ved* (6.63), whereas the minimum distance is between *have_V* and *get_toV* (1.3):

```
> max(caus.dist)
[1] 6.632803
> min(caus.dist)
[1] 1.300911
```

The results already indicate that the distributional and therefore semantic (dis)similarities are probably not motivated by the causative verb alone, since the constructions with the same auxiliary *get* are so dissimilar. We can explore these differences in a more systematic way by performing a cluster analysis.

15.2.4 Hierarchical cluster analysis

15.2.4.1 *Identifying the clusters*

There exist many kinds of cluster analysis. In this section, we will discuss hierarchical agglomerative clustering. It represents all objects as leaves or branches of a clustering tree. This tree is called a dendrogram. Unlike a normal tree, it 'grows' not from the root to the branches, but the other way round. In the beginning, each object (in our case, a constructional profile vector) represents its own cluster, or a 'leaf'. Next, the most similar objects (the ones for which the distance between the objects is the smallest) are merged. This procedure is repeated again and again. In the end, all leaves and branches are merged into one tree.

The function that we will need is `hclust()`. It offers many different options. We will use `method = "ward.D2"`, which usually produces compact and interpretable clusters. See Box "How do cluster trees grow?" on this and other possibilities. The dendrogram can be inspected visually in a plot.

```
> caus.hc <- hclust(caus.dist, method = "ward.D2")
> plot(caus.hc, hang = -1)
```

The resulting dendrogram can be seen in Figure 15.2. The argument `hang = -1` enables us to 'hang' all labels at the same height below the rest of the plot. The lower two elements are merged on the tree, the more similar the merged elements. The higher the merge, the more dissimilar the merged elements. The lowest merge is that of *have_V* and *get_toV*, which have the smallest distance, as you might recall.

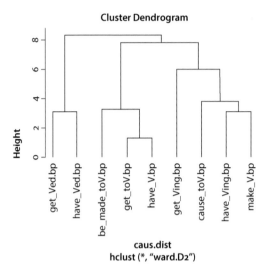

Figure 15.2. Hierarchical cluster dendrogram of the English causatives

How do cluster trees grow?

Cluster trees can grow in two ways: from roots to leaves, and from leaves to roots. The first method is called divisive clustering, whereas the second one is labelled agglomerative clustering. Agglomerative clustering, which is more popular, is implemented in `hclust()`. There are many different methods of agglomerative clustering, depending on how clusters are merged by the algorithm. The main ones are as follows:

- **Complete** (`method = "complete"`). The algorithm compares the **farthest neighbours** in all pairs of clusters and merges those clusters whose farthest neighbours are the closest. In Figure 15.3 (left) point X joins cluster A because the distance between X and the farthest member in cluster A is smaller than the distance between X and the farthest member in cluster B.
- **Single** (`method = "single"`). The algorithm compares the **nearest neighbours** in all pairs of clusters and merges those clusters whose nearest neighbours are the closest. In Figure 15.3 (centre) point X joins cluster B because the distance between X and the nearest member in cluster B is smaller than the distance between X and the nearest member in cluster A.
- **Average** (`method = "average"`). The algorithm compares the **average distances** between all pairs of clusters and merges those two clusters whose members have

the smallest average distance. In Figure 15.3 (right) Point X joins cluster B because the average distance from X to the members of cluster B is smaller than the average distance from X to the members of cluster A.

- **Ward** (`method = "ward.D2"`). The algorithm tries to minimize the increase in the variance in the distances between the members of clusters. This method usually produces compact clusters.

The merge procedure is repeated until all clusters are merged.

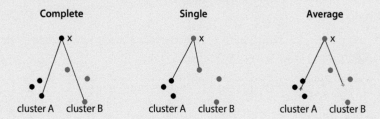

Figure 15.3. Different clustering methods. Left: complete. Centre: single. Right: average

For interpretation, it is often convenient to find the optimal number of clusters in a clustering solution. A useful statistic is the so-called average silhouette width. It shows the average well-formedness of the clusters in a given solution. Well-formedness means that the members of one cluster are close to one another and far away from the members of the other clusters. Average silhouette width ranges from 0 (no cluster structure in the data) to 1 (perfect separation of all clusters from one another). According to a rule of thumb, the average silhouette width below 0.2 should be interpreted as a lack of substantial cluster structure in the data (Kaufman & Rousseeuw 1990). We will use the function `silhouette()` from the package `cluster` to extract average silhouette widths. One can specify the number of clusters with the help of `cutree()` function. For example, this is how one can "cut" the tree in two large clusters:

```
> test.clust <- cutree(caus.hc, k = 2)
> test.clust
be_made_toV.bp   cause_toV.bp   get_toV.bp    get_Ved.bp
1                1              1             2
get_Ving.bp      have_V.bp      have_Ved.bp   have_Ving.bp
1                1              2             1
make_V.bp
1
```

The function cuts the tree into two clusters: one with *get_Ved* and *have_Ved* (value '2'), and the other with the remaining constructions (value '1').

We will begin with two clusters and then repeat the procedure until we have eight clusters. A one-cluster solution, which includes all objects, is not interesting and will not be tested. Nine clusters are theoretically possible if every causative construction forms its own cluster, but this case is not interesting, either. To see which number of clusters is optimal, we will need the function `silhouette()` from the package `cluster`.

```
> summary(silhouette(test.clust, caus.dist))$avg.width
[1] 0.2709663
```

To compute the silhouette widths for the number of clusters from 2 to 8, you can use the following code:

```
> asw <- sapply(2:8, function(x) summary(silhouette(cutree(caus.hc,
k = x), caus.dist))$avg.width)
> asw
[1] 0.2709663 0.3427721 0.3685310 0.2951836 0.2399533 0.2083129
[7] 0.1206189
```

The greatest silhouette width is approximately 0.369. It belongs to a four-cluster solution. One can explore the clustering information as we did above for the two-cluster solution, or, more conveniently, add the rectangles that correspond to the clusters directly to the plot:

```
> plot(caus.hc, hang = -1) # run if you have already closed the
graphics device
> rect.hclust(caus.hc, k = 4)
```

The result is shown in Figure 15.4. This solution also looks the most intuitive, although the three-cluster solution, which would merge *get_Ving* with the rest of the large left-hand cluster, has only a slightly smaller average silhouette width.

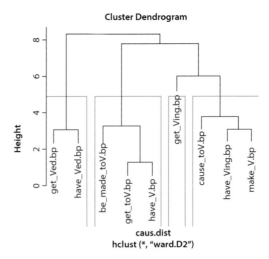

Figure 15.4. Rectangles with the optimal number of clusters, according to the average silhouette widths

15.2.4.2 *Interpretation of the cluster solution: Snake plots and effect size measures*

Let us begin with the cluster that contains *get_Ved* and *have_Ved* and compare it with the other constructions. How can we identify the features that are distinctive of this cluster? One of the options is to explore the absolute differences between the scores. First, we create two matrices, one with *get_Ved* and *have_Ved*, and the other one with all other constructions.

```
> c1 <- caus.bp[c(4,7),]
> c2 <- caus.bp[-c(4,7),]
```

Next, we compute the average proportion for every feature by using `colMeans()`.

```
> c1.bp <- colMeans(c1)
> c2.bp <- colMeans(c2)
```

Now we can compute the differences between the average values in both clusters and sort them. The function `sort()` can sort vectors in ascending (the default) and descending order:

```
> diff <- c1.bp - c2.bp
> sort(diff, decreasing = TRUE)
CrSem.Anim    CeSem.Anim      Poss.Yes      CdEv.Phys      Coref.Yes
0.32000000    0.25142857    0.16000000    0.09285714    0.06857143
CdEv.Soc      Neg.No          Neg.Yes        Coref.No       CdEv.Ment
0.03285714    0.03285714    -0.03285714    -0.06857143    -0.12571429
Poss.No       CeSem.Inanim    CrSem.Inanim
-0.16000000    -0.25142857    -0.32000000
```

For binary variables the results will be symmetric, e.g. 0.32 for `CrSem.Anim` and –0.32 for `CrSem.Inanim`. To visualize the differences, one can use the so-called snake plot (Divjak & Gries 2009). The *x*-axis shows the sorted scores (in ascending order), and the *y*-axis displays the variables according to their ranks. To create a plot with text labels, one should first create an empty plot (`type` = `"n"`), and next add the text as shown below:

```
> plot(sort(diff)*1.2, 1:length(diff), type = "n", xlab = "cluster
2 <--> cluster 1", yaxt = "n", ylab = "")
> text(sort(diff), 1:length(diff), names(sort(diff)))
```

The result can be seen in Figure 15.5. Some clarifications are necessary. The first argument of `plot()` is the sorted vector with differences arranged in ascending order. This vector contains the values plotted on the horizontal axis. The values are magnified slightly by multiplying them by 1.2 to ensure that there is enough space for the text labels. Alternatively, one can use `xlim`. The second argument tells R to plot the variables at different heights from 1 to 13, according to their ranks. The argument `type` = `"n"` is used when we want to create an empty plot first and to add text labels later. Next, `xlab` gives the name of the *x* axis; `yaxt` = `"n"` suppresses plotting any ticks on the y axis; and `ylab` = `""` suppresses adding any labels for the y axis.

The next line of code adds text labels to the plot. The first two arguments specify the coordinates of the labels. They are identical to the first arguments of the `plot()` function above, except for the multiplication by 1.2. The text labels are the names of the values in the sorted vector with differences. Finally, `cex = 0.8` specifies the relative size of text labels (by default, `cex = 1`). See Appendix 2 for other graphical options.

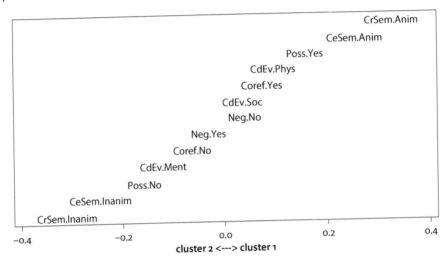

Figure 15.5. A snake plot of the differences between *get_Ved* and *have_Ved* ('cluster 1') and all other constructions ('cluster 2')

The snake plot demonstrates that *get_Ved* and *have_Ved* have a much higher proportion of animate Causers and Causees, as well as markers of the Causer's possession, and a higher proportion on non-mental effected predicates in comparison with the other causative constructions. This perfectly fits the semantics of these constructions as the ones related to inducive interpersonal causation, which is often related to service encounters, as in (1):

(1) a. *I had my car repaired (by a mechanic).*
     b. *I got my hair done.*

A more traditional way of identification of the most distinctive variables is by using effect size measures for contingency tables (see Chapter 9). To create a contingency table with two clusters as rows and the values of a contextual feature as columns, one should first create a factor with values '1' (*get_Ved* and *have_Ved*) and '2' (all other constructions). You can use any other values if you like.

```
> cluster <- as.character(caus$Cx)
> cluster[cluster == "get_Ved"|cluster == "have_Ved"] = "1"
> cluster[cluster != "1"] = "2"
> cluster <- as.factor(cluster)
```

Now one can cross-tabulate `cluster` with any variable and compute the effect size (we will use Cramér's V because the size of the table may vary) with the help of `assocstats` from the package `vcd`:

```
> assocstats(table(cluster, caus$CrSem))
                    X^2 df   P(> X^2)
Likelihood Ratio   66.191   1 4.4409e-16
Pearson            42.604   1 6.7038e-11

Phi-Coefficient     :0.308
Contingency Coeff.  :0.294
Cramer's V          :0.308
```

By repeating the procedure, one will find that the semantics of the Causer is indeed the variable with the strongest effect size. This finding supports the conclusions that we have made on the basis of the snake plot. One can also use multiple logistic regression and conditional inference trees and random forests with the cluster as the response variable to test if the selected variables remain significantly distinctive when the other variables are taken into account.

15.2.4.3 Validation of a cluster solution

We have used average silhouette widths to choose the best number of clusters, but how stable are the clusters and how well are they supported by the data? These questions can be answered with the help of multiscale bootstrap resampling in the package `pvclust`. There is an important difference: one has to use a transposed version of the data, so that each BP vector is represented by a column. It is the columns that are clustered. To transpose a matrix or a data frame, one can use the function `t()`. One has to specify the clustering method and the distance metric again. Note that computation may take some time. The results may slightly differ from one run to another.

```
> caus.pvc <- pvclust(t(caus.bp), method.hclust = "ward.D2", method.
dist = "canberra")
Bootstrap (r = 0.46)... Done.
Bootstrap (r = 0.54)... Done.
Bootstrap (r = 0.69)... Done.
Bootstrap (r = 0.77)... Done.
Bootstrap (r = 0.85)... Done.
Bootstrap (r = 1.0)... Done.
Bootstrap (r = 1.08)... Done.
Bootstrap (r = 1.15)... Done.
Bootstrap (r = 1.23)... Done.
Bootstrap (r = 1.38)... Done.
```

The essence of bootstrapping was discussed in Chapter 7. The algorithm takes a random sample with replacement from the original sample and computes the statistics of interest. The procedure is repeated many times. In the case of `pvclust()`, the default number of resamplings is 1000, but it can be changed if more precise results are needed by adding, for example, `nboot = 10000`. The computation can take quite some time if the number of iterations is very large.

The results can be seen in the plot (Figure 15.6):

```
> plot(caus.pvc, hang = -1)
```

The numbers are the probability values of obtaining the clusters in a bootstrap. You may have slightly different values every time you run `pvclust()`, unless you use the same random seed (see Chapter 14). The probability number on the left is the so-called AU (Approximately Unbiased) *p*-value, the other one is the BP (Bootstrap Probability) value. Note that the interpretation of the *p*-value is different here from our previous case studies: the closer the *p*-value to 1, the more empirical support the cluster has. The AU value is considered to be the more precise measure. We can visualize the *p*-values and highlight the clusters that have a *p*-value above 0.95 with the help of the following command:

```
> pvrect(caus.pvc, alpha = 0.95)
```

As one can see from Figure 15.6, only one cluster which contains *get_Ved* and *have_Ved* is supported by the data at the level of 0.95, although the other clusters are not particularly

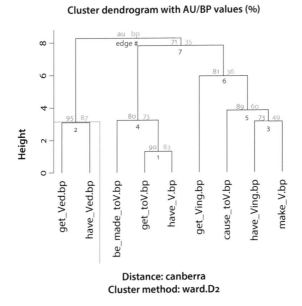

Figure 15.6. Hierarchical clustering with multiscale bootstrap *p*-values

weak, either. We have thus reasons to believe that this cluster may be observed if we use a different sample.

15.2.5   Partitioning methods

15.2.5.1   *General introduction*

Non-hierarchical cluster analysis groups objects into a pre-specified number of clusters. The process usually begins with a random classification of the objects. Next, the classification is refined by an iterative algorithm by reallocating the objects from one cluster to another until no further improvement can be made. Probably the best-known non-hierarchical method is k-means clustering. In this algorithm, observations are clustered around cluster centroids ('means'). These centroids are abstract 'prototypes', which are usually not identical to any particular member of their cluster. Another approach is partitioning around medoids, where the medoid is the most centrally located exemplar of a cluster, average distance from which to all other members of the cluster is minimal. Unlike centroids, medoids are always members of their clusters. The k-medoids algorithm is considered to be more robust that k-means with regard to outliers and noise. Below you can find information about both methods.

15.2.5.2   *Partitioning around centroids (k-means)*

The k-means algorithm is implemented in the function `kmeans()`. It requires two main arguments: a matrix with data (the clustered objects should be represented by the rows) and the number of clusters. It is also recommended to try several random sets for selecting initial means (one can simply choose a random number). For example, we can partition the BP vectors of the causatives into four clusters as follows:

```
> test.clust <- kmeans(caus.bp, 4, nstart = 25)
```

To see how the cluster membership, one can use the following code:

```
> test.clust$cluster
be_made_toV   cause_toV   get_toV      get_Ved    get_Ving
1             2           1            1          3
have_V        have_Ved    have_Ving    make_V
1             1           4            2
```

The classification is very different from the one obtained in the previous section. The main explanation is that k-means uses Euclidean distances, whereas we used Canberra distances. Therefore, high-frequency features matter more than low-frequency features. K-means clustering is also sensitive to outliers and often creates singleton clusters, as we see here (clusters 3 and 4).

How to choose the optimal number of clusters? In k-means, the main goodness-of-fit criterion is the so-called within-cluster sum of squares (WCSS). The algorithm tries to reallocate observations from one cluster to another in such a way as to minimize the sum of squared Euclidean distances between the members of the same cluster and the cluster mean. One can also compare the sum WCSS scores produced by different solutions with different numbers of clusters. Of course, the greater the number of clusters, the smaller the total WCSS. However, it is possible to select the number of clusters such that partitioning the data into more clusters will not bring any significant decrease in WCSS. One can compare different WCSS and decide on the number of clusters with the help of a **scree plot**. To obtain WCSS for a specific cluster solution, one can do the following:

```
> test.clust$tot.withinss
[1] 0.43024
```

If we repeat the procedure for the number of clusters from 1 (no partitioning) to 8 (the total number of objects minus one), we will obtain the following values, which can be plotted as shown in Figure 15.7. To speed up the procedure, you can use the following code with sapply(), which returns a vector of WCSS:

```
> wcss <- sapply(1:8, function(x) kmeans(caus.bp, x, nstart = 25)$tot.withinss)
> wcss
[1] 3.02124444 1.39204000 0.66037333 0.43024000 0.26853333
[6] 0.08213333 0.03813333 0.01600000

> plot(1:8, wcss, type = "b", main = "Scree plot of WCSS for n clusters", xlab = "n of clusters", ylab = "WCSS")
```

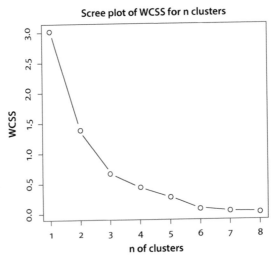

Figure 15.7. Within-cluster sums of squares for different numbers of clusters produced by the *k*-means clustering algorithm

How to interpret a scree plot? The rule of thumb is to find the point where the line 'elbows'. That means that after this point, adding new clusters does not help decrease WCSS very significantly. It seems that the best candidate is the point at $n = 3$. Of course, this is only a heuristic, and the ultimate judgment should be made on the basis of theoretical considerations. We will use this method for diagnostics in different modifications in the subsequent chapters, as well.

15.2.5.3 *Partitioning around medoids*

In this subsection, we will discuss the *k*-medoids algorithm. As has been mentioned already, it is considered more robust than *k*-means. In addition, the function `pam()` in the `cluster` package, where this algorithm is implemented, accepts both an initial matrix with numeric vectors and a distance matrix. This enables us to use any kind of distance. Let us use the Canberra distance matrix from our previous analysis and partition the data into four clusters, as above:

```
> caus.pam <- pam(caus.dist, k = 4)
```

If you want to use the original matrix, you only have choice between the Euclidean (the default) and Manhattan distances, e.g. `pam(caus.bp, k = 2, metric = "Manhattan")`.

To see the cluster membership, you can do the following:

```
> caus.pam$clustering
be_made_toV   cause_toV   get_toV   get_Ved   get_Ving
1             2           1         3         4
have_V        have_Ved    have_Ving   make_V
1             3           2           2
```

This solution coincides with the four-cluster solution in the hierarchical clustering. To obtain the medoids, one can use the following command:

```
> caus.pam$medoids
[1] "have_V"  "make_V"      "have_Ved" "get_Ving"
```

These are the prototypical members of the clusters. In our case, two clusters have only one or two members, so their medoids are not particularly informative.

Since the members of the four PAM-clusters are identical to the members of the four clusters discussed in the section about hierarchical cluster analysis, the average silhouette width values in both models should be identical. However, for didactic purposes, we will demonstrate how one can compute average silhouette widths for PAM-clusters:

```
> caus.pam$silinfo$avg.width
[1] 0.368531
```

To compare several solutions, you can use the following code:

```
> asw <- sapply(2:8, function(x) pam(caus.dist, k = x)$silinfo$avg.
width)
> asw
[1]  0.2191445  0.3427721  0.3685310  0.2951836  0.2399533  0.2083129
0.1206189
```

To summarize, the main conclusion that we can draw from this case study is that the distributional properties of the periphrastic causatives are not related directly to the auxiliary verbs only. Rather, we deal with full-fledged constructions with their individual semantic characteristics.

Hierarchical or non-hierarchical?

How can one choose, which clustering approach to use? As Manning & Schütze (1999: 500) suggest, hierarchical clustering is preferable for detailed data analysis, as it provides more information than non-hierarchical methods. Non-hierarchical partitioning approaches are convenient when the dataset is large. The *k*-means algorithm is conceptually simple, but it is restricted in its applications because it assumes a Euclidean space and does not allow one to use other types of distances. It is also less robust than *k*-medoids with regard to outliers and other noise.

15.3   Summary

In this chapter we have discussed Behavioural Profile vectors, different distance metrics and clustering methods. You have got acquainted with hierarchical and partitioning cluster algorithms, and have learnt how to decide on the optimal number of clusters with the help of average silhouette widths and scree plots. In addition, we have discussed how to validate a hierarchical clustering solution by using multiscale bootstrap.

It is important to realize that the techniques discussed in this chapter are exploratory. Different distance metrics and clustering methods may produce very different results. This is why it is recommended to try different methods, which enable one to see the data from different perspectives. Although some solutions can reflect the data structure better than others, they are still only heuristic methods that should be complemented by hypothesis-testing methods, such as regression analysis.

Reporting the results of a cluster analysis

When presenting the results of a cluster analysis, it is crucial that you are very clear about the clustered objects, the criteria for their comparison, as well as the distance metric and clustering method. It is also important that you can justify the number of clusters that you consider optimal, and, if available, report the results of cluster validation and the average silhouette width of the solution. If necessary, the dendrogram can be presented horizontally. See also `help(hclust)` for a few graphical options, such as how to avoid plotting the labels, or how to prune the tree up to *n* large clusters.

More on clustering methods

There exist many more clustering algorithms. It is worthwhile to explore the clustering functions in the `cluster` package. You can find such functions as `diana()`, which does divisive hierarchical clustering, `funny()`, which performs fuzzy clustering, and more. For creation of phylogenetic trees of language families, the neighbour-joining algorithm is particularly popular. See `nj()` in the package `ape`. You can represent different kinds of phylogenetic trees (unrooted, radial, cladograms, etc.). See `help(plot.phylo)`, the same package. An extensive discussion of clustering methods for historical linguistics and cladistics is offered in Johnson (2008: Ch. 6). For better general understanding of different clustering approaches, see Everitt et al. (2011).

CHAPTER 16

Introduction to Semantic Vector Spaces
Cosine as a measure of semantic similarity

What you will learn from this chapter:

> This chapter introduces Semantic Vector Spaces, another distributional approach to semantics. This method originates in Natural Language Processing. Unlike Behavioural Profiles discussed in the previous chapter, it uses automatically extracted co-occurrences of target words and contextual features. The characteristic features of the method are weighted co-occurrence frequencies and the use of the cosine as the most popular similarity measure. This chapter provides a general introduction to the method, with a case study of English cooking verbs as an illustration.

16.1 Distributional models of semantics and Semantic Vector Space models

The main idea behind the distributional approach was formulated by John Firth in his famous quotation, "You shall know a word by the company it keeps" (Firth 1957). To put it differently, words that occur in the same contexts tend to have similar meanings (Harris 1954). This idea lies at the core of Semantic Vector Space modelling. Originating in Computational Linguistics (e.g. Deerwester et al. 1990; Schütze 1992; Lin 1998), this approach is now finding its way into lexical semantics and other theoretical disciplines. Similar to Behavioural Profiles, Semantic Vector Spaces are based on comparing contextual environments of words or senses, but in a more computationally intensive way. Instead of a manually coded sample, researchers extract the distributional information automatically from large morphologically and syntactically annotated corpora. The weighted co-occurrence frequencies between target words and contextual features are combined in long vectors. One can compute the distances between the vectors in order to measure their semantic similarity, hence the term 'Vector Spaces'.

Implementations of Semantic Vector Spaces vary with regard to how one defines the context: as entire documents, 'bags of words' that contain a certain number of lexemes on the right and left from the target word, syntactic subcategorization frames, etc. The choice of the context type is crucial. If the context is defined as a bag of words, it will be particularly sensitive to topic-related contextual differences and semantic prosody. An example is Peirsman et al. (2010), who demonstrate the change in lexical associations of the word *islam* after the terrorist attacks of 9/11 in Dutch newspapers. However, the size of the context window around the target word also matters: smaller context windows help model semantic relationships, such as synonymy, hyper- and hyponymy, cohyponymy, whereas wider context windows are more useful in modelling topical similarity.

If the definition of context also takes into account the syntactic relationships between a word and its collocates, such models are better at capturing semantic similarity (Pado & Lapata 2007; Peirsman 2008). If the context is defined on the basis of purely syntactic features, e.g. subcategorization frames, the words tend to cluster according to more abstract grammatical distinctions, e.g. Levin-like verb classes and broad lexicosemantic noun classes in Levshina & Heylen (2014). In this case study we will explore a basic bag-of-words model. However, the principles of analysis are not fundamentally different for other definitions of contexts.

Why do contextual features work as a proxy for semantics? Some linguists and philosophers, including Wittgenstein, go as far as to suggest that meaning *is* context of use (see Stefanowitsch 2010: 368–370). A less radical interpretation of the role of contextual clues is that the latter are related to the conceptual structures associated with linguistic forms. It has been shown that the situational clues present in the context of a new word or construction are crucial in establishing their meaning, especially when learning non-basic vocabulary, which normally happens without immediate access to referents (Dąbrowska 2009). In psycholinguistics, Miller & Charles (1991) found experimental evidence that similarity judgments about words depend on the contexts in which the words appear. Some distributional models applied in psycholinguistic research, such as Latent Semantic Analysis (Landauer & Dumais 1997), have been quite successful in performing human lexical tasks, for example, a TOEFL test on synonyms.

16.2   A Semantic Vector Space model of English verbs of cooking

16.2.1   Theoretical background and data

For this case study you will need the data and functions from the two add-on packages. They should first be installed if you have not installed them yet. Next, you should load them.

```
> install.packages("cluster")
> library(Rling); library(cluster)
```

Semantic (conceptual) and lexical fields were a central topic in structuralist lexicology and anthropology. Every word in a lexical field was believed to acquire its meaning by its opposition to the other words in the same field. Some words can be more general (hypernyms) and some more specific (hyponyms). For instance, consider English verbs of cooking.[1] Figure 16.1 represents some of the verbs organized in a hierarchical network (an adapted version of analysis in Lehrer 1974). The verb *cook* is the superordinate term, which designates an irreversible process involving heat with a purpose of making food more desirable and/or nutritious and/or digestible (Lehrer 1974: 62). The other verbs inherit these properties. Figure 16.1 shows the most important semantic features that distinguish between the verbs, for instance +*water* or -*fat* (oil). The structure of the semantic field is quite complex. There are two kinds of *boil*: one of them is a superordinate term that designates cooking with water and without fat, and the other one is the former's hyponym with the feature +*vigorous* (*cooking*). This kind of semantic relationships is called autohyponymy. Some terms may have more than two superordinates: *grill* can be applied both to cooking food on an open grill, as a subordinate term of *broil*, and to the process of cooking with fat on a frying pan, as a subordinate term of *fry* (e.g. *grilled cheese sandwich*). The position of *roast* as a hyponym of both *bake* and *broil* can be explained by the changes in the cooking practices. Previously, foods used to be roasted on a spit in front of an open fire; traditionally, *roast* is similar to *broil* and its subordinate terms. However, nowadays the same effect can be achieved by putting food in an oven, similar to baking.

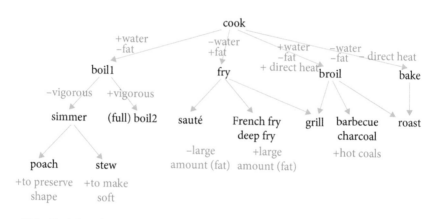

Figure 16.1. English verbs of cooking (a selection), an adjusted version of Lehrer (1974)

Although the abstract distinctive features play a crucial role, Lehrer observes that the lower the verb in the hierarchy, the greater role is played by its collocates (Lehrer 1974: 33). For instance, *poach* means that the food is carefully boiled in water so that the shape is preserved. A typical example is *poached eggs*. *Stew* means that the food is cooked slowly for a long time until it is soft, e.g. *stewed vegetables*. However, the phrase ?*poached vegetables* sounds strange, even if the vegetables are cooked so that their shape is preserved. On the

---

1. The graph represents the American English terms (around 1970s); in British English *grill* is used instead of *broil*.

other hand, ?*stewed eggs* is not fully acceptable, either, even if the eggs are cooked slowly. Another problem is the relationships between the subordinate and superordinate terms, which are not always transitive. For instance, *poached egg* is not equal to *boiled egg*. In the former case, unlike in the latter, the shell is removed before cooking.

The hypothesis of this case study is that collocates are important at all levels and that we can obtain a similar clustering of cooking verbs by only looking at their distributional properties. For the case study, a sample of ten verbs was selected: *bake, boil, broil, cook, fry, grill, poach, roast, simmer* and *stew*. All instances of these verbs were collected from the Corpus of Contemporary American English (Davies 2008 –). To ensure maximally that the verbs were used in the literal sense, the data were selected from magazines (where most uses come from recipes) and the verbs were used only in the initial [vv0] form, which over-laps with the imperative (e.g. *bake for 40 to 50 minutes*). For a bag-of-words vector space model, collocates (lemmas) were selected within the window of five words on the left and five words on the right. Next, a matrix of co-occurrences was created, which can be found in the data frame `cooking`:

```
> data(cooking)
> head(cooking)
            Bake Boil Broil Cook Fry Grill Poach Roast Stew Simmer
AB            2    0    0    0    0    0     0     0     0    0
ABOUTI        0    0    0    2    0    0     0     0     0    0
ABRAMS        0    0    0    0    0    1     0     0     0    0
ABSORB        0    0    0    0    0    0     0     0     0    14
ABSORBED-10   0    0    0    1    0    0     0     0     0    0
ABUNDANCE     0    0    0    0    1    0     0     0     0    0
```

The analysis is done in three steps:

Step 1. Creation of semantic vectors from weighted co-occurrence frequencies:
   a) computation of expected co-occurrence frequencies;
   b) computation of Pointwise Mutual Information scores;
   c) transformation of the latter into Positive Pointwise Mutual Information (PPMI) scores.

Step 2. Computation of similarity scores between the resulting PPMI vectors with the help of the cosine measure.

Step 3. Exploration of similarity scores – if necessary, with the help of cluster analysis.

16.2.2   Creating vectors of weighted co-occurrence frequencies

To begin with the analyses, we will first remove from the data frame `cooking` all rows that contain only zeros. These are collexemes that do not occur with any of the target verbs we are interested in.

```
> cooking <- cooking[rowSums(cooking) > 0, ]
```

The dataset contains 'raw' co-occurrence frequencies. It is common to weight them in order to give more prominence to surprising co-occurrences. The most popular weighting method in Semantic Vector Spaces is Pointwise Mutual Information scores. It is highly sensitive to combinations of less frequent targets and features. The formula of PMI of target word x and contextual feature y is presented below. Note that it is common to use the logarithm to base 2:

$$\text{PMI}(x, y) = \log_2 \frac{p(x, y)}{p(x)p(y)}$$

where $p(x, y)$ is the probability of co-occurrence of x and y, $p(x)$ is the probability of x, and $p(y)$ is the probability of y. This formula can be expressed in a more convenient form (cf. Chapter 10):

$$\text{PMI}(x, y) = \log_2 \frac{O_{xy}}{E_{xy}}$$

where O_{xy} is the observed frequency of co-occurrence of x and y, and E_{xy} is the expected frequency.

The notions of observed and expected frequencies were introduced in Chapter 9. To obtain a vector of expected frequencies for a verb and all its collocates, you can use the following code:

```
> exp.bake <- sum(cooking$Bake)*rowSums(cooking)/sum(cooking)
> exp.bake[1:5]
AB           ABOUTI      ABRAMS      ABSORB      ABSORBED-10
0.5737930    0.5737930   0.2868965   4.0165510   0.2868965
```

The result is a vector of expected frequencies for *bake* and each collocate. Now we can create a vector of PMI scores. Again, below is the code for *bake*:

```
> PMI.bake <- log2(cooking$Bake/exp.bake)
> PMI.bake[1:5]
AB         ABOUTI   ABRAMS   ABSORB   ABSORBED-10
1.801398   -Inf     -Inf     -Inf     -Inf
```

It has been shown in Bullinaria & Levy (2007) that the Positive Pointwise Mutual Information (PPMI) measure performs better than simple PMI scores. PPMI is essentially the same as PMI, but all negative values are replaced with zeros. Below is the code for *bake*:

```
> PPMI.bake <- ifelse(PMI.bake < 0, 0, PMI.bake)
> PPMI.bake[1:5]
AB         ABOUTI     ABRAMS     ABSORB     ABSORBED-10
1.801398   0.000000   0.000000   0.000000   0.000000
```

To apply this procedure to all verbs simultaneously, one can use the code below. First, we will turn the data frame into a matrix to facilitate further calculations.

```
> cooking <- as.matrix(cooking)
```

Next, we will compute expected frequencies for all cells in the data by using `chisq.test()`, which was introduced in Chapter 9:

```
> cooking.exp <- chisq.test(cooking)$expected
[warning message omitted]
```

After that, we compute the PMI and PPMI scores for all verbs and all collocates:

```
> cooking.PMI <- log2(cooking/cooking.exp)
> cooking.PPMI <- ifelse(cooking.PMI < 0, 0, cooking.PMI)
```

Now we are ready for the next step, computation of the cosine similarity values.

16.2.3   Cosine similarity

Now we need to compute the distances between the vectors. One option is to use the `dist()` function, as in the previous case study. Yet, it is more conventional to use the cosines of angles between distributional vectors as measures of (dis)similarity. Consider Figure 16.2. Angle θ_2 between the imaginary distributional vectors of the nouns *dog* and *cat* is smaller than the angle θ_1 between *dog* and *Universe*, since *dog* and *cat* are more semantically related and therefore should occur in similar contexts. For the angle between 0^0 and 180^0, the greater the angle, the smaller the cosine of that angle. If the angle between two PPMI vectors is 0^0, which means maximal distributional similarity, the cosine value is 1. If the angle between two PPMI vectors is 90^0, which indicates maximal dissimilarity, the cosine value is 0. So, the greater the similarity of two vectors, the greater the cosine value of the angle between them. In this example, the cosine similarity of *dog* and *cat* will be greater than that of *dog* and *Universe*.

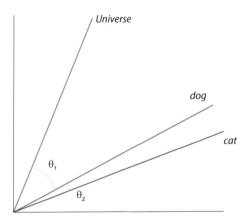

Figure 16.2. Cosine as a similarity measure

The code to compute the cosine between two vectors *a* and *b* can be represented as follows:

```
> cos <- sum(a*b)/(sqrt(sum(a *a)) *sqrt(sum(b *b))) # do not run
```

or, alternatively,

```
> cos <- crossprod(a, b)/sqrt(crossprod(a)*crossprod(b)) # do not run
```

For instance, the cosine between the distributional vectors of *bake* and *simmer* is as follows:

```
> crossprod(cooking.PPMI[, 1], cooking.PPMI[, 10])/
sqrt(crossprod(cooking.PPMI[, 1]) *crossprod(cooking.PPMI[, 10]))
          [,1]
[1,] 0.01160899
```

The cosine value for *boil* and *simmer* is greater, which means that the verbs are more similar distributionally:

```
> crossprod(cooking.PPMI[, 2], cooking.PPMI[, 10])/
sqrt(crossprod(cooking.PPMI[, 2]) *crossprod(cooking.PPMI[, 10]))

          [,1]
[1,] 0.07422152
```

It would be too time-consuming to compute all cosines pairwise. To speed up the process, one can use the function `cossim()` in the `Rling` package. Its argument is a matrix with distributional vectors as rows, so we will first transpose the matrix with PPMI scores:

```
> cooking1 <- t(cooking.PPMI)
> cooking.cos <- cossim(cooking1)
> round(cooking.cos, 2)
        Bake Boil Broil Cook Fry  Grill Poach Roast Stew Simmer
Bake    1.00 0.01 0.06  0.01 0.03 0.01  0.01  0.04  0.00 0.01
Boil    0.01 1.00 0.03  0.03 0.03 0.02  0.03  0.05  0.03 0.07
Broil   0.06 0.03 1.00  0.03 0.04 0.08  0.03  0.08  0.03 0.02
Cook    0.01 0.03 0.03  1.00 0.03 0.03  0.01  0.03  0.02 0.03
Fry     0.03 0.03 0.04  0.03 1.00 0.06  0.03  0.05  0.01 0.01
Grill   0.01 0.02 0.08  0.03 0.06 1.00  0.04  0.07  0.03 0.01
Poach   0.01 0.03 0.03  0.01 0.03 0.04  1.00  0.03  0.07 0.04
Roast   0.04 0.05 0.08  0.03 0.05 0.07  0.03  1.00  0.02 0.03
Stew    0.00 0.03 0.03  0.02 0.01 0.03  0.07  0.02  1.00 0.02
Simmer  0.01 0.07 0.02  0.03 0.01 0.01  0.04  0.03  0.02 1.00
```

This is a similarity matrix, the opposite of a distance matrix, which was discussed in Chapter 15. The diagonal elements are equal to 1 because a vector is maximally similar to itself. In contrast, the diagonal elements in a distance matrix are always zeros. If we examine the cosine values row by row or column by column, we can already detect some interpretable interesting patterns:

- *broil, roast* and *grill* have the highest similarity scores;
- *simmer* and *boil* are relatively similar to each other;
- *poach* and *stew* are relatively similar to each other.

It is also interesting that the superordinate *cook* is not particularly close to any other verb, having medium-range similarity scores (around 0.03) with most of them.

The cosine similarity measures can be transformed into distances. The easiest method would be simply to subtract each similarity score from 1. Here we will use another method. We will divide each similarity score by the maximum similarity (excluding one) in the data and subtract the result from one. This operation will produce normalized distance values more evenly distributed in a range from 0 to 1. The object can next be transformed into a full-fledged distance matrix with the help of as.dist():

```
> cooking.dist <- 1 - (cooking.cos/0.07958)
> cooking.dist <- as.dist(cooking.dist)
```

Now we are ready to perform clustering with the help of partitioning around medoids, which was introduced in Chapter 15. When using a partitioning clustering method, one should specify in advance the number of clusters into which the data will be classified. Since we do not know the optimal number of clusters in advance, we will try different solutions, from two to nine, and compare their average silhouette widths. As was discussed in Chapter 15, the average silhouette width is a convenient tool for estimating the optimal number of clusters. We will use the function pam() in the package cluster. Below you can see the code that can be used to compute the average silhouette width of a two-cluster solution.

```
> test.clust <- pam(cooking.dist, 2)
> test.clust$silinfo$avg.width
[1] 0.3664788
```

If we repeat the procedure for the number of clusters up to 9, we will see that the best solution seems to be the one with six clusters because it yields the highest average silhouette width 0.6. See the previous chapter (Section 15.2.5.3) on how to write one line of code to compute average silhouette width based on PAM-clustering.

Let us look at the six-cluster solution more closely.

```
> test.clust <- pam(cooking.dist, 6)
> test.clust$clustering
Bake  Boil  Broil  Cook  Fry  Grill  Poach  Roast  Stew  Simmer
 1     2     3     4    5     3      6      3      6     2
```

The largest cluster 3 includes three verbs: *broil, grill* and *roast*. Cluster 2 contains *boil* and *simmer*. Cluster 6 includes *poach* and *stew*. The other verbs (*bake, cook* and *fry*) form their own individual clusters.

The results are very close to Lehrer's classification. We have found that the co-hyponyms *poach* and *stew* cluster together, as well as *simmer* and *boil. Broil* clusters with its co-hyponyms, *grill* and *roast*. The verb *bake* is on its own, since it has unique properties, and so is *fry*. *Cook*, as the most general term, is on its own, as well. Note that Lehrer's hierarchy contained quite a few ambiguities due to polysemy, and further research is needed to take these nuances into account, for instance, by creating distributional vectors for each sense, rather than for a lexeme.

16.3 Summary

In this chapter, we have introduced the method of Semantic Vector Spaces. Unlike the Behavioural Profiles method, which involves individual corpus instances of constructions coded for categorical variables, normally selected on theoretical grounds, Semantic Vector Spaces are based on automatically collected co-occurrence frequencies of target words with many other words and/or syntactic relationships or frames, and represent a radically data-driven technique. In spite of all differences, there are two major assumptions shared by both Behavioural Profiles and Semantic Vector Spaces: first, distributional differences are interpreted as semantic differences, and second, these differences are treated as spatial distances. These distances were measured as cosines of angles between distributional vectors in semantic hyperspace.

How to report analyses based on Semantic Vector Spaces

There are no strict rules, and the procedure strongly depends on the specific task. However, one should mention the character and number of contextual features, the weighting method, and the similarity/distance measure. Usually the performance of a model is evaluated by comparing it with a 'gold standard', such as WordNet or results of psycholinguistic experiments.

In practice, Semantic Vector Spaces are created on much longer lists of target words, and contextual features are often carefully pre-selected (e.g. a thousand most frequent nouns). One also uses computationally efficient, fast algorithms written in other programming languages, such as Python or Java. However, the main aim of this chapter was to introduce the basic principles of Semantic Vector Spaces and demonstrate how semantics can be done in a data-driven, bottom-up fashion.

More on Semantic Vector Spaces

The literature on vector spaces in linguistics is abundant. For a linguist-friendly introduction, see Levshina & Heylen (2014). For more technical details and a broader picture, see Turney & Pantel (2010). An important application concerns compositional
semantics (e.g. Mitchell & Lapata 2010). See also a discussion of distributional Latent
Semantic Analysis in a pioneering paper by Landauer & Dumais (1997).

CHAPTER 17

Language and space
Dialects, maps and Multidimensional Scaling

What you will learn from this chapter:

> This chapter introduces another popular method that deals with distance matrices. This method is called Multidimensional Scaling. It is a dimensionality reduction technique that represents distances between objects in a low-dimensional space. You will learn how to perform different types of metric and non-metric scaling and carry out the diagnostics of solutions by using the scree plot, the Shepard plot and goodness-of-fit measures. The chapter also shows how one can use R for creation of geographical maps with points and text labels. Finally, you will learn how to measure the correlation between two distance matrices with the help of the Mantel test. The case studies are based on geographic coordinates and several linguistic features of varieties of English all over the world.

17.1 Making maps with R

In this section you will learn how to make maps with R on the basis of geographic coordinates. To reproduce the code below, you will need the following packages:

```
> install.packages("rworldmap")
> library(Rling); library(rworldmap)
```

The dataset is called eWAVE. It contains a fraction of the data about varieties of English from the Electronic World Atlas of Varieties of English (Kortmann & Lunkenheimer 2013).[1] The dataset contains 20 randomly selected features from 76 varieties of English, as well as their type and region. Finally, it contains the coordinates (longitude and latitude) that reflect the approximate location of varieties.

```
> data(eWAVE)
> str(eWAVE)
'data.frame': 76 obs. of 24 variables:
```

---

1. URL http://ewave-atlas.org/ (last access 21.11.2014).

```
$ F1: Factor w/ 6 levels "?","A","B","C",..: 3 1 5 4 3 5 3 2
5 6 …
$ F7: Factor w/ 6 levels "?","A","B","C",..: 2 1 2 3 2 3 2 2
2 6 …
[output omitted]
$ Region: Factor w/ 8 levels "Africa","America",..: 3 6 2 3 3 5 5
5 5 6 …
$ Type: Factor w/ 5 levels "English-based Creoles",..: 3 4 5 3 3 1
3 1 1 …
$ Lon: num 120 177.6 -79.5 149.1 147.3 …
$ Lat: num -25.2 -17.6 39.5 -35.2 -42.9 …
```

The row names contain the names of the varieties. For example, the first ten varieties are as follows:

```
> rownames(eWAVE)[1:10]
[1] "Aboriginal English"   "Acrolectal Fiji English"
[3] "Appalachian English"  "Australian English"
[5] "Australian Vernacular English" "Bahamian Creole"
[7] "Bahamian English" "Barbadian Creole (Bajan)"
[9] "Belizean Creole" "Bislama"
```

For the present case study, only the three last variables will be relevant. First, let us use the coordinates to create a world map where the geographic locations of varieties are displayed as symbols which represent the linguistic type of varieties. We will first create a numeric vector that represents the types as numbers.

```
> code <- as.numeric(eWAVE$Type)
> code
[1] 3 4 5 3 3 1 3 1 1 1 4 1 2 4 2 4 3 4 3 3 3 5 1
[24] 5 5 5 3 4 2 1 1 1 4 4 4 3 1 4 4 1 3 4 3 3 5 3
[47] 4 2 2 5 5 4 1 3 4 1 3 1 1 5 5 1 4 3 4 2 1 1 3
[70] 4 3 2 1 3 3 3
```

Now we are ready to create our first map with the help of some functions from the package rworldmap.

```
> dialmap <- getMap()
> plot(dialmap)
> points(eWAVE[, 23:24], pch = code + 20, col = code, bg = code)
```

The first two lines of code are needed to create an empty map of the world. The third line adds points to the map. The contour and filling colour of the symbols correspond to the five linguistic types. We add 20 to the pch argument because R symbols that can be filled with different colours are in the range from 21 to 25. Finally, we provide a legend:

```
> legend("bottomleft", legend = levels(eWAVE$Type), pch = 21:25,
col = 1:5, pt.bg = 1:5)
```

The result is shown in Figure 17.1.

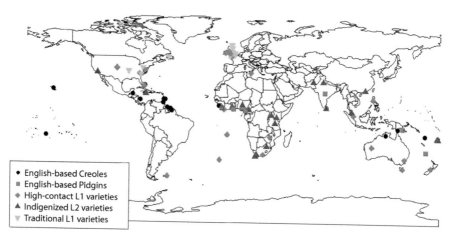

Figure 17.1. A map of the world with 76 varieties of English from eWAVE

To zoom in on a specific region, one can use `xlim()` and `ylim()`. The x coordinates specify the longitude, whereas the y coordinates stand for the latitude. As an illustration, let us zoom in on the USA mainland territory and display two varieties: Appalachian English and Chicano English. Their coordinates in eWAVE are found in rows 3 and 18, respectively. To zoom in on the USA territory, you can use the following code, which will create an empty map with country boundaries:

```
> plot(dialmap, xlim = c(-140, -40), ylim = c(30, 50), asp = 1)
```

You can try out different boundaries with the help of `xlim()` and `ylim()`, as well as projection types (`asp`). Next, let us plot the locations as points and add text labels, as shown in Figure 17.2:

```
> points(eWAVE[c(3, 18), 23:24], col = code[c(3, 18)], cex = 1.2,
pch = code[c(3, 18)] + 20, bg = code[c(3, 18)])
> text(eWAVE[c(3, 18), 23:24], labels = rownames(eWAVE)[c(3, 18)],
cex = 0.8, adj = c(0.5, 1.2))
```

The `adj` argument provides a small horizontal and vertical adjustment for the text labels, to avoid overplotting.

In the remaining part of the chapter, you will learn how to represent geographic and linguistic distances with the help of Multidimensional Scaling, as well as how to compute correlations between distance matrices.

Figure 17.2. Zooming in on the USA mainland territory and two U.S. varieties

More on maps in R

In this section, we have only discussed some basic plotting tools for creation of maps. There are many useful packages in R that can help you create attractive and informative maps. One of them is `ggmap`, which downloads data from Google Maps and uses a structure similar to `ggplot2`, adding layers incrementally. A relatively easy way of highlighting countries of interest in different colours by using their names or ISO codes is provided in the package `rworldmap`. See also pp. 309 – 321 in R Graphics Cookbook (Chang 2012) about how to make maps with `ggplot2`, use different colours to represent values of variables and create maps from a shapefile.

17.2   What is Multidimensional Scaling?

Multidimensional Scaling (MDS) is a method that represents distances between objects in a low-dimensional space. Imagine a table of distances between different cities. With the help of MDS, it is possible to obtain a two-dimensional representation of these distances, similar to a geographical map, with the cities represented as points. One can also visualize non-spatial relationships, such as similarities and dissimilarities between languages, language varieties, words or phonemes. The aim of MDS is to find a low-dimensional space that would represent these objects as points in the space, such that the distances between these points would match the original (dis)similarities between the objects as precisely as possible. The larger the dissimilarity (and the smaller the similarity) between two objects, the farther apart these objects should be in the MDS space.

There are many types of MDS. The most important distinction is that between metric and non-metric MDS. The purpose of **metric** MDS is to represent the objects in a low-dimensional space, so that the original distances or dissimilarities between them are represented as precisely as possible by the distances between the points on the MDS map. Perhaps the best-known type of metric MDS is the so-called **classical MDS**, or Principal Coordinates Analysis. In **non-metric** MDS, it is the ranking of dissimilarities between the objects that matters, rather than their actual numerical values. The purpose of non-metric MDS is to find a configuration of objects such that the rankings of the MDS distances between the objects correspond as closely as possible to the rank order of the original dissimilarities between the objects. Non-metric MDS is widely used in psychometrics, when one deals with similarity and dissimilarity ratings on the ordinal scale. Less strict than metric MDS, it should be used when the ordering is more important than the actual distances. Note, however, that non-metric MDS algorithms tend to be slower than metric, so the latter may be preferred if you have a very large dataset.

The better the original distances or dissimilarities are represented in a dimensionality-reduction solution, the less information is lost. For example, a two-dimensional map may not perfectly represent the driving distances between different cities because of the Earth curvature or differences in elevation. Such loss of information is called **stress**. The amount of stress in a solution is the most important goodness-of-fit measure in MDS. The smaller the stress, the better the fit.

A solution with zero stress, however, is not necessarily the optimal one. In principle, it is possible to represent the distances between n objects with 100% accuracy in a model with $n - 1$ dimensions. For example, the distance between two points can be represented by a one-dimensional straight line, whereas all distances between three points can be perfectly represented on a two-dimensional plane, and so on. Still, the heuristic value of MDS is determined by its ability to find a small number of interpretable dimensions that account for most variation in the data. Similar to other multivariate methods, the art of MDS consists in striking the balance between parsimony and accuracy. The evaluation and diagnostics of MDS solutions will be explained below. The next section introduces the classical MDS, which will represent geographical distances on two- and three-dimensional maps, whereas Section 17.4 shows how to fit the Kruskal non-metric MDS of linguistic distances based on categorical data.

17.3   Computation and representation of geographical distances

This section shows how one can represent geographical distances with the help of classical MDS. Although this task is not particularly common in linguistic studies, it offers a simple example that illustrates the basic principles of MDS. To reproduce the code in this section, you will need the following packages:

```
> install.packages(c("Rling", "fields", "rgl", "MASS"))
> library(Rling); library(fields); library(rgl); library(MASS)
```

The dataset of English varieties eWAVE was introduced in the previous section. Again, only the last two columns with the longitude and latitude will be relevant.

```
> data(eWAVE)
```

To demonstrate how geographical distances can be represented by MDS, we will compute the distances from the coordinates with the help of rdist.earth() from the package fields. This function computes distances between all pairs of objects on the basis of their longitude and latitude coordinates, taking into account the Earth curvature. The result is a matrix with geographic distances. One can compute the distances in miles (the default) or kilometres (as shown below). Next, we transform the matrix into a distance matrix object.

```
> geo.dist <- rdist.earth(eWAVE[, 23:24], miles = FALSE)
> geo.dist <- as.dist(geo.dist)
```

Now we can perform MDS. The main function for classical MDS is cmdscale(). The first argument is the distance matrix. The argument eig is optional. It 'tells' R to compute the **eigenvalues** of every dimension, i.e. the contributions of all possible dimensions to explaining variance. This information is useful for deciding on the optimal number of dimensions. The default number of dimensions is two.

```
> geo.mds <- cmdscale(geo.dist, eig = TRUE) #equivalent to
cmdscale(geo.dist, k = 2, eig = TRUE)
```

The object geo.mds contains, among other things, coordinates of all varieties in two dimensions (the default), as well as the eigenvalues. To decide on the optimal number of dimensions, it is useful to examine a scree plot of the eigenvalues. The scree plot in Figure 17.3 shows the eigenvalues of the first 20 dimensions.

```
> barplot(geo.mds$eig[1:20], xlab = "Number of dimensions", ylab =
"Eigenvalues", main = "Scree plot")
```

The scree plot demonstrates that there is a substantial decrease in the explanatory power of new dimensions after the thirst three ones. It seems that a three-dimensional solution is the optimal one (not surprisingly). However, let us begin our visual inspection with a

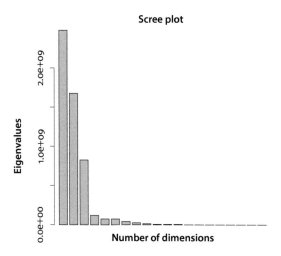

Figure 17.3. The scree plot of proportions of variance explained by the first 20 dimensions

two-dimensional plot. The code below demonstrates how one can create an empty MDS map and plot the text labels of the varieties onto it. Figure 17.4 displays the result.

```
> plot(geo.mds$points, type = "n", main = "MDS of geographic
distances between varieties of English")
> text(geo.mds$points, labels = rownames(eWAVE), cex = 0.6)
```

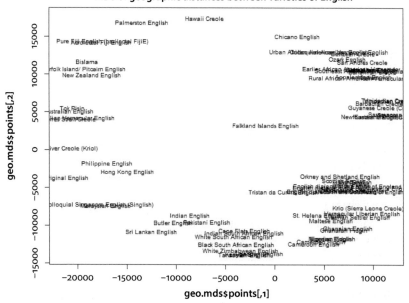

Figure 17.4. An MDS plot with text labels of the varieties of English

The plot has an empty centre and a densely populated periphery. A closer inspection reveals that the dialects are arranged in a specific order, as if one was looking on the globe from 'below', with the centre approximately at the South Pole. The upper part of the map with Americas roughly corresponds to the Western hemisphere, and the lower part with Europe, Asia and Africa to the Eastern hemisphere. The map does not represent the north/south distinctions (latitudes). To represent this information, it is necessary to add the third dimension. One can do it on a three-dimensional plot with the help of the package `rgl`. Before creating the plot, one should re-run `cmdscale()` with `k = 3` to obtain the coordinates on the third dimension.

```
> geo.mds.3d <- cmdscale(geo.dist, k = 3, eig = TRUE)
> plot3d(geo.mds.3d$points, type = "n")
> text3d(geo.mds.3d$points, texts = rownames(eWAVE), cex = 0.6)
```

The plot, shown in Figure 17.5, can be rotated with the help of the left button of the mouse or the touchpad. You can also zoom out and in by holding the right button and using the scroll wheel of the mouse or making sweeping movements with your touchpad.

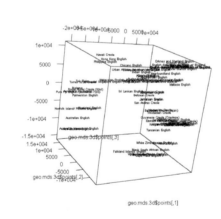

Figure 17.5. A 3D MDS plot of varieties of English based on geographic distances

A closer inspection of the 3D plot demonstrates that the varieties are plotted in a way that resembles their locations on the Earth surface. The labels, however, are located 'inside out', that is, the points that are on the left from the other points are located in 'real life' to the East from the other points. This mismatch is not a problem. It often happens in MDS that the coordinates are 'flipped', but a 'flipped' solution is just as good as an 'unflipped' one.

Although the solution looks interpretable, it is necessary to find out whether it represents the data well. The GOF component of the MDS object gives two goodness-of-fit measures, which give an idea about the quality of the model, similar to the R^2 statistic in linear regression. The higher the scores, the better.

```
> geo.mds.3d$GOF
[1] 0.7423278 0.9207068
```

Another way of estimating the goodness of fit is Kruskal's (1964) formula for computation of stress:

$$Stress = \left[\frac{\sum_{i<j}\left(d_{ij} - \hat{d}_{ij}\right)^2}{\sum_{i<j} d_{ij}^{\,2}} \right]^{1/2}$$

where d_{ij} is the actual distance between objects i and j, and $\hat{d}_{ij}$ is the fitted distance between the same objects in the MDS solution. In R, this can be computed as follows:

```
> sqrt(sum((geo.dist - dist(geo.mds.3d$points))^2)/sum(geo.dist^2))
[1] 0.1432637
```

Stress indicates the opposite of the GOF measures mentioned above. The smaller the stress, the better the fit. Below are some rules of thumb for interpretation of stress values in MDS solutions:

$0.2 \le$ Stress	Poor
$0.1 \le$ Stress < 0.2	Fair
$0.05 \le$ Stress < 0.01	Good
Stress < 0.05	Excellent

The GOF values and stress only show the general picture, but they do not tell us which individual distances are fitted well and which ones poorly. For that purpose, one can use the Shepard diagnostic plot in the MASS package. It shows how well the distances in the initial matrix are approximated by the fitted distances in the resulting solution. The method allows one to identify degenerate solutions and other problems (see Borg & Groenen 1997: Ch. 13).

```
> geo.sh <- Shepard(geo.dist, geo.mds.3d$points)
> plot(geo.sh, main = "Shepard plot", pch = ".")
> lines(geo.sh$x, geo.sh$yf, type = "S")
```

Figure 17.6 shows the Shepard plot of the data. The x-axis corresponds to the geographic distances between each pair of varieties, whereas the y-axis shows the distances between the varieties as they are represented by the MDS solution. The points that are remote from

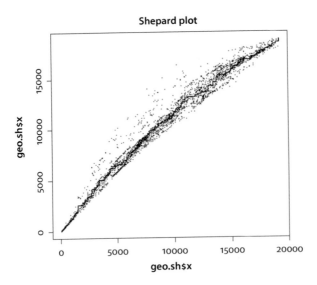

Figure 17.6. The Shepard plot for diagnostics of MDS solution

the diagonal are outliers. They contribute to the stress value the most. In this example, we do not observe serious problems with the fit of individual distances.

17.4   Computation and representation of linguistic distances: The Kruskal non-metric MDS

17.4.1   Recoding the dataset

This section will demonstrate how one can compute distances based on ordinal and other types of data and represent them in non-metric MDS. To reproduce the code, you will need the following packages:

```
> install.packages(c("Rling", "cluster", "MASS", "ggplot2"))
> library(Rling); library(cluster); library(MASS); library(ggplot2)
```

We will continue our analysis of the dataset eWAVE:

```
> data(eWAVE)
```

The first twenty columns in eWAVE dataset represent twenty randomly selected linguistic features from the Electronic World Atlas of Varieties of English.[2] The features represent different aspects of language structure, including morphology, syntax and organization of discourse. The Atlas has its own system of coding the presence or absence of linguistic

---

2.   See the full list of features at http://ewave-atlas.org/parameters (last access 24.06.2014).

features in varieties: 'A' means that the feature is pervasive or obligatory; 'B' says that the feature is neither pervasive nor extremely rare; 'C' means that the feature exists, but it is extremely rare; 'D' stands for an attested absence of the feature. There are two types of missing values: 'X' shows that the structural feature is not applicable given the structural make-up of the variety, and '?' indicates missing information.

This type of representation is typical of ordinal variables (see Chapter 1). It is not clear whether the difference between the categories 'A' and 'B' is the same as the difference between 'B' and 'C' or 'C' and 'D'. Ordinal categorical variables can be represented by ordered factors in R. In addition, it is necessary to recode 'X' and '?' into 'NA', so that the algorithms that will be used below can identify the missing values. This can be done as follows. First, we create a copy of the dataset. Next, the missing values are substituted with 'NA':

```
> eWAVE1 <- eWAVE
> eWAVE1[eWAVE1 == "?"] <- NA
> eWAVE1[eWAVE1 == "X"] <- NA
```

The next step is to order the factors, so that 'D' represents the smallest value, and 'A' represents the greatest value. To apply the transformation to all features simultaneously, one can use the function `lapply()`. Since the function returns a list of factors, it is necessary to combine them in a new data frame.

```
> eWAVE2 <- lapply(eWAVE1[, 1:20], function(x) ordered(x, levels =
c("D", "C", "B", "A")))
> eWAVE2 <- data.frame(eWAVE2)
```

The resulting data frame looks as follows:

```
> str(eWAVE2)
'data.frame': 76 obs. of 20 variables:
$ F1: Ord.factor w/ 4 levels "D"<"C"<"B"<"A": 3 NA 1 2 3 1 3 4...
$ F7: Ord.factor w/ 4 levels "D"<"C"<"B"<"A": 4 NA 4 3 4 3 4 4...
$ F48: Ord.factor w/ 4 levels "D"<"C"<"B"<"A": 4 3 3 NA NA 2 3 ...
[output omitted]
```

17.4.2 Computation of Gower distances

In Chapter 15, the distances were computed between vectors with continuous values. Here, the data are ordinal. To compute the distances between the varieties, we will use the Gower general coefficient of similarity, which can be computed for all kinds of variables, including categorical ones. In its most general form, it looks as follows (Gower 1971: 861):

$$S_{ij} = \sum_{k=1}^{v} s_{ijk} w_k \Big/ \sum_{k=1}^{v} \delta_{ijk} w_k$$

where S_{ij} is the general similarity between observations i and j, v is the number of variables, s_{ijk} is the similarity between i and j with regard to the variable k, and δ_{ijk} is the possibility of making comparison between i and j regarding k. This value is equal to 1 if both exemplars have non-missing values, and 0 otherwise. Finally, w_k is the weight of the variable k, which can be specified by the researcher. By default, all weights are equal to 1.

For ordinal and numeric variables, s_{ijk} is defined as 1 minus the absolute difference of both values divided by the total range of that variable. The values of ordinal variables are replaced by their integer representations. For example, in the English varieties data, 'A' will correspond to 4 and 'D' will correspond to 1.

For nominal variables, including binary ones, s_{ijk} equals 1 if the values of i and j are identical, and 0 if the values are different. From this follows that the Gower similarity coefficient returns the proportion of overlapping values in two vectors with categorical values with regard to the total number of possible comparisons.[3]

The Gower coefficient shows the degree of similarity. However, for MDS we need the opposite of similarities, namely, dissimilarities that can be represented as distances. The distances between exemplars are calculated by subtracting the similarity scores from 1.

The distance metric based on the Gower similarity coefficient, which is referred to as the Gower distance, is implemented in the `daisy()` function in the `cluster` package. This metric is chosen automatically if at least one variable in the data is not numerical.

```
> ling.dist <- daisy(eWAVE2)  # equivalent to daisy(eWAVE2, metric
= "gower")
> summary(ling.dist)
2850 dissimilarities, summarized:
Min.    1st Qu. Median  Mean    3rd Qu. Max.     NA's
0.00000 0.28070 0.35556 0.37555 0.45000 1.00000  8
Metric: mixed ; Types = O, O, O, O, O, O, O, O, O, O, O, O, O, O,
O, O, O, O, O, O
Number of objects: 76
```

There is one small problem with the distances. The MDS algorithms that will be introduced below do not accept missing values. As can be seen from the summary, the distance matrix contains eight 'NA's. They can be replaced with the mean distance value. Another solution would be to inspect the data and remove the varieties that contain too many missing values.

```
> ling.dist1 <- ling.dist
> ling.dist1[is.na(ling.dist)] <- mean(ling.dist, na.rm = TRUE)
```

---

3. In addition, a binary variable with values '1' and '0' can be treated asymmetrically. In that case, the weighting sigma equals 0 if both observations have '0'. See the help page of the function `daisy()` in the package `cluster` for more information and examples.

In addition, the MDS algorithm that we are going to use does not accept zero or negative distances. The zero values can be replaced with very small positive numbers:

```
> ling.dist2 <-ling.dist1
> ling.dist2[ling.dist2 == 0] <- 0.001
```

We will discuss a popular non-metric approach developed by Kruskal (1964). You will need the function isoMDS() from the package MASS. Its main arguments are a distance matrix and the preferred number of dimensions. Let us begin with a two-dimensional solution (the default). Since this function does not deal with zero distances, the distance matrix ling.dist2 will be used:

```
> ling.mds.kr <- isoMDS(ling.dist2) #equivalent to isoMDS(ling.
dist2, k = 2)
initial value 32.470515
iter 5 value 24.586167
final value 24.416368
converged
```

Number of iterations

Sometimes, the algorithm may stop after 50 iterations, as in the example with imaginary data below:

```
> test <- isoMDS(test.dist, k = 8) # do not run
initial value 6.601167
iter 5 value 1.934208
...
iter 50 value 0.428581
final value 0.428581
stopped after 50 iterations
```

The algorithm tries to find a stress-optimal configuration by re-scaling the data again and again until the next possible improvement is below a convergence criterion. The default number of iterations is 50. In this example, this number was not enough for the algorithm to reach the point of no further substantial improvement. To increase the number of iterations from 50 to 100 or another number, one can use the following code:

```
> test <- isoMDS(test.dist, k = 8, maxit = 100)
```

(Continued)

```
initial value 6.601167
iter   5 value 1.934208
...
iter  60 value 0.394103
final value 0.388977
converged
```

The solution can be represented with the help of `qplot()` in `ggplot2`. This function has been chosen because it can easily represent the text labels in different colours depending on the type of the variety, as shown below, or any other variable. It will also automatically add a legend. The resulting plot is shown in Figure 17.7.

```
> qplot(ling.mds.kr$points[, 1], ling.mds.kr$points[, 2], label =
rownames(eWAVE), cex = 0.5, col = eWAVE$Type, geom = "text")
```

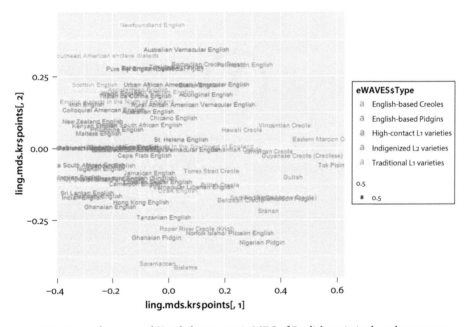

Figure 17.7. A two-dimensional Kruskal non-metric MDS of English varieties based on twenty linguistic features

The plot demonstrates a continuum from the traditional L1 varieties (mostly in the upper left sector) via the high-contact L1 varieties and indigenized L2 varieties to the creoles and pidgins. Although the corresponding areas overlap, the general tendency is still observed.

The next question is whether the two-dimensional representation is optimal. We can test it by fitting MDS models for different numbers of dimensions and comparing the relative decrease in the stress value with the help of a scree plot. The stress of the solution is printed out as the 'final value'. The stress of the two-dimensional solution was 24.42. This value is large. This means one loses much information. In this situation, one can increase the number of dimensions until acceptable quality is achieved.

Warning: degenerate MDS solutions

In some non-metric MDS solutions, the stress may be very low, but the solution may be poor. Consider the Shepard plot in Figure 17.8. The MDS stress is almost 0, but the solution is degenerate because the algorithm dichotomizes all fitted distances into 0 and 20. See Borg & Groenen (1997: 270–273) for a detailed explanation. A graphical indication of such problems is the presence of long horizontal lines.

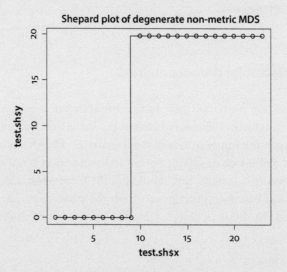

Figure 17.8. The Shepard plot of a degenerate MDS solution

A general recommendation in such situations is to use a stricter approach, that is, metric MDS.

Ties in non-metric MDS: how to treat similar distances?

When a distance matrix contains identical values, one can speak of **ties**. There are two main ways of tie treatment in MDS: primary (weak) and secondary (strong). If the primary treatment is used, ties impose no restrictions on the distances in the resulting MDS solution. The fact that the input distances are identical is simply not taken into account. The secondary treatment tries to represent equal input distances as equal distances in the resulting MDS model. To decide on the treatment method, one should consider how the identical distances arise in the first place and whether this is a true property of the objects or a mere artifact of measurement (Borg & Groenen 1997: 212–213). In case you want to take the identical values into account (for instance, if you have very few different values in your distance metric, and cannot afford losing any information), you can use the secondary approach to ties. This option is not available in `isoMDS()`, but you can use the `smacofSym()` function in the package `smacof`. The code will be as follows: `smacofSym(yourDistMatrix, type = "ordinal", ties = "secondary")`.

17.5   The Mantel test for distance matrices

An interesting question is whether one can find any correlation between the geographic distances and the linguistic differences between the varieties. One can compute simple correlations between the values in two distance matrices. However, since the distances are between pairs and the observations are not independent, it is not advisable to use a standard correlation test. Instead, one should use the Mantel test. Here we will discuss a version of this test based on permutation from the package `vegan`. To perform the test, you will need the distance objects from the previous case studies (Sections 17.3 and 17.4).

```
> install.packages("vegan")
> library(vegan)

> mantel(geo.dist, ling.dist, na.rm = TRUE) #equivalent to
mantel(geo.dist, ling.dist, method = "pearson", permutations = 999,
na.rm = TRUE)
```

```
Mantel statistic based on Pearson's product-moment correlation

Call:
mantel(xdis = geo.dist, ydis = ling.dist, na.rm = TRUE)

Mantel statistic r: 0.1213
      Significance: 0.001

Upper quantiles of permutations (null model):
90%      95%      97.5%    99%
0.0351   0.0525   0.0679   0.0877

Based on 999 permutations
```

Note that one has to add `na.rm = TRUE` because the original linguistic distance matrix `ling.dist` contains missing values. The default statistic is the Mantel statistic, which is in fact identical to the Pearson correlation coefficient r. To compute rank-based correlation coefficients, type in `method = "spearman"` or `method = "kendall"`. In all cases, the correlation is significant and positive, but weak. This means that there are other factors that influence the linguistic characteristics of the varieties. One of them is the amount and type of language contact.

17.6   Summary

Multidimensional Scaling is a convenient tool for visual exploration of multivariate data. Its advantage in comparison with cluster analysis is that MDS can represent both groupings and interpretable dimensions of variation, whereas cluster analysis only returns groupings. This is especially useful when one wants to model a continuum of linguistic categories or varieties.

How to present MDS results

When reporting the results of MDS, one should not forget to mention the quality of the solution (stress), the type of distance metric and the method. Of course, all relevant MDS maps should be provided and interpreted.

One of the weaknesses of traditional MDS, however, is that there is no straightforward way to interpret the location of the points with regard to the input variables. In the next two chapters, we will discuss several multivariate methods that allow one to retain information about the input variables and combine them with the information about the groups of objects. These methods are Principal Components Analysis, Factor Analysis (for quantitative data) and Correspondence Analysis (for categorical data).

More flavours of MDS

The `smacof` package also contains many useful functions for individual differences scaling, constrained MDS and other methods. For more theoretical information about those and other types of MDS, see Borg & Groenen (1997) and Cox & Cox (2001).

CHAPTER 18

Multidimensional analysis of register variation

Principal Components Analysis and Factor Analysis

What you will learn from this chapter:

> In this chapter you will learn about Principal Components Analysis and Factor Analysis. The aim of these methods is to reduce a large number of correlated quantitative variables to a small set of underlying dimensions. You will learn how to use these methods to perform corpus-based multidimensional analysis of register variation.

18.1 Multidimensional analysis of register variation

Knowledge of the repertoire of registers and linguistic features associated with them is an important part of one's language competence. Registers are language varieties associated with a particular situation of use, e.g. face-to-face conversations, emails, textbooks, fictional novels, lectures and Twitter messages. These situations can be characterized by such parameters as the channel of communication (speech, writing or signing), relationships between the participants (e.g. social status and personal relationships), communicative purpose (transfer of information, persuasion, entertainment, etc.) and settings (e.g. private or public place of communication). On the other hand, registers are also associated with specific linguistic features. For instance, face-to-face conversations contain a higher proportion of first- and second-person pronouns than textbooks, and a lower proportion of nouns and adjectives (e.g. Biber 1988).

In his famous multidimensional analysis of register variation, Douglas Biber (1988) used Factor Analysis to compare diverse texts along a relatively small number of interpretable dimensions of register variation, such as 'Involved versus Informational Production' or 'Narrative versus Non-narrative Concerns'. These dimensions emerge automatically from a large number of variables that describe the proportions of different linguistic features in a set of texts that represent a register. The registers and specific texts can then be mapped onto this register space according to their linguistic features. For instance, face-to-face and telephone conversations will have high scores on the involved pole of the dimension 'Involved versus Informational Production', whereas academic prose will have a high score on the informativity pole.

This type of analysis is usually performed with the help of exploratory Factor Analysis (FA). Since this method is closely related to Principal Components Analysis (PCA), both methods will be discussed in this chapter. Although both of them are used to simplify the data structure and classify variables and objects, FA is more appropriate for detecting theoretically relevant underlying dimensions in the data. However, PCA and FA usually yield similar results, especially if the variables are strongly correlated and the number of variables is large (Field et al. 2012: 760).

18.2   Case study: Register variation in the British National Corpus

18.2.1   The data and research question

You will need several add-on packages for this case study. They should be installed and then loaded.

```
> install.packages(c("psych", "FactoMineR"))
> library(Rling); library(psych); library(FactoMineR)
```

In this section we will carry out a multivariate analysis of register variation. The data are 69 subsections of the BNC coded for 11 variables, which represent normalized frequencies of different parts of speech in each subsection. The subsections represent five broadly defined metaregisters (the spoken part [mostly conversations], fiction, news, academic texts, non-academic prose) plus a 'miscellaneous' category. The data have the following structure:

```
> data(reg_bnc)
> str(reg_bnc)
'data.frame':  69 obs. of 12 variables:
$ Reg        : Factor w/ 6 levels "Acad","Fiction",..: 6 6 6 6 6 6
6 6 6 6 ...
$ Ncomm      : num 0.17 0.205 0.206 0.136 0.133 ...
$ Nprop      : num 0.02697 0.02498 0.0468 0.0112 0.00985 ...
$ Vpres      : num 0.0355 0.0391 0.0366 0.0485 0.0452 ...
$ Vpast      : num 0.0219 0.0298 0.0236 0.0189 0.0198 ...
$ P1         : num 0.0347 0.0208 0.018 0.0276 0.0455 ...
$ P2         : num 0.01832 0.01137 0.00775 0.03749 0.03703 ...
$ Adj        : num 0.0536 0.0585 0.0596 0.0407 0.0446 ...
$ ConjCoord  : num 0.0395 0.034 0.0335 0.0339 0.0384 ...
$ ConjSub    : num 0.031 0.0276 0.0232 0.0315 0.0283 ...
$ Interject  : num 0.00997 0.00414 0.00226 0.02173 0.04298 ...
$ Num        : num 0.0206 0.0192 0.0277 0.0414 0.0164 ...
```

All columns except the first one are numeric vectors that represent the proportions of various word classes in 69 BNC subsections. The latter are provided as the row names:

```
> rownames(reg_bnc)
[1] "S_brdcst_disc" "S_brdcst_doc" "S_brdcst_news" "S_classroom"
[5] "S_consult"     "S_conv"       "S_courtroom" "S_demonstratn"
[9] "S_interv_oral" "S_interview" "S_lect_arts" "S_lect_com"
[output omitted]
```

The main question of this study is as follows. Can we identify interpretable dimensions of register variation on the basis of the data and what are the relationships between the metaregisters, as well as more specific subsections, with regard to these dimensions? To answer this question, we will use PCA and FA. We will begin with PCA because it is conceptually less complex.

18.2.2 Principal Components Analysis

Before beginning the analyses, it is useful to check whether the data are actually appropriate for PCA and FA. There are two important conditions: on the one hand, the variables should be intercorrelated (otherwise, we cannot reduce the data to a smaller number of underlying components); on the other hand, the correlations should not be too high. Very high correlations are not a problem for PCA, but they can cause inaccurate estimates in FA, similar to multicollinearity in multiple regression (Field et al. 2012: 770–771). As a very approximate rule of thumb, the absolute values of correlations should not be lower than 0.3 and above 0.9. To examine the correlations between the variables, one can use cor():

```
> round(cor(reg_bnc[, -1]), 2)
          Ncomm Nprop Vpres Vpast P1    P2    Adj
Ncomm     1.00  0.23  -0.41 -0.21 -0.83 -0.75 0.86
Nprop     0.23  1.00  -0.34 0.36  -0.37 -0.50 0.13
Vpres     -0.41 -0.34 1.00  -0.46 0.42  0.50  -0.35
Vpast     -0.21 0.36  -0.46 1.00  0.03  -0.11 -0.16
P1        -0.83 -0.37 0.42  0.03  1.00  0.80  -0.79
P2        -0.75 -0.50 0.50  -0.11 0.80  1.00  -0.70
Adj       0.86  0.13  -0.35 -0.16 -0.79 -0.70 1.00
ConjCoord -0.13 -0.45 0.21  0.07  0.23  0.31  0.04
ConjSub   -0.52 -0.68 0.48  -0.22 0.57  0.57  -0.39
Interject -0.67 -0.39 0.41  0.02  0.70  0.79  -0.62
Num       0.21  0.28  -0.28 -0.13 -0.25 -0.16 0.03
          ConjCoord ConjSub Interject Num
Ncomm     -0.13     -0.52   -0.67     0.21
Nprop     -0.45     -0.68   -0.39     0.28
Vpres     0.21      0.48    0.41      -0.28
Vpast     0.07      -0.22   0.02      -0.13
P1        0.23      0.57    0.70      -0.25
```

P2	0.31	0.57	0.79	-0.16
Adj	0.04	-0.39	-0.62	0.03
ConjCoord	1.00	0.26	0.18	-0.41
ConjSub	0.26	1.00	0.36	-0.28
Interject	0.18	0.36	1.00	-0.09
Num	-0.41	-0.28	-0.09	1.00

The variable *Num* has many correlations with the absolute value slightly under 0.3. One may consider removing such variables. As for possible multicollinearity, this should not be a concern, since there are no highly correlated variables.

One can also use the Bartlett test for this kind of preliminary diagnostics. The null hypothesis of this test is that the variables are not correlated. In that case, it would not make sense to run further analysis. The test is available as cortest.bartlett() in the package psych.

```
> cortest.bartlett(reg_bnc[, -1])
R was not square, finding R from data
$chisq
[1] 536.3401

$p.value
[1] 4.109611e-80

$df
[1] 55
```

Since the *p*-value is well below the significance level, we can reject the null hypothesis of zero correlation between the variables and continue with the analyses.

We will begin with PCA, using PCA() from the FactoMineR package:

```
> reg.pca <- PCA(reg_bnc, quali.sup = 1, graph = FALSE)
```

The argument quali.sup = 1 tells R that the first variable, *Reg*, should be regarded as a qualitative supplementary variable. In contrast to active elements, supplementary elements do not contribute to the construction of principal components. They are added to the analysis for the purpose of interpretation or illustration. There are two types of supplementary variables, qualitative and quantitative. Next, the argument graph = FALSE suppresses the immediate creation of graphical output. Note that PCA is usually performed on standardized scores (see Chapter 3) rather than original ones because it is sensitive to scaling differences. This is the default option, which should not be changed.

The first question is how many dimensions are needed to account for register variation. The output of reg.pca$eig shows eigenvalues, proportions of variance explained by each component and cumulative explained variance. The eigenvalue is an important concept in multivariate analysis. As was mentioned in the previous chapter, an eigenvalue shows how much of the total variance is explained by each component. The higher the correlations between a component and the variables, the greater the component's eigenvalue. Note that the eigenvalue of every additional component is smaller than the previous one. The first component always explains the greatest portion of variance. However, the cumulative percentage of explained variance always increases, until it reaches 100%.

```
> head(reg.pca$eig)
  eigenvalue  percentage  of  variance  cumulative  percentage  of
  variance
comp  1  5.0682936  46.075396  46.07540
comp  2  1.8722103  17.020094  63.09549
comp  3  1.3758435  12.507669  75.60316
comp  4  0.7900757  7.182506   82.78566
comp  5  0.6451271  5.864791   88.65046
comp  6  0.4217144  3.833768   92.48422
```

There are different rules of thumb with regard to the optimal number of components: some statisticians believe that one should retain only those components whose eigenvalues are greater than 1 (the Kaiser criterion); others are less strict, and use 0.7 as a cut-off point (see a discussion in Field et al. 2012: 762–764). One can also inspect the values visually using a scree plot, as has been done in the previous chapters. Consider Figure 18.1. The *x*-axis of the bar plot represents the number of components from 1 to 11 (the number of rows in `reg.pca$eig`), which were created by the algorithm. The *y*-axis shows the percentage of variance explained by each dimension. These values can be found in the second column in `reg.pca$eig`. The R code is as follows:

```
> barplot(reg.pca$eig[,2], names = 1:nrow(reg.pca$eig), xlab =
"components", ylab = "Percentage of explained variance")
```

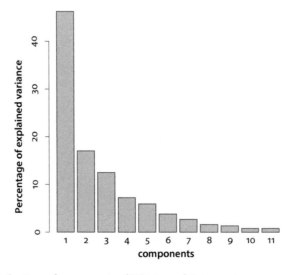

Figure 18.1. Contributions of components of PCA to explaining variance

Figure 18.1 shows no substantial increase in explanatory power after three dimensions, which also explain together 75.6% of variance. This is also the number of components according to the Kaiser criterion, since only the first three components have eigenvalues greater than 1.

Now we can begin interpreting the components, or dimensions. To visualize the variable space, one can use the following command:

```
> plot(reg.pca, choix = "var", cex = 0.8)
```

The argument `choix = "var"` is used to represent the variables. The result is displayed in Figure 18.2. By default, the algorithm creates a plot with individuals (in our case, the BNC subsections). Unless specified otherwise, the plot displays the first two components as two axes. The variables are represented as vectors pointing away from the origin. The angles between the vectors and the axes indicate how strongly the variables are correlated with the dimensions. The smaller the angle, the stronger the correlation. If two vectors point to almost the same direction, this means that the corresponding variables are highly correlated and therefore may represent the same underlying theoretical construct. The length of the vectors reflects how much variation in the variable is captured by this low-dimensional display, with the maximum length of 1 (limited by the circle). In other words, the length represents the quality of the representation of a variable on the plane.

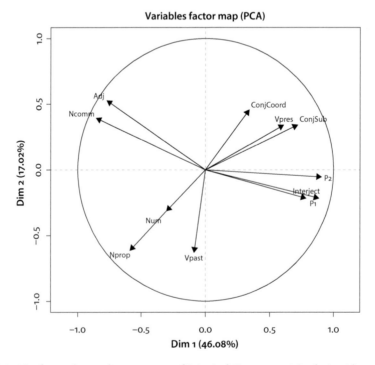

Figure 18.2. The first and second components of Principal Components Analysis with variables

The orientation of variables suggests that the first (horizontal) component relates to the well-known opposition between involved and informational communication. The variables which are the most strongly correlated with the dimension are the ones that represent the frequencies of the 1st and 2nd person pronouns and interjections. These are linguistic features associated with involved, interactive communication. They are opposed to common nouns and adjectives on the left – features that indicate high informational density of communication.

One can also examine the correlation coefficients by using dimdesc(). For the first dimension, the output is as follows:

```
> dimdesc(reg.pca)
$Dim.1
$Dim.1$quanti
               correlation   p.value
P2             0.9117524     0.000000e+00
P1             0.8958585     0.000000e+00
Interject      0.7913207     6.661338e-16
ConjSub        0.7268571     1.540101e-12
Vpres          0.6203029     1.311435e-08
ConjCoord      0.3461531     3.574209e-03
Num           -0.3236023     6.681150e-03
Nprop         -0.5825157     1.513793e-07
Adj           -0.7699620     1.056008e-14
Ncomm         -0.8551296     8.636119e-21

$Dim.1$quali
        R2            p.value
Reg   0.7783745     2.391373e-19

$Dim.1$category
               Estimate    p.value
Spok           3.100121    6.960014e-16
Fiction        1.259459    2.530881e-02
Acad          -1.256963    2.978404e-03
NonacProse    -1.272090    2.671066e-03
News          -1.427441    4.102683e-06
[output omitted]
```

The numbers support our previous observations based on the graphical representation: the top positively correlated features are the 1st and 2nd person pronouns and interjections. Their correlations are very strong, around 0.9. The strongest negative correlations are observed for common nouns and adjectives (–0.86 and –0.77, respectively). By default, the function returns only those estimates that are significant at the level of 0.05.

In addition, the function returns the estimates of regression coefficients for qualitative supplementary variables (in this example, the metaregisters). The response variable is the coordinates of the megaregisters on the dimension. The largest positive estimate (3.1) is observed for the spoken data. This means that it is the most strongly associated with involvement. The spoken data are followed by fiction. The values of the non-fiction written registers are negative, which reflects the informative orientation of the latter.

The second component has relatively high positive values for adjectives and coordinate conjunctions, and negative values for past forms of verbs and proper nouns. One can interpret this dimension tentatively as description vs. reporting of past events. The academic texts are significantly correlated with the positive values. The register that is significantly associated with the negative values on the second dimension is the news. As for the third dimension, it seems to correspond to the distinction between narrative and non-narrative texts. The strongly associated features are past tense verbs and coordinating conjunctions (positive correlation) and numerals (negative correlation). It distinguishes fiction from all other registers. One can visualize the second and third dimensions in a plot with the following command (see Figure 18.3):

```
> plot(reg.pca, axes = c(2,3), choix = "var", cex = 0.8)
```

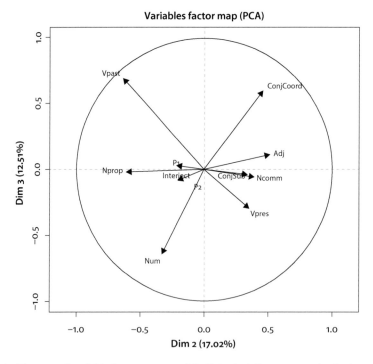

Figure 18.3. The second and third components of the Principal Components Analysis with variables

Finally, we will plot the individual subsections onto this space. Their labels will be in grey, size 0.8. The centroids of the five metaregisters are plotted, as well. Their positions can be interpreted as the prototypes of the corresponding metaregisters. To plot components 1 and 2, the following code can be used:

```
> plot(reg.pca, cex = 0.8, col.ind = "grey", col.quali = "black")
```

Plotting components 2 and 3 is done as follows:

```
> plot(reg.pca, axes = c(2, 3), cex = 0.8, col.ind = "grey", col.
quali = "black")
```

The results are shown in Figures 18.4 and 18.5. They show that the BNC subsections that belong to the same metaregister tend to cluster together.

The results seem to support one's intuitive ideas about registers. For example, spoken discourse is highly involved (component 1), neutral with regard to description/past event reporting (component 2) and slightly more non-narrative than narrative (component 3).

It is also possible to plot confidence ellipses around the centroids to estimate the amount of overlap of the prototypes of the registers (dimensions 1 and 2):

```
> plotellipses(reg.pca, label = "quali")
```

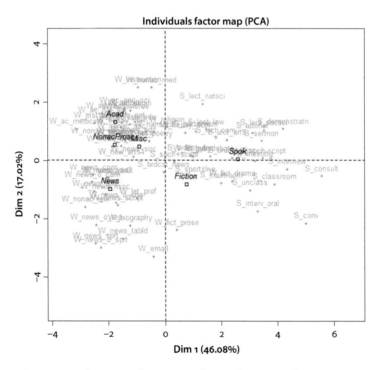

Figure 18.4. Orientation of 69 BNC subsections with regard to Principal Components 1 and 2. Grey text labels: subsections. Black text labels: register centroids

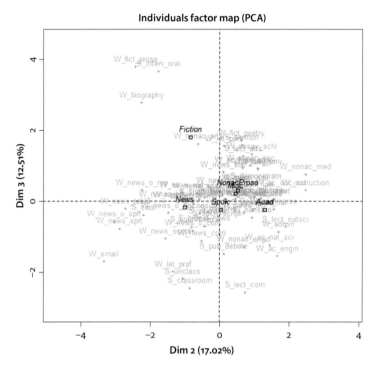

Figure 18.5. Orientation of 69 BNC subsections with regard to Principal Components 2 and 3. Grey text labels: subsections. Black text labels: register centroids

The argument `label = "quali"` tells R to plot only the labels of supplementary elements. Figure 18.6 shows the 95% confidence ellipses of the centroids. Note that the size of confidence ellipses depends on the number of points. The fiction ellipsis is very large, since this category is represented only by three BNC subsections. The large ellipsis of fiction overlaps with the ellipsis of the spoken data, and the category 'miscellaneous' overlaps with most other registers. The reader is encouraged to explore the second and third dimensions by adding `axis = c(2, 3)`. One can also compare the confidence ellipses around all individual subcorpora that represent a register, rather than around the register centroids by adding `mean = FALSE`.

To summarize, even though PCA is not a technique *par excellence* for discovering underlying constructs, we have found three more or less interpretable dimensions based on eleven linguistic variables. These dimensions capture important differences between the registers and text types. The `FactoMineR` package contains many more useful functions, and the reader is encouraged to explore them (see also Husson et al. 2010).

However, it is not entirely clear how dimension 2 is related to dimension 3. Dimension 2 opposes adjectives, coordinate conjunction and common nouns to past tense verbs and proper nouns, whereas Dimension 3 gives positive scores to past tense verbs and

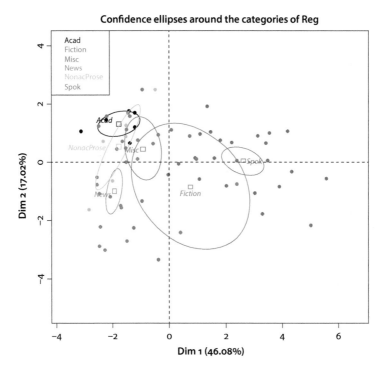

Figure 18.6. Confidence ellipses around the centroids of the registers, Principle Components 1 and 2

coordinate conjunctions, and negative scores to numerals. To achieve greater interpretability, one can try a different method, Factor Analysis, which is a more appropriate tool for finding theoretically interpretable dimensions of variation.

18.2.3   Factor Analysis

The aim of both PCA and FA is to simplify the structure of a set of variables. Yet, these methods have important differences. The main purpose of PCA is to find as few orthogonal (uncorrelated) components as possible while maximizing the total explained variance. It is used mainly to reduce dimensionality. In contrast, FA is more widely used for exploring theoretical constructs, or latent variables, which are called factors. There is also a major technical difference between the methods. Unlike PCA, FA 'rotates' the factors, trying to increase the load of variables on several common factors.

The main function for FA is `factanal()` in the basic R distribution. To perform FA, one has to specify the desired number of factors. We will use the optimal number of components in PCA, that is, three factors.

```
> reg.fa <- factanal(reg_bnc[, -1], factors = 3)
> reg.fa
```

```
Call:
factanal(x = reg_bnc[, -1], factors = 3)

Uniquenesses:
   Ncomm  Nprop  Vpres  Vpast  P1      P2      Adj     ConjCoord
   0.120  0.335  0.510  0.005  0.175   0.192   0.102   0.496
   ConjSub  Interject  Num
   0.438    0.416      0.726

Loadings:
          Factor1  Factor2  Factor3
Ncomm     -0.927            -0.125
Nprop     -0.214   -0.458   -0.640
Vpres      0.417    0.539    0.159
Vpast      0.138   -0.983
P1         0.868    0.118    0.240
P2         0.796    0.259    0.327
Adj       -0.940             0.107
ConjCoord                    0.709
ConjSub    0.480    0.336    0.467
Interject  0.716    0.101    0.248
Num       -0.109            -0.508

               Factor1  Factor2  Factor3
SS loadings      4.127    1.682    1.676
Proportion Var   0.375    0.153    0.152
Cumulative Var   0.375    0.528    0.680

Test of the hypothesis that 3 factors are sufficient.
The chi square statistic is 65.18 on 25 degrees of freedom.
The p-value is 1.95e-05
```

An important concept in FA is **factor loadings**. The stronger a variable loads onto a factor, the more strongly this variable defines the factor. Factor loadings are analogous to correlation coefficients between the variables and factors, although their numerical values can be sometimes greater than 1 or less than −1. As a rule of thumb, loadings with absolute (positive or negative) values greater than 0.3 are considered to be important. One can see that the first factor is very similar to the first Principal Component from the previous subsection, with strong positive correlations with the proportions of 1st and 2nd person pronouns and interjections, and strong negative correlations with the proportions of common nouns and adjectives. Thus, Factor 1 represents the distinction between involved and informational communication. This is also the factor that accounted for most variation in Biber's (1988) analysis. Factor 2, which distinguishes between past tense verbs and present tense verbs, looks similar to Biber's (1988) narrative vs. non-narrative dimension. Finally, Factor 3 contrasts coordinate (followed at some distance by subordinate) conjunctions, on the one hand, and proper nouns and numerals, on the other hand. This dimension looks intriguing. Let us have a look at the subcomponents and their scores. To make the algorithm return scores for the subcomponents, one can add `scores = "Bartlett"`.

```
> reg.fa <- factanal(reg_bnc[, -1], factors = 3, scores = "Bartlett")
> plot(reg.fa$scores[, 2:3], type = "n")
> text(reg.fa$scores[, 2:3], rownames(reg_bnc), cex = 0.7)
```

The resulting plot is shown in Figure 18.7.

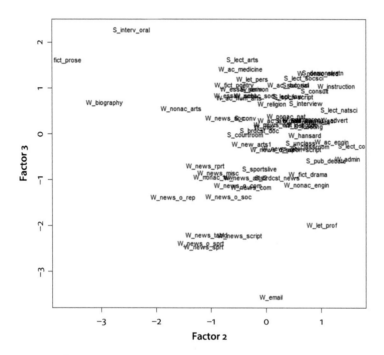

Figure 18.7. Scores of BNC subcorpora on Factor 2 and 3

It seems that the third factor relates to more or less elaborate development of ideas (fiction, interviews, lectures on arts) vs. concise informationally dense communication (news, emails).

When performing FA, one also has to address the question whether three factors are enough. This information can be obtained from the p-value in the bottom line of `reg.fa`. A p-value smaller than 0.05 indicates that the number of factors is insufficient. Unfortunately, there is much variation in the data that is left unexplained. Increasing the number of factors to six saturates the model ($p = 0.0738$), but does not help to arrive at a parsimonious theoretically interesting solution.

Finally, it is necessary to mention that there are two popular kinds of rotation, called Varimax and Promax. In the case of Varimax (a type of orthogonal rotation), factors are considered uncorrelated, whereas Promax (a type of oblique rotation) allows for some degree of correlation between factors. It is believed that behavioural data are more 'messy' and factors tend to be correlated. If we expect to find really clear-cut, unique factors, it is better to use Varimax, which is the default option. If one expects the resulting factors to be closely related, one can try Promax. To explore the latter option, one can use the following code:

```
> reg.fa <- factanal(reg_bnc[, -1], factors = 3, rotation = "promax")
> reg.fa$loadings
```

```
Loadings:
           Factor1   Factor2   Factor3
Ncomm      -1.005              -0.195
Nprop                -0.718     0.258
Vpres       0.331              -0.472
Vpast       0.259     0.113     1.066
P1          0.869
P2          0.735     0.205
Adj        -1.106     0.350    -0.102
ConjCoord  -0.220     0.853     0.216
ConjSub     0.314     0.448    -0.159
Interject   0.697     0.132
Num                  -0.596    -0.238

                 Factor1   Factor2   Factor3
SS loadings       4.347     2.012     1.615
Proportion Var    0.395     0.183     0.147
Cumulative Var    0.395     0.578     0.725
```

One can see that Factors 2 and 3 have swapped their order in comparison with the previous version, but otherwise the results are quite similar. Usually, Promax yields a better fit. Note that cumulative explained variance is greater than it was in the previous solution.

How reliable is your questionnaire?

Factor Analysis is frequently used on questionnaire data. But how reliable is the questionnaire? Does it reflect the underlying construct well? A popular measure of reliability is the Cronbach α ('alpha').

One could think of such questions as 'Do you like learning new languages?', 'Do you read books in foreign languages?' and 'Do you try to speak the local language when you stay in another country?' as measures of one's interest in foreign languages. To measure how related these questions are and how well they represent the underlying construct, one can use the `alpha()` function in the package `psych`:

```
> alpha(cbind(Question1, Question2, Question3)) # do not run
```

where the variables `Question1`, `Question2` and `Question3` are vectors with the subjects' responses on a scale. If some questions imply a reversed scale, one can specify that with the `keys` argument (see the help page). The function returns different versions of the coefficient, but the most traditional one is `raw_alpha`. The closer its value to one, the better, although extremely high values may suggest that the questions are tautological.

18.3 Summary

This chapter has introduced the basics of Principal Components Analysis and Factor Analysis. A multidimensional analysis of register variation in the BNC served as an illustration. With the help of these closely related methods we have managed to find interpretable dimensions of register variation. The chapter has also demonstrated how relationships between different text types/registers and linguistic variables can be explored with the help of biplots (i.e. plots that represent both rows and columns of a dataset in one common space). Of course, the results of this case study cannot be regarded as conclusive. The 'real' multidimensional analysis of registers requires many more linguistic variables than were considered in our case study. For example, Biber (1988) used almost 70 features.

Multidimensional analysis of register variation is not the only possible application of PCA and FA in linguistics. For example, one can use loadings of components or factors as input in regression analysis to solve the problem of multicollinearity or simplify the model.

How to report results of PCA and FA

Reporting PCA and FA is usually quite verbose. One should mention the sample size, the number of variables and the procedure, namely, how you made the decision about the number of components/factors, as well as the rotation method and the p-value. Crucially, one should include a table with factor loadings per each variable. Of course,

(Continued)

all relevant biplots should be provided, as well, if the purpose is also to obtain a classification of observations.

More on PCA and FA

A more traditional function for performing PCA is `princomp()` in the base package. To learn about other variants of rotation in FA (such as Quartimax, Oblimin, BentlerT, etc.) and other options, see the help page of `fa()` in the package `psych`. For an accessible explanation of the theory behind PCA and FA, see Field et al. (2012: Ch. 17). This chapter dealt only with exploratory FA, leaving out confirmatory FA. The latter is more complex and is typically used to test how well a hypothesized structure fits a set of data. For an introduction to confirmatory FA with R, see Everitt & Hothorn (2011: Ch. 7).

CHAPTER 19

Exemplars, categories, prototypes

Simple and multiple correspondence analysis

What you will learn from this chapter:

> This chapter introduces Correspondence Analysis. It is similar to PCA, but is designed for visualization and exploration of bivariate and multivariate categorical data. The first case study focuses on register variation of English Basic Colour Terms by using Simple Correspondence Analysis, which can be used for visualization of bivariate categorical data in two-dimensional contingency tables. In the second case study of German lexical categories *Stuhl* 'chair' and *Sessel* 'armchair', you will learn how to perform Multiple Correspondence Analysis with higher-dimensional tables.

19.1 Register variation of Basic Colour Terms: Simple Correspondence Analysis

19.1.1 The data and hypothesis

To reproduce the code in this case study, you will need several add-on packages. These packages need to be installed and loaded, if you have not done so previously.

```
> install.packages(c("vcd", "ca", "rgl"))
> library(Rling); library(vcd); library(ca); library(rgl)
```

The dataset for this case study was introduced in Chapter 4, which explored the dispersion of Basic Colour Terms (BCT) in a corpus. The dataset is called `colreg`. It contains the counts of eleven BCT in different registers from the Corpus of Contemporary American English (Davies 2008 –): spoken data on television and radio, fiction, academic prose and press (newspapers and magazines combined).

```
> data(colreg)
> colreg
```

	spoken	fiction	academic	press
black	20335	41118	26892	73080
blue	4693	22093	3605	21210
brown	1185	10914	1201	11539
gray	1168	12140	1289	6559
green	3860	14398	4477	26837
orange	931	3496	474	5766
pink	962	7312	584	6356
purple	613	3366	429	3403
red	7230	25111	5621	34596
white	14474	40745	26336	54883
yellow	1349	10553	1855	10382

The case study in Chapter 4 revealed that the frequencies of primary and secondary BCT are distributed across the registers unequally. More specifically, the secondary terms (*brown, gray, orange, pink* and *purple*) are less evenly distributed in the corpus than the primary terms (*black, white, red, green, yellow* and *blue*). The present case study will explore which terms are attracted to which register. A popular tool for visualization of categorical data is the mosaic plot:[1]

```
> mosaicplot(colreg, las = 2, shade = TRUE, main = "Register
variation of BCT")
```

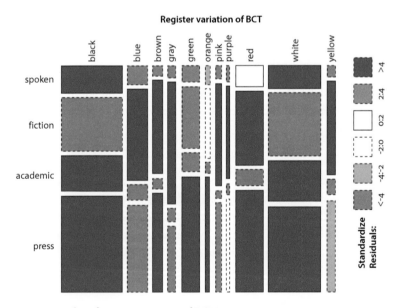

Figure 19.1. Mosaic plot of register variation of BCT

---

1.   This function is similar to *mosaic()* in vcd (see Chapter 9), which offers more graphical and structural options.

The result is shown in Figure 19.1. It shows which colour terms are overrepresented in a given register (blue-shaded rectangles) and which ones are underrepresented (pink- and red-shaded rectangles). See Chapter 9 for more information about how mosaic plots are interpreted. However, the mosaic plot is not particularly convenient when the number of categories is large. Moreover, it does not show any common dimensions of variation. A more appropriate method in this situation is Simple Correspondence Analysis (SCA).

19.1.2 Simple Correspondence Analysis

Correspondence Analysis (CA) is useful for identification of systematic relationships between variables and capturing the main tendencies in several dimensions. Similar to MDS, PCA and FA, it represents the objects of analysis as points in a low-dimensional space. We will use an implementation of SCA in the `ca` package. The code is very simple:

```
> ca.bc <- ca(colreg)
```

The details about the CA model can be obtained by using `summary()`. Of particular relevance is the upper part of the output, namely, the table with principal inertias, which show how much variation is explained by each dimension. Principal inertias are CA equivalents of eigenvalues in PCA, which was discussed in the previous chapter:

```
> summary(ca.bc)

Principal inertias (eigenvalues):

dim     value       %     cum%   scree plot
1       0.043730    77.9  77.9   ************************
2       0.010787    19.2  97.1   *****
3       0.001650    2.9   100.0

        ----        ---
Total:  0.056167    100.0
[output omitted]
```

The algorithm tries to represent the associations between variables in as few dimensions as possible. The two first dimensions represent together 97.1% of variation. This is a good approximation. Three dimensions are sufficient to capture all variation, without any loss of information.

What exactly are the associations between the registers and the colour terms like? To answer this question, one can explore a two-dimensional CA map (Figure 19.2):

```
> plot(ca.bc)
```

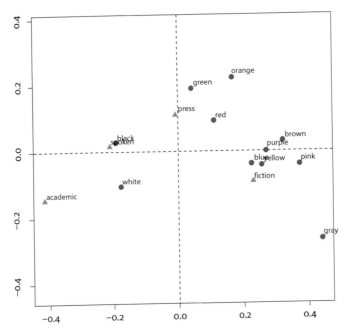

Figure 19.2. Associations between basic colour terms and registers in the Corpus of Contemporary American English (COCA). A two-dimensional correspondence analysis plot

CA plots display the labels of the levels of input variables in a low-dimensional space. In SCA, row labels are located close to one another if they contain similar proportions of counts in each column – in other words, if the rows have similar **profiles**. For example, the profile of *black* in `colreg` is [0.13, 0.25, 0.17, 0.45], and the profile of *white* is [0.11, 0.30, 0.19, 0.40]. The numbers are the actual frequencies divided by the row totals. Those profiles are more similar to each other than to the profile of *gray* [0.06, 0.57, 0.06, 0.31]. This explains why *black* and *white* are close on the map, and *gray* is far from both of them. CA maps represent the difference between profiles as the χ^2-distance. It is similar to the Euclidean distance, but is weighted by the inverse of the corresponding value in the average row profile. As a result, the stronger a row deviates from the average profile, the farther away from the other rows it will be located. The same holds for columns. Their labels are located close if they contain similar proportions of counts in each row, i.e. their profiles are similar. However, the interpretation of mutual proximity of rows (i.e. the BCT) and columns (i.e. the registers) is not straightforward. By default, the function creates a so-called symmetric plot. This means that the algorithm tries to overlay the BCT space on the register space in an optimal way. As a result of the rescaling, the distances between rows and columns are no longer meaningful. Therefore, the location of individual rows (BCT) should be interpreted with regard to the dimensions formed by the columns (i.e. the registers), rather than on the basis of their proximities with the individual columns.

Interpretation of symmetric (default) CA maps

It is easy to misinterpret a CA map. To be on the safe side, follow these rules:

- Row-to-row distances on the CA map represent the approximate χ^2-distances between the row profiles.
- Column-to-column distances on the CA map represent the approximate χ^2-distances between the column profiles.
- There is no direct interpretation of row-to-column or column-to-row distances. Interpret the dimensions first, and then examine how the profiles are located with regard to the dimensions of variation (Greenacre 2007: 72).

It seems that the first dimension (the horizontal axis) contrasts the achromatic primary colours (black and white), which are located in the left-hand part of the graph, with the other terms, which can be found in the right-hand area. This part of the plot also contains the labels of the spoken and academic subcorpora. In the right-hand part, one can find the label of fiction and those of the secondary colour terms. This is not surprising, since fiction writers tend to use more elaborate and varied attributes for objects than those one can expect to find in the other registers. Interestingly, the primary colours *yellow* and *blue* are also close to the secondary BCTs. The press subcorpus has an intermediary position with regard to the horizontal dimension and is located higher on the vertical dimension than the other registers. This orientation is shared by *red* and *green*, partly because of the political connotations of those colour terms (*Green Party*, *Red Army*), partly due to such proper names as *Red Cross* and *Green Bay Packers*, and partly due to food terms (red wine, green beans) in recipes and articles on nutrition. The secondary term *orange* is also found nearby. A closer inspection suggests a simple explanation: *orange* is frequently used in the sense 'made of oranges'. This use is frequent in recipes and articles on nutrition in the magazines.

To see if there are any interesting patterns that are missed when one looks at two dimensions only, it is possible to plot all three dimensions with the help of the `plot3d()` function in the same package. Although this is not really necessary for our analysis, since the two-dimensional solution captures nearly all variance, a three-dimensional solution will be explored for purposes of illustration. Note that you also have to install and load another package, `rgl`, to create three-dimensional interactive plots (see also Section 17.3 in Chapter 17).

```
> plot3d(ca.bc, labels = c(1,1))
```

The argument `labels = c(1, 1)` means that both row and column profiles should be shown as text labels, while `c(0, 0)` will produce only symbols on the plot, and `c(2, 2)` will show a combination of symbols and labels. The first number determines the representation of rows, and the second number determines how columns are represented. The result is a three-dimensional plot, which opens in a separate window and can be rotated with the help of the left button of the mouse or the touchpad. You can also zoom out and in by holding the right button and scrolling the mouse wheel or using your touchpad. Figure 19.3 displays the same solution in a three-dimensional space. A closer inspection shows that the third dimension slightly draws apart the 'black-and-white' academic and spoken registers.

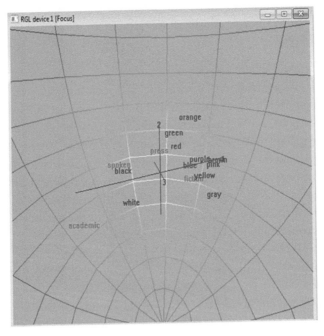

Figure 19.3. A three-dimensional plot of the BCT in four registers

To summarize, SCA has yielded interpretable results. Most secondary BCT, as well as *blue* and *yellow*, cluster together in the same part of the plot where one finds fiction. Note that *blue* and *yellow* are the closest to the secondary terms in Berlin and Kay's (1969) hierarchy.

The location of *green* and *red* is relatively high on Dimension 2, which is also the position of newspaper and magazine texts.

19.2   Visualization of exemplars and prototypes of lexical categories: Multiple Correspondence Analysis of *Stuhl* and *Sessel*

19.2.1   The data and theoretical background

The data and functions mentioned in this case study are available in several add-on packages, which should be installed and loaded:

```
> install.packages(c("FactoMineR", "ca", "rms"))
> library(Rling); library(FactoMineR); library(ca); library(rms)
```

Linguistics, in particular lexicology and semantics, has been influenced by categorization theories in psychology, especially Prototype Theory and, more recently, Exemplar Theory (e.g. Bybee 2001; Taylor 2012). According to Prototype Theory (e.g. Rosch 1975, Rosch & Mervis 1975), categorization of a new item is performed by comparing it with the prototype of an existing category. The prototype is the summary representation of a category. It contains all features of the category instances. Those features are weighted according to their frequency of occurrence in the subject's previous experience. For instance, most instances of the category BIRD have the feature 'can fly', and only some of them have the feature 'can swim'. The feature 'can fly' therefore will be weighted higher than the feature 'can swim'. In this sense, different members of a category can have different degrees of prototypicality, since they possess typical features to a different extent. Thus, a robin, which can fly and cannot swim, is a more prototypical member of the category BIRD than a penguin, who cannot fly but is an excellent swimmer.

Although Prototype Theory has been outperformed by more recent models, such as Exemplar Theory, most categorization theories of the present share a few basic assumptions. One of them is the crucial role of features in establishing the similarity between two exemplars. These features are highly intercorrelated. For instance, a typical bird can fly, has wings, and makes nests in trees. If it did not have wings to keep it in the air, it would not be able to fly. If it were not able to fly, it would make nests in other places.

The case study that illustrates Multiple Correspondence Analysis belongs to the domain of lexical semantics. It focuses on two German lexical categories, *Stuhl* 'chair' and *Sessel* 'armchair'. The categories have been investigated in a classic study by Gipper (1959). In his experiment, German-speaking subjects were asked to name the piece of furniture shown in a picture. Gipper studied the relative frequencies of *Stuhl* and *Sessel* in the subjects' responses. According to his proto-statistical analysis, the two lexical categories differed regarding the opposition between functionality (*Stuhl*) and comfort (*Sessel*). A theoretically important observation was that the boundaries between the categories were fuzzy, a fact that was against the mainstream structuralist view back then.

The dataset contains 188 instances of these two categories from online stores. The data are available in the dataset `chairs`. The first variable *Shop* represents one of the three online stores; the second one, *WordDE*, shows the exact lexical label of each chair or armchair, and the third variable, *Category*, corresponds to the lexical category (in most cases, the last element of the composite), 'Stuhl' or 'Sessel'. The instances were coded on the basis of online descriptions and pictures for 16 parameters represented by the remaining variables, most of which are self-explanatory.

```
> data(chairs)
> str(chairs)
'data.frame': 188 obs. of 19 variables:
$ Shop         : Factor w/ 3 levels "ikea.de","Moebel-Profi.de",..:
2 1 1 2 1 3 ...
$ WordDE       : Factor w/ 44 levels "3-in-1-Sessel",..: 2 17 38
41 23 13 25 15 ...
$ Category     : Factor w/ 2 levels "Sessel","Stuhl": 2 2 1 2 2 2
2 1 2 2 ...
$ Function     : Factor w/ 5 levels "Eat","NotSpec",..: 1 1 2 1 1
5 2 4 1 1 ...
$ Age          : Factor w/ 2 levels "Adult","Children": 1 2 1 1 2
1 1 1 1 1 ...
$ Back         : Factor w/ 4 levels "Adjust","High",..: 3 4 4 2 2
2 4 2 4 4 ...
$ Soft         : Factor w/ 3 levels "No","Pad","Yes": 1 1 1 3 1 3
1 3 1 1 ...
$ Arms         : Factor w/ 2 levels "No","Yes": 1 1 2 1 2 2 1 2 1
1 ...
$ Upholst      : Factor w/ 2 levels "No","Yes": 1 1 1 2 1 2 1 2 1
2 ...
$ MaterialSeat : Factor w/ 10 levels "Fabric","Leather",..: 6 10
8 1 6 1 10 2 10...
$ SeatHeight   : Factor w/ 3 levels "Adjust","High",..: 3 2 3 3 2
1 3 3 3 ...
$ SeatDepth    : Factor w/ 3 levels "Adjust","Deep",..: 3 3 3 3 3
2 3 2 3 3 ...
$ Swivel       : Factor w/ 2 levels "No","Yes": 1 1 1 1 2 1 1 1
1 ...
$ Roll         : Factor w/ 2 levels "No","Yes": 1 1 1 1 2 1 1 1
1 ...
```

```
$ Rock           : Factor w/ 2 levels "No","Rock": 1 1 1 1 1 1 1 1
1 1 ...
$ AddFunctions   : Factor w/ 3 levels "Bed","No","Table": 2 2 2 2 2
2 2 2 2 ...
$ Recline        : Factor w/ 2 levels "No","Yes": 1 1 1 1 1 1 1 1 1
1 ...
$ ReclineBack    : Factor w/ 2 levels "No","Yes": 1 1 1 1 1 1 1 2 1
1 ...
$ SaveSpace      : Factor w/ 3 levels "collapse","No",..: 2 2 3 2 2
2 1 2 2 2 ...
```

As one can imagine, many of the variables are intercorrelated. For instance, if a chair can swivel, it can usually roll. One can use the xtabs() function to cross-tabulate the variables.

```
> swivelRoll <- xtabs(~ chairs$Swivel + chairs$Roll)
> swivelRoll
            chairs$Roll
chairs$Swivel  No    Yes
No            133    1
Yes            14    40
> chisq.test(swivelRoll)

        Pearson's Chi-squared test with Yates' continuity correction

data: swivelRoll
X-squared = 117.1027, df = 1, p-value < 2.2e-16
```

The χ^2-test confirms our expectations that the variables *Swivel* and *Roll* are associated.

19.2.2   Multiple Correspondence Analysis

To analyse multivariate data with more than two categorical variables, one needs Multiple Correspondence Analysis (MCA). In this case study we will use the FactoMineR package, which offers a few useful options for visualization and interpretation of results. This package was also discussed in the previous chapter in the section about PCA.

Recall that the input data for SCA in Section 19.1 was in the form of a contingency table, which cross-tabulated the values of two categorical variables representing registers and Basic Colour Terms. The input data for MCA are normally in the data frame format, where the rows are individual observations and the columns are categorical variables. MCA, in addition to relationships between the values of categorical variables, can also represent individual observations. An individual is located at the same part of the plot as the values of variables it is characterized by. In most cases, one is interested in the relationships between the variables, i.e. how strongly they are associated and whether they can be interpreted in terms of common dimensions of variation. Plotting the individual members of a category can reveal the category structure, its centre and periphery, clusters of observations, which may correspond to more or less distinct subcategories.

Let us first create a map of 16 variables and the exemplars, using a two-dimensional representation, for reasons that will be addressed below. The first three columns of the data frame will be ignored at this point.

```
> chairs.ca <- MCA(chairs[, -c(1:3)], graph = FALSE)
```

Next, we create a customized version of the MCA map, specifying the size of the labels (cex = 0.7), the colours of the variables (col.var = "black") and the colours of individual exemplars (col.ind = "grey"). The result is displayed in Figure 19.4.

```
> plot(chairs.ca, cex = 0.7, col.var = "black", col.ind = "grey")
```

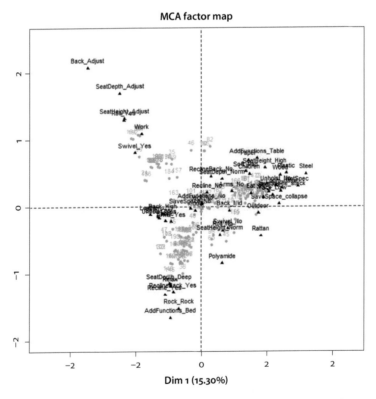

Figure 19.4. Multiple Correspondence Analysis map of *Stuhl* and *Sessel* data with features (black) and exemplars (grey)

The package `FactoMineR` offers many useful tools for interpretation. For example, one can retrieve the contributions of different variables to the first three dimensions by using the function `dimdesc()`, which was introduced in the previous chapter (only the first dimension is shown here):

```
> dimdesc(chairs.ca)
$'Dim 1'
$'Dim 1'$quali
                 R2              p.value
Unholst        0.72940952      1.094774e-54
MaterialSeat   0.74518860      3.215782e-48
Function       0.69158437      1.158923e-45
Soft           0.66568141      9.657154e-45
Swivel         0.40875670      5.393205e-23
Roll           0.38348403      2.728416e-21
SeatHeight     0.39565748      5.870717e-21
Back           0.36654364      3.802707e-18
Arms           0.21473392      2.133731e-11
SeatDepth      0.20909906      3.769585e-10
SaveSpace      0.19444992      2.058545e-09
Age            0.06521465      4.047690e-04
ReclineBack    0.06368029      4.764098e-04
Recline        0.04908474      2.246446e-03

$'Dim 1'$category
                   Estimate      p.value
Unholst_No         0.5083627    1.094774e-54
Swivel_No          0.4028109    5.393205e-23
Roll_No            0.4275049    2.728416e-21
NotSpec            0.6439510    2.149389e-16
Arms_No            0.2642196    2.133731e-11
Soft_No            0.3884948    1.476046e-10
SeatDepth_Norm     0.4470056    1.238635e-06
SeatHeight_High    0.5382304    1.615086e-06
Back_Low           0.7371337    1.713799e-06
Eat                0.2341430    2.409594e-05
Plastic            0.3465410    1.930598e-04
Back_Mid           0.3583736    4.033879e-04
Children           0.2361136    4.047690e-04
ReclineBack_No     0.1638759    4.764098e-04
Recline_No         0.1829562    2.246446e-03
Wood               0.2931048    3.379594e-03
SaveSpace_stack    0.2670527    1.904623e-02
Outdoor            0.3004254    4.625690e-02
Back_High         -0.2201617    5.628503e-03
```

```
Recline_Yes          -0.1829562    2.246446e-03
ReclineBack_Yes      -0.1638759    4.764098e-04
Adult                -0.2361136    4.047690e-04
SeatDepth_Adjust     -0.4374452    2.414491e-04
Back_Adjust          -0.8753456    1.980519e-08
SaveSpace_No         -0.5196558    2.724152e-09
Arms_Yes             -0.2642196    2.133731e-11
Soft_Yes             -0.5750871    5.276672e-13
Relax                -0.4635746    1.991433e-15
SeatHeight_Adjust    -0.6819107    7.910288e-18
Fabric               -0.7046046    3.058115e-19
Work                 -0.7149448    4.237029e-21
Roll_Yes             -0.4275049    2.728416e-21
Leather              -0.8350486    6.013338e-23
Swivel_Yes           -0.4028109    5.393205e-23
Unholst_Yes          -0.5083627    1.094774e-54
[output omitted]
```

The first set of numbers in $'Dim 1'$quali shows the statistics (R^2 of a linear regression model) that indicates how strongly each variable is associated with each dimension. Only significantly associated variables are displayed. One can see that the variables that are the most closely associated with the first dimension are the presence or absence of upholstery, function (eating, relaxing, work, etc.), softness of the seat, material and ability to move (swivel and roll). The second set of statistics $'Dim 1'$category provides information on the directionality of those associations. These are estimates of simple linear regression coefficients. If an estimate is positive (low back, high seat, multifunctional), then the feature will be located in the right-hand part of the plot with positive values of Dimension 1. If it is negative (e.g. made of leather or fabric, with an adjustable back and seat height and designed for work), then the feature will be found on the left. The greater the deviation from zero, the stronger the effect. It seems that the first dimension contrasts highly comfortable office and relaxation (arm)chairs on the left with less comfortable ones on the right.

An inspection of the second dimension reveals that functionality is still a distinctive feature, but this time chairs for relaxation are contrasted with (arm)chairs for work. The third dimension is more difficult to interpret. To summarize, there are three distinct categories of chairs: comfortable chairs for relaxation, comfortable adjustable chairs for work and multifunctional chairs for the household. In addition, in the middle part of the plot one can find comfortable chairs for the dining room, which share some properties of the above-mentioned subcategories.

How are these differences related to the lexical categories under investigation, *Stuhl* and *Sessel*? Similar to PCA, MCA enables one to add supplementary elements. Those are individuals or variables (both categorical and numeric) that do not take part in the creation of the semantic space and do not contribute to the orientation of its dimensions. Those observations or variables are added for the purposes of interpretation. In this case study, *Category*

('Stuhl' or 'Sessel') will be treated as a supplementary variable. For this purpose, we will add an argument `quali.sup = 1`, which will allow for treating the first column in our subset of the data frame (from the third variable on) as a supplementary qualitative (i.e. categorical) variable. Thus, the linguistic form is literally 'mapped' on the meaning represented by the semantic space created by intercorrelated features of the referents.

```
> chairs.cal <- MCA(chairs[, -c(1:2)], quali.sup = 1, graph = FALSE)
> plot(chairs.cal, invis = "ind", col.var = "darkgrey", col.quali.
sup = "black")
```

The models `chairs.ca` and `chairs.cal` are the same with regard to the coordinates of the points and interpretation of the dimensions. The difference is only in the presence or absence of supplementary variables. The resulting plot, which is shown in Figure 19.5, indicates that *Stuhl* is associated mostly with the features clustered in the upper right quadrant of the map. These features characterize simple practical chairs. However, it is relatively close to the centre because most office chairs for work (see the features in the upper left quadrant) are also categorized as *Stuhl*. The centroid of *Sessel* is located at the bottom, as are the features associated with comfortable chairs for relaxation. Thus, the results suggest that the functional differentiation is crucial. However, it is associated with a number of other referential features.

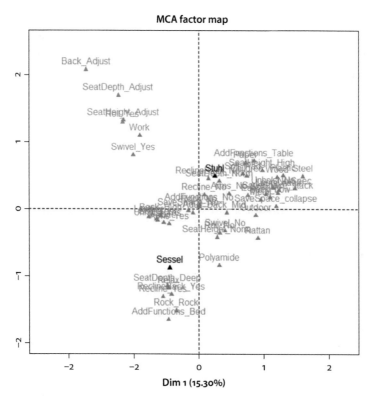

Figure 19.5. Multiple Correspondence Analysis map of *Stuhl* and *Sessel* data with supplementary variables (black) and features (grey)

This implementation of MCA also allows us to construct 95% confidence ellipses around the centroids of *Stuhl* and *Sessel*, which can be regarded as the prototypes of the categories.

```
> plotellipses(chairs.ca1, keepvar = 1, label = "quali")
```

The argument `keepvar = 1` specifies the variable that should be the criterion for classification of the individuals. This variable is *Category*, the first variable in our subset. The final argument `label = "quali"` means that only the labels of the supplementary factor will be plotted.

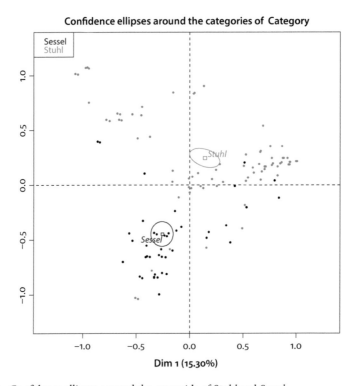

Figure 19.6. Confidence ellipses around the centroids of *Stuhl* and *Sessel*

Figure 19.6 displays the result. Since the confidence ellipses do not overlap, the prototypes can be regarded as distinct. Another option is to create 95% confidence ellipses around all exemplars that represent each category. To choose this option, you should add `means = FALSE`.

```
> plotellipses(chairs.ca1, means = FALSE, keepvar = 1, label =
"quali")
```

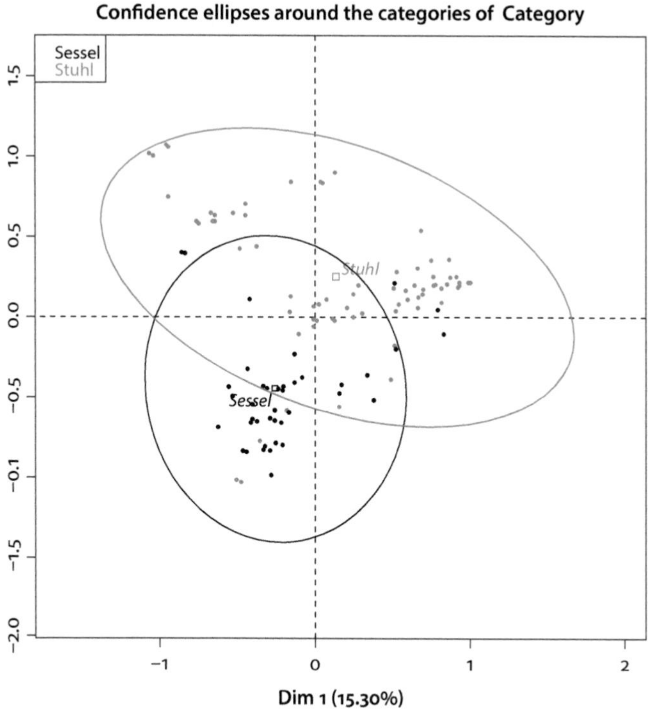

Figure 19.7. Confidence ellipses around the exemplars of *Stuhl* and *Sessel*

Figure 19.7 shows that the categories display a significant overlap, which supports Gipper's observation about the fuzzy boundaries between the categories.

Now it is time to come back to the problem of the number of dimensions. The dimensionality reduction methods discussed in previous chapters usually involve analysis of the proportion of variation explained by the dimensions. In MCA, unlike in Simple Correspondence Analysis, the proportion of explained variance tends to be very modest because the total variance is inflated (see Greenacre 2007: Ch. 19 for a discussion of the problem). The following code yields the eigenvalues, or principal inertias, expressed in absolute values, percentages and cumulative percentages (only the top ten are shown):

```
> chairs.ca$eig
     eigenvalue  percentage  of  variance  cumulative  percentage  of
variance
dim  1  0.3250725720   15.29753280    15.29753
dim  2  0.2576755177   12.12590671    27.42344
dim  3  0.1351901997    6.36189175    33.78533
dim  4  0.1229322264    5.78504595    39.57038
dim  5  0.1089102792    5.12518961    44.69557
```

```
dim   6  0.0961853064    4.52636736    49.22193
dim   7  0.0901939195    4.24441974    53.46635
dim   8  0.0861985147    4.05640069    57.52275
dim   9  0.0816542710    3.84255393    61.36531
dim  10  0.0726465359    3.41866051    64.78397
[output omitted]
```

One can see that the first two dimensions represent only 27.42% of the total variance. That seems to be a very modest result. Greenacre proposes a solution implemented in his `ca` package, namely, adjusted MCA, which estimates explained variation more realistically. Unfortunately, at the moment of writing this solution was not available in `FactoMineR`. One can compare the two-dimensional solution described above with the adjusted version, which is implemented in `mjca()` function in the `ca` package. The adjusted version is default. First, an MCA model of the same data is fit with the help of `mjca()`:

```
> chairs.ca2 <- mjca(chairs[, -c(1:3)])
> summary(chairs.ca2)

Principal inertias (eigenvalues):

dim    value      %     cum%   scree plot
1      0.078443   47.1   47.1   ************************
2      0.043342   26.0   73.2   **************
3      0.006012    3.6   76.8   **
4      0.004155    2.5   79.3   *
5      0.002451    1.5   80.8   *
6      0.001291    0.8   81.5
7      0.000873    0.5   82.1
8      0.000639    0.4   82.4
9      0.000417    0.3   82.7
10     0.000117    0.1   82.8
11     7.6e-050    0.0   82.8
12     1e-05000    0.0   82.8
       ----       ---
Total: 0.166428
[output omitted]
```

The summary suggests that two first dimensions represent 73.2% of inertia (i.e. variance). The horizontal scree plot made of asterisks shows that the subsequent dimensions do not add much to the model. Thus, the two-dimensional solution is correct. But are the non-adjusted and adjusted solutions equivalent? A correlation analysis of the coordinates of features of the first two dimensions (the reader can continue with further dimensions) shows that the solutions are practically identical, differing only in scale and the orientation of the second dimension in `chairs.ca2`, which is turned upside down (hence a negative correlation). In multivariate exploratory techniques, such 'flipping' is common and should not be a cause of concern (cf. Chapter 17, Section 17.3):

```
> cor(chairs.ca$var$coord[, 1], chairs.ca2$colcoord[, 1])
[1] 1
> cor(chairs.ca$var$coord[, 2], chairs.ca2$colcoord[, 2])
[1] -1
```

Therefore, our initial two-dimensional representation is not perfect, but it is acceptable for a pilot study. Adding more dimensions will not help to improve the fit significantly.

It was mentioned in Chapter 12 that the problem of multicollinearity can be solved by reducing the correlated variables to a smaller set of underlying dimensions. Intercorrelated features of categorical variables are pervasive in linguistic practice. For instance, if a verb depicts a mental state (*think, believe*), it is also very likely to have an animate (typically human) first argument (*I believe*), to be followed by a complement clause (*I believe you are right*), and not to be modified by an adverb of speed (**I quickly believe you are right*). Unfortunately, such data are difficult to model with the help of logistic regression, due to data sparseness and multicollinearity. A better option is to do regression on dimensions of MCA. We will demonstrate how one can use MCA dimensions as predictors in a logistic regression model (cf. Chapter 12).

```
> dim1 <- chairs.ca$ind$coord[, 1] #coordinates of individual
exemplars on the horizontal axis
> dim2 <- chairs.ca$ind$coord[, 2] # the same for the vertical axis
> m <- lrm(chairs$Category ~ dim1 + dim2)
> m

Logistic Regression Model
lrm(formula = chairs$Category ~ dim1 + dim2)
```

	Model Likelihood Ratio Test		Discrimination Indexes		Rank Discrim. Indexes	
Obs	188	LR chi2	118.82	R2	0.643	C	0.921
Sessel	67	d.f.	2	g	2.667	Dxy	0.842
Stuhl	121	Pr(> chi2)	<0.0001	gr	14.394	gamma	0.845
max |deriv|	2e-06			gp	0.386	tau-a	0.388
				Brier	0.094		

	Coef	S.E.	Wald Z	Pr(>|Z|)
Intercept	0.9833	0.2448	4.02	<0.0001
dim1	2.1780	0.5319	4.09	<0.0001
dim2	3.9151	0.5377	7.28	<0.0001

The results demonstrate that the two dimensions have a high predictive power in the choice between the lexical categories (*C* > 0.92). The coefficients show that the higher the value of an exemplar with regard to dimension 1 and dimension 2 in the MCA, the greater are the chances of it being categorized as a *Stuhl*. This supports our conclusions that were made after examining the supplementary variables and confidence ellipses.

MCA and Behavioural Profiles

A note should be made about MCA and the Behavioural Profiles approach (see Chapter 15). The methods require identical input data, with exemplars coded for a set of categorical variables. Each method has its advantages and disadvantages. The main advantages of MCA are as follows. First, it allows one to interpret the differences between categories with the help of features shown on the same biplot. Second, an MCA can show both tokens (exemplars) and types (categories) of constructions/words, whereas Behavioural Profile vectors deal only with types. A token-based representation allows one to see the centre and periphery of a category, as well as the overlap between similar categories. An advantage of Behavioural Profiles is that their dendrograms are easier to interpret and validate than the patterns observed in MCA maps. Multidimensional MCA solutions may be especially challenging for interpretation. However, in practice results of Correspondence Analysis tend to be similar to clusters of Behavioural Profiles. See, for example, Newman (2011), who uses both methods to compare verbs of slow movement, such as *trudge, plod* and *hobble*.

19.3   Summary

This chapter has discussed Simple and Multiple Correspondence Analysis – techniques developed specially for categorical data. Like PCA and FA, CA can be used to represent data in a few interpretable dimensions. While Simple Correspondence Analysis deals with two cross-tabulated variables, Multiple Correspondence Analysis visualizes the relationships between three and more categorical variables. We have discussed how to create and interpret CA maps, choose the optimal number of dimensions, use supplementary elements, draw 95% confidence ellipses, and other things. The chapter has also shown how one can use the dimensions of MCA as independent variables in regression analysis.

How to report results of Correspondence Analysis

In addition to the plots, one should provide the number of dimensions with the proportions of explained variance (inertia) and features that contribute to the orientation of dimensions. For SCA with two categorical variables, one also reports the χ^2-statistic, the degrees of freedom and the p-value (see Chapter 9). For MCA, it is recommended to add the results of a confirmatory logistic regression, if available (see Chapter 12).

More on Correspondence Analysis

Many other kinds of Correspondence Analysis are discussed in detail in Greenacre (2007). For more examples of use of MCA in `FactoMineR`, see Husson et al. (2010).

CHAPTER 20

Constructional change and motion charts

What you will learn from this chapter:

> This chapter introduces motion charts as a method for dynamic visualization of language change. More specifically, they enable one to detect and explore changes in the use of constructions by visualizing the relative frequencies of different lexemes that fill in the constructional slots. The method is illustrated with a case study that explores the changes in the use of future markers *will* and *be going to* by comparing the frequencies of infinitives that follow the markers.

20.1 The past and present of the future: Diachronic motion charts of *be going to* and *will*

20.1.1 Theoretical background and data

To perform this case study, you will need two add-on packages, which have to be installed and loaded:

```
> install.packages("googleVis")
> library(Rling); library(googleVis)
```

The landscape of future markers in English has been changing for centuries. On the one hand, the auxiliary *shall*, which used to be obligatory with the first person subjects, has given way to *will*. On the other hand, *be going to* has developed from a purposive motion construction to a full-fledged future marker. As a result, its frequency has been on the rise, as a screenshot of the Google Books Ngram viewer in Figure 20.1 demonstrates.

In this case study, we will zoom in on the 'division of labour' between *will* and *be going to*. How has their use changed since the beginning of the nineteenth century? More specifically, has *be going to* taken over some 'territory' of *will*?

We will use the data based on ngrams from the Corpus of Historical American English, or COHA (Davies 2011). In line with the distributional approach to semantics, we will investigate if there are any changes in the distribution of the infinitives that follow these markers. The infinitives were extracted from the ngram lists of *am/is/are going to + Inf* and *will + Inf*. The auxiliaries *be* and *have* were removed from the collexeme list. Only verbs that occur in all time periods (see below) were considered.

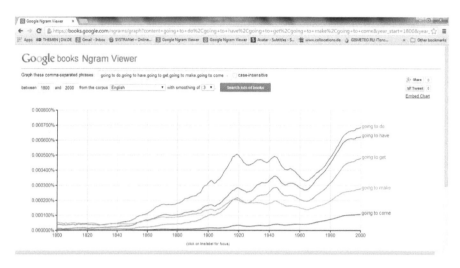

Figure 20.1. Google Ngram Viewer displaying frequencies of five ngrams with *going to +V* from 1800 to 2000

The dataset is called `fut`. It has the following structure:

```
> data(fut)
> str(fut)
'data.frame': 6973 obs. of 4 variables:
$ Verb : Factor w/ 367 levels "accept","accompany",..: 1 1 1 1 1 1
1 1 1 1 ...
$ Period: num 1820 1830 1840 1850 1860 1870 1880 1890 1900 1910 ...
$ will:    num   2.02  1.52   1.81   2.55   4.38 ...
$ goingto: num  0     0      0      0      0 ...

> head(fut)
Verb        Period   will        goingto
1 accept    1820     2.021075    0
2 accept    1830     1.524613    0
3 accept    1840     1.807208    0
4 accept    1850     2.546407    0
5 accept    1860     4.379536    0
6 accept    1870     3.385248    0
```

The number of unique verbs in the column `Verb` is 367. The periods examined are nineteen decades from the 1820s to the 2000s. In fact, COHA covers the period from the 1810s to the 2000s, but the subcorpus that represents the first decade is much smaller than the other subcorpora, so the 1810s were excluded. As a result, we have nineteen decades, which are shown in the column `Period`. The columns `will` and `goingto` contain the normalized frequencies (per million words) of the infinitives in the *will* and *be going to* construction, respectively.

20.1.2 Motion charts

To find out if there are any changes in the division of labour between these future constructions, we will use a visualization technique called motion charts. It was introduced to diachronic linguistic analysis by Martin Hilpert (2011).[1] Motion charts represent linguistic changes in time dynamically as changes in the position of some objects (for example, collexemes), with regard to two dimensions (typically, two near-synonymous constructions). This allows one to see how the associations between a word and the constructions change over time, which may be interpreted as evidence of semantic change. To construct motion charts, one can use the package `googleVis`. The function `gvisMotionChart()` creates an object referring to the Google Visualization API (Application Programming Interface). To view the output one needs a browser Flash and an Internet connection. In order to capture a motion chart for off-line presentation, e.g. in a PPT slideshow, one additionally needs screen-capturing software.

There are only three obligatory arguments of the function: the data frame itself, `idvar`, which specifies the column in the data frame that contains the identities of the points, and `timevar`, which specifies the column that corresponds to the time dimension. The other options are described on the help page of the function.

```
> mch <- gvisMotionChart(fut, idvar = "Verb", timevar = "Period")
> plot(mch)
```

The resulting plot, which is shown in Figure 20.2, opens in a web browser. The horizontal axis shows the normalized frequencies of the verbs after *will*. The vertical axis demonstrates the frequencies after *be going to*. The bubbles correspond to the individual verbs. They can be coloured in different colours if you choose this option from the drop-down menu *Color* in the top right corner. One can also change the size of the bubbles to represent their frequencies with either construction with the help of the drop-down menu *Size*. The frequencies are shown on the linear scale, although one can represent them on the logarithmic scale (see the buttons at the ends of the axes). In the latter case, the scale will be stretched at the lower range and shrunk for high frequencies.

One can see that the normalized frequencies of the verbs in the 1820s are much higher in the *will* construction. To see how they change over time, click on the *Play* button (the black triangle) at the bottom left corner of the plot. The circles will begin to move. The algorithm interpolates the frequencies for every year between the decades, so that the motion appears continuous. Slow motion corresponds to small changes in the frequencies, whereas quick motion shows that the changes are big. To stop the motion, one can click on the *Pause* button.

Figure 20.3 shows the verb frequencies in the 1900s. One can see that the frequencies of verbs in *be going to* future have increased. Still, the normalized frequencies of *will* have not decreased, either. For a few most frequent verbs, they have even slightly increased.

---

1.   See http://members.unine.ch/martin.hilpert/motion.html, where you can find video tutorials and a number of interesting examples (last access 11.06.2015).

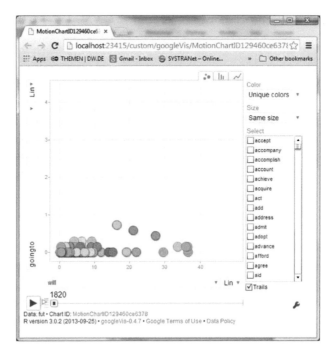

Figure 20.2. A screenshot of a motion chart of the verbs used with *be going to* and *will*: the 1820s

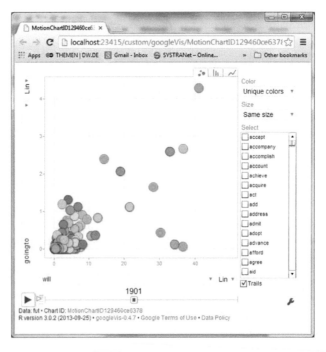

Figure 20.3. A screenshot of a motion chart of the verbs used with *be going to* and *will*: the 1900s

Figure 20.4 displays the frequencies in the 2000s, the last decade captured by the corpus. It is apparent that many verbs are now used more frequently with *be going to*. At the same time, the use of *will* has slightly decreased. Still, it would be wrong to say that *be going to* is the predominant marker because the weighted frequency of *will* is still greater than that of *be going to*. This will become obvious when you compare the units of the horizontal and vertical axes.

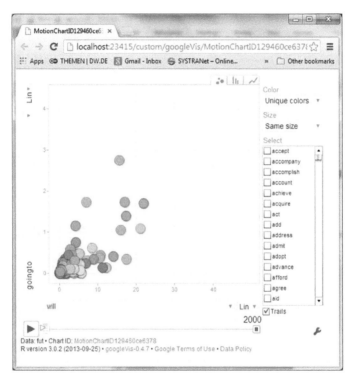

Figure 20.4. A screenshot of a motion chart of the verbs used with *be going to* and *will*: the 2000s

In addition to this general picture, one can also trace the changes in the patterns of use of individual verbs. One can click on the circles, or check the boxes corresponding to the individual verbs in the scrollable list on the right. One can also trace the trajectories of changes of a word by checking the *Trail* box in the bottom right corner (normally it should be checked by default). For instance, Figure 20.5 displays the trajectory of *take* over the entire period. It shows that the constructional preferences of *take* have somewhat shifted towards the future construction with *be going to*. However, this development was not linear. There was an intermediate period, when the verb had increasing frequencies with both *will* and *be going to*. Still, after this period the frequency of the verb with *will* has slightly decreased.

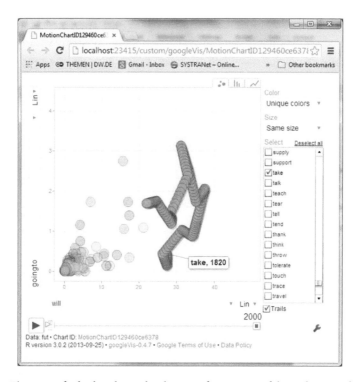

Figure 20.5. The trace of *take* that shows the changing frequencies of the verb in two future constructions

Thus, the motion charts suggest growing preferences for *be going to* and disprefer-ences for *will*-future, although the latter still remains the predominant marker. Let us now have a look at two verbs of motion, *come* and *go*. Figure 20.6 displays their traces in time. One can see that their patterns have changed in the direction from *will* to *be going to* in a similar fashion. The possibility of *be going to* followed by a verb of motion, especially *go*, indicates that the initial meaning of directed motion is bleached. This indicates that the grammaticalization of *be going to* was still going on in the time span covered by the motion chart.

These findings are in line with previous research. For instance, Hilpert (2013: Section 2.4.4) compared the relative frequencies of *be going to* and *will* in two periods, the 1960–1980s and 1990s. The proportion of *be going to* has increased slightly with time. However, he also found an interaction of register and time. Namely, *be going to* increased its relative frequency in informal registers, whereas *will* came to be used more often in formal contexts. Informalization of speech genres may be a possible explana-tion of the gradual shift towards *be going to*, but one needs a multivariate analysis, such as logistic regression (see Chapter 12), to disentangle different factors that may come into play.

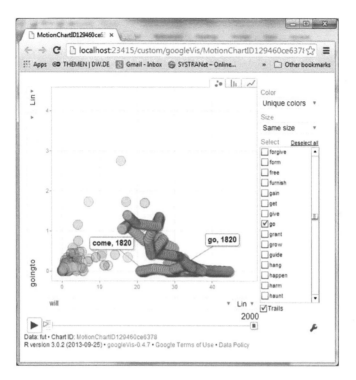

Figure 20.6. The traces of *come* and *go*

20.2   Summary

This chapter has presented motion charts, a method that has been used, among other things, for the visualization of changes in the division of labour between two constructions in time. A comparison of only two constructions may sometimes be all that is needed, but clearly human language is more complex. For example, it might be useful to include *gonna* + Infinitive in the analysis, as well as *shall* + Infinitive as a future marker, in addition to *going to* and *will*, in order to see a fuller picture. Hilpert (2011: Section 5; 2013: Section 2.6) discusses ways in which motion charts can be used to represent changes in more complex, mutivariate datasets. Still, even pairwise comparisons can help us formulate new research hypotheses, which can be later tested with the help of multivariate statistical methods, including those described in this book.

Epilogue

This book has demonstrated how one can use different statistical tests, graphs and other tools in linguistic research. Of course, many interesting topics remain outside the scope of the book. Recent trends in Bayesian statistics, graph theory, regression modelling (e.g. generalized additive models), spatial statistics and time series analysis can offer new insights and opportunities for specific linguistic problems. There is also a growing awareness in the community of the importance of efficient visualization techniques, with new spectacular graphical tools emerging daily as a result.

That said, the main goal of this book has been to equip the readers with enough R skills and understanding of fundamental statistical principles to perform common procedures in exploration, visualization, analysis and interpretation of linguistic data. If the book helps someone to become a creative user of R and a friend of statistics, the author's work has not been in vain.

The most important R objects and basic operations with them

If you need to know which class of R objects x belongs to, you can use the function `is(x)`. Alternatively, you can type `class(x)`, which will return only one value:

```
> x <- 1:3
> x
[1] 1 2 3
> is(x)
[1] "integer"        "numeric"        "vector"
[4] "data.frameRowLabels"
```

1 VECTORS

A vector is a sequence of numeric values, characters or logical (Boolean) values TRUE or FALSE.

1.1 Numeric vectors

– How to create a vector:
```
> v <- c(1:5, 10, 5) # creates a vector with all numbers from 1
to 5 inclusively, 10 and 5.
> v
[1] 1 2 3 4 5 10 5
> v1 <- seq(0, 100, 10) # creates a vector with numbers from 0
(inclusively) to 100 at an interval of 10
> v1
[1] 0 10 20 30 40 50 60 70 80 90 100
> v2 <- rep(1:5, 3) # creates a vector with the sequence of num-
bers from 1 to 5 repeated three times
> v2
[1] 1 2 3 4 5 1 2 3 4 5 1 2 3 4 5
```

– How to see the summary statistics of a vector:

```
> summary(v) # returns the minimum, 1st quartile, median, mean,
3rd quartile and maximum
Min. 1st    Qu.    Median    Mean    3rd Qu.    Max.
1.000       2.500  4.000     4.286   5.000      10.000
```

– How to sort a vector:

```
> sort(v) # sorts in increasing order
[1] 1 2 3 4 5 5 10
> sort(v, decreasing = TRUE) # sorts in decreasing order
[1] 10 5 5 4 3 2 1
```

– How to check how many elements a vector consists of:

```
> length(v)
[1] 7
```

– How to select elements of a vector:

```
> v[c(3, 6)] # returns only the 3rd and the 6th elements
[1] 3 10
> v[-1] # returns all elements except the first one
[1] 2 3 4 5 10 5
> v[v > 2] # returns the elements of vector v that are greater
than 2
[1] 3 4 5 10 5
> v[v != 5] # returns the elements of vector v that are not equal
to 5
[1] 1 2 3 4 10
> v[v < 3|v==10] # returns the elements of vector v that are
smaller than 3 OR are equal to 10
[1] 1 2 10
> v[v > 4 & v < 10] # returns the elements of vector v that are
greater than 4 AND smaller than 10
[1] 5 5
```

– How to obtain the indices of vector elements that meet some conditions:

```
> which(v == 5) # returns the indices of the elements of vector
v that are equal to 5
[1] 5 7
```

– How to sum all values of a vector:

```
> sum(v)
[1] 30
```

- How to combine two or more vectors into one:
```
> w <- c(20, 30, 40)
> y <- c(v, w)
> y
[1] 1 2 3 4 5 10 5 20 30 40
```

- How to perform basic arithmetic operations on all elements of a vector:
```
> v + 3 # adds 3 to every element of vector v
[1] 4 5 6 7 8 13 8
> v *2 # multiply every element of vector v by 2
[1] 2 4 6 8 10 20 10
> v^2 # raises every element of vector v to the power of 2
[1] 1 4 9 16 25 100 25
> log(v) # returns the natural logarithm of every element of
vector v
[1] 0.0000000 0.6931472 1.0986123 1.3862944 1.6094379 2.3025851
1.6094379
```

- How to round the elements of a vector:
```
> round(log(v), 2) # rounds the logarithmic values of vector v,
displaying only two digits after the decimal separator
[1] 0.00 0.69 1.10 1.39 1.61 2.30 1.61
```

1.2   Character vectors

A character vector is a special type of vectors that contain characters and/or character strings.

- How to create a character vector:
```
> charv <- c("do", "re", "mi", "do")
> charv
[1] "do" "re" "mi" "do"
```

- How to obtain the indices of the elements of a character vector that have a specific value:
```
> which(charv == "do")
[1] 1 4
> grep("d", charv) # returns the indices of all elements of
character vector charv that contain 'd'
[1] 1 4
```

–   How to replace characters in a character vector:

```
> gsub("m", "t", charv) # replace every 'm' in the elements of
the character vector charv with 't'
[1] "do" "re" "ti" "do"
> paste(charv, "!", sep = "") # add '! ' to every element of
character vector charv, without any graphical separators (the
default separator is a space)
[1] "do!" "re!" "mi!" "do!"
```

–   How to turn a character vector into a factor:

```
> f <- as.factor(charv)
> f
[1] do re mi do
Levels: do mi re
```

1.3   Logical vectors

–   How to create a logical vector:

```
> boolv <- c(TRUE, FALSE, FALSE, TRUE)
> boolv
[1] TRUE FALSE FALSE TRUE
```

–   How to obtain the indices of the elements of a character vector that have a specific value (TRUE or FALSE):

```
> which(boolv == TRUE)
[1] 1 4
```

2   FACTORS

A factor is a sequence of values of a categorical variable. The values are called levels.

–   How to create a factor:

```
> f <- factor(c("do", "re", "mi", "do"))
> f
[1] do re mi do
Levels: do mi re
```

See also how to transform a character vector into a factor.

–   How to see the levels of a factor:

```
> levels(f)
[1] "do" "mi" "re"
```

– How to change the order of the levels (the default order is alphabetic):

```
> f1 <- relevel(f, ref = "mi") # make mi the first (reference)
level
> levels(f1)
[1] "mi" "do" "re"
```

– How to see how many times each level of a factor occurs:

```
> table(f)
f
do  mi  re
2   1   1
```

Alternatively:

```
> summary(f)
do  mi  re
2   1   1
```

– How to turn a factor into a numeric vector:

```
> v3 <- as.numeric(f)
> v3
[1] 1 3 2 1 # the numbers correspond to the order of factor
levels
```

– How to turn a factor into a character vector:

```
> charv1 <- as.character(f)
> charv1
[1] "do" "re" "mi" "do"
```

– How to make an ordered factor:

```
> ord <- c("XS", "S", "M", "L", "XL")
> ord
[1] "XS" "S" "M" "L" "XL"
> ord <- ordered(ord, levels = c("XS", "S", "M", "L", "XL"))
> ord
[1] XS S M L XL
Levels: XS < S < M < L < XL
```

– How to cross-tabulate two factors:

```
> gender <- factor(c("M", "F", "M", "F", "M", "F"))
> gender
[1] M F M F M F
Levels: F M
```

```
> group <- factor(c("A", "A", "B", "A", "B", "B"))
> group
[1] A A B A B B
Levels: A B

> table(group, gender)
       gender
group   F   M
A       2   1
B       1   2
```

Alternatively:

```
> xtabs(~ group + gender)
       gender
group   F   M
A       2   1
B       1   2
```

3   MATRICES

A matrix is a two-dimensional array. Arrays can have any number of dimensions. Matrices can contain numbers, characters or Boolean values.

- How to create a matrix from scratch:
  ```
  > m <- matrix(c(2, 7, 5, 3, 8, 11, 2, 4, 5), nrow = 3)
  > m
        [,1]  [,2]  [,3]
  [1,]   2     3     2
  [2,]   7     8     4
  [3,]   5    11     5
  ```

- How to learn the number of rows and columns in a matrix:
  ```
  > dim(m)
  [1] 3 3
  ```

- How to select columns, rows and elements:
  ```
  > m[, 1] # selects column 1
  [1] 2 7 5
  > m[2, ] # selects row 2
  [1] 7 8 4
  > m[3, 3] # selects the element in row 3 and column 3
  [1] 5
  ```

```
> m[c(1, 3),] # selects rows 1 and 3
      [,1]   [,2]    [,3]
[1,]   2      3       2
[2,]   5     11       5
> m[, -2] # selects all columns except the second one
      [,1]   [,2]
[1,]   2      2
[2,]   7      4
[3,]   5      5
```

- How to add the names of rows and columns:

```
> rownames(m) <- c("A", "B", "C")
> colnames(m) <- c("X", "Y", "Z")
> m
   X   Y   Z
A  2   3   2
B  7   8   4
C  5  11   5
```

- How to obtain a vector with row or column sums:

```
# add na.rm = TRUE if the matrix contains missing values
> rowSums(m)
A   B   C
7  19  21
> colSums(m)
 X   Y   Z
14  22  11
```

- How to obtain a vector with row or column means:

```
> rowMeans(m)
A          B          C
2.333333   6.333333   7.000000
> colMeans(m)
X          Y          Z
4.666667   7.333333   3.666667
```

- How to apply a function to rows or columns:

```
> apply(m, 1, sd) # applies the function sd() to every row
A          B          C
0.5773503        2.0816660   3.4641016
```

- ```
  > apply(m, 2, var) # applies the function var() to every column
  X           Y           Z
  6.333333   16.333333    2.333333
  ```

- How to transpose a matrix, i.e. swap the rows and columns:
  ```
  > t(m)
       A   B   C
  X    2   7   5
  Y    3   8   11
  Z    2   4   5
  ```

- How to turn counts in a table into proportions:
  ```
  > prop.table(m)  # the sum of all cells is 1
       X            Y            Z
  A    0.04255319   0.06382979   0.04255319
  B    0.14893617   0.17021277   0.08510638
  C    0.10638298   0.23404255   0.10638298
  > prop.table(m, 1) # the sum of each row is 1
  X   Y           Z
  A   0.2857143   0.4285714    0.2857143
  B   0.3684211   0.4210526    0.2105263
  C   0.2380952   0.5238095    0.2380952
  > prop.table(m, 2) # the sum of each column is 1
       X           Y            Z
  A    0.1428571   0.1363636    0.1818182
  B    0.5000000   0.3636364    0.3636364
  C    0.3571429   0.5000000    0.4545455
  ```

4 Data frames

A data frame is an object that contains any kind of variable: numeric, character and logic vectors, as well as ordered and unordered factors. The rows are usually observations, and the columns represent variables.

- How to create a data frame:
  ```
  > group <- factor(c("A", "A", "B", "A", "B", "B")) # one can also
  create a simple character vector. The latter will be transformed
  into a factor automatically by data.frame().
  > gender <- factor(c("M", "F", "M", "F", "M", "F"))
  > grade <- c(2.3, 1.7, 5, 3, 1.3, 5)
  ```
  ```

```
> df <- data.frame(group, gender, grade)
> df
   group gender grade
1  A      M       2.3
2  A      F       1.7
3  B      M       5.0
4  A      F       3.0
5  B      M       1.3
6  B      F       5.0
```

- How to see the structure of a data frame:

```
> str(df)
'data.frame':    6 obs. of 3 variables:
$ group: Factor w/ 2 levels "A","B": 1 1 2 1 2 2
$ gender: Factor w/ 2 levels "F","M": 2 1 2 1 2 1
$ grade: num 2.3 1.7 5 3 1.3 5
> summary(df)
group   gender   grade
A:3     F:3      Min.     :1.30
B:3     M:3      1st Qu.  :1.85
                 Median   :2.65
                 Mean     :3.05
                 3rd Qu.  :4.50
                 Max.     :5.00
```

- How to add new variables:

```
> df$pass <- c(TRUE, TRUE, FALSE, TRUE, TRUE, FALSE)
> df
   group gender grade   pass
1  A      M       2.3    TRUE
2  A      F       1.7    TRUE
3  B      M       5.0    FALSE
4  A      F       3.0    TRUE
5  B      M       1.3    TRUE
6  B      F       5.0    FALSE
```

- How to select columns and/or rows of a data frame:

```
> df$group # selects the column group only
[1] A A B A B B
Levels: A B
> df[, 2:3] # selects columns 2 and 3
```

```
      gender   grade
1    M        2.3
2    F        1.7
3    M        5.0
4    F        3.0
5    M        1.3
6    F        5.0
> df[c("grade","pass")]  # selects columns grade and pass by
their names
      grade   pass
1    2.3      TRUE
2    1.7      TRUE
3    5.0      FALSE
4    3.0      TRUE
5    1.3      TRUE
6    5.0      FALSE
> df[c(2, 4, 6), ] # selects observations (i.e. rows) 2, 4 and 6
     group   gender   grade   pass
2    A       F        1.7     TRUE
4    A       F        3.0     TRUE
6    B       F        5.0     FALSE
> df[2:5, -1] # selects observations from 2 to 5 and all columns
except the first one
      gender   grade   pass
2    F         1.7     TRUE
3    M         5.0     FALSE
4    F         3.0     TRUE
5    M         1.3     TRUE
```

- How to select only observations that meet specific criteria:

```
> df[df$gender == "F", ] # returns observations with gender F
     group   gender   grade   pass
2    A       F        1.7     TRUE
4    A       F        3.0     TRUE
6    B       F        5.0     FALSE
> df[df$gender == "F" & df$grade < 5, ] # returns observations
with gender F AND grade smaller than 5
     group   gender   grade   pass
2    A       F        1.7     TRUE
4    A       F        3.0     TRUE
```

```
> df[df$gender == "F" | df$group == "A", ] # returns observa-
tions with gender F OR group A
  group     gender   grade    pass
1 A         M        2.3      TRUE
2 A         F        1.7      TRUE
4 A         F        3.0      TRUE
6 B         F        5.0      FALSE
```

- How to obtain the indices (row names) of observations that meet certain criteria:
```
> which(df$gender=="F" & df$grade < 5)
[1] 2 4
```

- How to sort a data frame by values in one or more columns:
```
> df[order(df$grade), ] # sorts the data frame by grade in
ascending order
  group     gender   grade    pass
5 B         M        1.3      TRUE
2 A         F        1.7      TRUE
1 A         M        2.3      TRUE
4 A         F        3.0      TRUE
3 B         M        5.0      FALSE
6 B         F        5.0      FALSE
> df[order(-df$grade), ] # sorts the data frame by grade in
descending order
  group     gender   grade    pass
3 B         M        5.0      FALSE
6 B         F        5.0      FALSE
4 A         F        3.0      TRUE
1 A         M        2.3      TRUE
2 A         F        1.7      TRUE
5 B         M        1.3      TRUE
> df[order(df[,1], -df[,3]), ] # sorts the data frame first by
group in alphabetic order and then by grade in descending order
  group     gender   grade    pass
4 A         F        3.0      TRUE
1 A         M        2.3      TRUE
2 A         F        1.7      TRUE
3 B         M        5.0      FALSE
6 B         F        5.0      FALSE
5 B         M        1.3      TRUE
```

- How to read a data frame from a file:
  ```
  > df <- read.table("C/yourDirectory/yourFile", header = TRUE)
  # reads a file with tab-separated columns (e.g. a copy of an
  ```
  Excel spreadsheet) and treats the first line as column names. By default, header = FALSE. You can specify the column separator by adding, for example, sep = "\t" (a tab).
  ```
  > df <- read.csv("C/yourDirectory/yourFile") # reads a file with
  ```
  comma-separated columns. The first line in the file is treated as column names.

- How to export a data frame to a file:
  ```
  > write.table(df, file = 'C/yourDirectory/yourFile', sep = "\t",
  quote = FALSE) # the separator is a tab (by default, the separa-
  tor is a space). The values in character vectors or factors are
  not surrounded by double quotes (by default, they are). The row
  and column names are saved by default.
  ```

- How to edit a data frame with the help of an editing interface:
  Select *Edit > Data editor* in the main menu of the R GUI and enter the name of the data frame that you want to edit. A spreadsheet will open, where you can edit the data.

  Alternatively:

  ```
  > fix(df)
  ```

  After you have finished editing, simply close the window with the spreadsheet. The changes will be saved.

Main plotting functions and graphical parameters in R

1 A scatter plot with text labels

A scatter plot represents individual observations (rows) as points in a two-dimensional space delimited by the *x*- and *y*-axis. For illustration, we will use a small sample from the dataset ELP (English Lexicon Project) data:

```
> library(Rling)
> data(ELP)
> data <- ELP[31:40, ]
> data
      Word        Length   SUBTLWF   POS   Mean_RT
31  ordinances    10       0.16      NN    796.59
32  ovary         5        0.51      NN    694.13
33  reared        6        0.41      VB    736.19
34  nudist        6        0.65      NN    752.58
35  exportation   11       0.02      NN    1121.00
36  unhurt        6        0.10      JJ    759.00
37  jackpot       7        3.71      NN    598.18
38  medieval      8        2.96      JJ    752.97
39  hangover      8        3.90      NN    616.55
40  quintet       7        0.51      NN    881.25
```

First, we will plot the points (stimuli) according to their log-transformed corpus frequency (the *x*-axis) and mean reaction time (the *y*-axis) and next add the text labels (the words):

```
> plot(log(data$SUBTLWF), data$Mean_RT, pch = 16, cex = 1.2, main
= "Corpus frequency and mean reaction times", sub = "Data from
English Lexicon Project", xlim = c(-5, 2), ylim = c(500, 1200), xlab
= "Log-transformed corpus frequency", ylab = "Mean reaction time,
ms", cex.lab = 0.8, cex.axis = 0.8)
```

The result is shown in Figure A1. Some comments are due:

- log(data$SUBTLWF) are the *x*-coordinates of plotted points.
- data$Mean_RT are the *y*-coordinates of plotted points.
- pch = 16 determines the type of plotted points, by default pch = 1.
- cex = 1.2 specifies the size of plotted text and symbols, by default cex = 1.
- main = "Corpus..." gives the plot a title.

- `sub = "data…"` provides a subtitle of the plot.
- `xlim = c(-5, 2)` determines the range of *x*-values on the plot.
- `ylim = c(500, 1200)` determines the range of *y*-values on the plot.
- `xlab = "Log…"` provides a text label for the *x*-axis.
- `ylab = "Mean…"` provides a text label for the *y*-axis.
- `cex.lab = 0.8` specifies the size of axis marks, relative to the current setting of `cex`.
- `cex.axis = 0.8` specifies the size of axis labels, relative to the current setting of `cex`.

```
> text(log(data$SUBTLWF), data$Mean_RT, labels = data$Word, adj =
c(1.2, 0), cex = 0.7, font = 4)
```

- `log(data$SUBTLWF)` provides the *x*-coordinates of the text labels.
- `data$Mean_RT` contains the *y*-coordinates of the text labels.
- `labels = data$Word` specifies the text labels.
- `adj = c(1.2, 0)` are adjustments for text labels. The first number is the horizontal adjustment (negative: right, positive: left), and the second one is the vertical adjustment (negative: up, positive: down). The adjustments are added to the *x* and *y*-values provided in the first two arguments.
- `cex = 0.7` determines the font size of text labels (1 by default).
- `font = 4` specifies he font type for text: '1' for plain text (the default), '2' for bold face, '3' for italic, '4' for bold italic (here).

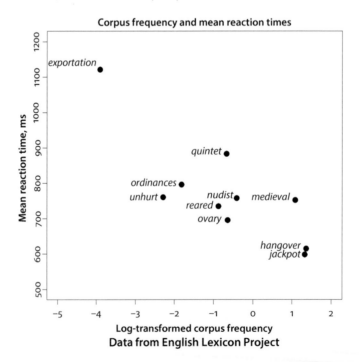

Figure A1. A scatter plot of experimental lexical data with points and text labels

Now we can try to plot the words that belong to different parts of speech (nouns vs. non-nouns) as different symbols. We will also use different colours for their text labels. First, it is necessary to get the indices of all observations that represent nouns:

```
> NN <- which(data$POS == "NN")
> NN
[1] 1 2 4 5 7 9 10
```

These are the rows which contain nouns. Next, we create an empty plot without any points with the help of `type = "n"`. The axes and titles remain the same.

```
> plot(log(data$SUBTLWF), data$Mean_RT, type = "n", main = "Corpus
frequency and mean reaction times", sub = "Data from English Lexicon
Project", xlim = c(-5, 2), ylim = c(500, 1200), xlab = "Log-
transformed corpus frequency", ylab = "Mean reaction time, ms",
cex.lab = 0.8, cex.axis = 0.8)
```

Now we can plot the points, first, the ones that correspond to the nouns, and next those that correspond to other parts of speech:

```
> points(log(data$SUBTLWF)[NN], data$Mean_RT[NN], cex = 1.2)
> points(log(data$SUBTLWF)[-NN], data$Mean_RT[-NN], cex = 1.2, pch
= 2, col = "grey40")
```

Finally, we add text labels, which differ in the font effects and colour (`font = 2` is for italic).

```
>    text(log(data$SUBTLWF)[NN],    data$Mean_RT[NN],    labels    =
data$Word[NN], adj = c(1.2, 0), cex = 0.7, font = 4)
>    text(log(data$SUBTLWF)[-NN],    data$Mean_RT[-NN],    labels    =
data$Word[-NN], adj = c(1.2, 0), cex = 0.7, font = 2, col = "grey40")
```

To add a legend, one can do the following:

```
> legend("topright", pch = c(1, 2), col = c("black", "grey40"),
legend = c("Nouns", "Other POS"), cex = 0.8, bty = "n")
```

Comments:

- "bottomright"   specifies the position of the legend. The other options are "top", "bottom", "left", "right", "center", "topleft", "topright" and "bottomleft". Alternatively, one can use coordinates, e.g. c(1, 1).
- pch = c(1, 2) specifies the symbols that should be plotted.
- col = c("black", "grey40")   determines the colours of the symbols.
- legend = c("Nouns", "Other POS") is the text of the legend.
- bty = "n" says that no box should be added around the legend. By default, there is a box.

The result is shown in Figure A2.

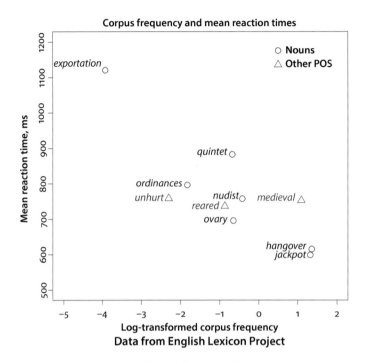

Figure A2. A scatter plot of experimental lexical data with different symbols and colours

2   Line chart

A line chart shows one or more lines. It is especially useful in diachronic studies. We will compare the normalized frequencies of the nouns *nerd* and *geek* in the Corpus of Contemporary American English in five periods from 1990 to 2012. The matrix with the frequencies can be created as follows:

```
> data <- rbind(c(1.74, 1.81, 2.36, 2.43, 3.06), c(0.77, 1.89, 3.72,
3.88, 3.56))
> rownames(data) <- c("nerd", "geek")
> colnames(data) <- c("1990-1994", "1995-1999", "2000-2004", "2005-
2009", "2010-2012")
> data
      1990-1994  1995-1999  2000-2004  2005-2009  2010-2012
nerd  1.74       1.81       2.36       2.43       3.06
geek  0.77       1.89       3.72       3.88       3.56
```

First, we plot the frequencies of *nerd*. The *x*-axis corresponds to the time periods, whereas the *y*-axis shows the normalized frequencies per million words.

```
> plot(data[1,], type = "o", pch = 2, ylim = range(0, data[1, ],
data[2, ]), axes = FALSE, xlab = "Periods", ylab = "Frequency per
million words", main = "nerd and geek in COCA")
```

Comments:

- `data[1,]` gives the frequencies of *nerd*.
- `type = "o"` ('overplotted') will produce both lines and points.
- `pch = 2` specifies the type of points (empty triangles).
- `ylim = range(0, data[1, ], data[2, ])` gives the range of *y*, from 0 (the minimum value) to the maximum frequency from the frequencies of *nerd* and *geek*.
- `axes = FALSE` suppresses the plotting of axes.
- `xlab = "Periods"` specifies the text label for the *x*-axis.
- `ylab = "Frequency per million words"` specifies the text label for the *y*-axis.
- `main = "nerd and geek in COCA"` provides the title of the plot.

Next, we draw the axes: first, the horizontal, and then the vertical one:

```
> axis(1, at = 1:5, labels = colnames(data))
> axis(2)
```

This will add a box around the plot:

```
> box()
```

Now it is time to add the second line with the frequencies of *geek*:

```
> lines(data[2,], type = "o", lty = 2, pch = 0, col = "darkgrey")
```

- `lty = 2` specifies the line type (dashed). The other options are '1' (solid, default), '3' (dotted), '4' (dot-dash), '5' (long-dash), and '6' (two-dash).
- `pch = 0` specifies the points (empty squares).
- `col = "darkgrey"` specifies the colour of the line and the points.

Finally, we add a legend:

```
> legend("bottomright", lty = c(1, 2), col = c("black", "darkgrey"),
pch = c(2, 0), legend = c("nerd", "geek"))
```

See comments to the legend in a scatter plot. Figure A3 displays the results.

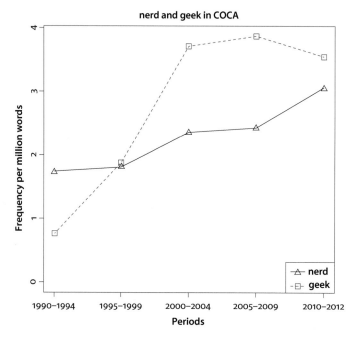

Figure A3. The frequencies of *nerd* and *geek* in COCA

3   Bar plots

Bar plots show numeric values as bars of different height. You can plot a single vector, or several. They can be stacked or juxtaposed. We will plot the frequencies of eleven basic colour terms in four registers of the Corpus of Contemporary American English (the data set `colreg` in `Rling`). The data look as follows:

```
> library(Rling)
> data(colreg)
> colreg
        spoken    fiction   academic   press
black   20335     41118     26892      73080
blue    4693      22093     3605       21210
brown   1185      10914     1201       11539
gray    1168      12140     1289       6559
green   3860      14398     4477       26837
orange  931       3496      474        5766
pink    962       7312      584        6356
purple  613       3366      429        3403
red     7230      25111     5621       34596
white   14474     40745     26336      54883
yellow  1349      10553     1855       10382
```

First, we will plot only the sum frequencies of every colour term, sorted in descending order. To do so, we first compute the sum frequencies and sort them:

```
> colreg_sums <- sort(rowSums(colreg), decreasing = TRUE)
> colreg_sums
black   white   red    blue   green   brown  yellow  gray    pink
orange  purple
161425  136438  72558  51601  49572   24839  24139   21156   15214
10667   7811
```

Now we can make our bar plot. We can easily plot the bars in the colours that correspond to the colour terms:

```
> barplot(colreg_sums, main = "Basic Colour Terms in COCA", ylab =
"frequency", las = 3, col = names(colreg_sums))
```

The result can be seen in Figure A4. Some comments are due:

– colreg_sums is a vector with the frequencies to plot.
– main = "Basic Colour Terms in COCA" provides the title.
– ylab = "frequency" names the *y*-axis.
– las = 3 makes the annotation of both axes vertically oriented. The other options are '0' (always parallel to the axes, the default), '1' (always horizontal) and '2' (always perpendicular to the axes).
– col = names(colreg_sums) specifies the colours of the bars.

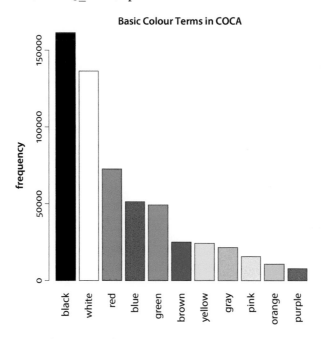

Figure A4. A bar plot of frequencies of Basic Colour Terms in COCA

We have just created a simple bar plot of only one vector. It is also possible to combine two and more vectors. Let us compare the frequencies of the colour terms in the spoken data, fiction and academic prose. First, we create a stacked bar plot with a legend. The bars are stacked by default. Note that we will have to subset and transpose the matrix colreg.

```
> barplot(t(colreg[, 1:3]), las = 3, main = "Frequencies of Basic
Colour Terms in COCA", ylab = "Frequency", col = c("black", "grey",
"white"))
```

- t(colreg[, 1:3]) is the transposed version of the initial matrix with only three first columns ("spoken", "fiction" and "academic"). These columns become rows in the transposed version.
- las = 3 makes the annotation of both axes vertically oriented. See the comments above.
- main = "Frequencies of Basic Colour Terms in COCA" provides the title of the plot.
- ylab = "Frequency" gives the name to the *y*-axis.
- col = c("black", "grey", "white") provides colours for the bars that relate to the registers.

```
> legend("top", fill = c("black", "grey", "white"), legend =
c("spoken", "fiction", "academic"))
```

- "top" specifies the position of the legend (at the top).
- fill = c("black", "grey", "white") provides the colours for the small filled squares.
- legend = c("spoken", "fiction", "academic") specifies the text of the legend.

See the result in Figure A5.

Another version of the bar plot is with bars next to one another. The code is the same, with the exception of one additional argument, beside = TRUE:

```
> barplot(t(colreg[, 1:3]), las = 3, main = "Frequencies of Basic
Colour Terms in COCA", ylab = "Frequency", col = c("black", "grey",
"white"), beside = TRUE)
> legend("top", fill = c("black", "grey", "white"), legend =
c("spoken", "fiction", "academic"))
```

See the result in Figure A6.

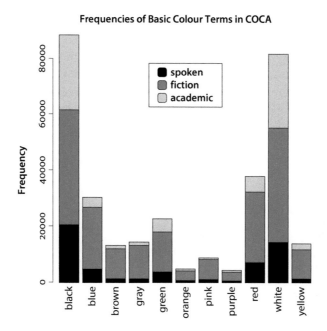

Figure A5. A bar plot of Basic Colour Terms in four registers of COCA. The bars are stacked

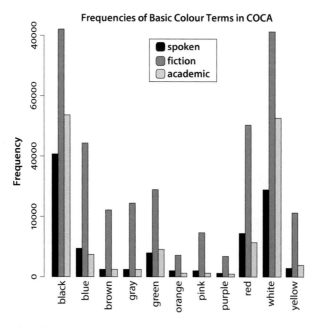

Figure A6. A bar plot of Basic Colour Terms in four registers of COCA. The bars are grouped (unstacked)

4 Dot charts

A dot chart shows basically the same information as a bar plot, but numeric values are displayed as dots at a certain distance from the origin. Below is a dot chart of the Basic Colour Term frequencies from the previous section. Note that a dot chart displays the first values in a vector at the bottom and the last values at the top, so we have to sort the vector again to put the more frequent terms at the top.

```
> dotchart(sort(colreg_sums), xlab = "frequency", main = "Basic
Colour Terms in COCA")
```

See the result in Figure A7.

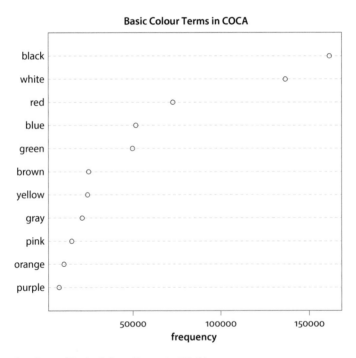

Figure A7. A dot chart of Basic Colour Terms in COCA

5 Pie charts

A pie chart displays the proportions of different categories as pieces of a pie. The larger a piece, the greater the proportion. We create a pie chart of frequencies of *although* in different registers of COCA. The frequencies are as follows:

```
> although <- c(9749, 13134, 25233, 20184, 52837)
> although
[1]  9749 13134 25233 20184 52837
```

The five frequencies relate to five registers in the following order: spoken, fiction, magazines, newspapers and academic. To make a pie chart, we will need to define the colours of the pie pieces:

```
> although_col <- c("black", "grey40", "grey70", "grey90", "white")
```

It is also useful to add the percentages of each register to the plot. First, we compute the percentages and then turn them into a character vector by pasting '%'.

```
> although_percent <- round(prop.table(although)*100, 1)
> although_percent
[1]  8.0 10.8 20.8 16.7 43.6
> although_percent <- paste(although_percent, "%", sep = "")
> although_percent
[1] "8%"      "10.8%" "20.8%" "16.7%" "43.6%"
```

Now we are ready to make our pie chart:

```
> pie(although, col = although_col, labels = although_percent, main
= "although in COCA")
> legend(c(1, 1), fill = although_col, legend = c("spoken", "fiction",
"magazine", "newspaper", "academic"))
```

See the previous plots and help pages for more details. The result can be found in Figure A8.

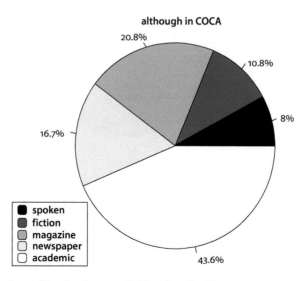

Figure A8. A pie chart of the distribution of *although* in the COCA registers

6   Some additional tips

– how to choose colours in R

To see the list of colours in R, type `colors()`. You will see a list with 657 colours that you can select for your plot. You can use colour names from the list, indices, hexadecimal or RGB values (see `help(rgb)`). When you want to use many colours, it may be convenient to use one of the ready-made palettes, such as `rainbow`, `heat`, `terrain`, `gray`, etc. See `help(rainbow)` for more details. Below is an illustration of how one can make the pie chart from the previous section colourful by using the rainbow palette:

```
> pie(although, col = rainbow(5), labels = although_percent,
main = "although in COCA")
> legend("bottomleft", fill = rainbow(5), legend = c("spoken",
"fiction", "magazine", "newspaper", "academic"))
```

`rainbow(5)` specifies the palette and the number of colours on the palette. The result is shown in Figure A9.

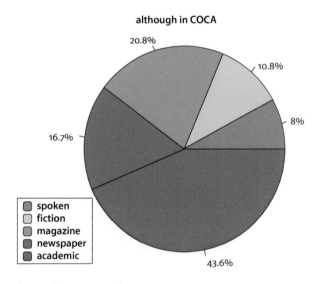

Figure A9. A pie chart with `rainbow` colours

– how to plot two or more graphs next to one another

```
> x <- 1:3
> par(mfrow = c(1, 2))
> barplot(sort(x, decreasing = TRUE))
> barplot(x)
```

This will allow two graphs to be plotted next to each other. See Figure A10.

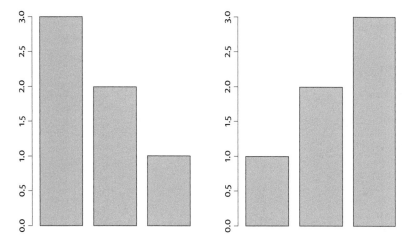

Figure A10. Two bar plots next to each another

```
> par(mfrow = c(5, 10))
> barplot(x)
… [repeat 49 times]
```

This will create fifty plots arranged in five rows and ten columns (see Figure A11).

Note that the layout will be reproduced until you change it explicitly (e.g. `par(mfrow = c(1, 1))`) or close the graphical device, which will restore the default settings.

–   how to use the arguments `pch` and `cex`

     The former argument specifies the type of point symbol. The top row in Figure A12 shows possible values of `pch` from `pch = 0` to `pch = 20` and the symbols that they produce. The argument `cex` specifies the size of symbols and text labels. The default value is 1. The bottom row in Figure A12 shows a few examples of different values from `cex = 1` to `cex = 5`. Note that you can use decimals, as well, e.g. `cex = 0.8`.

7   The structure of `ggplot2` functions

Creating graphs with `ggplot2` is different from using other graphical utilities in R. The package is based on Leland Wilkinson's grammar of graphics. This grammar is quite complex, and this section only provides a basic introduction into the most common options. In `ggplot2`, a plot is built up layer by layer. These layers are as follows:

Figure A11. Fifty bar plots arranged in five rows and ten columns

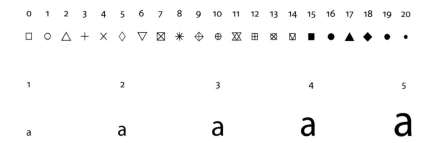

Figure A12. Top: different values of pch. Bottom: different values of cex

- ggplot() initiates a new plot. Here you normally declare the data frame and specify the values of *x* and *y* (when necessary) by using ggplot(df, aes(x = Var1, y = Var2)). The package also offers qplot(), a quick plot whose syntax resembles the basic R plotting functions.
- 'geoms', the layer that specifies the type of the plot. Some of the most popular geoms are as follows:
  - geom_bar() creates bar plots
  - geom_boxplot() creates box-and-whisker plots
  - geom_errorbar() plots error bars
  - geom_histogram() creates histograms
  - geom_density() creates density plots
  - geom_line() draws lines that connect ordered *x*-values
  - geom_point() creates scatter plots
  - geom_text() adds text annotations

  Here you can specify additional graphical parameters, e.g. geom_bar(fill = "white", colour = "black", width = 0.5) will result in a bar plot with white bars with black outline and the width of 0.5 units. One can also override the default way the plot statistics are computed, e.g. geom_bar(stat = "identity") instead of the default stat = "bin" will use the bar heights provided by the user. In this case, the heights should be specified as the *y*-variable in ggplot(df, aes(x = Var1, y = Var2)).
- statistical transformations, which should be specified if they are different from the default ones in the geoms.
  - stat_bin() is similar to table(). It counts the number of observations in bins (e.g. in each factor level). This is the default statistics for geom_histogram(). Here you can specify the bin width, e.g. stat_bin(binwidth = 0.2).
  - stat_boxplot() summarizes the data for a box-and-whisker plot. This is the default transformation for geom_boxplot().

- – `stat_density()` computes 1D kernel density estimates, which are used in `geom_density()`.
  - – `stat_identity()` makes no transformations and plots the data as is.
- – 'aesthetics' `aes()` specifies the mapping of variables to different parts of the plot, e.g. `aes(x = Var1 and y = Var2)`
- – coordinate systems
  - – `coord_flip()` flips the x- and y-axis
  - – `coord_polar()` uses the polar coordinate system, which is useful for creation of pie charts
- – position adjustments
  - – `position_dodge()` is used for creation of plots with grouped (unstacked) bars
  - – `position_jitter()` is used to add some jitter to avoid overplotting
- – title and axes
  - – `ggtitle("Title")` provides a title for the plot
  - – `labs(x = "Label of x", y = "Label of y")` provides the labels for x and y
  - – `xlim(), ylim()` specify the limits of the axes, as in conventional R plots
- – `ggsave()` saves the last displayed plot (by default). You need to supply the file name, e.g. `ggsave(file = "YourDirectory/YourPlot.png)`.

These elements are concatenated, e.g. `ggplot(df, aes(x = Var1)) + geom_bar() + coord_flip()`. See the examples in the book. For more details, see Chang (2013), Wickham (2009) and http://docs.ggplot2.org/.

References

Agresti, A. (2002). *Categorical Data Analysis* (2nd ed.). Hoboken, NJ: Wiley. DOI: 10.1002/0471249688

Allan, L.G. (1980). A note on measurement of contingency between two binary variables in judgment tasks. *Bulletin of the Psychonomic Society*, 15, 147–149. DOI: 10.3758/BF03334492

Anishchanka, A. (2013). *Seeing it in color: A usage-based perspective on color naming in advertising*. Ph.D. diss., University of Leuven.

Arppe, A., Han, W., & Newman, J. (2013). Polytomous logistic regression with Shanghainese topic markers. Vignette, CRAN-R Project. http://cran.r-project.org/web/packages/polytomous/vignettes/shanghainese.pdf (last access 13.12.2014).

Atkins, B.T.S. (1987). Semantic ID tags: Corpus evidence for dictionary senses. The uses of large text databases. *Proceedings of the Third Annual Conference of the UW Centre for the New Oxford English Dictionary* (pp. 17–36). Waterloo, Canada.

Baayen, R.H. (2008). *Analyzing Linguistic Data. A Practical Introduction to Statistics Using R*. Cambridge: Cambridge University Press. DOI: 10.1017/CBO9780511801686

Balota, D.A., Yap, M.J., & Cortese, M.J., et al. (2007). The English Lexicon Project. *Behavior Research Methods*, 39(3), 445–459. DOI: 10.3758/BF03193014

Barnbrook, G., Mason, O., & Krishnamurthy, R. (2013). *Collocation: Applications and Implications*. Basingstoke, Hampshire: Palgrave Macmillan. DOI: 10.1057/9781137297242

Bates, E., & Goodman, J.C. (1997). On the inseparability of grammar and the lexicon: Evidence from acquisition, aphasia and real-time processing. *Language and Cognitive Processes*, 12(5/6), 507–586. DOI: 10.1080/016909697386628

Berlin, B., & Kay, P. (1969). *Basic Color Terms: Their Universality and Evolution*. Berkeley, CA: University of California Press.

Biber, D. (1988). *Variation Across Speech and Writing*. Cambridge: Cambridge University Press. DOI: 10.1017/CBO9780511621024

Bloomfield, L. (1935). *Language*. London: Allen & Unwin.

Borg, I., & Groenen, P. (1997). *Modern Multidimensional Scaling: Theory and Applications*. New York: Springer. DOI: 10.1007/978-1-4757-2711-1

Boroditsky, L. (2001). Does language shape thought?: Mandarin and English speakers' conceptions of time. *Cognitive Psychology*, 43, 1–22. DOI: 10.1006/cogp.2001.0748

Bowerman, M., & Choi, S. (2003). Space under construction: Language-specific spatial categorization in first language acquisition. In D. Gentner & S. Goldin-Meadow (Eds.), *Language in Mind: Advances in the Study of Language and Thought* (pp. 387–427). Cambridge, MA: MIT Press.

Bresnan, J., & Hay, J. (2008). Gradient Grammar: An effect of animacy on the syntax of *give* in New Zealand and American English. *Lingua*, 118(2), 245–259. DOI: 10.1016/j.lingua.2007.02.007

Brugman, C. (1988 [1981]). *The Story of Over: Polysemy, Semantics and the Structure of the Lexicon*. New York: Garland.

Bullinaria, J.A., & Levy, J.P. (2007). Extracting semantic representations from word co-occurrence statistics: A Computational Study. *Behavior Research Methods*, 39, 510–526. DOI: 10.3758/BF03193020

Bybee, J. (2001). *Phonology and language use*. Cambridge: Cambridge University Press. DOI: 10.1017/CBO9780511612886

Chambers, J. (2008). *Software for Data Analysis: Programming with R*. New York: Springer. DOI: 10.1007/978-0-387-75936-4

Chang, W. (2012). *R Graphics Cookbook*. Sebastopol, CA: O'Reilly Media.

Chomsky, N. (1957). *Syntactic Structures*. The Hague: Mouton.

Conover, W.J. (1999). *Practical Nonparametric Statistics* (3rd ed.). New York: Wiley.

Conover, W.J., Johnson, M.E., & Johnson, M.M. (1981). A comparative study of tests for homogeneity of variances, with applications to the outer continental shelf bidding data. *Technometrics, 23*, 351–361. DOI: 10.1080/00401706.1981.10487680

Cox, T.F., & Cox, M.A.A. (2001). *Multidimensional Scaling* (2nd ed.). Boca Raton, FL: Chapman and Hall/CRC Press.

Crawley, M.J. (2007). *The R Book*. Chichester: Wiley. DOI: 10.1002/9780470515075

Dąbrowska, E. (2009). Words as constructions. In V. Evans & S. Pourcel (Eds.), *New Directions in Cognitive Linguistics* (pp. 201–223). Amsterdam: John Benjamins. DOI: 10.1075/hcp.24.16dab

Davies, M. (2008). The Corpus of Contemporary American English: 450 million words, 1990 – present. Available online at http://corpus.byu.edu/coca/.

Davies, M. (2011). N-grams and word frequency data from the Corpus of Historical American English (COHA). Available online at http://www.ngrams.info.

Davies, M. (2013). Corpus of Global Web-Based English: 1.9 billion words from speakers in 20 countries. Available online at http://corpus2.byu.edu/glowbe/.

de Leeuw, J. (1977). Applications of convex analysis to multidimensional scaling. In J. Barra, F. Brodeau, G. Romier, & B. V. Cutsem (Eds.), *Recent Developments in Statistics* (pp. 133–145). Amsterdam: North Holland Publishing Company.

Deerwester, S., Dumais, S.T., Furnas, G.W., Landayer, T.K., & Harshman, R. (1990). Indexing by Latent Semantic Analysis. *Journal of the American Society for Information Science, 41*, 391–407. DOI: 10.1002/(SICI)1097-4571(199009)41:6<391::AID-ASI1>3.0.CO;2-9

Diessel, H. (2007). Frequency effects in language acquisition, language use, and diachronic change. *New Ideas in Psychology, 25*, 108–127. DOI: 10.1016/j.newideapsych.2007.02.002

Divjak, D. (2003). On trying in Russian: A tentative network model for near(er) synonyms. In *Belgian Contributions to the 13th International Congress of Slavicists*, Ljubljana, 15–21 August 2003. Special issue of *Slavica Gandensia*. (pp. 25–58).

Divjak, D., & Gries, S. Th. (2006). Ways of trying in Russian: Clustering behavioral profiles. *Corpus Linguistics and Linguistic Theory, 2*, 23–60. DOI: 10.1515/CLLT.2006.002

Divjak, D., & Gries, S. Th. (2009). Corpus-based cognitive semantics: A contrastive study of phasal verbs in English and Russian. In K. Dziwirek & B. Lewandowska-Tomaszczyk (Eds.), *Studies in Cognitive Corpus Linguistics* (pp. 273–296). Frankfurt am Main: Peter Lang.

Dunning, T. (1993). Accurate methods for the statistics of surprise and coincidence. *Computational Linguistics, 19*(1), 61–74.

Ellis, N. (2006). Language acquisition as rational contingency learning. *Applied Linguistics, 27*(1), 1–24. DOI: 10.1093/applin/ami038

Ellis, N., & Ferreira-Junior, F.G. (2009). Constructions and their acquisition: Islands and the distinctiveness of their occupancy. *Annual Review of Cognitive Linguistics, 7*, 188–221. DOI: 10.1075/arcl.7.08ell

Ember, C.R., & Ember, M. (2007). Climate, econiche, and sexuality: Influences on sonority in language. *American Anthropologist, 109*(1), 180–185. DOI: 10.1525/aa.2007.109.1.180

Everett, D. (2005). Cultural Constraints on Grammar and Cognition in Pirahã: Another Look at the Design Features of Human Language. *Current Anthropology, 46*, 621–646. DOI: 10.1086/431525

Evert, S. (2004). *The Statistics of Word Cooccurrences: Word Pairs and Collocations*. IMS, University of Stuttgart.

Everitt, B., & Hothorn, T. (2011). *An Introduction to Applied Multivariate Analysis with R*. New York: Springer. DOI: 10.1007/978-1-4419-9650-3

Everitt, B.S., Landau, S., Leese, M., & Stahl, D. (2011). *Cluster Analysis* (5th ed.). Chichester: Wiley. DOI: 10.1002/9780470977811

Faraway, J.J. (2009). *Linear Models with R*. Boca Raton, FL: Chapman and Hall/CRC Press.

Fox, J. (2008). *Applied Regression Analysis and Generalized Linear Models* (2nd ed.). Thousand Oaks, CA: Sage Publications.

Field, A., Miles, J., & Field, Z. (2012). *Discovering Statistics Using R*. Los Angeles: Sage.

Firth, J.R. (1957). A synopsis of linguistic theory 1930–1955. In J. R. Firth (Ed.), *Studies in Linguistic Analysis* (pp. 1–32). Oxford: Blackwell.

Friendly, M. (1996). Paivio et al. Word List Generator, Online application. Retrieved April 28, 2013, from http://www.datavis.ca/online/paivio/

Geeraerts, D. (1999). Idealist and empiricist tendencies in cognitive linguistics. In T. Janssen & G. Redeker (Eds.), *Cognitive Linguistics: Foundations, Scope, and Methodology* (pp. 163–194). Berlin/New York: Mouton de Gruyter. DOI: 10.1515/9783110803464.163

Geeraerts, D. (2010). *Theories of Lexical Semantics*. Oxford: Oxford University Press.

Gilquin, G. (2006). The place of prototypicality in corpus linguistics: Causation in the hot seat. In S. Th. Gries & A. Stefanowitsch (Eds.), *Corpora in Cognitive Linguistics: Corpus-Based Approaches to Syntax and Lexis* (pp. 159–191). Berlin/New York: Mouton de Gruyter.

Gilquin, G. (2010). *Corpus, Cognition and Causative Constructions*. Amsterdam: John Benjamins. DOI: 10.1075/scl.39

Gipper, H. (1959). Sessel oder Stuhl? Ein Beitrag zur Bestimmung von Wortinhalten im Bereich der Sachkultur. In H. Gipper (Ed.), *Sprache – Schlüssel zur Welt: Festschrift für Leo Weisgerber* (pp. 271–92). Düsseldorf: Schwann.

Goldberg, A.E., Casenhiser, D., & Sethuraman, N. (2004). Learning argument structure generalizations. *Cognitive Linguistics, 14*(3), 289–316.

Gower, J.C. (1971). A general coefficient of similarity and some of its properties. *Biometrics, 27*, 857–874. DOI: 10.2307/2528823

Greenacre, M. (2007). *Correspondence Analysis in Practice* (2nd ed.). Boca Raton, FL: Chapman and Hall/CRC Press. DOI: 10.1201/9781420011234

Gries, S. Th. (2004). Coll.analysis 3. A program for R for Windows 2.x.

Gries, S. Th. (2006). Corpus-based methods and Cognitive Semantics: The many senses of to run. In S. Th. Gries & A. Stefanowitsch (Eds.), *Corpora in Cognitive Linguistics. Corpus-based Approaches to Syntax and Lexis* (pp. 57–99). Berlin/New York: Mouton de Gruyter.

Gries, S. Th. (2008). Dispersions and adjusted frequencies in corpora. *International Journal of Corpus Linguistics, 13*(4), 403–437. DOI: 10.1075/ijcl.13.4.02gri

Gries, S. Th. (2009). *Quantitative Corpus Linguistics with R: A Practical Introduction*. New York/London: Routledge. DOI: 10.1515/9783110216042

Gries, S. Th. (2012). Behavioral Profiles: A fine-grained and quantitative approach in corpus-based lexical semantics. In G. Jarema, G. Libben, & C. Westbury (Eds.), *Methodological and Analytic Frontiers in Lexical Research* (pp. 57–80). Amsterdam: John Benjamins. DOI: 10.1075/bct.47.04gri

Gries, S. Th. (2013). *Statistics for Linguistics with R*. Berlin/New York: De Gruyter Mouton. DOI: 10.1515/9783110307474

Gries, S. Th., Hampe, B., & Schönefeld, D. (2005). Converging evidence: Bringing together experimental and corpus data on the association of verbs and constructions. *Cognitive Linguistics*, *16*(4), 635–676. DOI: 10.1515/cogl.2005.16.4.635

Gries, S. Th., & Stefanowitsch, A. (2004). Extending collostructional analysis: A corpus-based perspective on 'alternations'. *International Journal of Corpus Linguistics*, *9*(1), 97–129. DOI: 10.1075/ijcl.9.1.06gri

Hanks, P. (1996). Contextual dependency and lexical sets. *International Journal of Corpus Linguistics*, *1*(1), 75–98. DOI: 10.1075/ijcl.1.1.06han

Harrell, F.E. (2001). *Regression Modeling Strategies. With Applications to Linear Models, Logistic Regression, and Survival Analysis*. New York: Springer.

Harris, Z. (1954). Distributional structure. *Word*, *10*(2/3), 146–162.

Hilpert, M. (2011). Dynamic visualizations of language change: Motion charts on the basis of bivariate and multivariate data from diachronic corpora. *International Journal of Corpus Linguistics*, *16*(4), 435–461. DOI: 10.1075/ijcl.16.4.01hil

Hilpert, M. (2013). *Constructional Change in English: Developments in Allomorphy, Word Formation, and Syntax*. Cambridge: Cambridge University Press. DOI: 10.1017/CBO9781139004206

Hosmer, D.W., & Lemeshow, S. (2000). *Applied Logistic Regression*. New York: Wiley. DOI: 10.1002/0471722146

Hothorn, T., Hornik, K., & Zeileis, A. (2006). Unbiased recursive partitioning: A conditional inference framework. *Journal of Computational and Graphical Statistics*, *15*(3), 651–674. DOI: 10.1198/106186006X133933

Huck, S.W. (2009). *Statistical Misconceptions*. New York/London: Routledge.

Husson, F., Lê, S., & Pagès, J. (2010). *Exploratory Multivariate Analysis by Example Using R*. Boca Raton, FL: Chapman and Hall/CRC Press. DOI: 10.1201/b10345

Itkonen, E. (1980). Qualitative vs. quantitative analysis in linguistics. In T. A. Perry (Ed.), *Evidence and Argumentation in Linguistics* (pp. 334–366). Berlin: Mouton.

Johnson, K. (2008). *Quantiative Methods in Linguistics*. Malden, MA: Blackwell Publishing.

Kaufman, L., & Rousseeuw, P.J. (1990). *Finding Groups in Data: An Introduction to Cluster Analysis*. New York: Wiley-Interscience.

Kay, P., & McDaniel, C.K. (1978). The linguistic significance of the meanings of Basic Color Terms. *Language*, *54*(3), 610–646. DOI: 10.1353/lan.1978.0035

Kepser, S., & Reis, M. (2005). Evidence in Linguistics. In S. Kepser & M. Reis (Eds.), *Linguistic Evidence: Empirical, Theoretical and Computational Perspectives* (pp. 1–6). Berlin/New York: Mouton de Gruyter. DOI: 10.1515/9783110197549.1

Keuleers, E., Lacey, P., Rastle, K., & Brysbaert, M. (2012). The British Lexicon Project: Lexical decision data for 28,730 monosyllabic and disyllabic English words. *Behavior Research Methods*, *44*(1), 287–304. DOI: 10.3758/s13428-011-0118-4

Kortmann, B., & Lunkenheimer, K. (Eds.). (2013). *The Electronic World Atlas of Varieties of English*. Leipzig: Max Planck Institute for Evolutionary Anthropology. Retrieved from http://ewave-atlas.org

Kruskal, J.B. (1964). Multidimensional Scaling by optimizing goodness of fit to a nonmetric hypothesis. *Psychometrica*, *29*(1), 1–27. DOI: 10.1007/BF02289565

Kučera, H., & Francis, W.N. (1967). *Computational Analysis of Present-day American English*. Providence: Brown University Press.

Lakoff, G., & Johnson, M. (1980). *Metaphors We Live By*. Chicago: University of Chicago Press.

Landauer, T.K., & Dumais, S.T. (1997). A solution to Plato's problem: The Latent Semantic Analysis theory of the acquisition, induction, and representation of knowledge. *Psychological Review, 104*, 211–240. DOI: 10.1037/0033-295X.104.2.211

Langacker, R.W. (1987). *Foundations of Cognitive Grammar: Theoretical Prerequisites.* Stanford, CA: Stanford University Press.

Larson-Hall, J. (2010). *A Guide to Doing Statistics in Second Language Research Using SPSS.* New York: Routledge.

Lehrer, A. (1974). *Semantic Fields and Lexical Structure.* Amsterdam: North Holland Publishing Company.

Levshina, N. (2011). *Doe wat je niet laten kan [Do what you cannot let]: A usage-based analysis of Dutch causative constructions.* Ph.D. diss., University of Leuven.

Levshina, N. (2014). Geographic variation of *quite* + ADJ in twenty national varieties of English: A pilot study. *Yearbook of the German Cognitive Linguistics Association, 2*, 109–126. DOI: 10.1515/gcla-2014-0008

Levshina, N. (In preparation). Convergent evidence of divergent knowledge: A study of the associations between the Russian ditransitive construction and its collexemes.

Levshina, N., Geeraerts, D., & Speelman, D. (2011). Changing the world vs. changing the mind: Distinctive collexeme analysis of the causative construction with doen in Belgian and Netherlandic Dutch. In F. Gregersen, J. Parrot, & P. Quist (Eds.), *Language variation – European perspectives III. Selected papers from the 5th International Conference on Language Variation in Europe, Copenhagen, June 2009* (pp. 111–123). Amsterdam: John Benjamins. DOI: 10.1075/silv.7.09lev

Levshina, N., Geeraerts, D., & Speelman, D. (2013). Towards a 3D-Grammar: Interaction of linguistic and extralinguistic factors in the use of Dutch causative constructions. *Journal of Pragmatics, 52*, 34–48. DOI: 10.1016/j.pragma.2012.12.013

Levshina, N., & Heylen, K. (2014). A radically data-driven construction grammar: Experiments with Dutch causative constructions. In R. Boogaart, T. Colleman, & G. Rutten (Eds.), *Extending the Scope of Construction Grammar* (pp. 17–46). Berlin/New York: Mouton de Gruyter.

Leys, C., Ley, C., Klein, O., Bernard, P., & Licata, L. (2013). Detecting outliers: Do not use standard deviation around the mean, use absolute deviation around the median. *Journal of Experimental Social Psychology, 49*, 764–766. DOI: 10.1016/j.jesp.2013.03.013

Lijffijt, J., & Gries, S. Th. (2012). Correction to "Dispersions and adjusted frequencies in corpora". *International Journal of Corpus Linguistics, 17*(1), 147–149. DOI: 10.1075/ijcl.17.1.08lij

Lin, D. (1998). Automatic retrieval and clustering of similar words. *Proceedings of the 17th International Conference on Computational linguistics*, Montreal, Canada, August 1998 (pp. 768–774).

Louviere, J.J., Hensher, D.A., & Swait, J.D. (2000). *Stated Choice Methods: Analysis and application.* Cambridge: Cambridge University Press.

Lund, K., & Burgess, C. (1996). Producing high-dimensional semantic spaces from lexical co-occurrences. *Behavior Research Methods, Instruments, & Computers, 28*, 203–208. DOI: 10.3758/BF03204766

Manning, C., & Schütze, H. (1999). *Foundations of Statistical Natural Language Processing.* Cambridge, MA: MIT Press.

Matloff, N. (2011). *The Art of R Programming: A Tour of Statistical Software Design.* San Francisco: No Starch Press.

Michelbacher, L., Evert, S., & Schutze, H. (2011). Asymmetry in corpus-derived and human word associations. *Corpus Linguistics and Linguistic Theory, 7*(2), 245–276. DOI: 10.1515/cllt.2011.012

Miller, G.A., & Charles, W.G. (1991). Contextual correlates of semantic similarity. *Language and Cognitive Processes*, 6(1), 1–28. DOI: 10.1080/01690969108406936

Mitchell, J., & Lapata, M. (2010). Composition in distributional models of semantics. Cognitive Science, 34(8), 1388–1439. DOI: 10.1111/j.1551-6709.2010.01106.x

Newman, J. (2011). Corpora and cognitive linguistics. *Brazilian Journal of Applied Linguistics*, 11(2), 521–559.

Núñez, R.E., & Sweetser, E. (2006). With the future behind them: Convergent evidence from Aymara language and gesture in the crosslinguistic comparison of spatial construals of time. *Cognitive Science*, 30, 401–450. DOI: 10.1207/s15516709cog0000_62

Pado, S., & Lapata, M. (2007). Dependency-based construction of Semantic Space Models. *Computational Linguistics*, 33(2), 161–199. DOI: 10.1162/coli.2007.33.2.161

Peirsman, Y. (2008). Word Space Models of semantic similarity and relatedness. In *Proceedings of the ESSLLI-2008 Student Session*, Hamburg, Germany.

Peirsman, Y., Heylen, K., & Geeraerts, D. (2010). Applying Word Space Models to sociolinguistics. Religion names before and after 9/11. In D. Geeraerts, G. Kristiansen, & Y. Peirsman (Eds.), *Recent Advances in Cognitive Sociolinguistics* (pp. 111–137). Berlin/New York: Mouton de Gruyter.

Paivio, A., Juille, J.C., & Madigan, S. (1968). Concreteness, imagery, and meaningfulness values for 925 nouns. *Journal of Experimental Psychology*, 76(1, Pt. 2), 1–25. DOI: 10.1037/h0025327

Paradis, C. (1997). *Degree Modifiers of Adjectives in Spoken British English*. Lund: Lund University Press.

Rosch Heider, E., & Olivier, D.C. (1972). The structure of the color space in naming and memory for two languages. *Cognitive Psychology*, 3, 337–345. DOI: 10.1016/0010-0285(72)90011-4

Rosch, E. (1975). Cognitive representation of semantic categories. *Journal of Experimental Psychology*, 104(3), 192–233. DOI: 10.1037/0096-3445.104.3.192

Rosch, E., & Mervis, C.B. (1975). Family resemblances: Studies in the internal structure of categories. *Cognitive Psychology*, 7, 573–605. DOI: 10.1016/0010-0285(75)90024-9

Salkind, N.J. (2011). *Statistics for People Who (Think They) Hate Statistics* (4th ed.). Los Angeles: Sage.

Schmid, H.-J. (2000). *English Abstract Nouns as Conceptual Shells. From corpus to cognition*. Berlin/New York: Mouton de Gruyter.

Schütze, H. (1992). Dimensions of meaning. In *Proceedings of Supercomputing 92* (pp. 787–796). Minneapolis, MN.

Senghas, A., & Coppola, M. (2001). Children creating language: How Nicaraguan Sign Language acquired a spatial grammar. *Psychological Science*, 12(4), 323–328. DOI: 10.1111/1467-9280.00359

Senghas, A., Kita, S., & Özyürek, A. (2004). Children creating core properties of language: Evidence from an emerging Sign Language in Nicaragua. *Science*, 305(5691), 1779–1782. DOI: 10.1126/science.1100199

Sheskin, D.J. (2011). *Handbook of Parametric and Nonparametric Statistical Procedures*. Boca Raton, FL: Chapman and Hall/CRC Press.

Speelman, D., & Geeraerts, D. (2009). Causes for causatives: The case of Dutch 'doen' and 'laten'. In T. Sanders & E. Sweetser (Eds.), *Causal Categories in Discourse and Cognition* (pp. 173–204). Berlin/New York: Mouton de Gruyter.

Steels, L. (Ed.). (2012). *Experiments in Cultural Language Evolution*. Amsterdam: John Benjamins. DOI: 10.1075/ais.3

Steen, G.J., Dorst, A.G., Herrmann, J.B., Kaal, A.A., Krennmayr, T., & Pasma, T. (2010). *A Method for Linguistic Metaphor Identification. From MIP to MIPVU*. Amsterdam: John Benjamins. DOI: 10.1075/celcr.14

Stefanowitsch, A. (2001). *Constructing causation: A construction grammar approach to analytic causatives*. Ph.D. diss., Rice University.

Stefanowitsch, A. (2010). Empirical Cognitive Semantics: Some thoughts. In D. Glynn & K. Fischer (Eds.), *Quantitative Methods in Cognitive Semantics: Corpus-driven Approaches* (pp. 355–380). Berlin/New York: De Gruyter Mouton.

Stefanowitsch, A., & Gries, S. Th. (2003). Collostructions: Investigating the interaction of words and constructions. *International Journal of Corpus Linguistics, 8*(2), 209–243. DOI: 10.1075/ijcl.8.2.03ste

Stefanowitsch, A., & Gries, S. Th. (2005). Covarying collexemes. *Corpus Linguistics and Linguistic Theory 1*(1), 1–43.

Sweetser, E. (1990). *From Etymology to Pragmatics*. Cambridge: Cambridge University Press. DOI: 10.1017/CBO9780511620904

Szmrecsanyi, B. (2010). The English genitive alternation in a cognitive sociolinguistics perspective. In D. Geeraerts, G. Kristiansen, & Y. Peirsman (Eds.), *Advances in Cognitive Sociolinguistics* (pp. 141–166). Berlin/New York: Mouton de Gruyter.

Tagliamonte, S., & Baayen, R.H. (2012). Models, forests and trees of York English: Was/were variation as a case study for statistical practice. *Language Variation and Change, 24*(2), 135–178. DOI: 10.1017/S0954394512000129

Talmy, L. (1985). Lexicalization patterns: Semantic structure in lexical forms. In T. Shopen (Ed.), *Grammatical Categories and the Lexicon, Vol. III* (pp. 57–149). Cambridge: Cambridge University Press.

Talmy, L. (2000). *Toward a Cognitive Semantics*. Cambridge, MA: MIT Press.

Taylor, J. (2012). *The Mental Corpus. How Language is Represented in the Mind*. Oxford: Oxford University Press. DOI: 10.1093/acprof:oso/9780199290802.001.0001

Teetor, P. (2011). *R Cookbook*. Sebastopol. CA: O'Reilly Media.

Turney, P.D., & Pantel, P. (2010). From frequency to meaning: Vector Space Models of semantics. *Journal of Articial Intelligence Research, 37*, 141–188.

Urdan, T.C. (2010). *Statistics in Plain English* (3rd ed.). New York: Routledge.

Verhagen, A., & Kemmer, S. (1997). Interaction and causation: Causative constructions in modern standard Dutch. *Journal of Pragmatics, 24*, 61–82. DOI: 10.1016/S0378-2166(96)00003-3

Verhoeven, J., De Pauw, G., & Kloots, H. (2004). Speech rate in a pluricentric language: A comparison between Dutch in Belgium and the Netherlands. *Language and Speech, 47*(3), 297–308. DOI: 10.1177/00238309040470030401

Wickham, H. (2009). *ggplot2: Elegant Graphics for Data Analysis*. New York: Springer.

Wiechmann, D. (2008). On the computation of Collostruction Strength. *Corpus Linguistics and Linguistic Theory, 4*(2), 253–290. DOI: 10.1515/CLLT.2008.011

Wierzbicka, A. (2006). *English: Meaning and Culture*. Oxford: Oxford University Press.

Winke, P., Gass, S., & Sydorenko, T. (2010). The effects of captioning videos used for foreign language listening activities. *Language Learning and Technology, 14*(1), 65–86.

Wolk, C., Bresnan, J., Rosenbach, A., & Szmrecsanyi, B. (2013). Dative and genitive variability in Late Modern English: Exploring cross-constructional variation and change. *Diachronica, 30*(3), 382–419. DOI: 10.1075/dia.30.3.04wol

Wulff, S. (2006). Go-V vs. go-and-V in English: A case of constructional synonymy? In S. Th. Gries & A. Stefanowitsch (Eds.), *Corpora in Cognitive Linguistics. Corpus-based Approaches to Syntax and Lexis* (pp. 101–125). Berlin/New York: Mouton de Gruyter.

Wulff, S., Gries, S. Th., & Stefanowitsch, A. (2007). Brutal Brits and persuasive Americans: Variety-specific meaning construction in the into-causative. In G. Radden, K.-M. Köpcke, T. Berg, & P. Siemund (Eds.), *Aspects of Meaning Construction* (pp. 265–281). Amsterdam: John Benjamins. DOI: 10.1075/z.136.17wul

Zipf, G.K. (1935). *The Psycho-Biology of Language*. Cambridge, MA: MIT Press.

Zipf, G.K. (1949). *Human Behavior and the Principle of Least Effort. An Introduction to Human Ecology*. Cambridge, MA: Addison Wesley.

Subject Index

Index of R functions and packages